Hands-On
Low-Code
Application
Development
with Salesforce

Build customized CRM applications that solve
business challenges in just a few clicks

Enrico Murru

BIRMINGHAM—MUMBAI

Hands-On Low-Code Application Development with Salesforce

Commissioning Editor: Kunal Chaudhari

Acquisition Editor: Alok Dhuri

Senior Editor: Nitee Shetty

Content Development Editor: Tiksha Lad

Technical Editor: Pradeep Sahu

Copy Editor: Safis Editing

Project Coordinator: Deeksha Thakkar

Proofreader: Safis Editing

Indexer: Tejal Daruwale Soni

Production Designer: Vijay Kamble

First published: October 2020

Production reference: 1151020

Published by Packt Publishing Ltd.
Livery Place
35 Livery Street
Birmingham
B3 2PB, UK.

ISBN 978-1-80020-977-0

www.packt.com

*To our dear Steven, and all friends and relatives whom Covid-19
took from us.*

-Enrico Murru

`Packt.com`

Subscribe to our online digital library for full access to over 7,000 books and videos, as well as industry leading tools to help you plan your personal development and advance your career. For more information, please visit our website.

Why subscribe?

- Spend less time learning and more time coding with practical eBooks and Videos from over 4,000 industry professionals

- Improve your learning with Skill Plans built especially for you

- Get a free eBook or video every month

- Fully searchable for easy access to vital information

- Copy and paste, print, and bookmark content

Did you know that Packt offers eBook versions of every book published, with PDF and ePub files available? You can upgrade to the eBook version at `packt.com` and as a print book customer, you are entitled to a discount on the eBook copy. Get in touch with us at `customercare@packtpub.com` for more details.

At `www.packt.com`, you can also read a collection of free technical articles, sign up for a range of free newsletters, and receive exclusive discounts and offers on Packt books and eBooks.

Contributors

About the author

Enrico Murru is a 20 times Salesforce certified solution and technical architect at WebResults (an Engineering Spa company), an Italian platinum Salesforce partner. After the electronic engineering MSc (University of Cagliari, 2007), he started working as a Java developer at a local software house. In 2009, he joined WebResults as a junior Salesforce developer, learning all about Salesforce. In 2013, he launched his first blog (Nerd @ Work). From 2016 to 2019, he was nominated as the first Italian Salesforce MVP due to his commitment to the Salesforce community. In 2016, he started one of his most popular projects, the ORGanizer for Salesforce browser extension, a productivity booster for Salesforce professionals. Find him on Twitter at @enreeco.

I want to thank my lovely wife, Alessandra, who lets me give time and effort to my side projects with support and understanding, even on this second book and during this awful pandemic. You are my rock and I cannot think of a better companion to have for the rest of my life.

Thank you to my colleagues and friends, old and new, for helping me to leverage my experience with new challenges in my daily work.

I also want to thank the whole Packt team who worked with me on this new adventure: Alok, Prajakta, Tiksha, and all the other guys who had to review my once horrible English writing!

About the reviewer

Fabrice Cathala is a three-time Salesforce MVP who's been working for over 20 years in the IT industry. He started his career in the world of the data center. In 2001, he moved to implement enterprise-class on-premise applications. Then, in 2004, he discovered cloud computing with Salesforce and has been a cloud evangelist ever since. He's run several blogs on the subject.

Today, Fabrice is a Salesforce Technical Architect working in the UK. He currently holds 9 certifications and over 400 Trailhead badges. Outside of work, he is an active member of the Salesforce community.

He is also keen on non-computer activities such as going for a swim with his daughter Macy-Anaïs at the local swimming pool.

> *I want to say thank you to my wife, Kate, for giving me the freedom to spend a lot of time on my geeky hobbies.*

Packt is searching for authors like you

If you're interested in becoming an author for Packt, please visit `authors.packtpub.com` and apply today. We have worked with thousands of developers and tech professionals, just like you, to help them share their insight with the global tech community. You can make a general application, apply for a specific hot topic that we are recruiting an author for, or submit your own idea.

Table of Contents

3

Mastering Formulas

4

Cleaning Data with Validation Rules

5

Handling Dynamic Configuration

6

Security First – The "Who Sees What" Paradigm

Section 3: Automation Tools

7

Be a Workflow Champion

8

Setting Up Approval Processes

Section 4:
Composing the User Interface

12
All about Layouts

13
The Lightning App Builder

14
Leveraging Customers and Partners Power with Communities

Section 5:
Data Management

Section 6:
Ready to Release?

17
The Sandbox Model

18
Deploying Your Solution

Section 7:
Before We Say Goodbye

19
Salesforce Ohana – The Most Amazing Community Around

Other Books You May Enjoy

Index

Preface

Since the beginning of my career in the Salesforce ecosystem as a Salesforce junior developer in 2009, it was clear to me that learning Salesforce was not a hard path if you had the right guidance. It's also been a long time from the point that I actually understood that what I know can be profitable for other professionals, since I realized that I badly wanted to write a book for beginners to help them learn the platform by way of examples, transferring to people what I have learned in more than 10 years of projects, trial and error, and consultancy.

According to **Burning Glass Report**, on the whitepaper titled *Skilling Up for the Future: The Growing Demand for Salesforce Talent* (available at `https://developer.salesforce.com/resources2/career2017/docs/Skilling+Up+for+the+Future.pdf`), 4.2 million jobs will be created in the Salesforce ecosystem worldwide, making Salesforce one of the most in-demand technologies (third place in 2018). The increased need for Salesforce professionals elevates the urgency for well-defined career paths with clear trails and goals, delivering to this ecosystem technical specialists (such as developers and architects) that should have strong IT backgrounds, but also less technical skilled people such as business analysts or administrators, roles that ideally anyone with any background can reach.

This urgency brought Salesforce to deliver one of the coolest e-learning portals ever, `http://www.trailhead.com`, which, along with a wonderful community of professionals, users, technology starters, an incredibly rich help portal, and thousands of blogs, videos, and books, makes learning Salesforce and related products a reachable task, even if you haven't ever worked on the platform.

The goal of this book is focused on the Salesforce CRM platform, the oldest and most available product of the Salesforce ecosystem, and specifically on its implementation with a low-code approach. One of the key principles of Salesforce customization is that you don't need to know any programming language to administer a Salesforce organization and understand the concepts in this book, which will be a guide for your Salesforce administrator, developer, or consultant starting paths.

I tried to infuse my own experience into the narration and, although it may seem excessive for a beginner audience, even advanced concepts on Salesforce configuration, because I believe that a book should be a guide and so it may be read more than once, where each read becomes clearer thanks to the knowledge the reader will take in day by day.

As I always say during public speeches, Salesforce is the love of my life (I mean of my *professional* life, otherwise my wife would be really disappointed) and this book is a way to say thank you to a technology that made me a (professional) man.

Who this book is for

If you are an experienced developer with no Salesforce experience, if you are a technical or solution architect coming from CRM implementations based on other products, if you want to start your career in information technology but you don't have a degree in computer programming, if you are a Salesforce user and want to learn how Salesforce CRM works, if you are a Salesforce developer but lack some administration skills, or if simply you are planning to take your Salesforce Administrator or Salesforce Application Builder certifications, this book is right for you.

The only prerequisite is the desire to learn and get the most out of the Salesforce world.

What this book covers

Chapter 1, A Brief Introduction to Salesforce, consists of a quick history of the Salesforce company and the basics of the platform.

Chapter 2, Building the Data Model, explains how to customize Salesforce objects with fields and relationships.

Chapter 3, Mastering Formulas, covers how to write formulas and create formula fields.

Chapter 4, Cleaning Data with Validation Rules, explains how to leverage validation rules to maintain data consistency.

Chapter 5, Handling Dynamic Configuration, covers how to use Custom Settings and Custom Metadata types to add a configuration layer to your customizations.

Chapter 6, Security First – The "Who Sees What" Paradigm, explains how to configure data access to enhance security.

Chapter 7, Be a Workflow Champion, explains what automation is with Workflow Rules.

Chapter 8, Setting Up Approval Processes, covers defining rules on records to adhere to business approval processes.

Chapter 9, Process Builder – Workflow Evolution, expounds a more modern version of Workflow Rules for process automation.

Chapter 10, Designing Lightning Flows, covers delivering Flows to implement even more complex automation processes in addition to using visual screens to interact with users.

Chapter 11, Interacting with Actions, explains the power of complex actions on data in a one-click style.

Chapter 12, All about Layouts, entails defining record layouts to show the right data when needed.

Chapter 13, The Lightning App Builder, shows you how to build powerful apps leveraging Salesforce components.

Chapter 14, Leveraging Customers and Partners Power with Communities, explains how to interact with external users from within the CRM.

Chapter 15, Importing and Exporting Data Declaratively, covers managing your data with the built-in Import and Export functionalities and with the Data Loader.

Chapter 16, Learning about Data Reporting, empowers your reporting skills to monitor business processes.

Chapter 17, The Sandbox Model, shows you how to design your sandbox strategy to deliver the right environments for the right usage.

Chapter 18, Deploying Your Solution, covers releasing your customizations into production.

Chapter 19, Salesforce Ohana – The Most Amazing Community around, discusses the Salesforce community, which you should join to empower your professional network and unleash your trailblazer skills.

To get the most out of this book

There are no specific requirements for this book; you just need a laptop, an internet connection, and a web browser.

The only limitation is in the browsers supported by the Salesforce platform, the latest version of Google Chrome being the preferred browser.

For an updated list of the supported web browsers, refer to Salesforce Help at `https://help.salesforce.com/articleView?id=getstart_browsers_sfx.htm&type=5`.

If you are using the digital version of this book, we advise you to type the code yourself or access the code via the GitHub repository (link available in the next section). Doing so will help you avoid any potential errors related to the copying and pasting of code.

Download the example code files

You can download the example code files for this book from GitHub at `https://github.com/PacktPublishing/Hands-On-Low-Code-Application-Development-with-Salesforce`. In case there's an update to the code, it will be updated on the existing GitHub repository.

Refer to the *Deploying with packages* section of *Chapter 18, Deploying Your Solution*, for a quick guide on how to release each chapter's code into your development Salesforce org.

We also have other code bundles from our rich catalog of books and videos available at `https://github.com/PacktPublishing/`. Check them out!

Download the color images

We also provide a PDF file that has color images of the screenshots/diagrams used in this book. You can download it here:

`https://static.packt-cdn.com/downloads/9781800209770_ColorImages.pdf`.

Conventions used

There are a number of text conventions used throughout this book.

`Code in text`: Indicates code words in text, database table names, folder names, filenames, file extensions, pathnames, dummy URLs, user input, and Twitter handles. Here is an example: "What happens if the `Sales` department is renamed to, let's say, `Sales Dept.` and the Division to `Huge Clients`?"

A block of code is set as follows:

```
AND (
  OR (
    $User.Department != "Sales",
```

```
    $User.Division != "Big Customers"
  ),
  Amount > 500000
)
```

When we wish to draw your attention to a particular part of a code block, the relevant lines or items are set in bold:

```
AND (
  OR (
    $User.Department !=
            $Setup.Sales_Settings__c
                .Sales_Department_Name__c,
    $User.Division !=
            $Setup.Sales_Settings__c
                .Big_Customers_Division__c
  ),
  Amount > $Setup.Sales_Settings__c.Amount_Threshold__c
)
```

Bold: Indicates a new term, an important word, or words that you see onscreen. For example, words in menus or dialog boxes appear in the text like this. Here is an example: "To enable Salesforce communities, click on **Setup | Feature Settings | Communities | Communities Settings** and flag the **Enable communities** option."

> **Tips or important notes**
> Appear like this.

Get in touch

Feedback from our readers is always welcome.

General feedback: If you have questions about any aspect of this book, mention the book title in the subject of your message and email us at customercare@packtpub.com.

Errata: Although we have taken every care to ensure the accuracy of our content, mistakes do happen. If you have found a mistake in this book, we would be grateful if you would report this to us. Please visit www.packtpub.com/support/errata, selecting your book, clicking on the Errata Submission Form link, and entering the details.

Piracy: If you come across any illegal copies of our works in any form on the Internet, we would be grateful if you would provide us with the location address or website name. Please contact us at copyright@packt.com with a link to the material.

If you are interested in becoming an author: If there is a topic that you have expertise in and you are interested in either writing or contributing to a book, please visit authors.packtpub.com.

Reviews

Please leave a review. Once you have read and used this book, why not leave a review on the site that you purchased it from? Potential readers can then see and use your unbiased opinion to make purchase decisions, we at Packt can understand what you think about our products, and our authors can see your feedback on their book. Thank you!

For more information about Packt, please visit packt.com.

Section 1: What Is Salesforce?

Let's introduce Salesforce and see how it delivers a rich platform with an abundance of "click-not-code" features.

This section comprises the following chapter:

- *Chapter 1, A Brief Introduction to Salesforce*

1

A Brief Introduction to Salesforce

We will start our journey through the Salesforce platform customization with a quick overview of the history of the company, by highlighting the key milestones across its 20+ years of life.

Then, we'll briefly see what's inside the platform and how it works, describing the multitenant architecture that lets multiple Salesforce customers be located on the same physical servers without harming one another this is the core of how Salesforce works and the reason of its successfully scalable and reliable architecture.

As this is a learning book, we'll also have a look at Trailhead, the fantastic learning platform that's rapidly becoming a founding brick of Salesforce knowledge-sharing philosophy. At the end of almost each chapter you'll see a *Blaze your trail* section that will contain Trailheads content related to the specific chapter's topic.

To test our new skills, we'll also see how to create a free environment (called a Salesforce Developer Edition org, or simply a DE org) activated with all the main platform features so that you can learn along with reading this book.

In this chapter, we'll focus on the following topics:

- Salesforce company history
- How the Salesforce platform is built

- How to have fun learning Salesforce with Trailhead
- How to create a Developer Edition org to learn with examples

Understanding Salesforce

Defining Salesforce as a **Software as a Service (SaaS) Customer Relationship Management (CRM)** is reductive nowadays. A *CRM* is a software meant to help and manage customer relationships (mostly sales and service processes) while integrating with legacy systems (where most of the data comes from, such as shipping tracking details or product logistic details, to name just a few), while *SaaS* means that the software is in the cloud and you have access to it without the need to take care of all the hardware and infrastructure you would need for other competitors' products.

> **Further reading**
>
> Read the post at `https://crm.org/crmland/what-is-a-crm` for a deeper explanation of what a CRM is; it will take you some time to understand how companies benefit from a well-structured and reliable CRM system.

Today, Salesforce is much more than a CRM, after successful and smart acquisitions, making the Salesforce ecosystem one of the most important cloud companies out there, bringing marketing automation features, custom application development with any language, e-commerce solutions, powerful analytics solutions, and, recently, a lot of artificial intelligence.

For the sake of this book, we'll cover the center of this ecosystem, and the oldest and richest of features, the Salesforce CRM platform, which will let you customize an environment to do practically anything you want, which might go beyond *simple* customer management.

Why is Salesforce so special? You decided to purchase a book about Salesforce customization, so you must have come into contact with the technology in some way.

The technological aspect is surely one of the most important aspects: the CRM platform is the center of the whole product ecosystem and it can be used to centralize all data (this is the so-called *Customer 360* platform), and we can say that Salesforce is one of the first companies that centered its business in the cloud.

But in my opinion, what differentiates Salesforce from other companies and competitors is its genuine will to make people, whether they are customers, consultants, employees, or partners (let's generically call everyone stakeholders), feel part of an amazing community where profit is only one of the driving factors.

We'll talk about the Salesforce community and the Ohana value in *Chapter 19, Salesforce Ohana – The Most Amazing Community Around.*

Let's highlight the most important milestones in Salesforce's history, so we can have a better view of how huge Salesforce has become in these 20 years of its history.

Unfolding the evolution of Salesforce

Salesforce's growth in the last 20 years has been incredible: by 2024, it is expected that the net revenue of Salesforce's industry will exceed $1 trillion (that is, $1,000,000,000,000).

> **Further reading**
>
> Have a read at the *The Salesforce Economic Impact* white paper by IDC, available at `https://www.salesforce.com/content/dam/web/en_us/www/documents/reports/idc-salesforce-economy-report.pdf`, for a complete analysis of the Salesforce industry economic impact worldwide.

Everything started in March 1999, just like in the old fashioned Silicon Valley start-up fables: four buddies started a company at Telegraph Hill, San Francisco, in a one-bedroom apartment (have a look at the actual pictures at `https://www.salesforce.com/blog/2019/02/salesforce-san-francisco-1999.html`).

It was Marc Benioff's house (founder and current CEO at Salesforce), along with Parker Harris, Frank Dominguez, and Dave Moellenhoff.

Their aim was to create business applications with the SaaS model, designing adaptable applications without high maintenance and development costs, following the same paradigm of Amazon.com: an easy-to-use site but for business applications. They developed the basis of the first SaaS CRM in just 1 month!

It was in 2000 that the Salesforce.com company moved to 1 Market Street (San Francisco) and launched the product, along with the famous and controversial **No Software** brand, which soon become synonymous with Salesforce. Of course, this does not mean that a SaaS application doesn't require any lines of code, but rather that your company will rely on cloud software only, and so *no legacy software* is needed anymore (but, as you can imagine, *No Software* alone is quite catchy!).

The Salesforce CRM software continued to evolve, and its features were presented in so-called *City Tours*, a few hour-long events handled in diverse US cities. But it was in 2003 that Salesforce launched one of its most iconic events, **Dreamforce**, a few-day event held in San Francisco where all Salesforce customers could meet each other and learn what was going on with their CRM software (there were around 1,000 participants).

In 2004, Salesforce.com Inc. went public on the NYSE with the *CRM* stock code (although I consider myself totally illiterate in financial education, I love that stock symbol choice!).

In 2006, the **AppExchange** portal was launched: the apps economy was just starting, and Salesforce partners could build reusable artifacts (or packages) that other packages could use to enhance their Salesforce customizations, reducing implementation and maintenance efforts. Apple's App Store was launched later on, and, as you read at `https://www.salesforce.com/blog/2019/02/steve-jobs-inspired-appexchange.html`, the `appstore.com` domain and trademark was gifted by Marc Benioff to Steve Jobs as an act of gratitude for having inspired such a successful business model.

At the 2006 Dreamforce event, the **Apex** on-demand programming language was presented, and that changed the way the Salesforce CRM could be customized; a lot of lines of code could run on Salesforce infrastructure to enhance automation customizations. In the same event, the **Visualforce** framework was also presented, granting Salesforce partners the ability to build complex user interfaces.

In 2008, the **Force.com** platform was delivered, which, thanks to Apex and Visualforce, let customers implement their own customized applications side by side with the usual *standard* CRM processes: this was the advent of the **Platform as a Service (PaaS)** model.

I joined the *Salesforce Ohana* (refer to *Chapter 19, Salesforce Ohana – The Most Amazing Community Around*, for more details on the *Ohana movement*) in early 2009, as a Salesforce junior developer at WebResults (an engineering group). It was a risky bet for our former CEO, Lorenzo Coslovi, and our CTO, Alessandro Plebani, who, a few years earlier, decided to start investing in the Salesforce world, when Salesforce was not really known in the Italian market and its market share was really small. They created a fantastic team of professionals, and I'm really grateful to both of them for letting me be part of this Salesforce revolution.

In 2012, ExactTarget was acquired and presented at the same year's Dreamforce as the new **Salesforce Marketing Cloud**, a product completely focused on B2C customer marketing.

2013 saw the birth of the **Salesforce1** platform, which brought the whole Salesforce desktop experience to the mobile channel, anticipating the **Lightning** platform, which was presented a few years later.

In 2014, **Trailhead** was launched, a fun way to learn Salesforce-related stuff at no cost at all; anyone can create an account and access thousands of free learning modules.

In 2015, the new **Lightning Experience** look and feel was applied across devices (desktop, mobile, tablets, and so on) after 16 years of almost no great user interface change. It was a new and modern way to access the Salesforce data; regardless of whether you are a Lightning Experience supporter or not, you have to admit that the Salesforce guys' efforts to bring innovation to their platform is commendable. Developers have to learn a new development platform, called the *Aura framework*, the precursor of the recent **Lightning Web Components** (**LWC**) framework, a JavaScript-based framework introduced in 2018 that significantly increases Lightning Experience performances and code reusability.

This whole book, with an exception made for some small cases, is based on the look and feel of Lightning Experience.

2016 was the year of artificial intelligence, with the **Einstein** product released, meant to improve every single product by delivering the easiest machine learning functionality to the Salesforce platform. The Einstein artificial intelligence was presented in front of 170,000 attendees at that year's Dreamforce (170x more attendees than the first 2003 Dreamforce). In the same year, Salesforce acquired over 10 companies (including Quip, SteelBrick as CPQ, and DemandWare as B2C Commerce Cloud, to name a few).

In 2018, **MuleSoft** was acquired, bringing another important piece of technology to the platform – that is, the ability to connect legacy systems in the cloud, unleashing digital transformation with ease.

In 2019, it was time for another acquisition, **Tableau**, one of the leading companies in data visualization and business intelligence.

In this book, we'll be concentrating on the core of the Salesforce platform, *the SaaS CRM*, to find the ways to customize it and let Salesforce adapt to each company's business processes with a low-code approach – that is, a lot of point ing and clicking and little-to-no coding.

To tell how the Salesforce CRM has changed throughout the years, have a look at the following figure, which shows all the different user interfaces that have evolved over more than 20 years:

Figure 1.1 – Salesforce user interface evolution from 1999 to 2020

To understand how old I am (not that old really, but relative to the life of Salesforce, quite a bit), I was introduced to the platform in the second stage in the preceding figure.

Ah, good old times!

Further reading

To get inspired by what Marc Benioff and his folks did, refer to Marc Benioff's books, *Behind the Cloud: The Untold Story of How Salesforce.com Went from Idea to Billion-Dollar Company-and Revolutionized an Industry* (2009) and *Trailblazer: The Power of Business as the Greatest Platform for Change* (2019). For a quick and inspirational deep dive into Salesforce's history, check out the Salesforce Ben blog post at `https://www.salesforceben.com/brief-history-salesforce-com/`.

Let's have a quick look at how the Salesforce platform is shaped to deliver a reliable and trusted service to its customers.

Explaining the Salesforce architecture

The power of the Salesforce platform is its cloud nature: everything is stored in a safe and trusted cloud with data centers spread across the world.

This architecture doesn't simply mean that your code and data is stored in someone else's computer (that's how cloud haters ironically describe the cloud), but that your data is placed in data centers with the highest levels of security (that would cost your company many dollars to run the same, in terms of hardware, resources, people, and maintenance).

The most important feature of this cloud is **multitenancy**. Multitenancy refers to a software architecture in which a single instance of software (the Salesforce platform itself) runs on a specific server and serves multiple tenants, where a tenant is a group of users (your company's CRM) who share common access and privileges on that software instance (your CRM's specific customization).

This means that your CRM customizations (called metadata) and data are *in the same place* where other Salesforce customers' metadata and data reside, but the architecture is so well structured and secure that you will never be able to access that data and customizations (you'll only see what you own).

As pictured in the Trailhead module at `https://trailhead.salesforce.com/content/learn/modules/starting_force_com/starting_understanding_arch`, you can think of Salesforce as an apartment building: your specific CRM owns one or more apartments and has neighbors with which your company shares some of the resources (stairs, elevator, electricity, water supplies, common spaces, and so on). Regardless of your own apartment size, Salesforce guarantees the same level of service, such as computing power, data storage, access performance, and core features (authentication, reporting performances, and so on).

This is a winning approach, as it delivers the following:

- **Scalability**: A multi-tenant infrastructure makes it easy to increase capacity when more resources are required. If a server is upgraded, the whole client base takes advantage of it.

- **Performance**: The nature of multitenancy allows optimum performance maximization, letting any client use the right amount of resources it needs.

- **Service**: With a single platform to administer, the Salesforce cloud shares maintenance plans and software upgrades (*one software code base to rule them all*) among all its clients.

- **Upgrades**: Given that there is a single centralized software that runs the base of the platform, software updates are seamless, which leads to more robust software and the possibility of constantly delivering new and upgraded features (each Salesforce main release takes place in about 5 minutes). The Salesforce platform provides three main upgrades a year – winter, spring, and summer releases – which usually brings tens of new features as well as platform improvements and bug fixes. If you are curious about all the different logos each release has produced, take a look at **SFDC Monkey**'s blog attempt to list them all, at `https://sfdcmonkey.com/salesforce-release-logo-journey/`. Jump to `https://www.salesforce.com/releases/` to have a look at the latest release.

- **Metadata**: Metadata is just *data about data*, which means that metadata describes how data is shaped and accessed, defining user interfaces, automation processes, and security access rules (and way more than this). Metadata is stored in the Salesforce platform along with actual data, so each Salesforce customer can define its own way to represent and use its data through metadata definitions, without affecting other customers in the same multitenant architecture and without being affected by frequent platform seamless upgrades.

It is no surprise that this whole book is focused on the ways that the platform lets you manipulate metadata and data with low code usage.

Before starting our journey through Salesforce customization, let's talk about a fun way to learn stuff about Salesforce.

Empowering learning with Trailhead

One of the coolest things that made me fall in love with the Salesforce world in my early days as a Salesforce developer was the absolutely publicly accessible documentation, whether you are a platform administrator, user, or developer. I tried to learn other cloud CRM technologies at that time, but had no luck with getting training environments or free learning resources – you had to become a partner, pay the fee, and get the documents.

This is an awful approach, and I believe it is one of the main reasons why I learned the technology so fast that I become one of the key Salesforce experts in my company, despite still being a junior developer.

I remember the passion and curiosity I had when I was practically eating the Apex and Visualforce Developer Guides, and how many questions I made to my senior colleagues – it all seemed so easy; if I had a question, I would simply ask them or search Google, and I was pretty sure someone would have had the same issue.

I believe that the free-to-learn model provided the foundation for the vital and vibrant Salesforce technical community, which led, in 2014, to the presentation of the Trailhead service, meant to let anyone learn the Salesforce platform with ease and fun through gamification.

The portal can be accessed by anyone for free; simply jump to `https://trailhead. salesforce.com` and register with your Google, LinkedIn, or Salesforce account (you can use all of them together, actually). You'll be met with a Trailhead home page similar to the one shown in the following screenshot:

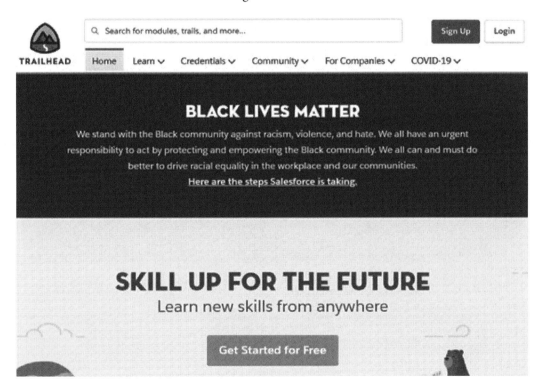

Figure 1.2 – Trailhead home page

Once registered, you are free to browse among hundreds of quick modules to learn about Salesforce products usage, administration, design, and customization from `https://trailhead.salesforce.com/modules`. The following screenshot shows the modules searching page:

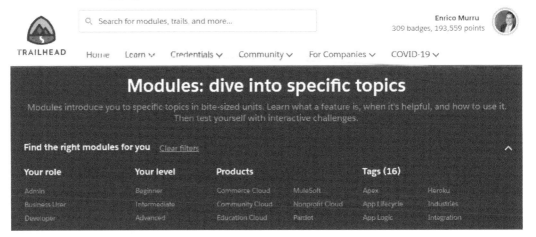

Figure 1.3 – Trailhead modules filter options

You can filter modules based on your roles, experience level, or products. In the following example, we'll filter to show just administrator beginner-level modules on the **Chatter** product:

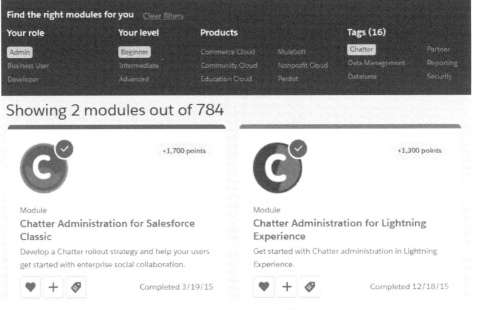

Figure 1.4 – Active modules filtering

Each module is characterized by a completion time of no more than 60 minutes (learning is fun when it is quick!) divided into small units of 10–20 minutes each so that you can learn in your free time between business meetings or working tasks; innovation should be at the core of any technical job, making learning easy and fast, so you can at least remain updated on the latest trends of the platform.

Each unit is composed of a subject-related explanation, which is the core of the learning part, and a final quiz to test your new skills (with a multiple-choice question or a hands-on exercise). By passing each unit, you can get between 25 to 500 points (depending on the question type and the number of failures), and when all the units are completed, you'll get a badge for the corresponding module (that is gamification done right!).

If you want more structured learning, you can choose Trailhead trails at `https://trailhead.salesforce.com/trails`, which are a coherent set of modules related by the same subject. For example, if we choose the **Admin Beginner** trails for **Salesforce Platform**, we'll get a bunch of trails, as shown in the following screenshot:

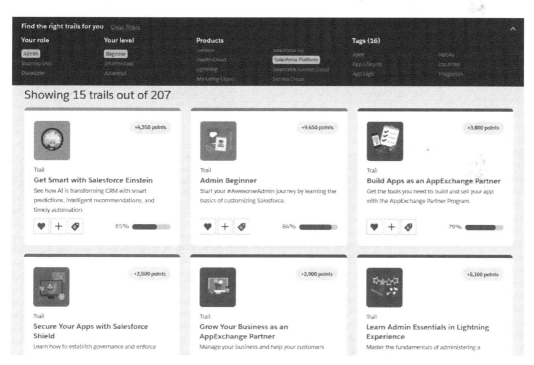

Figure 1.5 – Trailhead trails filtering

Here, as we said, each trail is focused on a specific subject.

Recently, Trailhead has also been used to start your certification process for certain certifications (you need to complete some peculiar modules called *Super Badges* to pass a certification, such as for *Platform Developer II*) and to execute certification maintenance (at each release, once a year, maintenance modules are released, and by passing them, your certification is validated for another year until the next platform release).

Trailhead users can create their own *Trailmixes*, as shown in the following screenshot, just like the one I've built for this book, available at `https://trailhead.salesforce.com/users/enreeco/trailmixes/hands-on-salesforce-application-development-without-code`:

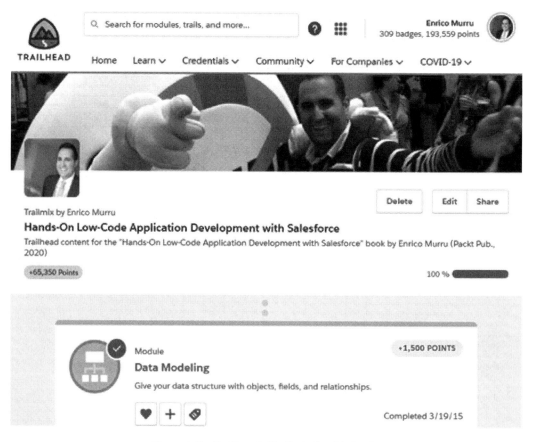

Figure 1.6 – Trailhead's Trailmix for this book

This Trailmix contains all the referenced Trailhead modules and trails that are included at the end of almost every chapter of this book in the *Blaze your trail* sections.

Before getting our hands dirty with Salesforce CRM low-code customization, let's see how to create a new Developer org, which you'll use to follow this book's examples.

Learning with examples – creating a Developer org

Developer Edition orgs (or DE orgs) are simplified environments that should not be used for commercial use, and that any Salesforce professional can create to get their hands on the technology, with no risk at all.

These environments come with almost all features and licenses present (such as Sales and Service Cloud and Communities, to name a few), so you can test them easily but with lower allocations, such as only 5 MB of data storage or the fact that you could only have two full Salesforce-licensed users. Moreover, these kinds of orgs cannot be used for commercial purposes.

> **Further reading**
>
> For a complete list of org allocations for DE orgs, refer to Salesforce Help at `https://help.salesforce.com/articleView?id=overview_limits_general.htm&type=5` and refer to the **Developer Edition** column.

Remember that DE orgs are not forever: if you don't access them for at least 6 months, they will automatically be deleted (but a friendly Salesforce email will notify you about the upcoming deletion, so you can log in to the org if you, for some reason, want it to stay active).

To create a brand new Developer Edition org (you can create as many as you want), do the following:

1. Go to `https://developer.salesforce.com` and click the **Sign-Up** button.

2. Compile the registration form and take care to use a disposable username with a similar email format (like `demo01@gianni.com` or `myfirstdemo@wow.it`).

3. Wait for the activation email.

4. Click on the activation link.

5. Reset your password and add a security question.

The following screenshot shows all the steps (my laptop language is set to Italian, so you'll see the email and reset password form in the following screenshot in Italian):

Figure 1.7 – Developer org registration process

If you plan to grow your career on Salesforce and this is your first DE org, try to write this username down so that you'll be able to access it in later years. I'm a romantic developer at heart, and being able to access my first ever DE org is something that reminds me how young I was when I first used the platform:

Company Information
WebResults.it
The organization's profile is below.

Organization Detail

Organization Name	WebResults.it
Primary Contact	Enrico Murru
Division	
Address	24048 Bergamo IT
Fiscal Year Starts In	January
Activate Multiple Currencies	☐
Newsletter	☐
Admin Newsletter	✓
Hide Notices About System Maintenance	☐
Hide Notices About System Downtime	☐

Created By	Enrico Murru, 03/02/2009 10.28

Figure 1.8 – Company info details of my first DE org

Once the registration is complete, you'll soon receive an activation email with a link you'll be able to reset your password with.

> **Tip**
> If you plan to use diverse orgs (different customers, different DE orgs, and so on), install a browser extension (you'll probably use Chrome or Firefox browsers to work your implementations). I suggest you give the **ORGanizer for Salesforce Chrome and Firefox** extension a try, an extension made by me that has credential storage features and many more Salesforce customization helping tools. The tool is available at `https://organizer.enree.co?#getit` on the Chrome Web Store, the Firefox add-on site, and on AppExchange for free.

Now that you have logged in to your brand-new DE org, you are ready to start your low-code Salesforce customization journey: fasten your seatbelt!

Summary

In this chapter, we briefly saw what the Salesforce platform is and how it has evolved over the last few years, thanks to Marc Benioff's long-term vision of what a cloud company should offer its customers, by delivering innovation through a completely customizable, trusted, and reliable platform and the introduction of new products to fill in diverse feature gaps thanks to smart acquisitions.

Then, we explored the Salesforce platform architecture and its multitenancy format, which lets Salesforce customers share the same cloud infrastructure and resources, in a scalable and reliable virtual *apartment building*, where each customer is granted the same amount of computational resources to smoothly run their Salesforce customizations, provided each customer is allowed to access their own data and metadata (data about data).

We introduced the Trailhead portal, which has rapidly become the main place where Salesforce learning takes place and whose modules are referenced throughout this book.

Finally, we saw how to create a DE Salesforce org so that you are free to learn what's explained in this book, to let you test the examples safely and with no risk to the Salesforce CRM's feature customizations.

In the next chapter, we'll start our low-code customization journey with data model customization, the first piece of metadata that tells the platform how the data should be modeled.

Section 2:
Data Modeling

In this section, we will learn how to build our data model with objects, fields, and formulas. We will build validation rules to guarantee data quality.

This section comprises the following chapters:

- *Chapter 2, Building the Data Model*
- *Chapter 3, Mastering Formulas*
- *Chapter 4, Cleaning Data with Validation Rules*
- *Chapter 5, Handling Dynamic Configuration*
- *Chapter 6, Security First – The "Who Sees What" Paradigm*

2
Building the Data Model

Data is at the heart of any company, and designing the right data model delivers an effective and productive CRM. We'll learn how to build the perfect data model using standard and custom Salesforce objects to conform to business needs. We'll then customize objects with custom fields and all flavors of relationships to link data together and create complex record hierarchies.

In this chapter, we'll cover the following topics:

- What is a data model?

- How to create custom Salesforce objects

- How to customize standard and custom objects with custom fields

- Which relationships are available to link objects together

Technical requirements

The code for the chapter can be found at the following link:

```
https://github.com/PacktPublishing/Hands-On-Low-Code-
Application-Development-with-Salesforce
```

What is a data model?

As you may already know, the business world revolves around information: the more data a company has, the more chance it has of enhancing its business and, thus, being more effective in the market.

But data is nothing without control, and a proper structure that makes data easy to read and understand. That's where the term *model* comes in: a data model is a structured way of storing data in an application, whether it is a desktop app, a web portal, a spreadsheet, a text file, or our beloved Salesforce CRM.

Again, data and data models need to be properly viewed and modified: all of this is represented by the **Model View Controller (MVC)** pattern, which is a way to *separate the concerns* or to avoid mixing the data, the business logic that handles data changes, and the artifacts used to display that data. This pattern can be pictured as follows:

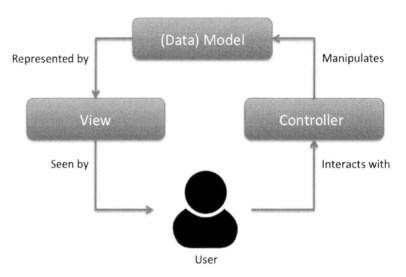

Figure 2.1 – Representation of the Model View Controller (MVC) pattern

From the figure, we can see the following:

- The **user** is the entity that interacts with the application (for example, a call center operator).

- The **controller** interacts with the user and manipulates the data model state to produce results (for example, creating a new customer record, updating a shipment status, or adding a lead to a marketing campaign).

- The (**data**) **model** holds the core of the business of an application and has its own structure that reflects the application's needs (for example, a sales application may contain a model that represents customers, products, payment methods, and contact info, among other things)

- The **view** is the way data is displayed to the **user** in a readable way (for example, a web form, a page layout, or a call center console).

In this scenario, a controller can also control the view (for example, by scrolling a long page to display diverse information) using the preceding data model, or it can use the view to get input from the user (for example, a wizard to add products to a chart). In addition, the data model can notify controllers when its state changes (for example, actions on data being executed by outside actors such as payment systems, billing printers, and so on).

How can we relate this to the Salesforce platform?

In Salesforce, the MVC pattern is at the core of the platform. The pattern consists of the following:

- **Data model**: Salesforce objects, fields, and relationships

- **Controller**: Workflows, Process Builder, Lightning Flow, **Approval Processes**, actions, Apex classes, and triggers (and even more automation tools)

- **View**: Page Layouts, Lightning pages, community pages, Visualforce Pages, and Lightning components

Throughout the book, we'll cover much of this list (excluding the coding part for Apex Classes and Triggers) to have a clear view of all the possibilities that you, as a developer, have for effectively customizing your Salesforce organization without needing to code.

In this chapter, we'll dig into how to create and manage Salesforce objects and customize them with fields and relationships in order to deliver a perfect data model.

Salesforce objects

Salesforce Platform is a product that you may use with little to no customization, provided that what the CRM provides as built-in features are enough for your business requirements.

This applies to data models as well: Salesforce comes with some pre-built models, called **Salesforce objects**, which are standard data structures that *Salesforce scientists* came up with after years of experience in the sales and service domain.

Jump to the developer org we created in the previous chapter, click on the **App Launcher**, and select the **Sales** app as pictured:

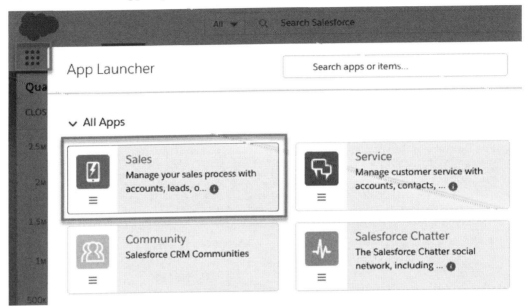

Figure 2.2 – Selecting the Sales standard app from the App Launcher

> **Tip**
> Feel free to play around with the other apps to make yourself comfortable with the Salesforce user interface.

The first thing you'll notice is the abundance of tabs that you can browse:

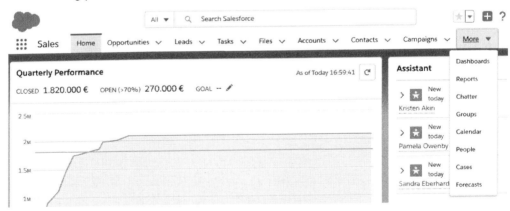

Figure 2.3 – The standard Sales app with a set of standard Salesforce objects

These tabs are the so-called **standard Salesforce objects** that are a part of the data model that the platform gives you as included with your licensed org. This app is focused on the sales process, and it includes the following tabs:

- **Home**: This is the app's home page, and it can be customized using Lightning Pages and the Lightning App Builder, as we'll see in the next chapters.

- **Opportunities**: This tab records sold or pending deals.

- **Leads**: This tab records prospective customers or simply people that may be interested in your business.

- **Tasks**: This tab records activities to be completed (such as a recurring phone call with a customer).

- **Files**: This tab is for managing your files.

- **Accounts**: This tab records persons or organizations involved in your business (a customer, a partner, a vendor, and so on).

- **Contacts**: This tab usually stores contact data of a person.

- **Campaigns**: This tab records marketing or sales campaigns.

If you click on the **Service** app or any other app, you'll see a different set of tabs, as the processes of handling sales or services for customers provide different kinds of data (that is, a different data model):

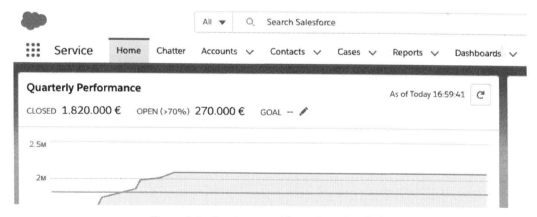

Figure 2.4 – Service app with service-related tabs

In this scenario, the apps are included in the **View** part of the MVC pattern, as they show different objects depending on their scope.

If you click on the **Contacts** tab and select the **All Contacts** list view in the top-right corner of the **Contacts** home page, this is what you will see:

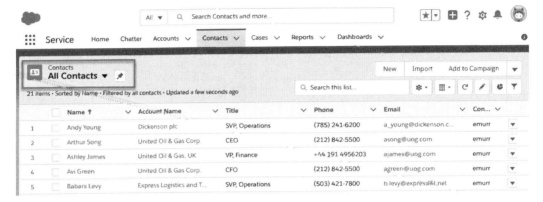

Figure 2.5 – Contacts home page with All Contacts selected

Here, you can filter the contacts using some built-in list views (such as **Recently Viewed**, **My Contacts** or **Birthdays This Month**) and you can customize or create new lists that adhere to your needs.

> **Further reading**
>
> List views are a simple and easy feature to master. Refer to Salesforce Help at `https://help.salesforce.com/articleView?id=` `customviews_lex.htm&type=5` for a detailed guide on list view customization.

Now, click any link in the **Name** column to have a look at the details of a contact:

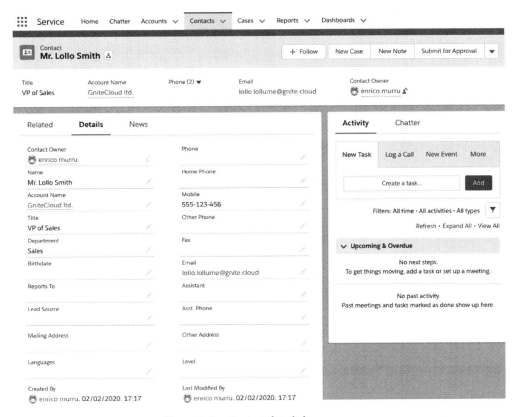

Figure 2.6 – Contact details home page

Under the name of the contact, where the **Related**, **Details**, and **News** tabs lie, click on the **Details** tab to have a look at the contact's fields (as shown in the preceding screenshot): this is the record layout view where the object fields are shown. For this specific object, we can see the **Name**, the related **Account Name** (the company that the contact belongs to; this is a relation field that links the **Contact** and **Account** object), **Mobile**, and some other data.

From what we have seen so far, Salesforce objects are containers of fields that refer to a specific kind of data (so don't expect real data to be put inside a contact object; if you do that, you may need to reconsider your data model).

> **Further reading**
>
> As a future designer of Salesforce solutions, you need to understand Salesforce standard objects and fields and their use cases. For a detailed list of all standard Salesforce objects, refer to Salesforce Help at https://developer. salesforce.com/docs/atlas.en-us.object_reference. meta/object_reference/sforce_api_objects_list.htm.

Let's consider an example to better understand how Salesforce objects can shape your business.

Your company, Amazing Ads Ltd., sells advertisement spaces (such as the big billboards you see on the side of roads) and wants to start a CRM project using Salesforce. The main actors involved in their business processes are as follows:

- Customers that pay to see their ads on billboards
- People related to customers, so they can save customer contact information
- Offer packages for ads to be offered to their customers
- Advertisement deals related to customers and specific packages
- Official contracts when the deal is closed with the details of contract start and end dates
- Details of a specific advertisement (such as title, frequency, and graphics)

Most of this data can be easily translated into standard Salesforce objects:

- **Account**: This represents any organization that has a link with our business, and being a customer is such a link.
- **Contact**: This holds all contact data of a given person.
- **Product** and **Price Book**: They contain product details that our company sells to our customers.
- **Opportunity**: This is the sales object, representing the entire sales journey from the first contact with a customer to the deal closing.
- **Contract**: When a deal is closed, a contract states that there is a business link between our company and an account, which has purchased our products/services.

Regarding the details of a specific ad, there is apparently nothing specific in Salesforce that can be applied. This is understandable as it is impossible to figure out every combination of company and business type. But that's where the power of Salesforce customization comes in.

Before talking about our first customization using custom objects, let's summarize what we have said so far: each business is based on data, and this data needs to be structured appropriately with a data model. Salesforce is not an empty app that has to be developed from scratch; instead, it holds its own data model (primarily for sales and services, but many more processes have been added in the last few years) that can be used and adapted to a company's business needs. This data model is organized in Salesforce objects as information units that hold a specific actor data of a business, where each object contains a set of fields that are the real holders of data (for example, contact phone number, customer name, and product price).

Customizing a data model with custom objects

To expand a data model, new information units can be created with custom Salesforce objects and, using relationships, we can link them with other standard or custom objects (we'll see relations later on). We'll be using the **Object Manager** tab for any object-related customization.

To create a new custom object, click on **Setup | Object Manager | Create | Custom Object**, as shown in the following screenshot:

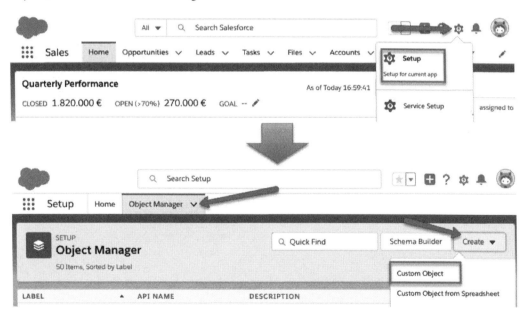

Figure 2.7 – Getting to the custom object creation wizard

> **Note**
>
> We've just entered the customization part of the Salesforce CRM, called **Setup**. From this page, you'll be able to customize almost any part of the platform. If you are not yet comfortable with this part of Salesforce, you'll surely be by the end of this book.

Let's see all the information you need to provide to create a new object in the following sections.

Custom object information

The **custom object** wizard contains all the information required to create a new object:

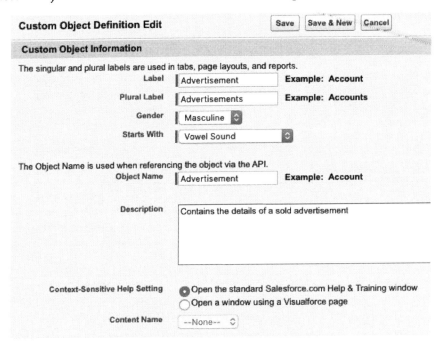

Figure 2.8 – Custom Object Information section

Let's review each field and what it records:

- **Label**: Object label (for example, **Advertisement**).

- **Plural Label**: Plural label (for example, **Advertisements**).

- **Gender**: **Masculine** or **Feminine** (this is needed for gendered languages).

- **Starts With**: **Consonant/Vowel sound** or **S** (plus consonant) or **Z** (it may be important depending on your default language, such as the need for an article such as *an* instead of *a*).

- **Object Name**: This is the technical name (usually called the API name) that is used to technically reference the object (for example, inside a SQL query, in a formula or in Apex code) and must be unique across all objects. It also must contain letters, numbers, and the underscore character; it must start with a letter, and it cannot contain more than one underscore in sequence (for example, **Advertisement**). After creation, Salesforce appends the __c suffix (so the object's API name becomes Advertisement__c), and this is the main way to distinguish standard and custom objects.

- **Description**: A meaningful description of why the object has been created.

> **Note**
>
> When a **Description** field is displayed to you in a wizard, take care to fill it in even if it's optional: you'll thank your past-self for this when after months or even years you get back to that object or field to understand what it was meant for.

Enter Record Name Label and Format

Then we have the **Enter Record Name Label and Format** section:

Enter Record Name Label and Format

The Record Name appears in page layouts, key lists, related lists, lookups, and search results. For example, the Record Name for Account is "Account Name" and for Case it is "Case Number". Note that the Record Name field is always called "Name" when referenced via the API.

Record Name	Advertisement Code	**Example: Account Name**
Data Type	Auto Number	
Display Format	A{YYYY}-{0000000}	**Example: A-{0000}** <u>What Is This?</u>
Starting Number	1	

Figure 2.9 – Object name field details section

Record Name is the label of the **Name** field that is automatically created by Salesforce on this object (for example, **Advertisement Code**)

In **Data Type**, the standard **Name** field can be of two different types:

- **Text**: The **Name** field can be filled in with any text value
- **Auto Number**: When a new record is created, the **Name** field is automatically populated with a unique value. When you select this value, the **Display Format** and **Starting Number** textboxes appear: they are used to define a specific format for the unique value. For example, we want the advertisement code to be formatted like A-YEAR-XXXXXXXX, where X is a sequence from 1 to 999999999. The previous screenshot shows how we have filled in the fields. We'll see shortly what it will look like on the record's layout.

Further reading

For more details on the Auto Number format, have a look at Salesforce Help at `https://help.salesforce.com/articleView?id=custom_ field_attributes.htm&type=5#DisplayFormat`.

Additional fields and options

Here, we will cover the remaining fields and their options for creating a custom object, shown in the following screenshot:

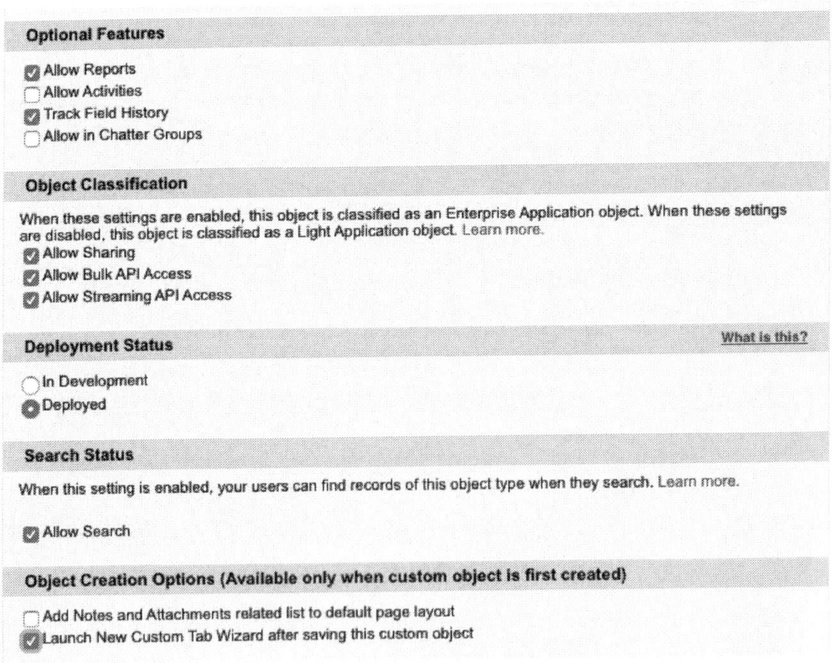

Figure 2.10 – Last options before creating the Advertisement custom object

We will start with **Optional Features** and **Object Classification**:

- **Optional Features**:

  Allow Reports: This object can be included in a report.

  Allow Activities: Tasks and events can be related to this object.

  Track Field History: Enables the tracking of field history (we'll see this feature later).

  Allow in Chatter Groups: This object can be used within the Chatter Publisher in Chatter Groups (more info about Chatter at `https://help.salesforce.com/articleView?id=collab_chatter_parent.htm&type=5`).

- **Object Classification**:

  Allow Sharing: Allows sharing on its records

  Allow Bulk API Access: Allows access via the Bulk API (a feature used by tools such as Data Loader to speed up data import/export)

  Allow Streaming API Access: Allows access to Streaming API (a feature used by external services to subscribe to object modification in real time, for example, when a record is changed, an event is fired and the external service outside Salesforce is notified and, thus, can execute its business logic)

With regard to the three options under **Object Classification**, let's say that disabling them causes the platform to be more responsive. While enabling them causes the platform to be less responsive on this specific object, it conveys some more useful features (for example, limiting the visibility of records using sharing, something we'll briefly see later on).

Now let's move on to **Deployment Status**, **Search Status**, and **Object Creation Options**:

- **Deployment Status:**

  In Development / Deployed: By flagging an object as **Deployed**, you are sure that the object can be seen by users other than you (if you are working on it and don't want other people to see what you are doing until it's ready, select **In Development**: you can change it later when your development is ready).

- **Search Status:**

  Allow Search: The object can be searched using the global search textbox. If you have created a tab for this object, the object is searchable by default.

- **Object Creation Options (Available only when custom object is first created):**

  Add Notes and Attachments related list to default page layout: If selected, a notes and attachments related list is added to the object layout (in Lightning Experience, the attachments have been replaced by the **File** object), so let's leave it unchecked.

  Launch New Custom Tab Wizard after saving this custom object: This launches a new tab creation wizard after completing the **Custom Object** wizard, so let's keep this option checked.

Custom object creation wizard

Now click the **Save** button to launch the **Custom Object** tab creation wizard (you can start this wizard from **Setup | Home | User Interface | Tabs** and select the **New** button in the **Custom Object Tabs** section, then select the **Tab Style** (among the tens of images displayed, this will select the icon associated with this object):

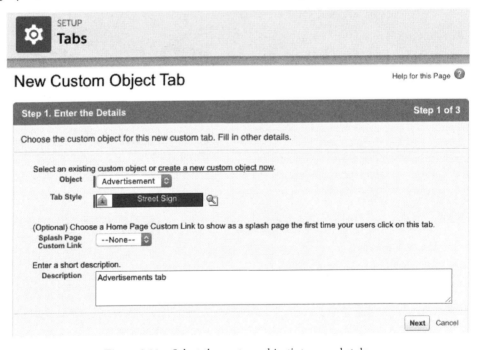

Figure 2.11 – Select the custom object's type and style

Click **Next** to select which user profiles can access this tab (let's leave the default values) and click **Next** again to jump to the final step of **Tab** creation:

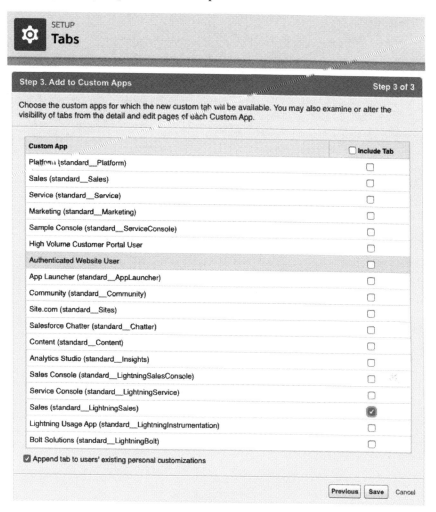

Figure 2.12 – Select the applications the tab will be added to

In the final step, select the applications where you want the tab to be added: we have chosen the **Sales** app only (take care to choose **standard_LightningSales** and not **standard_Sales** as we want to add the tab to the Lightning Experience app).

Now click **Save** to complete the creation, and you'll be redirected to the new custom object setup page:

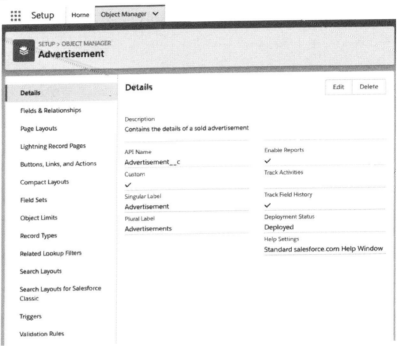

Figure 2.13 – Main custom object setup page

On the left menu shown in Fig 2.13, all the main object configuration options are available:

- **Fields & Relationships**: Manage the object's fields
- **Page Layouts**: Configuration of record layouts for the right field display for users
- **Lightning Record Pages**: Any Lightning Page created to display object data in Lightning Experience
- **Buttons, Links, and Actions**: Manage custom actionable items on records
- **Compact Layouts**: Manage record's key field layouts (for mobile or Lightning Experience quick view)
- **Field Sets**: Define a group of fields that can be managed by Visualforce/Apex

- **Object Limits**: A page showing all the main limits for a given object (such as the number of fields or relationships)

- **Record Types**: Record type management (we'll have a quick look at record types shortly)

- **Related Lookup Filters**: This object is used in a related lookup filter from another standard/custom object

- **Search Layouts**: Manage which fields are shown on search results

- **Triggers**: List of Apex Triggers created for this object

- **Validation Rules**: Manage all validation rules related to this record (to keep the data clean, we'll look at validation in the next chapters)

To edit any information, you can use the **Edit** button (almost any data that we have just inserted). With **Delete**, we can delete the object but be careful that all related data will also be deleted, as shown in the following confirmation popup:

Deleting a custom object does the following:

- Deletes all the data that currently exists in all records of that custom object
- Deletes all tracked history data associated with the custom object
- Deletes the custom tab and list views for the object
- Deletes workflow rules and actions that use the object
- Hides the custom object definition and all related definitions
- Hides the object's data records and all related data records
- Disables report types for which this is the main object
- Disables custom reports for which this is the main object
- Deactivates custom formula fields on the object
- Deactivates custom validation rules and approval processes on the object
- Deactivates and deletes the Lightning Pages associated with the custom object.

In order to preserve a record of data for future reference, run a data export before deleting custom objects by clicking Data | Data Export.

After you've deleted this custom object, it appears in the deleted objects list for 15 days. During that time, you can either undelete it to restore it and all the data stored in it, or delete it permanently. When you undelete a custom object, some of its properties might be lost or changed. After 15 days, the object and its data are permanently deleted.

Figure 2.14 – Delete popup shown on object deletion

If you click on the **Object Manager** tab now, you can spot our new custom object:

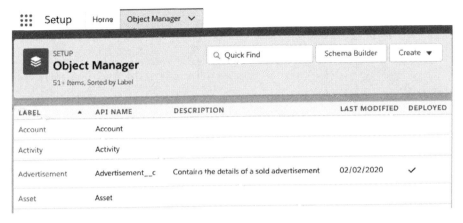

Figure 2.15 – List of standard and custom objects from the Object Manager tab

Before proceeding with customizing the object, we will take a little break to see what's just happened on the Sales app.

Checking the tab on the Sales app

Click on the **App Launcher** icon (the square icon with nine dots next to **Setup**) and select the **Sales** app (you may have a tab with the Sales app already open, just refresh it). Click on the **More** tab and select **Advertisements**. We have no records to display:

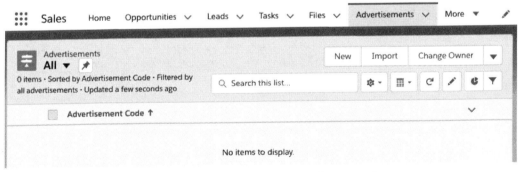

Figure 2.16 – Advertisements tab with no records

Let's create a new record with the **New** button:

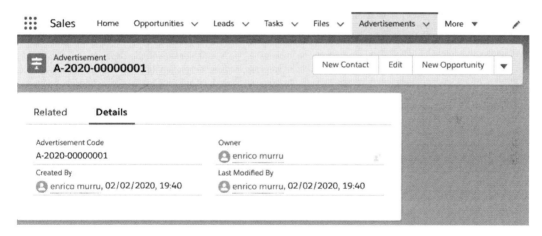

Figure 2.17 – Advertisement creation form

We haven't defined any field other than the **Advertisement Code** field, which is an auto-number field so it is set by Salesforce automatically. In this form, the **Owner** is already set up; the owner is the user who is responsible for the record. Click **Save** to save the record:

Figure 2.18 – Record details page

Advertisement Code is successfully updated with the format we configured in the object details (A-YEAR-XXXXXXXXX) and two new fields pop up, **Created By** and **Last Modified By**, that simply state by who and when the record has been created and updated. After the record is created, the owner can be easily changed using the change owner icon next to the **Owner** name.

Let's go on and see how to customize objects using custom fields.

Enhancing Salesforce objects with custom fields

Like Salesforce objects, the platform offers standard and custom fields, which are fields that are part of the Salesforce data model, and fields that can be created from scratch on any Salesforce object to increase the amount of data included in a single object, respectively.

Let's see an example by opening the **Account** page from **Setup | Object Manager | Account | Fields & Relationships**:

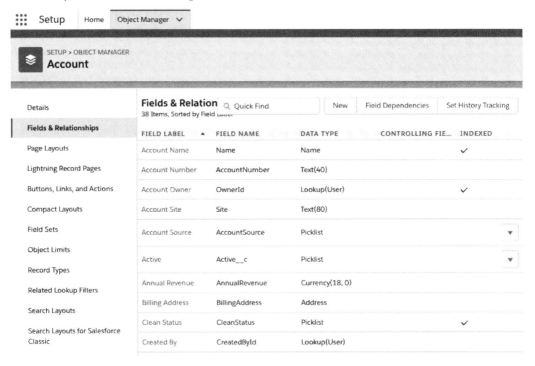

Figure 2.19 – Account fields list

Do you see something strange?

There is a field whose **FIELD NAME** (or API Name) ends with __c: this is a custom field that has been created by Salesforce on the developer org that you can delete without any problem. There are also other standard fields, which relate to how Salesforce modeled the account object (for example, Source, Addresses, Number, and so on).

> **Further reading**
>
> For a complete list of all available standard fields for standard objects, refer to Salesforce Help at https://developer.salesforce.com/docs/atlas.en-us.sfFieldRef.meta/sfFieldRef/salesforce_field_reference.htm.

What about our **Advertisement** custom object? It appears in a few fields, as can be seen in the following screenshot:

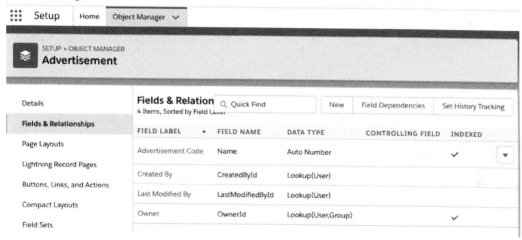

Figure 2.20 – Standard fields on a custom object

We've already talked about these fields:

- **Advertisement Code**: The **Name** field set up from the object's details page

- **Created By**: The user who created the record, which is related to the **Created Date** field not shown in this list that contains the creation date

- **Last Modified By**: Like the previous field but related to who last updated the record, and a **Last Modified Date** for the update date

- **Owner**: A relation with a user object that is used to state which user is the current record manager

As discussed before, the **Advertisement** object needs some more fields, as these standard fields alone don't give the right quantity of data to describe an advertisement.

So, let's add the following fields:

- **Installation Date**: The date when the ad will be installed.

- **Installation Address**: The whole address of the installation in plain text.

- **Is Active**: Whether the ad is still in place or not.

- **Months of Availability**: The number of months the ad will be active.

- **Price**: The amount paid by the customer.

- **Customer**: The customer who purchased the ad.

- **Deal**: The opportunity related to this advertisement.

- **Expected Dismission Date**: The date when the ad should be dismissed.

- **Renewal Status**: If the advertisement is about to be dismissed (or has already been dismissed), this field represents the renewal status: for example, **Renewing**, **Not interested**, or **To be recalled**.

To create a new field, click on **Setup | Object Manager | Advertisement | Fields & Relationships | New**:

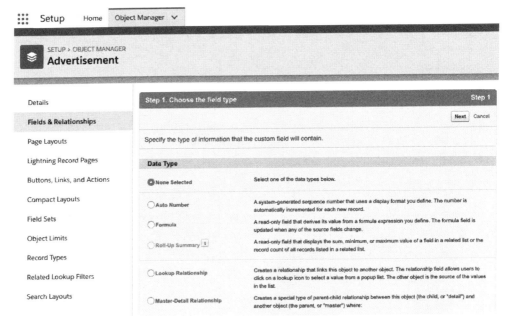

Figure 2.21 – Custom field creation wizard: type selection

The first step of this wizard is used to assign what kind of data the field will contain:

- **Auto Number**: Assigns a unique code to the object (like we did with the **Name** field).

- **Formula**: This is a calculated field (we'll see formulas in the next chapters).

- **Roll-Up Summary**: A special calculated field that can count the number of records related to this record with Master-Detail relationships (we'll see this field in the next section).

- **Lookup Relationship/Master-Detail Relationship/External Relationship**: Represents different kinds of relations between the current object and other records (covered in the next section).

- **Checkbox**: A field that can have two values only: true or false.

- **Currency**: Contains a currency (the company's currency is displayed along with the number).

- **Date** or **Date/Time**: Includes a date value or a date with time.

- **Email**: Contains an email, formatted value.

- **Geolocation**: Holds latitude and longitude values.

- **Number**: A generic number (integer or decimal).

- **Percent**: A percentage (displayed with the % symbol).

- **Phone**: Contains a phone number (Salesforce tries to format the phone number correctly).

- **Picklist**: A constrained list of text values where the user can select a single value.

- **Picklist (Multi-Select)**: A constrained list of text values where the user can select more than one value.

- **Text**: A simple short text field (input with a textbox component).

- **Text Area**: A simple short text field (input with a text area component that spans more rows).

- **Text Area (Long)**: A bigger text field.

- **Text Area (Rich)**: A text field with longer text and rich text capabilities (input with a WYSIWYG component, like a text editor).

- **Text (Encrypted)**: A simple short text that is encrypted (like a password field).

- **Time**: Contains a time value only.

- **Url**: Contains a URL text (displayed as a hypertext link).

Taking our **Advertisement** example, we can match the following fields:

- **Installation Date**: Date.

- **Installation Address**: Text area (long).

- **Is Active**: Checkbox.

- **Months of Availability**: Number.

- **Price**: Currency.

- **Customer** and **Deal**: This is a relation, so it must be some kind of lookup.

- **Expected Dismission Date**: **Date**, but it seems to be something related to the **Installation Date** *plus* the **Months of Availability**, so it must be something that's calculated.

- **Renewal Status**: Picklist.

Let's see some of this kind of custom field configuration. Click on the **New** button of the **Fields & Relationships** object setup page's tab and select one of the previous field types to see how to configure them.

> **Note**
> Before starting to customize your org, disable browser caching from **Setup | Security | Session Settings** and deselect the **Enable** secure and persistent browser caching option to improve the performance option under Caching: this will avoid frustrating delays in seeing your setup changes coming up on your browser. Do this in production only if absolutely necessary.

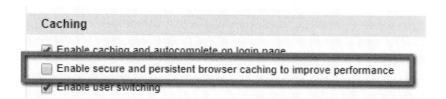

Figure 2.22 – Switching off browser caching to improve the setup experience

For the following sections, I've created a new **Example** custom object, dedicated to testing all field types.

Auto-number

We've seen the auto-number type for the standard **Field Name** field of the **Advertisement** object:

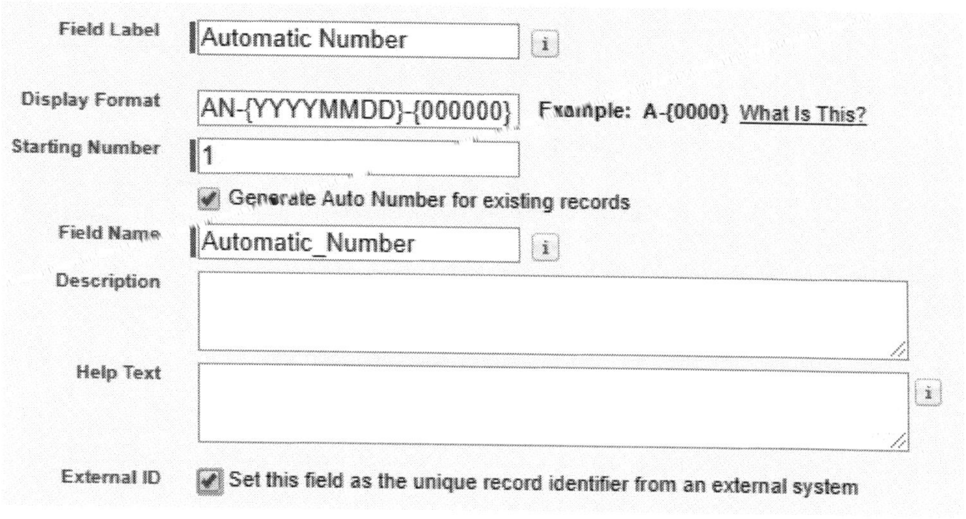

Figure 2.23 – Auto-number type configuration

From the preceding screenshot, we can observe the following:

- **Field Label** and **Field Name** behave as we saw with the object's **Label** and **Name** fields (a readable label and an API name that should not change once established).

- **Description** is used to state what the field is meant for (this is internal metadata, never shown to users).

- **Help Text** is used to help users with the meaning of the field (it's something that will appear on the record's view with a help icon).

- **Display Format** and **Starting Number** states how the auto-numbering is done.

- **Generate Auto Number for existing records** makes Salesforce calculate the field for any record already created (after all, you can create this field when you are already using the object).

- **External ID** is a feature used to speed up SOQL queries, as this field becomes an indexed field and can be used to directly refer to this record (be careful that this field is not necessarily unique across all records if not flagged on an auto-number field). This field can also be used for *upsert* operations, that is, updating or creating a record based on a record with the same value as a specific field (this is so useful when you don't want to check whether a record exists and are using an external database that you are absolutely sure contains the master of the record).

> **Further reading**
>
> Find out more about external IDs on Salesforce Help at `https://help.salesforce.com/articleView?id=000325076&language=en_US&type=1&mode=1`.

This is the final result once you complete the creation wizard:

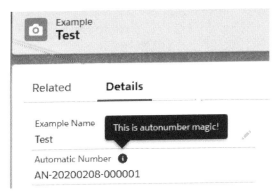

Figure 2.24 – Automatic Number field with help text

Checkbox

The **Checkbox** field, which holds two values only, true or false, is straightforward:

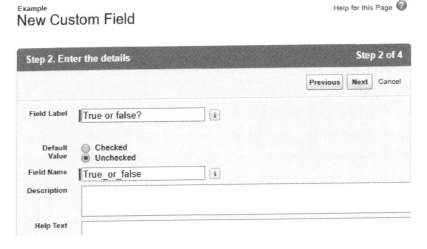

Figure 2.25 – Checkbox field creation

We can set up a default value to be flagged or not, leading to the following layout representation:

True or false?

Figure 2.26 – Checkbox view on a record's page

Date and Date/Time

This type holds the date or the date with time, shown in the current user's time zone format:

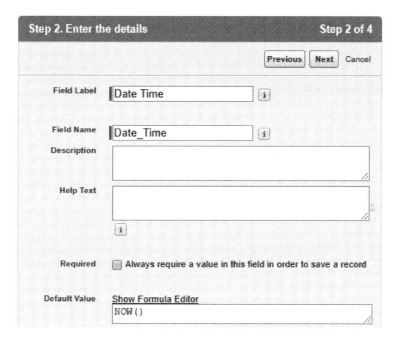

Figure 2.27 – Date and date/time configuration

From the preceding screenshot, we observe the following:

- **Required**: This field is required and is enforced at the layout level.

- **Default Value**: A formula (we'll see formulas in the next chapters) used in case the field is not filled in on save. In this case, we're setting up the field to have a default value with the NOW() function, which simply adds the current date/time value (with the **Date** field, we should use the TODAY() function, which only uses the date without the time value).

The field is displayed as follows (in edit mode):

Figure 2.28 – Date/time layout display

The small calendar and clock icons are actionable icons to select the date and time (the **Date** type has only the date selection textbox).

Email

This type is meant for email types of values:

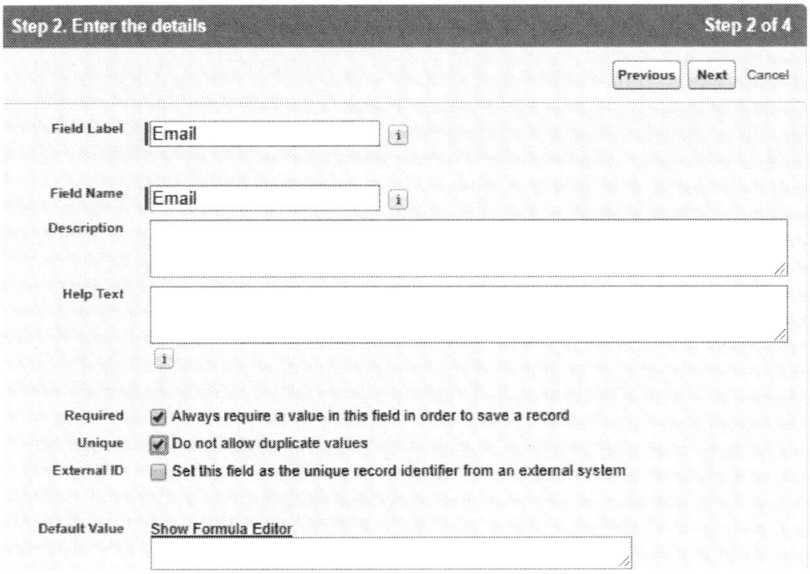

Figure 2.29 – Email type configuration

The **Unique** field guarantees that there cannot be any other record with the same value for this field.

If you try to add an invalid email value or a value already on the database, an error is shown:

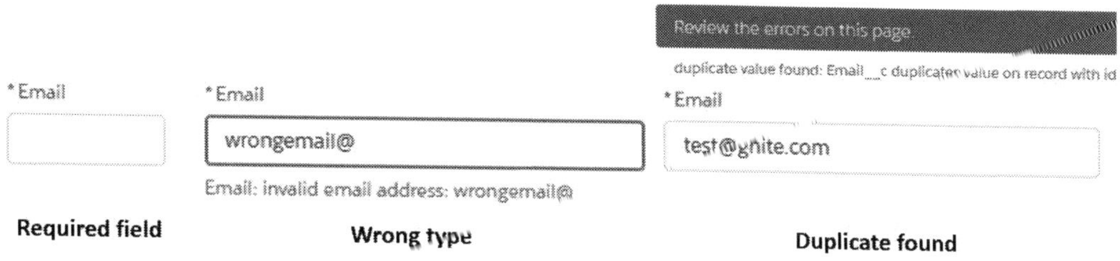

Figure 2.30 – Error types on the same field

Number, currency, and percentage

You can define a type for a generic number, a currency (in the main company's currency definition), and a percentage:

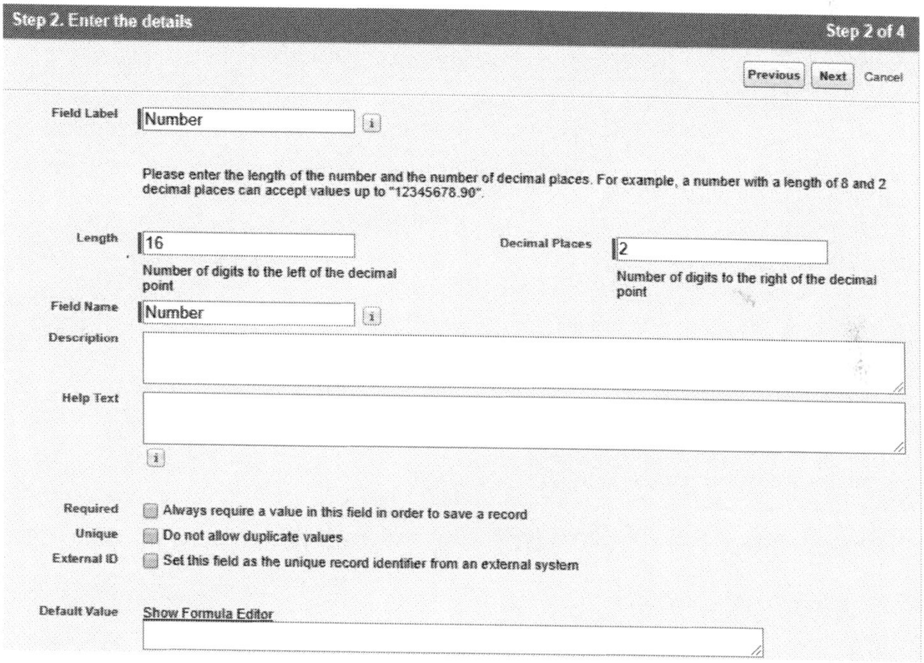

Figure 2.31 – Numeric field configuration

Only the **Numeric** type can be **Unique** and/or **External ID**.

Length defines the maximum number of integer digits, and **Decimal** is the number of decimal digits, and this works only if the total is 18.

This is the output:

Figure 2.32 – Numeric field types

When filling up a number, you can use the *M* and *K* characters to avoid hitting the *0* character, so that:

- 1.5M becomes 1,500,000
- 25K becomes 25,000

> **Tip**
> The use of the *dot* or *comma* as a decimal separator depends on the user's locale settings: refer to `https://help.salesforce.com/articleView?id=admin_language_locale_currency.htm&type=5` for more on setting up locales.

If your organization holds a multi-currency configuration, you'll be able to choose which currency your **Currency** field is filled with.

> **Further reading**
> There are more details on multi-currency on Salesforce Help at `https://help.salesforce.com/articleView?id=admin_enable_multicurrency.htm&type=5`.

Phone and URL

These are typed in to contain specific phone and URL types. No configuration is needed other than that which we described earlier.

Picklist

This is a very popular field type; it is basically a text field where you can specify a list of constrained values:

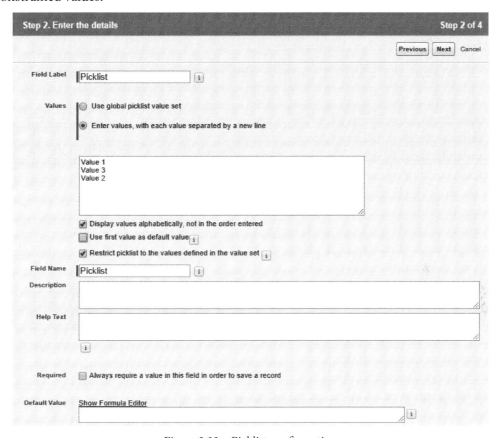

Figure 2.33 – Picklist configuration

The list of values can be set up with the following options:

- **Global picklist value set**: A set of values that can be used across objects (for example, a specific address toponym list such as *Street*, *Avenue*, or *Square*) that you may use in different places.
- **Manual list**: Enter the list of values manually, like in *Figure 2.33*.

Further reading

For more information on how to create global picklist value sets, refer to Salesforce Help at `https://help.salesforce.com/articleView?id=fields_creating_global_picklists.htm&type=5`.

While using **Global Value Sets**, the user is always required to fill in an allowed value (using manual values you can decide if you wish to restrict); to sort values in alphabetical order; and to use the first value as the default one.

Note

Restriction is important if data can come from different channels that are not necessarily a human: if your CRM is fed by an external system (such as a billing system or an order management system), the data coming in may have different value domains (so instead of *Street* the billing system sends *St.*). It's up to you and your design to choose whether or not the field is to be restricted (provided that users will only be able to use the provided values).

This is how the field is displayed:

Figure 2.34 – Picklist display

Multi-select picklist

Like picklists, multi-select picklists can contain a defined list of values, but instead of just one value they can hold many of them.

The configuration is the same as for the picklist type seen previously, but there is an exception made for the **# Visible Lines** options:

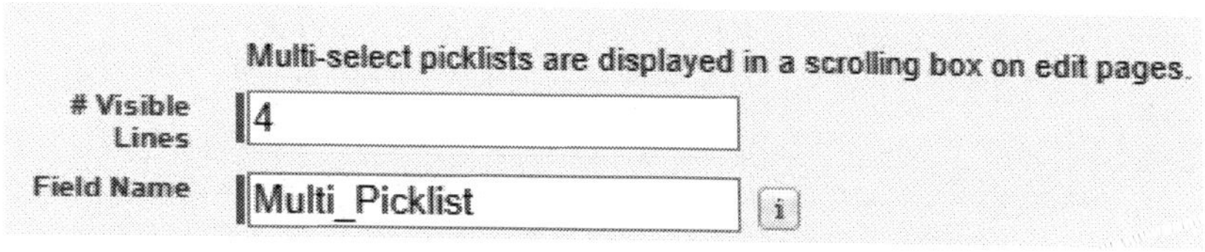

Figure 2.35 – Multi-select picklist configuration exception

The **# Visible Lines** field states how many values must appear on the user's side. The output of a multi-picklist is slightly varied to the usual ones:

MultiPicklist

Available   Chosen

Multi 2   ▶   Multi 1

Multi 3   Multi 4

◀

Figure 2.36 – Multi-select picklist display

Further reading

To understand the limitations involved in using picklist and multi-select picklist fields, refer to Salesforce Help at `https://help.salesforce.com/articleView?id=picklist_limitations.htm&type=5`.

Text and Text Area

Text and **Text Area** types are meant to host a simple text with a size of no more than 255 characters. While the simple **Text** field is displayed as input text, **Text Area** can contain multi-line values:

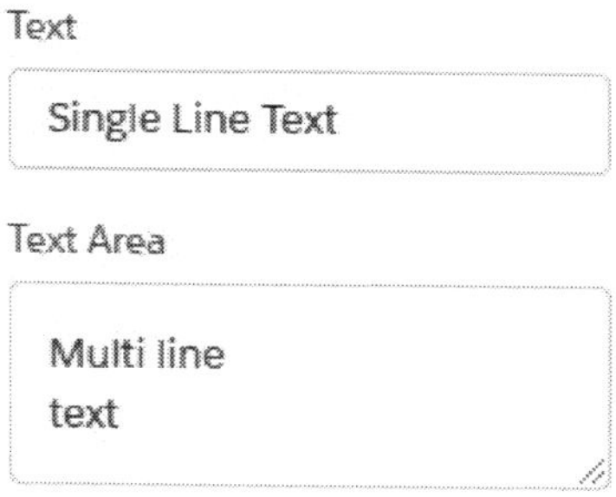

Text

Single Line Text

Text Area

Multi line
text

Figure 2.37 – Text and Text Area display

If you need more length (more than 255 characters) for a long description field or a notes field, use **Text Area Long**, which can hold up 131,072 characters (you can have a maximum of 1,638,400 characters across different long text area fields on the same object). When setting up the field, you can use the **# Visible Lines** field to show a specific number of lines in the text area.

If you need rich (for example, HTML-like) text, use the **Rich Text Area**, which allows you to add formatted text and images with an inline WYSYWYG editor, as you can see in the following screenshot:

Figure 2.38 – Text Area Long and Rich Text Area display

Further reading

Find more about text area type limitations on Salesforce Help at `https://help.salesforce.com/articleView?id=fields_rich_text_area_limitations.htm&type=5`.

Encrypted text

If you need to store some basic encrypted data (using Salesforce encryption at rest), use the **Encrypted** field type:

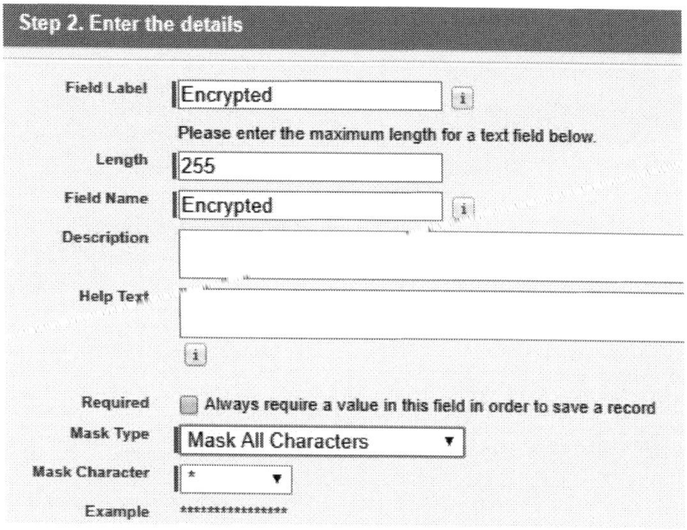

Step 2. Enter the details

Field Label	Encrypted
	Please enter the maximum length for a text field below.
Length	255
Field Name	Encrypted
Description	
Help Text	
Required	☐ Always require a value in this field in order to save a record
Mask Type	Mask All Characters ▼
Mask Character	* ▼
Example	**************

Figure 2.39 – Encrypted text type configuration

Only users with the **View Encrypted Data** permission checked will be able to see the values in encrypted custom fields.

You can select the **Mask Type** and the **Mask Character** (the format of the hidden value) and you cannot exceed 175 characters. When you fill in an encrypted text field, you'll be able to see what you are writing (unlike usual password input boxes), but it is subsequently encrypted upon save:

Figure 2.40 – Encrypted field display

Further reading

For more info about Encrypted Text limitations, refer to Salesforce Help at `https://help.salesforce.com/articleView?id=fields_about_encrypted_fields.htm&type=5`.

If you need to encrypt other field types, Salesforce Shield Platform Encryption is the way to go, but it involves a separate license type and more complex configurations and considerations (refer to `https://help.salesforce.com/articleView?id=security_pe_concepts.htm&type=5`).

Time

The **Time** type is used to host a simple **Time** value, without any reference to the user's time zone.

> **Further reading**
>
> For more considerations on **Time** fields, refer to Salesforce Help at `https://help.salesforce.com/articleView?id=custom_field_time_overview.htm&type=5`.

Closing the custom field creation wizard

Once the field type configuration is completed, click **Next** to select the **Field Level Security** options for the record, as shown in the following screenshot:

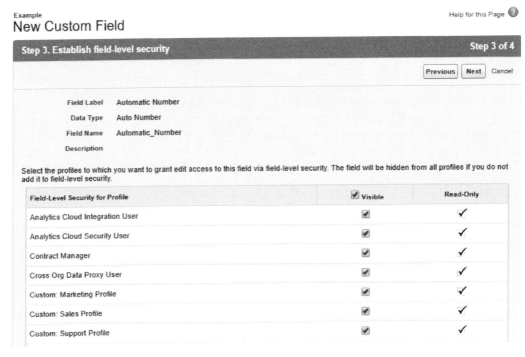

Figure 2.41 – Selecting field-level security for the new field

You can select which profiles can access the new field:

- **Visible**: The profile can view the field.

- **Read-Only**: The profile can only read the field and cannot write it.

These are the basic security configurations at the field level (who can see which field): in this specific case where we are creating an auto-number field (which cannot be updated manually), the **Read-Only** option is selected for all profiles.

Click **Next** to see the layout options:

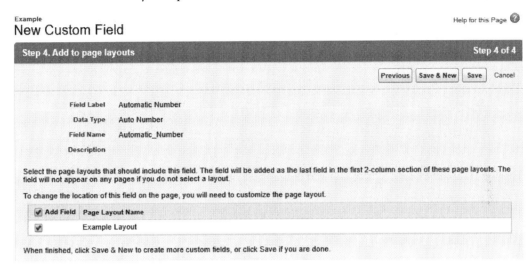

Figure 2.42 – Adding a field to a page layout

As we'll see in upcoming chapters, an object can have different layouts depending on the way we want to show its data: each layout can be related to one or more profiles, so each profile will see the record in a different way (for example, some fields may be too technical and of no interest to sales managers).

Click **Save** to complete the new field wizard (or **Save & New** if you want to start a new field creation wizard).

> **Further reading**
>
> For a deeper knowledge of all the different flavors of custom field configuration fields, refer to Salesforce Help at `https://help.salesforce.com/articleView?id=custom_field_attributes.htm&type=5`.

Field history

You can enable field history tracking on any object that you want to track specific field changes on. You can track up to 20 fields and retain the list of changes for up to 24 months (if changes are made through APIs, that is, from external systems) or 18 months (if changes are made by users from the user interface).

To enable field history tracking, click on the **Set History Tracking** button on the **Fields & Relationships** tab of any standard or custom object and select up to 20 fields (the following screenshot shows the history tracking configuration for a generic **Example** object):

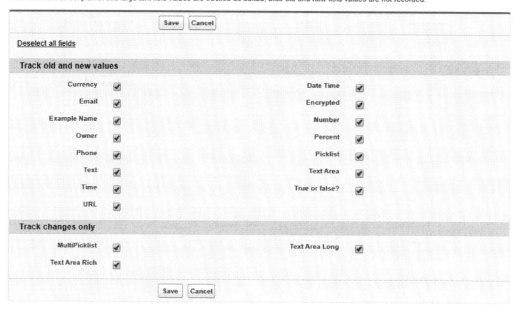

Figure 2.43 – Field history tracking configuration

Once tracking is enabled, you need to add the **Field History** related list to the object layout (unless you haven't already enabled **Field History Tracking** on object creation, as seen earlier).

Create a new record, save the record, then edit it, and update some of its fields. Now click on the **Related** tab of the record's page and have a look at the **Example History** (click the **View All** link if you have many entries):

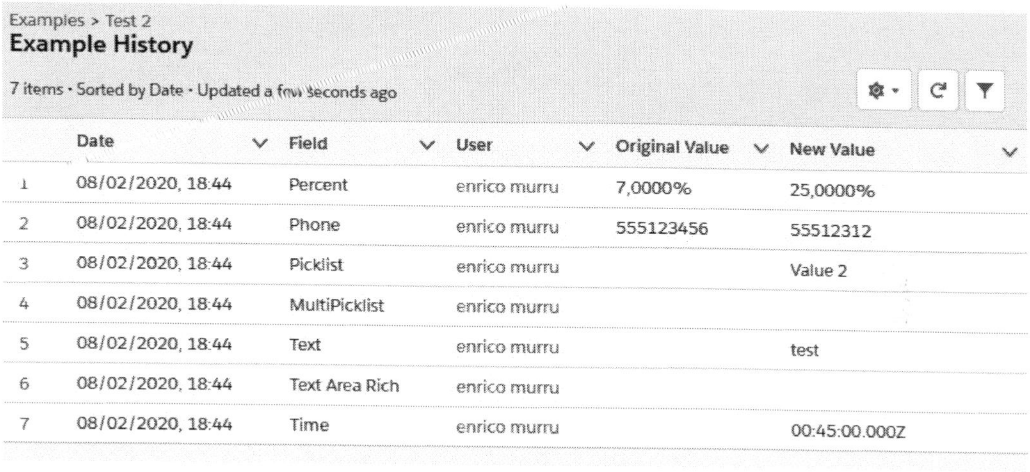

Examples > Test 2

Example History

7 items · Sorted by Date · Updated a few seconds ago

	Date	Field	User	Original Value	New Value
1	08/02/2020, 18:44	Percent	enrico murru	7,0000%	25,0000%
2	08/02/2020, 18:44	Phone	enrico murru	555123456	55512312
3	08/02/2020, 18:44	Picklist	enrico murru		Value 2
4	08/02/2020, 18:44	MultiPicklist	enrico murru		
5	08/02/2020, 18:44	Text	enrico murru		test
6	08/02/2020, 18:44	Text Area Rich	enrico murru		
7	08/02/2020, 18:44	Time	enrico murru		00:45:00.000Z

Figure 2.44 – Field history tracking related list

You will see a clear list of which fields have been changed and by who: long and rich text areas won't show the old/new values.

> **Further reading**
>
> You can increase the limitations of history tracking with **Field Audit Trail**: for more info refer to Salesforce Help at `https://help.salesforce.com/articleView?id=field_audit_trail.htm&type=5`.

Focusing on relationships

When defining a data model, it is common to take an object-oriented approach: represent your information units as objects and link them to organize their relationships.

Let's consider the following data model:

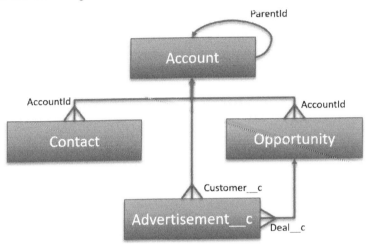

Figure 2.45 – Relationships between objects

It's easy to identify different relationships:

- **Contact to Account**: A contact can be related to an account with the `AccountId` lookup field, and more contacts can look up the same account.

- **Opportunity to Account**: An opportunity must be related to an account with the `AccountId` lookup field, and more opportunities can look up the same account.

- **Advertisement to Account and Opportunity**: An advertisement is related to both an account and an opportunity, and both relationships are one to many, that is, many advertisements can be related to the same account and/or opportunity, using custom relationship fields.

- **Account to itself**: An account can be related to another account using the `ParentId` lookup field.

We can identify three types of relationships:

- **Lookup**: An object may or may not be related to a parent object (a contact may not be related to an account)

- **Data Sensitivity Level Compliance Categorization Detail**: An object needs to be related to a parent object, without which it has no meaning (an opportunity is a deal that has to be done with a customer, or the advertisement needs a customer and/or a deal to be defined)

- **Self-Lookup**: An object can relate to the same object, creating a hierarchy at the object level.

Salesforce offers four kinds of relationship field types:

- Master-detail relationship

- Lookup relationship

- External lookup relationship

- Hierarchical relationship

Let's review all of them in the following sections.

Master-detail relationships

The master-detail field strongly connects two objects, so that the child object cannot exist without the parent. That's why when you create a new master-detail field, Salesforce requires that no record has ever been created, otherwise the data model, which requires this strong relationship, would break.

> **Tip**
>
> If you don't want to delete all records, create a lookup relation (check the next section), populate all records with a corresponding parent record, then change the field type (with the **Change Field Type** button on the custom field's **Edit** form).
>
> Remember that you cannot create a master-detail field on a standard object, but you can create a master-detail field that references a standard or custom object.

What is peculiar about master-detail relationships? If you delete the parent record, all children will be deleted as well, in a so-called cascading delete, and if you undelete the parent using the Recycle Bin (which you can access from **App Launcher | Recycle Bin**) the children are undeleted as well.

Let's create a master-detail relationship field (I'm using the **Example** object, but at the end of the chapter, try by yourself to create the relationships needed on the **Advertisement** object):

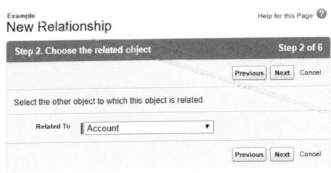

Figure 2.46 – Master-detail relationship creation

The first thing to do is the parent object selection (we have chosen the **Account** object); click **Next** to go on:

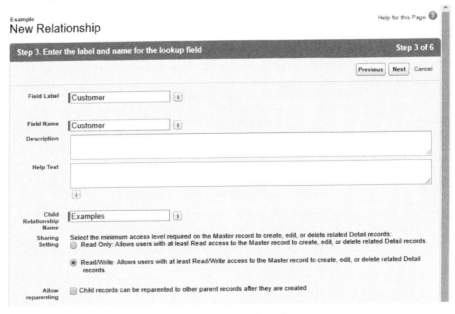

Figure 2.47 – Master-detail configuration

We can use some options like the following for understanding the configurations:

- **Child Relationship Name**: This is the name of the relationship that is established between **Account** and **Examples** (this field is used internally for integration purposes or for SOQL queries that involve child objects when querying the parent, that is, you can query an **Account** and get along all the contacts related in one shot).

- **Sharing Setting**: This defines how record sharing (that is, which user can see the record; we'll talk about sharing in the upcoming chapters) is defined for the current relationship. Generally speaking, the child object's sharing setting is mastered by the parent's sharing settings. With this configuration, you can state whether anyone that can at least read the parent has full access to the record (create, edit, and delete) or they need full `read/write` access on the parent (in the second case, if a user has only `read` access on a specific `Account` record, she will only be able to read any example record related to that **Account**).

- **Allow Reparenting**: You can flag this option if you want a child record to be reparented to another account.

There is another section that you can configure (not shown in Figure 2.48) titled **Lookup Filters**, which is used to filter out parent records when selecting them from the child object layout. You can use this option, for example, to filter only active accounts or opportunities that have been won.

Here is an example of the account's relationship filter:

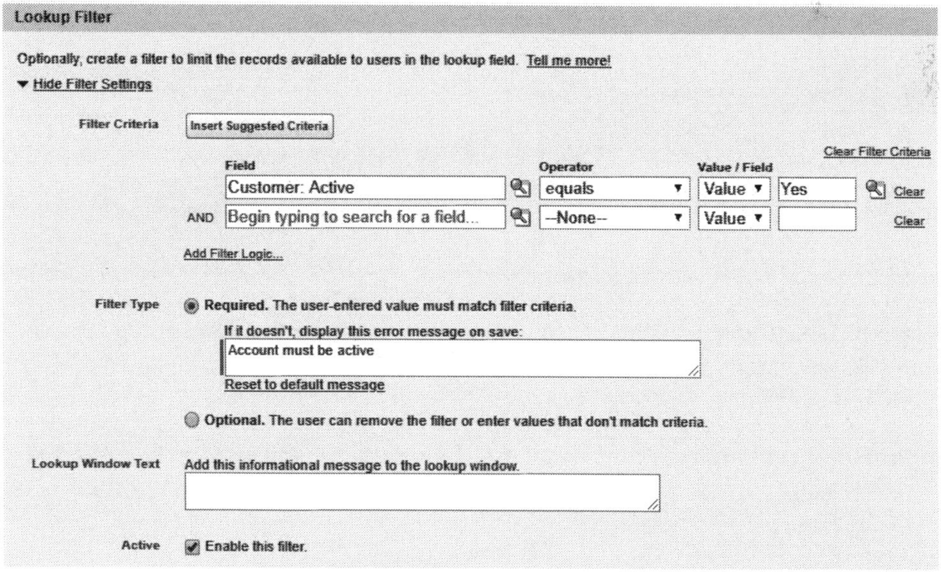

Figure 2.48 – Filter example on an account master-detail relationship

Click **Next** twice to jump to a new custom field wizard step, which allows you to select all the parent object layouts where you want the child related list to be shown:

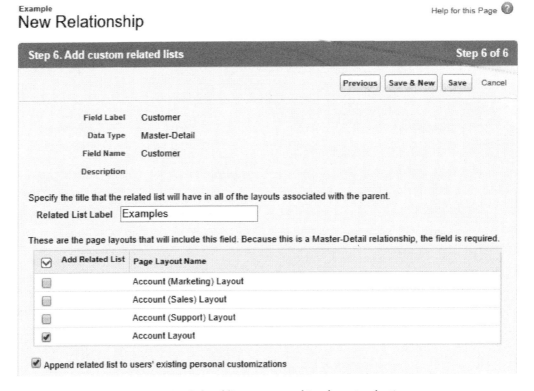

Figure 2.49 – Related list on parent object layouts selection

With this configuration, you are telling Salesforce to put the **Examples** related list on each of the following **Account** layouts (remember to have more layouts for different ways to display a record based on the user's profile). We have chosen to apply the related list on one layout only.

Now jump to the new object from **App Launcher** | **Advertisements** (or **Examples** if you have created a tab for the **Example** object) and click the **New** button to create a new record:

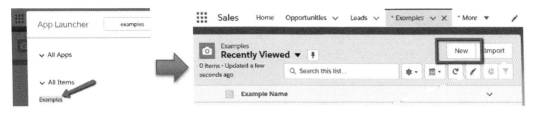

Figure 2.50 – Creating a new record

You should see something like this (depending on how many custom fields you have created):

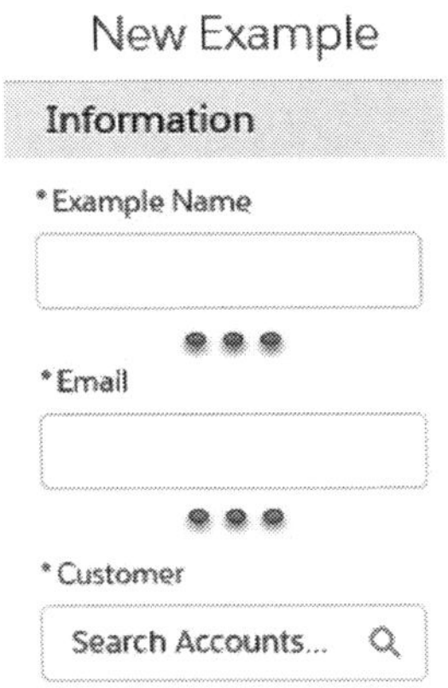

New Example

Information

* Example Name

* Email

* Customer

Search Accounts...

Figure 2.51 – Mandatory fields on the Example object

Non-required fields have been removed from the preceding screenshot (you may not have the **Email** field as well).

The master-detail field is a special field that, once clicked, allows you to search for a related object by simply showing you the most recent records you have viewed or a quick search result from what you have typed:

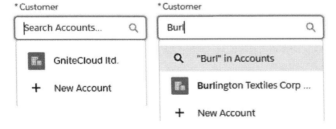

Figure 2.52 – Master-detail result

If you hit the *Enter* key, a full search modal shows up so you can select the right account if there is more related data provided:

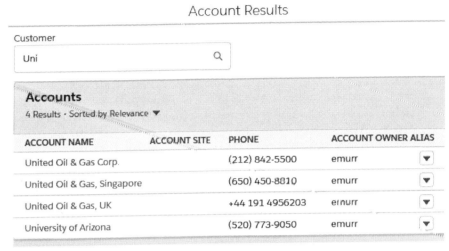

Figure 2.53 – Master-detail record search

There is a base limitation when using master-detail relationships: you can only have two master-detail fields per object.

Roll-up summary fields

When talking about master-detail fields, we must also mention **Roll-up** fields. What are they? Imagine you have several opportunities on accounts and you want to calculate the total amount of opportunities won, related to a specific customer. This means that we need to do the following:

- Pick up an account and open its layout.
- Create some sort of calculation on all related opportunities in a closed won stage.

This can be easily done by creating a roll-up field on the parent object, if and only if you have a master-detail relationship that points from the opportunity to the account object. This is a standard relationship, but as we've just created a master-detail on an **Example** object pointing to **Account**, we could create a roll-up field on the **Example** children as well.

Let's create a new roll-up on the **Account** object (from the **Setup | Object Manager | Account | Fields & Relationships | New** button). Select **Roll-Up Summary** on the first step of the custom field creation wizard and click **Next**. Let's name it **Won Opportunities**:

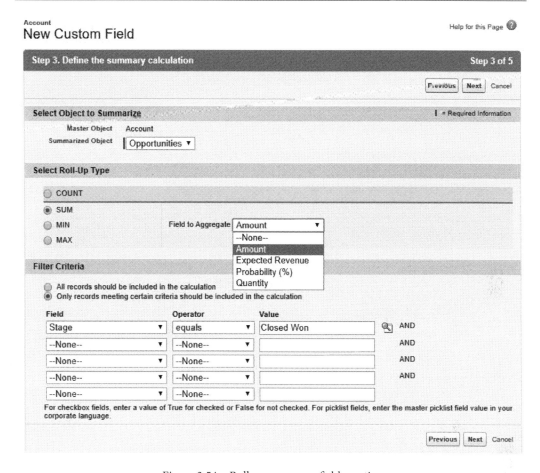

Figure 2.54 – Roll-up summary field creation

These are the options:

- **Summarized Object** (in our example, **Opportunities**)

- The **Roll-up Type**, which is the summarization function that we want to use:

  COUNT: Counts the number of children

  SUM: Sums up a given aggregated field (such as **Amount** or **Quantity**) for all children objects

  MIN/MAX: Gets the minimum or maximum value of a given aggregated field across all children

- An optional set of conditions on child object fields to filter out children (in our example, we filter all opportunities where **Stage** equals **Closed Won**)

Complete the custom field creation wizard, then jump to an **Account** with some opportunities, like the following:

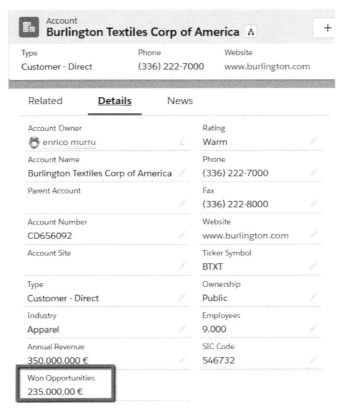

Figure 2.55 – Opportunities on an example account

Jump to the **Account's** details page and have a look at the value of the **Won Opportunities** field:

Figure 2.56 – Roll-up field example on Account record

The field is the sum of the opportunities in **Closed Won**, which is only one in our example.

> **Further reading**
>
> For more details on roll up summary fields, refer to Salesforce Help at `https://help.salesforce.com/articleView?id=fields_about_roll_up_summary_fields.htm&type=5`.

Many-to-many relationships

A special kind of relationship is involved when you need a multiple relationships between two objects.

This is what happens with **Products** and **Price Books** (where the same Product can be related to more than one Price Book) or **Contact** and **Accounts** (when the same contact can be related to more Accounts): these are standard many-to-many relationships and are realized using special **Junction** objects called **Pricebook Entry** and **Account Contact Relationship** objects (the latter feature has to be explicitly enabled; have a look at the following Trailhead module: `https://trailhead.salesforce.com/en/content/learn/modules/admin_intro_accounts_contacts/admin_intro_accounts_contacts_relationships`).

Junction objects contain two master-detail relationships (linked to both objects) and allow an easy way to link many records of a type to many other records of another type.

You can create custom Junction objects to make your own many-to-many relationships, like in the following screenshot:

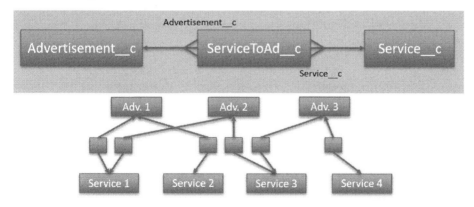

Figure 2.57 – Many-to-many relationship example with custom objects

In this scenario, an **Advertisement** can be related to many **Services** (which is any additional service the company gives along with an advertisement billboard). Technically speaking, the `Advertisement__c` master-detail relationship on the `ServiceToAd__c` junction object is the *master* relation (which one is the master depends on your needs; the master is always the first relation ever created on the custom junction object).

Lookup relationships

When you don't need a child object to have a strong relationship with its parent (that is, no need to cascade delete children when the parent is deleted) use simple **Lookup** relationship fields.

The configuration of lookup fields is similar to master-detail fields:

1. Select the parent object (for example, **Contract**).

2. Define all properties (including filters).

As there is no strong relation with the parent, there is no sharing stuff to configure, only some different behavior in the relationship management:

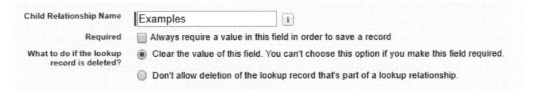

Figure 2.58 – Lookup field relationship options

Apart from the **Required** flag (remember, the master-detail relationship field is always required), the wizard asks what to do when the parent is deleted:

*   Clear current relationship field

*   Throw an error when deleting a parent

The second option forces the user to change the parent lookup (that is, setting the lookup field with another parent record) before deleting the parent.

There is a special power: Salesforce support can enable a third option, called **Delete this record also**, which brings the superpower of cascading delete to lookup relationships (again, no sharing stuff here).

Finally, if you select the same object type as a parent object, you are creating a *self-relationship*.

External lookup relationships

We'll not cover external relationships in detail here, but why not spend a few minutes on them?

To create external lookups, we need to set up **external data sources**, which is a declarative way to link up Salesforce and an external system data source. You need to access this external data but there is no need to import that data into Salesforce. The systems have to talk using a protocol called OData (other protocols are also available): when an **External Data Source** is enabled, Salesforce creates one or more **External Objects**, which map the external database into Salesforce, treating them as Salesforce objects (you can do queries, set up layouts, and link them to Salesforce objects to name a few).

Once **External Objects** are live, you can define two new kinds of relationship:

- **External lookup**: Used to link a standard or custom Salesforce object to an external object
- **Indirect lookup**: Used to link an external object to a standard or custom Salesforce object

> **Further reading**
>
> A cool Trailhead module explains how to set up external data sources at
> `https://trailhead.salesforce.com/en/content/learn/`
> `modules/lightning_connect`.

Hierarchical relationships

Hierarchical relationships are a special kind of lookup field that is uniquely creatable on the **User Salesforce** object and is used to create, guess what, **user** hierarchies!

When you create a new custom field on a **user** object, you see only one option for relationships:

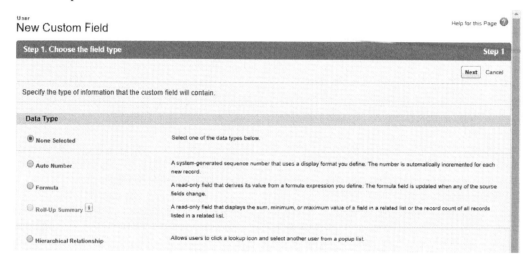

Figure 2.59 – User object new custom field creation

This relationship enforces hierarchical relationships, that is, it allows you to only pick up a User record that is not currently below the hierarchy of the current **User** record:

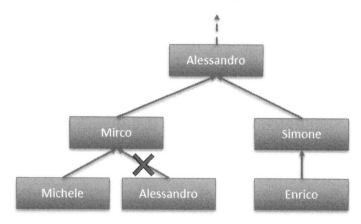

Figure 2.60 – User hierarchy with a hierarchical relationship

In the previous figure, the user Alessandro cannot be configured to report to Mirco, who turns out to be reporting to Alessandro already.

> **Further reading**
>
> For more considerations on Salesforce relationships, refer
> to Salesforce Help at `https://help.salesforce.`
> `com/articleView?id=relationships_`
> `considerations.htm&type=5`.

Major custom field limits

There are some object-related limitations that you should be aware of.

Go to **Setup | Object Manager**, select a Salesforce object, then click on the **Object Limits**
side tab to have a look at a given object's limitations regarding your Salesforce org:

Object Limits

10 Items, Sorted by Item

ITEM	USAGE	LIMIT	% USED
Active Lookup Filters	0	5	0%
Active Validation Rules	2	100	2%
Active Workflow Rules	0	50	0%
Approval Processes	0	500	0%
Custom Fields	25	500	5%
Custom Relationship Fields	2	40	5%
Sharing Rules (Both Owner- and Criteria-based)	0	300	0%
Sharing Rules (Criteria-based Only)	0	50	0%
Total Workflow Rules	0	500	0%
VLOOKUP Functions	0	10	0%

Figure 2.61 – Object Limits page

Be aware that the following limits apply on your objects:

- **Total number of custom fields**: 500 for Enterprise and Developer Edition and 800
  for Unlimited and Performance Edition (for other editions, refer to the link at the
  end of this section)
- **Custom Relationship Fields**: 40
- **Active Lookup Filters**: 5

There is also a **custom object** limit, which is set to 2,000 for Unlimited and Performance editions, 400 for Developer Edition, and 200 for Enterprise Edition (for other editions, refer to the link at the end of this section).

Further reading

To have a look at major limits and allocations related to Salesforce editions, refer to Salesforce Help at `https://help.salesforce.com/articleView?id=overview_limits_general.htm&type=5`.

Blaze your trail

Here is a list of useful Trailhead modules to enhance your knowledge related to data modeling, custom objects, custom fields, and relationships:

- Data Modeling: `https://trailhead.salesforce.com/en/content/learn/modules/data_modeling?trail_id=force_com_admin_beginner`

- Customizing an App with Lightning Object Creator: `https://trailhead.salesforce.com/en/content/learn/projects/quick-start-customize-an-app-with-lightning-object-creator`

- Customizing a Salesforce Object: `https://trailhead.salesforce.com/en/content/learn/projects/customize-a-salesforce-object`

- Administrator Certification Prep: Setup and Objects: `https://trailhead.salesforce.com/content/learn/modules/administrator-certification-prep-setup-and-objects`

- Picklist Administration: `https://trailhead.salesforce.com/en/content/learn/modules/picklist_admin?trail_id=force_com_admin_intermediate`

- External Services: `https://trailhead.salesforce.com/en/content/learn/modules/external-services?trail_id=force_com_admin_intermediate`

- Implementing Roll-Up Summary Fields: `https://trailhead.salesforce.com/content/learn/modules/point_click_business_logic/roll_up_summary_fields`

Summary

So far, we have become data model experts by learning how to customize Salesforce objects with custom fields of different types, in order to put the right data in the right place. Thanks to relationships, we can now link together Salesforce objects to deliver the most complex needs of data modeling that are required for the different use cases.

In the next chapter, we'll see how to master a peculiar kind of custom field, the **Formula** field, which we'll master to make calculations based on our objects' data (we're going to write some algorithms!).

3
Mastering Formulas

In this chapter, we'll discover what a formula is and where it is used across the Salesforce platform. We'll dig into its syntax and all of the available building blocks (that is, *functions*) that the formula framework delivers. Then we'll learn how to build a custom formula field using the custom formula editor wizard.

We'll cover the following topics in this chapter:

- How to define a formula's syntax
- Available formula functions
- How to build a formula field

Defining the formula syntax

A formula can be defined as a list of ingredients with which something is made, which is also a way to describe a *recipe*; and indeed, a formula is nothing more than a collection of values mixed together to get a resulting value that differs from the individual values put in. In mathematical terms, a formula is an algorithm that outputs a value based on other values, expressions, or fields.

In the previous chapter, we already saw a formula when defining the default value for a given custom field or when seeing the custom formula field type, which is one of the subjects of this chapter.

Let's create some examples of conditions that can be written with formulas:

- If a case is related to an **Account** that is active and is open for more than 1 week, output a flagged checkbox named **Urgent!** (formula field).

- Update the **Stage** field on the **Opportunity** object to **Closed Lost** if the opportunity is open for more than 2 months (the workflow rule's field update).

- If the **Fiscal Code** is not filled in on the **Contact** object and there is no **Account** related to the record, the **Contact** cannot be saved, and an error message should be displayed (validation rule).

- When a new **Advertisement** custom object and the **Profile** of the current user is **Sales Manager**, the **Installation Date** must be set to 14 days from the current date (the default custom field value).

There are plenty of places in the Salesforce platform where formulas can be used to achieve complex logic. The following are but a few of them:

- **Approval Process**: This is the criteria a record must meet to enter an approval process (we'll see approvals in the automation-related chapters).

- **Approval Step**: This is the criteria a record must meet to enter an approval step.

- **Assignment Rules for Leads/Cases**: These are the criteria a Lead/Case must meet to be assigned.

- **Auto-Response rules for Lead/Cases**: These are the criteria that trigger an auto-response.

- **Case Escalation Rules**: These are the criteria a case must meet to be escalated.

- **Custom Links and Buttons**: This is the algorithm to execute actions with links and buttons.

- **Custom Fields**: These are the calculated custom fields based on other fields, expressions, and values.

- **Custom Summary Formulas (Reports)**: These are the calculations on report summaries.

- **Validation Rules**: These are the criteria to validate a record that is being created/updated.

- **Default Field Values**: This is a formula to calculate a value as the default value of a given field on record creation if no value is set on creation.

- **Formula Fields**: As mentioned earlier, this is a specific custom field type that is used to create a calculated field based on expressions, fields, and values.

- **Workflow Rules**: These are the criteria a record must meet to trigger workflow rules.

- **Workflow Field Update**: This is a formula to calculate the value of a given field (this can be triggered by a Workflow Rule or an Approval Process).

Generally speaking, a formula should output a value of the same or a similar type as the feature it is being used with, as follows:

- If we are using a formula to set a default value of a numeric field, the formula should output a numeric value (currency, percent, or numeric).

- If we are using a formula as criteria to trigger a workflow rule, its output should be a *Boolean* value for sure (a checkbox - style value, that is, a value that can have only two values, `true` or `false`).

- If we are comparing dates, we can use date and date/time values.

The formula framework provides diverse *functions*, *operators,* and *expressions* to create complex algorithms or simply convert values from one type into another (for example, convert a number into text or vice versa or create a date value given three different numeric or text values containing day, month, and year).

Let's have a look at the following simple formula on the Opportunity object, which encapsulates all key formula elements. Here, we calculate commissions to be delivered to the sales representative based on an opportunity:

Here we are calculating the commission based on the `Amount` field:

```
IF ( Amount >= 1000000, Amount * 0.1, 0) + 1000
```

This formula can be read as follows: if the `Amount` field is greater than or equal to 1M ($ or whatever currency is set up for your organization), it calculates 10% of the amount value, 0 or otherwise, then sums up the returned value (that is, 10% of the amount or 0) with 1,000. This means that if the sales representative doesn't succeed in closing an opportunity with more than $ 1M, they only get $1,000 commission, otherwise, they get the same commission plus $100,000 (a pretty unfair algorithm!).

This formula is characterized by the following components:

- **Literal values**: These are static values that cannot change, such as `10,00,000`, `0.1`, `0`, and `1,000`. When using text values (also called strings), enclose the literal value within double or single quotes (for example, `'Closed Won'`).

- **Field Reference**: This pertains to any reference to a standard or custom field on the current object or any related object using relationships (we looked at relationships in the previous chapter). In this example, the field reference is `Amount`, which is referenced twice. They are usually called **merge fields** because the formula engine takes those fields and merges them with their corresponding values for the engine to complete the formula calculation.

- **Function**: In this example, we can see the `IF` function, which is a system-defined formula that takes input (in our example, the comparison between the `Amount` field and the literal `1000000`) and outputs a calculated value (in our example, the value of the calculated commission). There are plenty of available functions, which we'll see in the next chapter.

- **Operator**: This is a symbol used to execute a specific calculation (in our example, we found `>=`, `*`, and `+`), define the precedence of the calculations, and/or define formulas (the parentheses).

- **Comment**: Comments are a great way to document complex formulas as they are completely ignored by the formula calculation engine but are extremely useful to understand what's going on. If you are a coder, you'll recognize the multiline code style of C/C++, Java, or JavaScript languages (to name a few) with the `/* ... */` syntax. We can even use comments to comment out pieces of a formula to do a debugging session (for example, to understand why a formula is not behaving correctly). Don't comment out a formula completely, otherwise, you'll get an error while saving it.

In the next section, we'll have a look at most of the built-in system formulas and operators available on the Salesforce platform and then we'll see how to actually build a custom formula field on any Salesforce object.

Functions vade mecum

The Formula framework provides numerous built-in **functions** and **operators** that can be used depending on the context of execution (for example, summary functions are only available on reporting and some other functions are not available on custom formula fields or specific workflow types).

To master formulas, you need experience, for sure, but also a sort of ingenuity to combine the available building blocks to get to your algorithm.

Most of the functions in the following sections can be tested on custom formula fields, validation rules, or workflow rules, so you can test them while reading this chapter for hands-on experience.

We'll see how to build a custom formula field in depth in the next sections, but remember that functions' documentation can be found in the **Advanced Formula** editor shown in the following screenshot (available when building custom formula fields, validation rules, and workflow rules, for example):

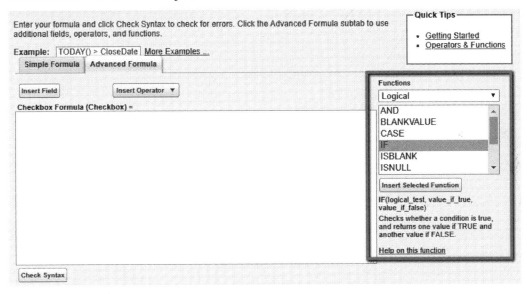

Figure 3.1 – Advanced formula editor with the built-in functions documentation explorer

We will start with a review of the available operators.

Operators

Operators are at the core of algorithms and you are already aware of them: math operators such as *sum* or *multiplication* or logical operators used to compare values such as *greater than* or *less than*.

As we have seen, operators can relate object fields with literals or even other expressions (we have summed up the result of the IF function with the literal 1000). Operators can also be chained to create a more complex concatenation of operations (such as summing more than two fields): each operator has its own precedence so be careful when chaining operations (also known as PEDMAS or BODMAS). Take the following formula as an example:

```
Amount + 1000 / 100 * 50
```

In this formula, we want to calculate 50% of the amount plus $ 1000, but due to operator precedence, the result won't be as expected. Indeed, the formula engine calculated the division and multiplication operations first (dealing with 1000 / 100 * 50, which always returns the value 500) and then applies the result to the Amount field. But this is not the behavior we expect.

> **Note**
> For a detailed explanation of operator precedence, refer to Wikipedia at
> https://en.wikipedia.org/wiki/Order_of_operations.

To fix things up, you could simply use the *parenthesis* operator, which changes the precedence of operations:

```
( Amount + 1000 ) / 100 * 50
```

Now the 50% calculation will be correctly applied to the Amount value plus $ 1,000.

As mentioned earlier, we have two types of operators available: math and logical. We'll see both of them in the next sections.

Mathematical operators

Here is the list of available **mathematical operators**. They are fairly self-explanatory, but we will review them nonetheless to better understand some rules for their use in Salesforce.

- + (**Add**): It sums up two or more numeric elements. Here's an example:

Here we see 5 days added after record creation date:

```
CreatedDate + 5
```

Here, the sum of all won, closed, and running opportunities on Account are added:

```
Won_Opportunities__c
+ Lost_Opportunities__c
+ Ongoing_Opportunities__c
```

Be careful when summing date or date/time fields with a number as the sum is applied using *day* as the unit of measure.

- - (**Subtract**): It simply subtracts one operand from another, as in this example.

Here we are subtracting the number of managers from the number of employees to get the number of workers for a given account:

```
NumberOfEmployees - Number_of_Managers__c
```

If the first operand is a date or date/time, you can subtract a number of days from that date. You can even subtract date or date/time fields and get back the number of days.

- * (**Multiply**): It multiplies two operands of numeric type only.

It calculates the 25% of the Amount field:

```
Amount * 0.25
```

- / (**Divide**): It divides two operands of numeric type only. If the divisor operand is 0, the formula doesn't output any value (it throws an error).

This divides the number of employees on managers to get the average number of employees per manager: it won't output if Number_of_Managers__c is 0:

```
NumberOfEmployees / Number_of_Managers__c
```

- `^` (**Exponentiation**): It raises a number to a power of a specified number. Again, it's applicable for numeric types only. The exponent number/expression must be a positive integer, otherwise, no value is output.

  This calculate the amount to be squared:

  ```
  Amount^2
  ```

- `()` (**Open and close parentheses**): As mentioned, parentheses change the order of precedence of operators, but they are also used to enclose function parameters.

  Here we are changing the order of precedence of operators, as follows:

  ```
  NumberOfEmployees^(NumberOfEmployees - 1)
  ```

This covers all of the mathematical operators. Now, let's review the logical operators.

Logical operators

The framework delivers some **logical operators**, which are used to compare values rather than calculate them: their output is always a *Boolean* value, that is, they output `true` or `false` only.

Boolean logic is at the base of algorithm programming: after all, it sets an output based on conditions of values, expressions, and operators, and a condition is nothing more than an assertion that something (a variable) *is* or *is not* something else (the condition statement). This is just another way of saying whether something is `true` or `false`.

Let's review the logical operators available at our disposal:

- `=` and `==` (**Equal**): It returns `true` if two values are equivalent. You can use the operator in the `=` and `==` form. They're just two ways to represent the same operator; the double format originates from C. Let's see an example where the following formula returns true if number of employees equals 5:

  ```
  NumberOfEmployees == 5
  ```

  If you need to check whether a field is not filled in (for example, is null), use the `IsBlank()` function instead.

- `<>` and `!=` (**Not Equal**): It returns `true` if two values are not equivalent. You can use the operator in the `<>` and `!=` forms.

- <, <= (**Less Than** and **Less Than or Equal To**): It returns `true` if the first value is less than (or less than or equal to) the right value. So here, this formula returns `true` if number of employees is lower or equal then 5:

```
NumberOfEmployees <= 5
```

- >, >= (**Greater Than** and **Greater Than or Equal To**): This is the same as the preceding but with the *greater* operation.

- && (**AND**): It returns true if **all** the conditions are `true`. With the **OR** operator (see next), they are called *Boolean operators* because they are used to operate on Boolean values/variables (a *variable* is just a placeholder for a value that can *vary* value over time, just like a Salesforce field). This operator can be used on behalf of the `AND()` function. You can chain more than one &&, as in the following example where if case is closed on create but is escalated and something is wrong, it should output an error message, as follows:

```
IF( IsEscalated && IsClosedOnCreate && FromWeb__c,
    This escalated too quickly!,
    All is ok! )
```

- || (**OR**): This returns true if at least one condition evaluates to `true`. This operator can be used on behalf of the `OR()` function. You can chain more than one ||, as in the following example where it outputs a text message if at least one condition on the number of employees is true:

```
IF (NumberOfEmployees > 100
    || Number_of_Managers__c > 5
    || AnnualRevenue ==10000000,
  Big company,
  Not so big company)
```

> **Note**
>
> When chaining a mixed sequence of && and ||, be clever to properly make use of parentheses; otherwise, unless you are an expert of Boolean logic, you'll get unwanted behavior from your formula (refer to the `VALUE()` function in the *Text functions* section).
>
> If you want to explore more about Boolean logic, refer to the Wikipedia article at `https://en.wikipedia.org/wiki/Boolean_algebra`.

To keep formulas readable, use *indentation*: add a new line just before a new Boolean operator or a comma whenever possible, and after each logical line break add 2 or more blank spaces; this will create an easy to read structure that will help you to understand what's going on.

There is one last operator that deals with text (or, in technical language, strings) and that is used to merge strings into one:

- & (**Concatenate**): It connects two strings and can be used with chaining if it outputs some brief details of a case in the form. This is case XXXXXX and has been created on XX/XX/XXXX:

```
This is case
    & CaseNumber
    &  and has been created on
    & CreatedDate
```

This concludes our look at operators. Now, let's move on to functions.

Functions

At the time of writing (*Summer '20* platform release), the Formula framework delivers 93 built-in formulas that can be roughly divided into the following:

- **Date and Time functions**
- **Logical Functions**
- **Math Functions**
- **Text Functions**
- **Summary Functions**
- **Advanced Functions**

From this list, we'll be concentrating on the first four categories as they are the key functions that you're likely to find useful in your daily work.

> **Note**
>
> For a complete list of all available functions, refer to Salesforce
> Help at `https://help.salesforce.com/`
> `articleView?id=customize_functions.html&type=5`.

Date and time functions

Let's begin with the most relevant date and time functions for our general purposes.

ADDMONTHS

Given a date and a value containing the number of months (with a positive or negative integer value), it returns a date after (positive integer) or before (negative integer) the input date. So if CreatedDate is January 31st, the resulting date is February 28th (or 29th if leap year)::

```
ADDMONTHS( CreatedDate, 1)
```

If the resulting date is in a month where the number of days is less than the starting date, the function outputs the last date.

DATE

It returns a `Date` value given 3 integer inputs for the year, month (1-12), and day; in the event of an incorrect day number, the formula throws an error. So for July 18, 1982, it is::

```
DATE(1982, 7, 18)
```

DATEVALUE

This function is used to convert a date/time value or a text value (which must be a string with the `YYYY-MM-DD` format, that is, four digits for the year and two digits each for the month and day) into a simple date value like for July 18, 1982, we have::

```
DATEVALUE(1982-07-18)
```

This can output the date value of the date/time of creation:

```
DATEVALUE(CreatedDate)
```

If the input value is a date/time, the function removes the time part and aligns with the current user's time locale (exceptions are applied when running on reports); if the input is a malformed string, the formula outputs an error.

DATETIMEVALUE

Just like DATEVALUE(), it is used to convert a date or text value into a date/time value. The time is always calculated using GMT. If the input is a date value, the time is set to midnight of the same day in GMT (and the user will see the date/time value with their own time zone). If the input is a string value, the format must be YYYY-MM-DD HH:MM:SS, that is, the same date format as the DATEVALUE() function concatenated with a blank space to two digits for the hour, colons, two digits for the minutes, colons, and two more digits for the seconds. An error is displayed if the format is not correct So, if we have July 18, 1982 10:15pm (if GMT) user or July 19, 1982 00:15am (if CET) shown as follows::

```
DATETIMEVALUE(1982-07-18 22:15:00)
```

This outputs the date value of the date/time of creation, as follows:

```
DATETIMEVALUE (Date__c)
```

Here is an example of a user within a CET time zone who sees two custom formula fields shaped like the previous code:

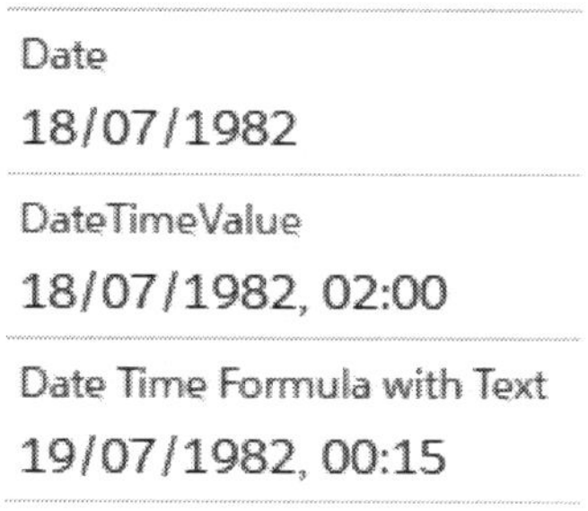

Date
18/07/1982

DateTimeValue
18/07/1982, 02:00

Date Time Formula with Text
19/07/1982, 00:15

Figure 3.2 – DATETIMEVALUE function display examples

TIMEVALUE

Just like previous functions, this is used to get the time value of a given date/time or text value. The text input needs to be formatted, hence: HH:MM:SS.msc, where msc represents three digits for milliseconds. The time is displayed with local organization time zone settings:

```
TIMEVALUE(CreatedDate)
TIMEVALUE(2020-02-22 22:22:22.222)
```

TODAY, NOW, and TIMENOW

To get the current date, date/time, or time, use the DATE(), NOW(), or TIMENOW() functions, which output, respectively, the date, the date and time (given the user's time zone) or just the time (In GMT). All functions don't need any input value but require parentheses to be executed correctly. The following tells if End_Date_c field is in the past or not::

```
IF (
    (DATEVALUE(End_Date__c) <= TODAY(),
    Created in the past,
    Created in the future
)
```

Other date-related functions

There are several other date-related functions that can be used to extract a date/time component (such as the day, month, and year). We're listing them in alphabetical order:

- DAY(date)
- HOUR(time)
- MILLISECOND(time)
- MINUTE(time)
- MONTH(date)
- SECOND(time)
- WEEKDAY(date)
- YEAR(date)

Logical functions

We've already seen some logical operators and learned that the && and || operators can be used instead of the AND() and OR() functions. Let's dig into them and other useful logical functions available on the framework.

AND and OR

`AND()` and `OR()` functions are used to support the `AND` and `OR` Boolean operators: as these operators can be chained, the functions can contain a varied number of input values. We can re-write the previous examples on `AND/OR` operators using functions:

If case is closed on create but is escalated and something is wrong, it should output an error message

```
IF (
    AND (
        IsEscalated,
        IsClosedOnCreate,
        FromWeb__c
    ),
    This escalated too quickly!,
    All is ok! )
```

Here's the other example which outputs a text message if at least one condition on the number of employees is true:

```
IF (
    OR (
        NumberOfEmployees > 100,
        Number_of_Managers__c > 5,
        AnnualRevenue ==10000000
    ),
    Big company,
    Not so big company)
```

Regarding readability, `AND()` and `OR()` functions obtain greater readability at the expense of using more characters (we'll see that this is one of the limitations of formulas).

BLANKVALUE and ISBLANK

Sometimes it is useful to be aware of whether a field has a value or not. If a variable is not set, we refer to it as having a `null` value (for example, a date field not filled in a record layout evaluates to `null`). Being aware of null values can be important when dealing with numeric formulas (for example, dividing a number by `null` leads to errors). In the case of text fields, they can be set to a blank value (which is an empty string, or `" "`).

Thanks to the ISBLANK() function, we are able to understand whether an expression has a value or not, and with BLANKVALUE(), we can replace that expression with another value if no value is found (it works for all kinds of field types):

So if the number of managers for an Account is not set up or is 0, the number of employees per manager is defaulted to 0

```
IF (
  OR (
      ISBLANK(Number_of_Managers__c),
      Number_of_Managers__c == 0
  ),
  0,
  BLANKVALUE(NumberOfEmployees, 0) / Number_of_Managers__c
)
```

Don't use ISNULL() and NULLVALUE(), which are the *old* functions and didn't take into account the blankness of string values.

CASE

Along with the IF() function, CASE() is used to output a result conditionally based on input conditions. This function evaluates an input expression and enumerates all possible values and an output expression for each value, ending with a default output in the case that no value is matched by the input expression:

```
CASE ( WEEKDAY(CloseDate),
    1, Sunday,
    2, Monday,
    3, Tuesday,
    4, Wednesday,
    5, Thursday,
    6, Friday,
    7, Saturday,
    No value no party!)
```

The last expression is commonly called the *else* expression.

Ensure that all conditional and output expressions have the same data type (in the example, we used numbers for the conditional expressions and text strings as the output expressions).

IF

The `IF()` function determines the output expression depending on the input expression being `true` or `false`: the *if/then/else* construct forms the basis of algorithms and of your daily life decisions (if I do A, then B could happen, otherwise, C will happen). If the input expression is evaluated and if it evaluates to `true`, then the first output expression is returned, otherwise, the last is returned.

This formula calculates the opportunity CloseDate if the Amount is greater then $ 1M or not

```
IF (
  Amount > 1000000,
  TODAY() + 60,
  TODAY() + 30
)
```

ISCLONE

This function is used on validation rules to check whether a record that is being created is actually a clone of another record: this function cannot be used within custom formula fields.

We can use this function in a validation rule to check whether a key date field is not in the past if the record is cloned:

This formula evaluates to true (and thus triggers a validation rule) if the estimated end date is in the past and the record is a clone

```
AND (
  ISCLONE(),
  Estimated_End_Date < TODAY()
)
```

ISNEW

`ISNEW()` returns true if the current record is a new record. This cannot be used inside a custom formula field as well. This can be used as a workflow rule criterion to set up a default field on record creation, accessing the current record's fields (which is not possible from a default field value's formula):

```
AND (
  ISNEW(),
  OR (
    ISBLANK(NumberOfEmployee),
```

```
      NumberOfEmployee == 0
   )
)
```

ISNUMBER

The `ISNUMBER()` function returns true if the input text value can be converted into a number:

```
IF(
   ISNUMBER(YearStarted),
   VALUE(YearStarted) + 1,


)
```

The function returns false if the input value is blank/null; it's also not aware of the user's locale, so `ISNUMBER(1,23)`, which is a valid decimal number in the Italian locale, returns false. It also supports scientific formatting such as `1E12` or `111.222..`

NOT

The `NOT()` function is used to negate an input expression, that is, it outputs true if the input is false and vice versa.

This validation rule evaluates to true (and thus throws an error) if the `CloseDate` is filled and no `Amount` has been set:

```
AND(
   NOT(
      ISBLANK(ClosedDate)
   ),
   OR(
      ISBLANK(Amount),
      Amount = 0
   )
)
```

PRIORVALUE

To get the previous value of a given field, use the `PRIORVALUE()` function. This function cannot be used in custom formula fields and in workflow rules if the evaluation criteria are set to **Evaluate the rule when a record is: created, and every time it's edited** (refer to the *Automation Tools* section).

To give an example, you can use this function in a validation rule to avoid setting a key field to blank (for example, the `Amount` field if the `Opportunity` is `Closed`):

```
AND (
    ISBLANK(
        PRIORVALUE(Amount)
    ),
    IsClosed,
    IsWon
)
```

If you are creating a record (so there is no actual prior value), the function returns the actual field value, but if it is blank, then the default value is set up.

ISCHANGED

The `ISCHANGED()` function returns true if the field has just changed its value: it is extremely useful in validation rules, for example, if you want to avoid a value from being changed, as in the following example where this validation rule criteria prevents an Opportunity from being re-opened when it was closed won::

```
AND (
    ISCHANGED(IsClosed),
    ISPICKVAL(PRIORVALUE(StageName), Closed Won)
)
```

If a record is being created, all fields are evaluated to false. This function can only be used in the following formulas:

- Assignment rules

- Validation rules

- Field updates

- Workflow rules if the evaluation criteria are set to **Evaluate the rule when a record is: created, and every time it's edited**

Math functions

The formula engine supports diverse math functions that can be used to make all kinds of calculations within formulas (they all work with numeric values/expressions):

- ABS (): The absolute value of a number (that is, the number without its sign)
- CEILING (): Rounds a number up to the nearest integer (for example, CEILING (1.2) outputs 2), away from zero if negative
- EXP (): Returns Euler's number, e, to the power of an input number
- FLOOR (): Rounds a number down to the nearest integer (for example, FLOOR (1.2) outputs 1), toward zero if negative
- LN (): Calculates the natural logarithm of an input number
- LOG (): Calculates the base 10 logarithm of an input number
- MAX (): Gets the maximum number given an input list of numbers (for example, MAX (1,2,3,4) outputs 4)
- MCEILING (): Like CEILING () but toward zero if negative
- MFLOOR (): Like FLOOR () but away from zero if negative
- MIN (): Gets the minimum number given an input list of numbers (for example, MIN (1,2,3,4) outputs 1)
- MOD (): Returns the remainder of a division (for example, MOD (5,4) outputs 1)
- ROUND (): Returns the nearest number to the input value, close by a specific number of digits (for example, given 0 decimal places, ROUND (1.7, 0) outputs 2 or given 2 decimal places, ROUND (130.009) outputs 130.01)
- SQRT (): Returns the positive square root for an input number (returns an error if a negative number is passed as input)
- GEOLOCATION (): Returns a geolocation value given latitude and longitude input values
- DISTANCE (): Calculates the distance in miles or kilometers of 2 geolocation fields (for example, DISTANCE (asset_location__c, GEOLOCATION (39.2238,9.1217), 'km'))

Text functions

Text functions are used to manipulate text input, for example, for searching a specific sequence of characters, handling picklist values, or trimming/splitting a string and more.

We'll dig into text functions and try to group them into homogeneous categories based on their functionality.

Find text – BEGINS, CONTAINS, FIND

The `BEGINS()`, `CONTAINS()`, and `FIND()` functions are used to tell whether a specific string is found inside input text:

- `BEGINS()` returns true if a text begins with the search string.
- `CONTAINS()` returns true if the first input text contains the second input text.
- `FIND()` returns the character index of the first input string where the second input string is found. This function can be called with an optional third parameter (an integer index) that tells the function from which index the search should be executed.

Here are some examples of usage:

If asset's serial number starts with `999`, that means it is a medical device

```
IF (
   BEGINS (SerialNumber, 999),
   Medical Device,
   Other Device
)
```

Depending con Case's `Description`, returns an urgency value

```
IF (
   CONTAINS (Description, Complain),
   HIGH,
   IF (
      CONTAINS (Description, Payment),
      MEDIUM,
      LOW
   )
)
```

Gets contact's email address and outputs a domain URL based on email's domain

```
www. + RIGHT (Email, LEN (Email) - FIND (@, Email) )
```

Be careful that the string match with these functions is **case-sensitive**. BEGINS () and CONTAINS () always match a blank text field on workflow rules and validation rules (for example, BEGINS (UniqueCode__c, 999) returns true if UniqueCode__c is blank), while FIND () always returns index 0 if the input text is blank or no match is found.

Picklist value management – ISPICKVAL and INCLUDES

When dealing with picklist fields, you cannot simply take the field and compare it with a string. For instance, this example will get you an error.

If an Opportunity is won, it calculates the commissioning amount by 20%

```
IF (
   StageName == Closed Won,
   Amount * 0.2,
   0
)
```

If you try to create a custom formula field with this content, you'll get the following error:

Field StageName is a picklist field. Picklist fields are only supported in certain functions.

To handle this comparison, you have two options: using the ISPICKVAL () function or converting the picklist into text using the TEXT () function (which we'll see shortly).

The previous example could have been written as follows:

```
IF (
   ISPICKVAL (StageName, Closed Won),
   Amount * 0.2,
   0
)
```

Remember that the picklist field and the string literal (the value you are matching the picklist field against) cannot be expressions. If you need to check more than one value for a single picklist field, you can use the CASE () function. If you need to check the previous value of a given picklist field, use the following formula:

```
ISPICKVAL ( PRIORVALUE ( StageName ), Negotiation/Review )
```

When you need to deal with multi-select picklist fields, use the INCLUDES() function instead. Given the multi-select Enabled_Product_Families__c on the Account object that states which Product Family values a partner can sell, if you want to calculate a commission for a specific product family, you could use something like the following example:

```
IF(
   INCLUDES( Enabled_Product_Families__c, Hardware ),
   0.2,
   0.1
)
```

The INCLUDES() function returns an error if the text literal is blank: like ISPICKVAL(), the first function parameter and the literals cannot be expressions. The same consideration about the use of PRIORVALUE() remains.

Text manipulation functions

There are several text manipulation functions, which are easy to explain and powerful to use to manipulate text:

- BR(): It adds a line break to a string. This function makes sense when dealing with multiline outputs:

```
/* outputs:
   XXXXX
   The reason

   Case description....
*/
CaseNumber & BR() & Reason & BR() & BR() & Description
```

- LEFT() and RIGHT(): They return the specified number of chars from the left/right of a string:

Outputs Hello

```
RIGHT( Hello Ohana!, 5)
```

Outputs Ohana!

```
RIGHT( Hello Ohana!, 6)
```

- LEN(): It returns the length of a text in terms of the number of characters it contains.

  So depending on the length of a serial number, we can assume the family of an asset:

  ```
  IF( LEN(SerialNumber) == 15, Software, Other Family )
  ```

- LOWER() and UPPER(): They convert a string into lower- and uppercase, respectively.

  So outputs for lollo@gnitmail.bg is:

  ```
  LOWER(LOLLO@GNITMAIL.bg)
  ```

- LPAD() and RPAD(): They add a selected character or sequence of characters to the left or right part of a text, respectively, to reach a specified length. If the length is less than the text's length, the result is a truncated value. Provided we want to manipulate the contact's FirstName field that contains the word Joe, this is what we would do:

  Outputs: Jo
  ```
  LPAD(FirstName, 2)
  ```

  Outputs: --Joe
  ```
  LPAD(FirstName, 5, -)
  ```

  Outputs: .-.-.-.Joe (the padding string is added until length is reached
  ```
  LPAD(FirstName, 10, .-)
  ```

  Outputs: Joe<<
  ```
  RPAD(FirstName, 5, <)
  ```

- SUBSTITUTE(): It replaces any occurrence of a string with another string. Consider a custom managed template for a case description that is generalized using the {0} string as a placeholder to be replaced with the case's contact FirstName field (we've not talked about cross-object relations in formulas yet—the following example simply gets FirstName from the Contact relation on the Case object). Refer to the following example for a workflow field update executed on case creation on the Description field:

  ```
  SUBSTITUTE(Description, {0}, Contact.FirstName)
  ```

  If Description defaults to Hello {0}, we are taking care of your case!, the **Description** field will be filled by the workflow field update with the value, Hello **Enrico**, we are taking care of your case!.

- `TEXT()`: It converts picklist, percent, number, date, date/time, or currency values into plain text values. Returned values are not sensitive to the user's locale, so a number/currency is always converted with the same formatted number, and dates are output with the `YYYY-MM-DD` format and date/time with `YYYY-MM-DD HH:MM:SSZ`.

- `TRIM()`: It removes all spaces and tabs from the beginning and end of a text string.

- `VALUE()`: It converts a text into a number. It returns an error if the text doesn't contain a numeric value or contains special characters other than a decimal point (period) or a minus sign for negative numbers.

Other useful text functions

It is also worth mentioning some other text-related functions.

The `HYPERLINK()` function is used to create a link for custom formula fields. It supports three parameters:

- It supports a valid URL (for example, `https://success.salesforce.com`).

- It also supports a friendly name (for example, `Trailblazer Community`).

- It supports an optional target, that is, the window or frame where the link should be opened: if you don't set a target the link is opened in a new browser window. Common values for this parameter are `_blank` (opens in a new unnamed window), `_self` (opens in the same frame/window), `_parent` (opens in the parent window if the current link is displayed in a frame), and `_top` (opens in the main window, discarding any parent frame).

Let's see an example:

Creates a link for googling Account's name on google

```
HYPERLINK(
   https://www.google.com/search?q= & Name,
   Search on Google...,
   _blank
)
```

If you want to add an image to a custom formula field (and why not, using a hyperlink too), use the `IMAGE()` function. The following example shows how a custom formula field can output a link referring to a contact's Twitter handle (custom field), showing a Twitter icon:

```
HYPERLINK(
   https://twitter.com/ & Twitter_Handle__c,
```

```
  IMAGE(
https://upload.wikimedia.org/wikipedia/it/0/09/Twitter_bird_
logo.png,
  Twitter_Handle__c,
  50,
  50)
)
```

The function requires the following:

- The image URL (this can be an expression)
- An alternative text (in this example, the Twitter handle)
- Optional integers for width and height for the image

This is how a custom formula field using an IMAGE() function is displayed:

Figure 3.3 - Custom formula field with the IMAGE() function

This formula can be used to display a different icon based on specific values, which is based on specific fields in the contact's record.

To complete the list of common usage functions, we need to mention the REGEX() function, which is used to compare a text against a **Regular Expression**: a regular expression is a sequence of characters that can be used to define the format a string should have.

REGEX() returns true if a string matches the provided regular expression. A typical example is checking in a validation rule whether a string matches a specific format.

The following example shows a validation rule criterion that enforces a string to contain a date in the YYYY-MM-DD format:

```
NOT(
  REGEX(
```

```
    Text_Date__c,
    ([12]\d{3}-(0[1-9]|1[0-2])-(0[1-9]|[12]\d|3[01])))
  )
)
```

Note that the NOT() function is used because a validation rule criteria, as we'll see in the *Chapter 4 Clean data with Validation Rules*, matches an error criteria.

> **Note**
> For more details on regular expressions, check out this Wikipedia article at
> `https://en.wikipedia.org/wiki/Regular_expression`.

Cross-object formulas

We've seen so far that a formula works by using functions, expressions, operators, literal values, and object fields. What if we need to access the account's fields when we are creating a custom formula field on the Case object or we are implementing a validation rule on the Campaign Member object but we need the Campaign details?

We'll use the so-called **cross-object formulas**: they allow us to reference parent object fields to be used as a merge field on a formula—it is possible to go back to an object ancestor up to 10 relationships away. So, for example, if we are creating a formula field on the **Case** object, we can access the following:

- Case fields
- Case.Contact fields
- Case.Contact.Account fields
- Case.Contact.Account.Owner (**User**) fields

If the parent object we want to access is available through a standard relationship field, simply use the relationship field name followed by a dot followed by the field you want to reference: pay attention that standard relationship fields usually have a trailing ID on their name, which you need to skip. So, for example, if you need to access the Contact fields of the *Case* you'll be using Contact.FirstName and not ContactId.FirstName.

If the relationship is a custom one (for example, a lookup from the Case object to the custom Advertisement object with API name Advertisement Reference__c), you'll use the __r trailing sequence instead of the __c provided by the custom field name, so we'll use Advertisement_Reference__r.Price__c instead of Advertisement_Reference__c.Price__c (which will generate an error when trying to save the formula).

If you recall, we used a cross-object formula when talking about the SUBSTITUTE() text
function (a formula based on the **Case** object):

```
SUBSTITUTE(Description, {0}, Contact.FirstName)
```

Before closing this chapter, we'll see how to create a new custom field, showing all of the
possibilities the custom formula field editor delivers.

Building a custom formula field

To create a new custom formula field, jump to **Setup | Object Manager**, select a standard
or custom object (I selected the **Example** object), then select **Fields & Relationships**, click
the **New** button and select the **Formula** option, and click **Next**:

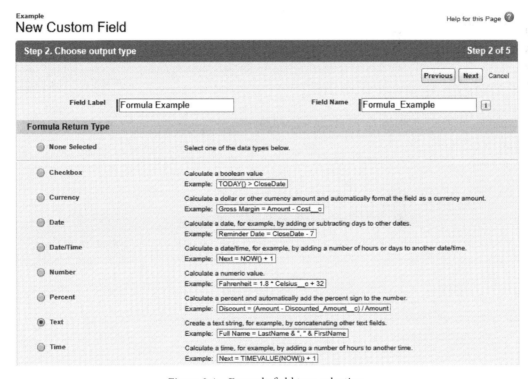

Figure 3.4 – Formula field type selection

By selecting the type, you are defining what will be the expected output for the formula. Let's select **Text** and fill in the field's label and name then click **Next**:

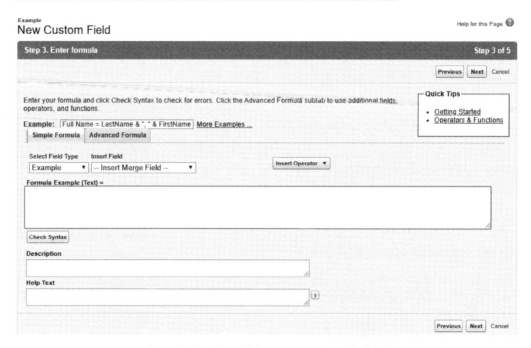

Figure 3.5 – Customizing a custom formula field

This step is meant to define the formula body and the usual **Description** and **Help Text** fields. Unless you can type the formula all by yourself, the page gives you helpers to select lists and buttons to compile the formula with no need to remember each field.

The **Select Field Type** and **Insert Field** lists show the list of available objects and their fields:

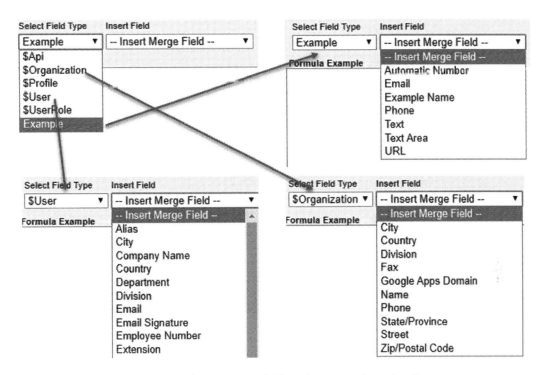

Figure 3.6 – Selecting merge fields in the custom formula editor

Each time you select the **Insert Field** list, the corresponding field is copied in the formula body text area:

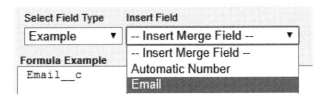

Figure 3.7 – Merge field copied into the formula body text area

Besides the current objects fields, you can access the following system objects:

- **API**: Fields to access some common Salesforce API endpoints and a valid session ID (this is something developers may be using to execute some highly custom automation on external systems)

- **Organization**: Fields related to the current org such as company name and address

- **User/Profile /User Role**: Fields related to the current user

The **Insert Operator** shows the & (concatenate) text operator (not so useful).

But what about cross-object fields?

The **Example** custom object has a master-detail lookup on the **Account** object but there seems to be no way that the editor can help us to retrieve the relationship name (if you are as forgetful as me, you certainly won't remember every single field name on your organization!).

Let's switch to the **Advanced Formula** mode:

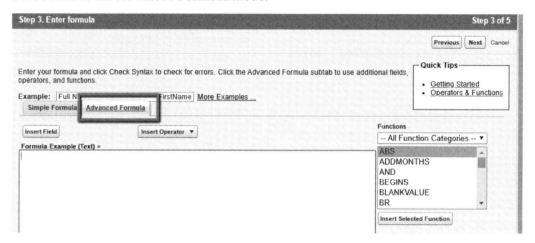

Figure 3.8 – Formula editor in the Advanced Formula mode

Here you can access the following:

- Whole parental relationships with the **Insert Field** button
- The whole set of operators with the **Insert Operator** button
- All available functions and a quick help guide with the **Functions** select list

Click **Insert Field** to display the inserted field helper popup:

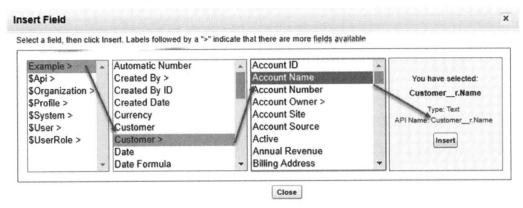

Figure 3.9 – Insert Field helper popup

We are able to explore all of the relationships and get the right field name or cross-object relation. You can achieve a quite complex combination , such as the one displayed in the following screenshot:

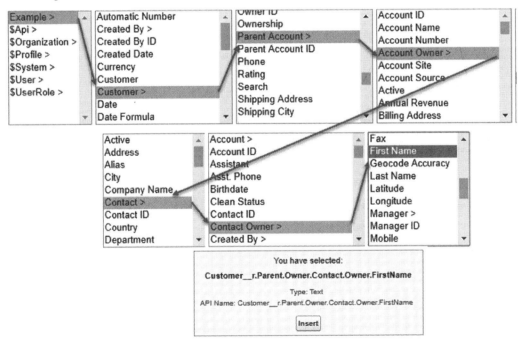

Figure 3.10 – A complex cross-object formula

The **Insert Operator** button shows all available operators that we've seen in the previous sections (it's up to you to choose the right one):

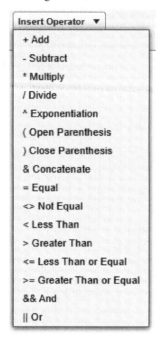

Figure 3.11 – Operators available in the editor

The **Functions** list gives you quick help on available functions:

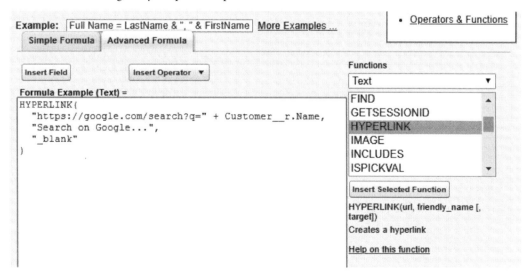

Figure 3.12 – Functions help select list

Finally, the **Check Syntax** button is needed to *compile* the formula before saving it with the **Next** button. If a compilation problem is found, a red error is shown at the bottom of the text area or a green success message instead:

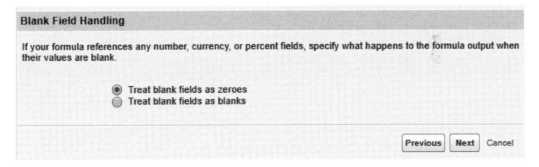

Figure 3.13 – The Check Syntax button's error and success messages

The **Advanced Formula** editor shows two more options regarding blank field handling at the page's bottom:

Blank Field Handling

If your formula references any number, currency, or percent fields, specify what happens to the formula output when their values are blank.

- Treat blank fields as zeroes
- Treat blank fields as blanks

Previous   Next   Cancel

Figure 3.14 – Blank field options

It depends on the calculation you are doing with your formula (probably a blank value in a numeric formula should be treated as a 0, while in a text formula as a blank value).

The editor wizard closes like a normal custom field (field accessibility by profile selection and a list of object layouts where you want to add the formula).

> **Note**
>
> Remember that a formula field is a **read-only** field and so it cannot be changed by the user directly but only by changing any referenced merge field (which the user may not be aware of as the formula body is never shown). Formula fields are never displayed while the record is in edit mode.

Do you remember **Expected Dismission Date,** explained in *Chapter 3*, regarding *Building the Data Model* the **Advertisement** object, which should display the expected dismission date of an advertisement based on **Installation Date** and the number of **Months of Availability**? This is a formula field that can be easily written as follows:

```
ADDMONTHS(
  Installation_Date__c,
  IF(
    ISBLANK(Months_of_availability__c),
    0,
    Months_of_availability__c
  )
)
```

And this is how it displays in the formula field editor:

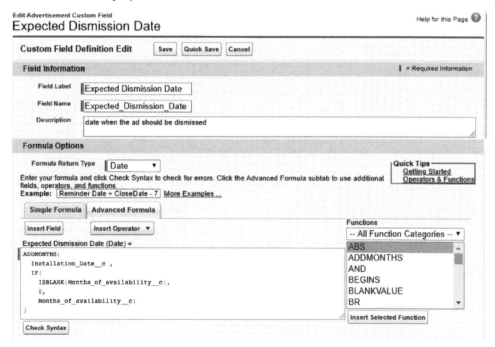

Figure 3.15 – The Expected Dismission Date formula field on the Advertisement custom object

Using formulas with default values

You can also write a formula for a field's default value as shown in the following screenshot:

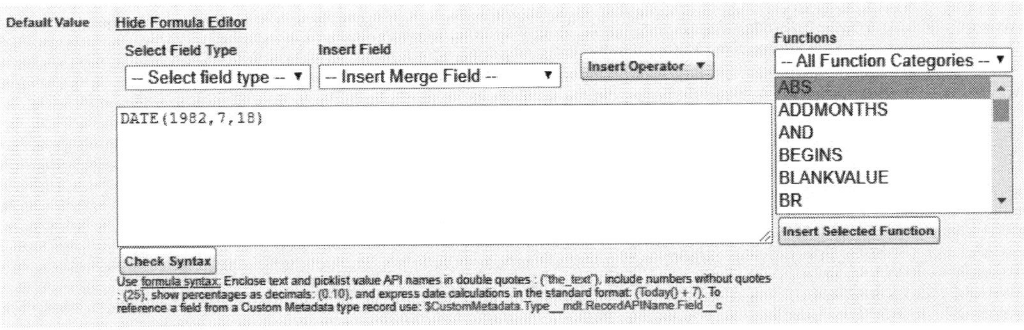

Figure 3.16 – The formula editor in the Default Value section of field editor

You cannot use any object fields nor any cross-object fields. Remember that the **Default Value** must match the field type as well.

Formula limits

The main limitation on formulas, that is, the first limit you encounter when you'll be building complex formulas, is the **number of characters a formula can contain** which, as of *Summer '20*, is **set to 3,900 characters** including spaces, line breaks, and comments.

> Tip
>
> If you need more formula space, create a separate formula field and chain it in another formula.

Another important limit is that **a formula can only show a maximum of 13,000 characters** (so you are not allowed to output bigger text content).

When a formula is saved, it is converted **into a compiled format, which must not exceed 4,000 bytes** and **when it is actually compiled** (by adding any other related formula)**, it cannot exceed 5,000 bytes**: there is no direct correlation between the formula size and its saved or compiled size in bytes.

Moreover, remember that you **cannot reference more than 15 objects in cross-object formulas** for a given object, that is, you cannot link more than 15 object types across all formulas in a given object (this applies for all kind of formulas, from custom fields to field updates, validation rules, and so on).

> **Note**
>
> To have a look at the major limits and allocations related to Salesforce editions, refer to Salesforce Help at `https://help.salesforce.com/articleView?id=overview_limits_general.htm&type=5`.

You **cannot use long text area, encrypted, and Description fields in formulas**: this is to enforce the computation time of formula value and to limit the possible output size.

To avoid infinite loops, **the value of a field cannot be related to a formula that uses the same field**.

Finally, you **cannot delete a field that is referenced in a formula**.

> **Note**
>
> There is a cool document with tips and hints to reduce formula size at `https://resources.docs.salesforce.com/224/latest/en-us/sfdc/pdf/salesforce_formula_size_tipsheet.pdf`.

Blaze your trail

If you want to enhance your knowledge on formulas, take a look at the following Trailhead modules:

- Using formula fields: `https://trailhead.salesforce.com/content/learn/modules/point_click_business_logic/formula_fields`

- Advanced formulas: `https://trailhead.salesforce.com/en/content/learn/modules/advanced_formulas`

- Evaluating report data with formulas: `https://trailhead.salesforce.com/en/content/learn/projects/rd-summary-formulas`

- Improving data quality for a recruiting app: `https://trailhead.salesforce.com/en/content/learn/projects/improve-data-quality-for-a-recruiting-app`

- Improving data quality for your sales and support teams: `https://trailhead.salesforce.com/en/content/learn/projects/improve-data-quality-for-a-cleaning-supply-app`

Summary

In this chapter, we explored the available options for building a formula and applying the concepts of diverse formula examples, closing with a detailed example of how to build a custom formula field. We learned the basic syntax of formulas, with operators and literals, and then we described the principal functions that the formula framework delivers, such as date/time functions, logical functions, math functions, and text functions, including concepts about cross-object formulas.

In the next chapter, we'll apply these formula concepts to validation rules to keep up with our organization's data quality.

4

Cleaning Data with Validation Rules

In the previous chapter, we saw how to build formulas and all the main building blocks that the Salesforce platform delivers, with a focus on operators and functions. We've learned that formulas can be used in a wide range of Salesforce components, from fields to default values, from workflow rules to approval processes, and so on.

In this chapter, we'll be diving into the creation and management of validation rules, a key Salesforce feature that you can use to deliver better quality data through formulas that identify incorrect/unwanted data states.

We'll learn about the following topics:

- What a validation rule is
- How to create and manage validation rules
- Considerations and limitations of validation rules

Technical requirements

The code for the chapter can be found here:

```
https://github.com/PacktPublishing/Hands-On-Salesforce-
Application-Development-without-Code
```

Defining data validation

Data validation is crucial for your business: if data is misaligned, dirty, or simply missing key pieces, it can rapidly become useless and even dangerous for your business. Would you drive a car without the lights on? I don't think so.

That's why the Salesforce platform delivers different ways to provide data validation on your CRM. Here, I cite the most often used methods of data validation:

- **Field type** built-in validation
- Field marked as **required**
- **Validation rules**
- Apex **triggers** / **Lightning components**

> **Note**
>
> **Apex triggers** give you the most freedom in defining validation criteria on record creation/update, bringing automation to the next level: it requires strong Apex coding skills though. The same applies to **Lightning components**, which are used to build user interfaces to deliver highly customized user experiences.

> **Further reading**
>
> We won't cover Apex triggers in this book (as this is a pure coding topic) but if you come from the no-to-low code world, you may be curious to explore the Apex world: take a look at Trailhead "Apex Basics & Database" at `https://trailhead.salesforce.com/en/content/learn/modules/apex_database?trail_id=force_com_dev_beginner` and "Apex Triggers" at `https://trailhead.salesforce.com/en/content/learn/modules/apex_triggers?trail_id=force_com_dev_beginner` on the Developer Beginner trail.
>
> If you want to explore building Lightning web components, refer to the Trailhead trail "Build Lightning Web Components" at `https://trailhead.salesforce.com/en/content/learn/trails/build-lightning-web-components`.

Validating data through field types

Custom fields deliver data validation through **field type** definition, as they support basic data validation capabilities to match data types (we've seen that putting the wrong email format in an email field causes an error, that a numeric field won't accept text values, and that a picklist field is displayed to allow the selection of specific kinds of values, and so on).

Another way to provide validation is by marking a field as required.

Universally required fields

Along with field type restrictions, the **required** option is a strong constraint because it makes the field be required *globally* or *universally*: the record can be created from any *channel* (user interface, massive import tool, automations such as Process Builder, external systems via Salesforce APIs, and so on) and its required fields will be mandatory without any exceptions.

> **Tip**
> You can mark a field as required on a specific layout (we'll have a look at layouts later in this book), but this way you are only acting at the user interface level: a user, assigned to a profile that is related to a specific layout where the field is marked as required, will be allowed to save a record unless the specific required field is not filled in; but nothing will happen if the same user fires an automation that updates the same record, setting the **layout required** field to blank.

The following is a list of custom field types that can be set as *universally* required:

- Currency
- Date
- Date/Time
- Email
- Lookup Relationship
- Master-Detail Relationship (*always required by design*)
- Number
- Percent
- Phone

- Picklist

- Text

- Text Area

- URL

There are some considerations regarding setting a universally required field:

- You can only mark custom fields as "required."

- If a field is universally required but a user doesn't have access to that field (see *Field Level Security* in the next chapters), then the user won't be able to successfully save the record. A required field cannot be removed from layouts and is automatically added at the end of a layout on creation.

- They cannot be read-only or optional fields.

- The Quick Create feature does not enforce required fields.

> **Further reading**
>
> For more details about the Quick Create feature, refer to Salesforce Help at
> `https://help.salesforce.com/articleView?id=basics_`
> `creating_records_with_quick_create.htm&type=5`.

- If you import the date with any tool, the field must be included in the operation (for example, using the Data Import Wizard we'll see this in the next chapters regarding data manipulation).

- If a field is used in a field update automation that sets the field as blank, this field cannot be marked as required.

- A field can be blank on records that were created before the field was marked as required: this means that when anyone tries to edit these records, they must set a value on the field for the save operation to successfully complete.

- Universally required fields may be useful for critical fields that should always be filled in no matter what, why, how, and when. If you need a more granular configuration of a required field, such as dependence on other record fields or related record fields, the validation rule should be your choice.

Creating validation rules

The cool thing about validation rules is that they can be easily adapted to your business needs by validating record fields based on diverse conditions on the current user and other fields in the object hierarchy you want to validate.

A validation rule basically works with criteria shaped by a formula that correlates fields by generating a single **true** or **false** value, indicating whether the criteria have been matched or not, and so whether the record should raise a validation error or not.

> **Tip**
> Remember that a validation rule's criteria must always return a **Boolean** value (that is, true or false) and that `true` indicates that the rule found an error condition.

This is the basic flow involving validation rules:

1. The user creates/updates a record.
2. They then click the **Save** button.
3. The engine checks all active validation rules on that object.

   If no rule is raised, the record is successfully saved on the database.

   If at least one rule is matched, the record is not saved and the user is notified with specific error messages (part of the validation rule configuration).

Remember that validation rules are applied even if the field being used is not displayed on the record layout and, just like **globally required** fields, they are not enforced when using the **Quick Create** feature.

> **Note**
> Just like any other feature you customize, it is highly recommended to test validation rules with all combinations of profiles and layouts, and with all other automations and inbound channels that can create and update a record.

Validation rule example with our example custom object

To create a new validation rule, click **Setup | Object Manager** and then select an object (we'll keep using our **Example** custom object), click on the **Validation Rules** side tab, and finally, click the **New** button:

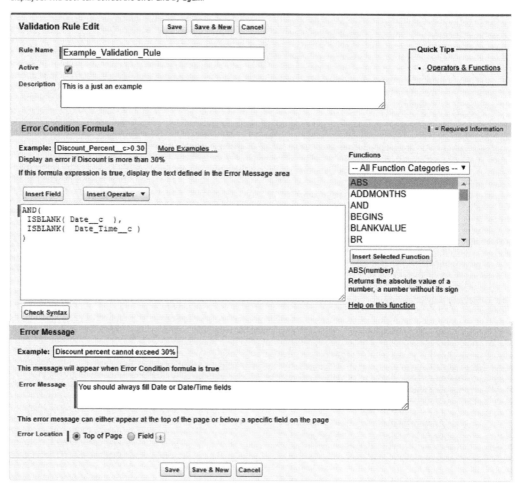

Figure 4.1 – Example of the validation rule creation wizard

The creation wizard needs the following fields to create a new validation rule:

- **Rule Name**: A unique name with no spaces or special characters.

- **Active**: A flag to indicate whether the rule should be evaluated.

- **Description**: The purpose of this rule.

- **Error Condition Formula**: The formula that, if evaluated to true, raises the error.

- **Error Message**: The error displayed if criteria evaluate to true.

- **Error Location**: We can tell Salesforce to display the error message at the top of the page or next to a specific field (if this makes sense; if more than one field is used within criteria, it doesn't make any sense to display the error next to a specific field). This option is only needed for user interface errors.

To create the **Error Condition Formula** shown in the preceding screenshot – *that the Date or Date/Time fields should always be filled* – use what you learned in the previous chapter: in our example, we are simply checking whether the `Date__c` or `Date_Time__c` custom fields are blank. If this happens, an error is thrown.

> **Note**
> If you don't have any of the fields above or you decided to use another Salesforce object, you can choose whatever fields you want.

Let's click the **Save** button to validate the rule and activate it:

Example Validation Rule

Back to Example

Validation Rule Detail		Edit	Clone			
Rule Name	Example_Validation_Rule			Active	✓	
Error Condition Formula	AND(ISBLANK(Date__c), ISBLANK(Date_Time__c))					
Error Message	You should always fill Date or Date/Time fields			Error Location	Top of Page	
Description	This is a just an example					
Created By	enrico murru, 29/02/2020, 17:12			Modified By	enrico murru, 29/02/2020, 17:25	

Edit   Clone

Figure 4.2 – Validation rule successfully created

Now let's click on **App Launcher** and look for the **Examples** tab, and then create a new **Example** record and try not to fill in any fields. You may encounter the following errors (if you configured the fields as in the previous chapters):

- The **Example Name** field is mandatory.

- The **Email** field is mandatory.

- The **Customer** field is mandatory.

The following screenshot shows this condition (the layout has been modified to show these fields first):

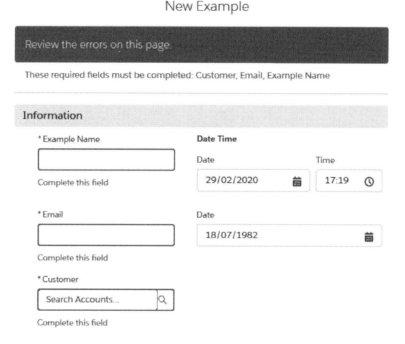

Figure 4.3 – Required field errors

As you can see, there is no error so far on the **Date** and **Date Time** fields: this is caused by the fact that the *required* field check is done before any other kind of validation.

There is something that I should warn you about with this configuration: we have stated that the error on the validation rule must be shown only if either the **Date** or **Date Time** field is blank, but here we can clearly see that the fields are filled by default with two dates (NOW() for the **Date Time** field and a hardcoded date for the **Date** field, which we did in the previous chapter).

This means that if we compile the **Example Name**, **Email**, and **Customer** fields, no actual validation rule is fired, and the record is saved.

> **Tip**
> Take your time to evaluate your data model configuration along with the validation rules to check and test whether any unwanted condition can happen on your business processes' configurations on the CRM.

Let's complete all the required fields: leave both the **Date** and **Date Time** fields blank and click the **Save** button:

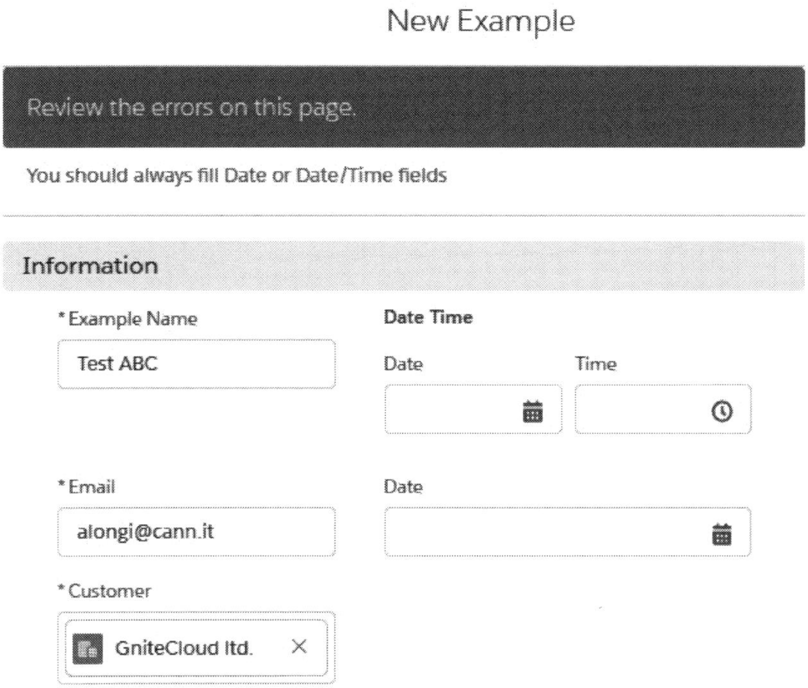

Figure 4.4 – Error on the validation rule match

If you try to complete either the **Date Time** or **Date** field, the record is successfully saved.

But what happens if you have more than one validation rule active at the same time?

Create a validation rule on the **Number** custom field as per the condition shown in the following screenshot – *that the Number field should be filled and must be greater than 1000*:

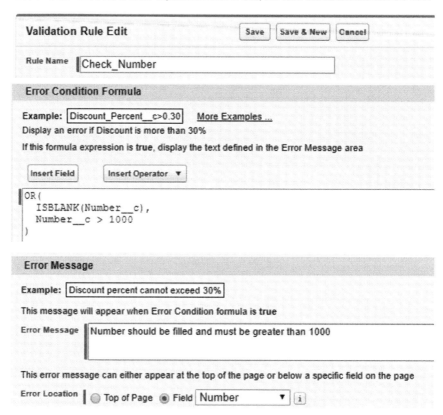

Figure 4.5 – A new validation rule on the Number field

This time the criteria are based solely on the **Number** custom field and we want the error to be displayed next to the **Number** field: the field has been moved on the layout right below the **Date** custom field (you'll become a wizard in layout manipulation further on).

Now, reload the tab where you were creating a new **Example** object, complete the required fields (**Example Name**, **Email**, and **Customer**) and leave every other field blank:

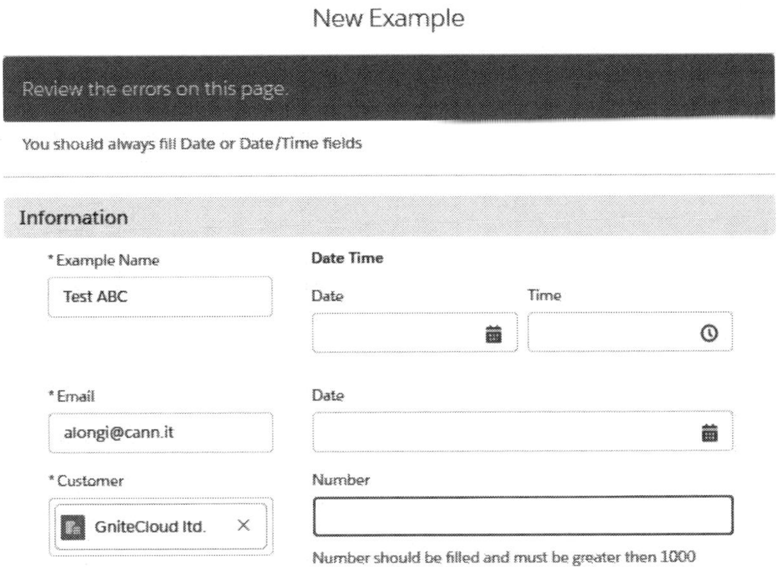

New Example

Figure 4.6 – Firing multiple validation rules

You can see more than one validation rule evaluated at the same time.

If we just set the **Error Location** option of the **Number** - related validation rule to **Top of page**, the error moves to the top of the page as expected:

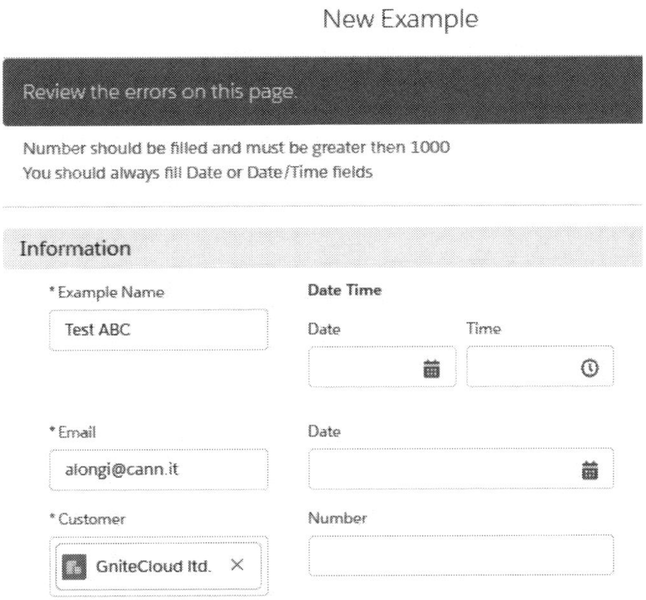

Figure 4.7 – Multiple validation rule errors at the top of the page

When dealing with validation rules, we can take the following actions:

- *Create / Edit*: as shown earlier.
- *Clone*: by using the **Clone** button; this is useful when you need a new version of the rule and want to start from a previously created validation rule.
- *Activate / Deactivate*: by using the **Active** checkbox on the rule definition, you can use activation/deactivation to test different versions of the same rule.

> **Note**
> The number of allowed active rules per object varies depending on the Salesforce edition (more details in the next section).

Now that we know how to create and manage data validation with validation rules, let's talk about some limitations and considerations.

Limitations and considerations

The first thing you need to understand is that there is a limit to the number of validation rules that can be active at the same time for a given object.

As of the *summer 2020 release*, depending on your edition, you can have the following number of active validation rules per object:

- **500**: Unlimited and Performance Edition
- **100**: Enterprise and Developer Edition
- **20**: all other editions

> **Further reading**
> To have a look at major limits and allocations related to Salesforce editions, refer to Salesforce Help at `https://help.salesforce.com/articleView?id=overview_limits_general.htm&type=5`.

If you want to know the limits specific to your organization, go to **Setup | Object Manager**, select a Salesforce object, and then click on the **Object Limits** side tab:

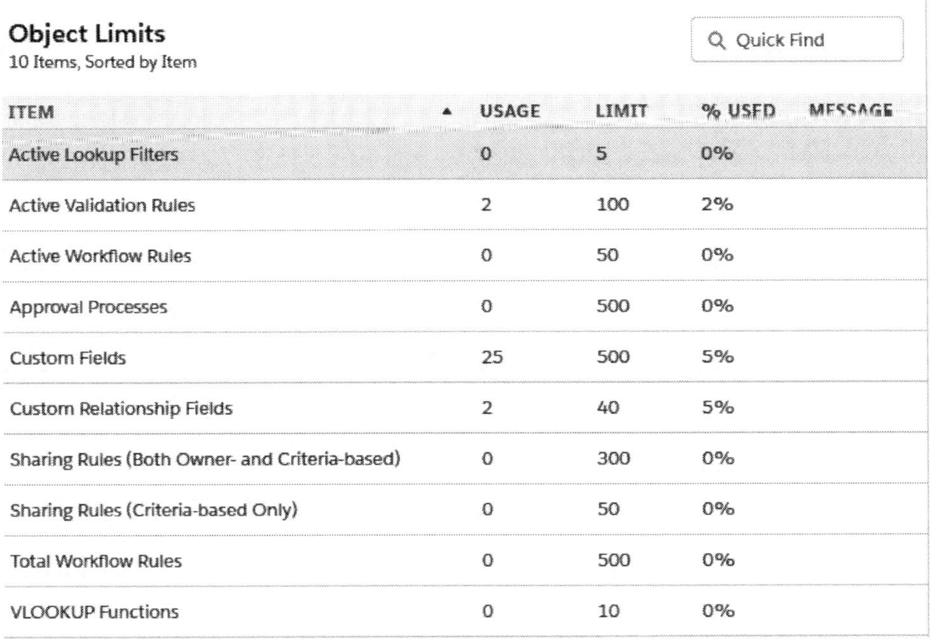

Object Limits
10 Items, Sorted by Item

Q Quick Find

ITEM ▲	USAGE	LIMIT	% USED	MESSAGE
Active Lookup Filters	0	5	0%	
Active Validation Rules	2	100	2%	
Active Workflow Rules	0	50	0%	
Approval Processes	0	500	0%	
Custom Fields	25	500	5%	
Custom Relationship Fields	2	40	5%	
Sharing Rules (Both Owner- and Criteria-based)	0	300	0%	
Sharing Rules (Criteria-based Only)	0	50	0%	
Total Workflow Rules	0	500	0%	
VLOOKUP Functions	0	10	0%	

Figure 4.8 – Object Limits page

There is another feature specific to validation rules, that is, the **VLOOKUP function**.

The VLOOKUP function

The VLOOKUP() function is a special kind of function that can *only be used within validation rules.*

This advanced function recalls Microsoft Excel's **VLOOKUP** function and it is actually used to "look up" a value from a given record set (that is, a set of records from another Salesforce object).

A good use case could be the need to validate a postal code for a given region/country.

Let's say we have a Salesforce object called **Postal Code** (with the API name Postal_Code__c) that handles the following custom fields:

- **City** (City__c): contains the city where a given postal code is used
- **Code** (Name): this is the standard **Name** field of the custom object (whose label has been renamed) and contains the postal code

We can create a new validation rule on the **Account** object with the following **Error Condition Formula**:

```
AND (
    NOT ( ISBLANK ( BillingPostalCode ) ),
    NOT ( ISBLANK ( BillingCity ) ),
    BillingCountry == "ITALY",
    VLOOKUP (
        $ObjectType.Postal_Code__c.Fields.City__c,
        $ObjectType.Postal_Code__c.Fields.Name,
        BillingPostalCode
    ) != BillingCity
)
```

So what's happening here? This validation rule fires if the following occurs:

- There is a value for postal code and billing city

- The billing country is set to ITALY (no other countries considered): to be safe, you could also use the IT abbreviation using the expression **OR (BillingCountry == "ITALY", BillingCountry == "IT")**

- There is no match on the **Postal Code** object between any of its records' **Name** fields and the current **Account Postal Code** value or if it doesn't match the **Account's** billing city value

> **Tip**
> `$ObjectType.OBJECT_API_NAME.Fields.FIELD_API_NAME`
> syntax is used to uniquely identify field names on an object.

What VLOOKUP() does is it simply makes a query against the Postal_Code__c object asking for the City__c field of the first record found, with the value of the Name field equal to the **Account's** BillingCity field.

The rule fires if no record is found on the **Postal Code** record set, and doesn't fire if a record is matched and the **Account** has the correct value:

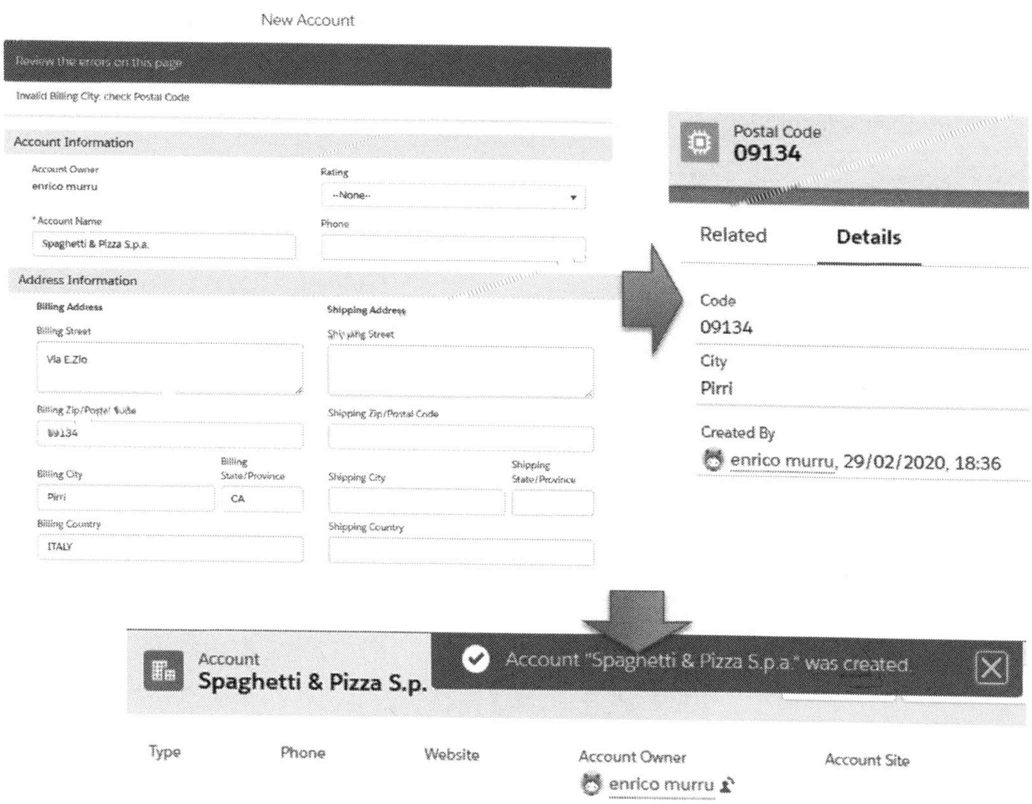

Figure 4.9 – VLOOKUP example on Account's validation rule

Remember that matching fields must have the same values (that is, **Account**'s `BillingPostalCode` and **Postal Code** `Name` fields) and that `VLOOKUP()` can only return fields of the types auto-number, roll-up summary, lookup, master-detail, checkbox, date, date/time, email, number, percent, phone, text, text area, or URL. Moreover, the external object matching field must be a **Name** field.

Only custom objects are supported within `VLOOKUP()` functions.

Further reading

For more fine-grained details on validation rule limitations, refer to Salesforce Help at `https://help.salesforce.com/articleView?id=fields_validation_considerations.htm&type=5`.

Some real-life examples

To complete the chapter, let's see some real-life examples of validation rules you may need in your implementations:

- Validate that an address postal code (that is, on **Account**) must be numeric, five characters long, and start with a zero:

```
AND (
    LEN ( ShippingPostalCode ) == 5,
    ISNUMERIC ( ShippingPostalCode ),
    LEFT ( ShippingPostalCode, 1) == "0"
)
```

- Validate the billing state for Italian addresses (aka provinces):

```
AND (
    BillingCountry = "ITALY",
    LEN(BillingState) == 2,
    NOT (
        CONTAINS("AG:AL:AN:AO:AR:AP:AT:AV:...", BillingState)
    )
)
```

A complete list of Italian provinces is available on Wikipedia at `https://en.wikipedia.org/wiki/Provinces_of_Italy`.

- Validate the mailing country values on contact against ISO 3166 code (Wikipedia at `https://en.wikipedia.org/wiki/ISO_3166-1`):

```
AND (
    LEN(BillingCountry) == 2,
    NOT (
        CONTAINS (
            "AF:AX:AL:DZ:AS:AD:AO:AI:AQ:AG:AR:AM:" &
            "AW:AU:AZ:BS:BH:BD:BB:BY:BE:BZ:BJ:BM:BT:BO:" &
            ". . .",
            BillingCountry
        )
    )
)
```

- Check whether an **Account's** annual revenue is within a specific range based on industry (and no less than $500,000):

```
OR (
   AnnualRevenue < 500000,
   AND (
      ISPICKVAL(Industry, "Banking"),
      AnnualRevenue < 100000000
   ),
   AND (
      ISPICKVAL(Industry, "Constructing"),
      AnnualRevenue < 1000000
   )
)
```

- Prevent cases from being re-opened if they have already been canceled:

```
AND (
   PRIORVALUE(IsClosed),
   IsClosed == false,
   ISPICKVAL( PRIORVALUE( Status ), "Canceled" )
)
```

- Check whether web-originated cases have the reason and description fields filled in:

```
AND (
   ISPICKVAL(Origin, "Web"),
   OR (
      ISBLANK( TEXT( Reason ) ) ),
      ISBLANK( Description )
   )
)
```

- Check the proper format for phone numbers with a trailing prefix (that is, +39 for Italy, +1 for the USA):

```
NOT (
   REGEX (
      Phone,
      ^[+]*{0,1}[0-9]{1,4}{0,1}[-\s\./0-9]*$
```

```
        )
    )
```

- Check whether a custom date field matches the current month:

```
MONTH( Date__c ) != MONTH ( TODAY() )
```

- Ensure that the opportunity close date is the first day of the next month:

```
AND(
    ISCHANGED( CloseDate),
    IF( MONTH( TODAY() ) < 12,
        CloseDate ==
            DATE( YEAR( TODAY() ), MONTH( TODAY() ) + 1, 1),
        CloseDate ==
            DATE( YEAR( TODAY() ) +1, 1, 1)
)
```

- Prevent certain users from creating/updating opportunities with an amount greater than $500,000:

```
AND(
    OR(
        $User.Department != "Sales",
        $User.Division != "Big Customers"
    ),
    Amount > 500000
)
```

Blaze your trail

Check out the following Trailhead modules to enhance your knowledge:

- Creating Validation Rules: https://trailhead.salesforce.com/en/content/learn/modules/point_click_business_logic/validation_rules

- Improving Data Quality for a Recruiting App: https://trailhead.salesforce.com/en/content/learn/projects/improve-data-quality-for-a-recruiting-app

- Customizing a Salesforce Object: `https://trailhead.salesforce.com/en/content/learn/projects/customize-a-salesforce-object`

- Improving Data Quality for Your Sales and Support Teams: `https://trailhead.salesforce.com/en/content/learn/projects/improve-data-quality-for-a-cleaning-supply-app`

Summary

So far, we have learned how to keep CRM data within our business standards by deploying validation rules based on record fields and unleashing formula functions, as seen in the previous chapter.

We've analyzed the differences between universally required fields and validation rules and even what the limits of validation rules are as well, completing our function's vade mecum with the advanced `VLOOKUP()` function to extract data from another Salesforce object.

Finally, we saw some real-life examples of validation rules to enhance our knowledge and fix the subject.

In the next chapter, we'll dig into custom settings and custom metadata types, a cool way to implement configurations.

5
Handling Dynamic Configuration

So far in the book, we've seen how to build a data model and how to create formulas to manage dynamic values, such as default values or custom formula fields and validations, to keep your data clean. We've also said that formulas could be used with many other Salesforce platform features that we'll see later, such as workflow rules, field updates, and approval processes.

In this chapter, we'll see how to add a powerful layer of configurations to such formulas with **Custom Settings** and **Custom Metadata Types**. This way, you'll never be required to edit a formula's body to update a threshold or a status text value that the formula is checking against an object's field; you'll simply change a **Custom Setting** or **Custom Metadata Type** value and the formula will change its behavior instantly. These features are also really useful when dealing with different organizations: if your project uses different sandboxes (jump to *Chapter 17, The Sandbox Model*, to learn more about sandboxes), you can easily set up different configuration values for each single org.

In this chapter, we'll be learning how to create dynamic formulas by doing the following:

- Managing custom settings, to create settings based on the current user
- Managing custom metadata types, to create global constant settings

Technical requirements

The code for the chapter can be found here:

```
https://github.com/PacktPublishing/Hands-On-Low-Code-
Application-Development-with-Salesforce
```

Setting up custom settings

Since the beginning of my Salesforce career as a developer (a *devmin* actually, as I usually did both developer and administration tasks), it was clear that the Salesforce platform was missing an important part of building efficient and maintainable algorithms. It required a way to define some sort of variables (or placeholders of values) that could be referenced in formulas and whose values could be changed on the fly when needed, without the need to update the formula itself.

Let's perform the following practical example and take one of the validation rules we saw in *Chapter 4, Cleaning Data with Validation Rules* (based on the **Opportunity** object):

```
AND (
   OR (
      $User.Department != "Sales",
      $User.Division != "Big Customers"
   ),
   Amount > 500000
)
```

This checks whether the current user who is creating/updating an **Opportunity** is in the `Sales` d**epartment** or in the `Big Customers` division and the amount is greater than `500000` dollars. If these conditions are not matched, the validation fires its error message.

What happens if the `Sales` department is renamed to, let's say, `Sales Dept.` and the division to `Huge Clients`?

And what if your business changes and the **Amount Threshold** should be raised to $1M?

Changes usually happen months after the CRM has been customized, so you'll have to check formula by formula to see where you are using the `Department` or `Division` or `Amount` fields and whether they are compared with the changing values. After this, you need to update each formula manually and bring the changes into production (we'll see how to deliver changes between your testing org, a sandbox, and your production org, where all your business data is laid down, toward the end of this book).

This procedure can lead to errors because of the following:

- You may miss some occurrences
- You may update the wrong value

After changes are applied, strong no-regression testing should be executed to check whether formula changes impact business operativity.

Wouldn't it be cool if we could have put some kind of placeholder instead of literal strings and numbers?

Custom Settings have been introduced with this great aim, making algorithms even more dynamic with an added layer of configurability.

Let's see how to build a **custom setting**:

1. Click on **Setup | Custom Code | Custom Setting** and click the **New** button to start the creation wizard:

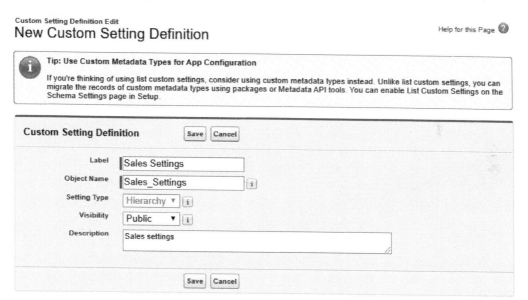

Figure 5.1 – Custom Setting creation wizard

2. Like custom object configuration, select a **Label** and an **Object Name** (or **API Name** – no spaces or special characters except for the underscore), leave the **Visibility** field as **Public,** and add a valuable description.

3. The **Visibility** field may be set to **Protected** and this is an important configuration if you are building a *packaged application*, that is, an application that you may deliver through **AppExchange** (`www.appexchange.com`), Salesforce's app store.

   With this visibility option, you set up a custom setting that your package's code can see and update but that the subscribing organization (that is, the org where the package is being installed) cannot. This is something that you probably won't need for a while.

> **Further reading**
>
> If you want to explore package creation, refer to Salesforce Help at `https://help.salesforce.com/articleView?id=package_distribute_apps_overview.htm&type=5`.

Selecting the right custom Setting Type

Let's have a look at the **Setting Type** option.

This picklist is disabled, and the `Hierarchy` value is defaulted to. A few years ago, this was not the standard behavior, although indeed you could also select the `List` value.

So then, what is the difference? Let's see here:

- **Hierarchical**: **Custom Settings** let you define a specific set of values related to a custom setting per org (default), user, or profile bases, letting the engine choose the most matching configuration (for example, if user Y has profile X and we have configured different values of the custom setting for profile X and user Y, the engine chooses the value set related to the user Y configuration): we'll see this behavior in action in a while.

- **List**: **Custom Settings**, on the other hand, are not related to user/profile hierarchy and are a defined list of values that can be accessed usually from Apex code. They are not enabled on **Point & Click** configurations such as formulas. Think of a list of postal codes as a good use case or specific product codes to be used within a customer acquisition wizard. For storage and performance reasons, Salesforce suggests using **Custom Metadata Types** instead of **List Custom Settings**.

If you find yourself working on an org that uses **List Custom Settings** and want to test them on your personal Developer Edition org, you can easily enable this option from **Setup | Data | Schema Settings** and select the **Manage list custom settings type** flag as shown in the following screenshot:

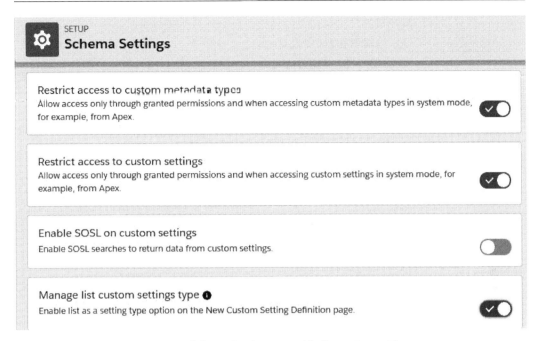

Figure 5.2 – Schema Settings to enable list custom settings

On this page, we can see other settings that we'll analyze further.

Go back to the **Custom Settings** creation and click the **Save** button:

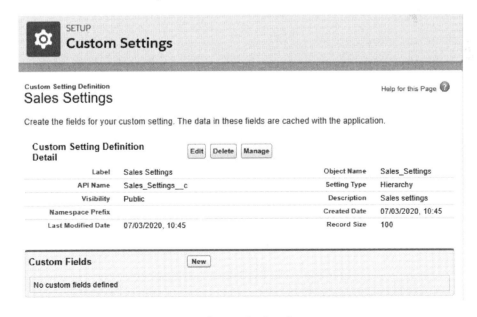

Figure 5.3 – Custom Settings home page

Our new **Sales Settings** custom setting homepage recalls a custom Salesforce object configuration page where the following applies:

- The API name ends with __c (such as `Sales_Settings__c`)
- **Custom Fields** can be added just as with custom objects

That's why, in the **Schema Settings** we've just seen, there was the **Enable SOSL on custom settings** option, which allows SOSL queries (that is, text search queries) to be executed on **Custom Settings** values (which is a feature we won't use in this book). **Custom Settings** are a special kind of Salesforce custom object that are cached by the platform so you don't need to make any queries to retrieve their values and are available in almost any execution context (a custom formula field, a validation rule, a workflow rule, an Apex trigger, a Lightning web component).

> **Tip**
>
> Once you select the **Type** of custom setting, you won't be able to change it anymore (even with the **Edit** button) but, as you'll hopefully follow the suggested best practice, you probably won't need any **List Custom Setting** at all.

Let's see how to add custom fields to our brand new custom setting.

Defining custom fields

On the **Custom Settings** home page (*Figure 5.3*), we can see a special field that is something that we haven't seen for a regular custom object, **Record Size** (which evaluates to **100**).

The platform allows you to store a small quantity of data coming from **Custom Settings** because each custom setting is cached (this means that it is always loaded into each user session, so it's accessible on the fly with relatively low latency). So, it enforces a maximum limit, that is, a minimum between the following (as of *summer 2020*):

- 10 MB
- 1 MB multiplied by the number of full-featured licenses

This means that if you have only 5 full licenses, you'll be able to store up to 5 MB, but if you have more than 100 full licenses, you'll be able to store up to 10 MB of **Custom Settings** data.

The **Record Size** field tells you how many bytes each record consumes on the overall count: the more fields you add, the more **Custom Settings** storage the record will consume.

Let's create a new field with the **New** button in the **Custom Fields** section:

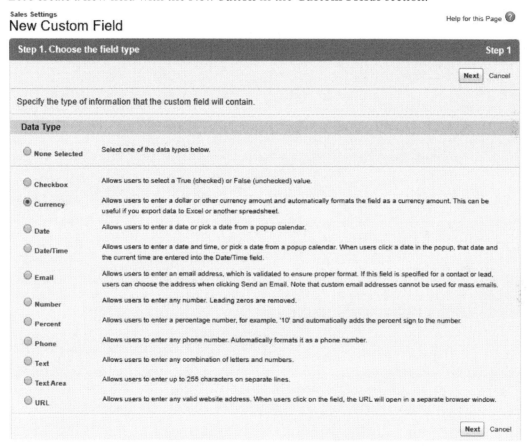

Figure 5.4 – Custom field creation on a custom setting

Only certain types of fields are allowed; no lookup relationships nor long text areas, for instance. We'll choose the **Currency** type and click **Next**:

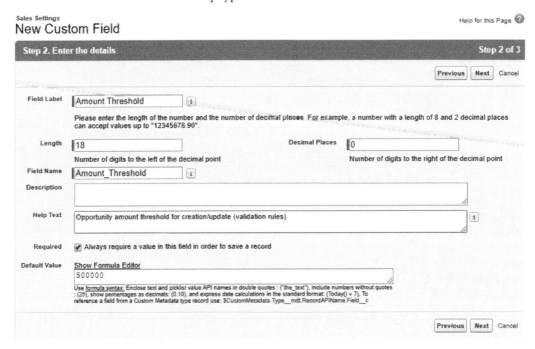

Figure 5.5 – Custom field definition on a custom setting

Click **Save** twice to create the record. Despite regular custom field creation, you won't be asked for layout- or field-level security options as the field is related to a setup object that won't generally be accessed by normal users.

Let's create some more string fields, which we'll use to replace string literals using the preceding validation rule, which we'll call `Sales Department Name` and `Big Customers Division` (as you create each field, take a look at how the **Record Size** field changes):

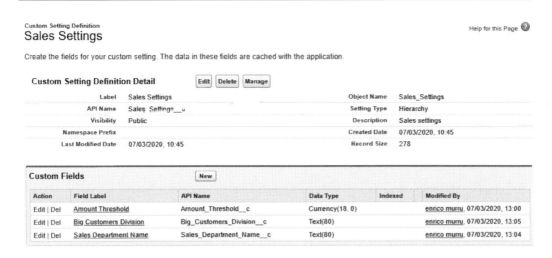

Figure 5.6 – Custom settings with three custom fields

The **Record Size** field now has a value of 278, which is composed of the following:

- 100: base custom setting record size

- 18: currency custom field

- 80: each text field counts as 80 bytes (1 per character)

Before changing the validation rule's formula, let's set a value on the record in the next section.

Managing custom settings

To create records for the **custom settings** configuration, click the **Manage** button on the **Custom Settings** home page or on the **Manage** link on the **Custom Settings** list page:

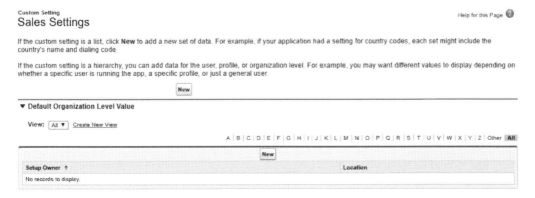

Figure 5.7 – Custom Setting value management page

The power of **Custom Settings** is that you can define a default value (valid for all users in the org) and/or different values based on different profiles or users. This way, when a user is running a specific formula, the formula engine dynamically calculates the value of the formula depending on the value that is related to the current user.

Let's click the **New** button in the **Default Organization Level Value** section to check this:

Figure 5.8 – Setting up the default custom setting value

We have the default values shown in *Figure 5.8* and, once saved, the record is output as follows:

Figure 5.9 – Default custom setting value layout

The **Location** field states the name of your company (set on the **Setup | Company Information** page).

Click **Back to List** to configure a specific value based on the user's profile, and then click the **New** button in the lower section:

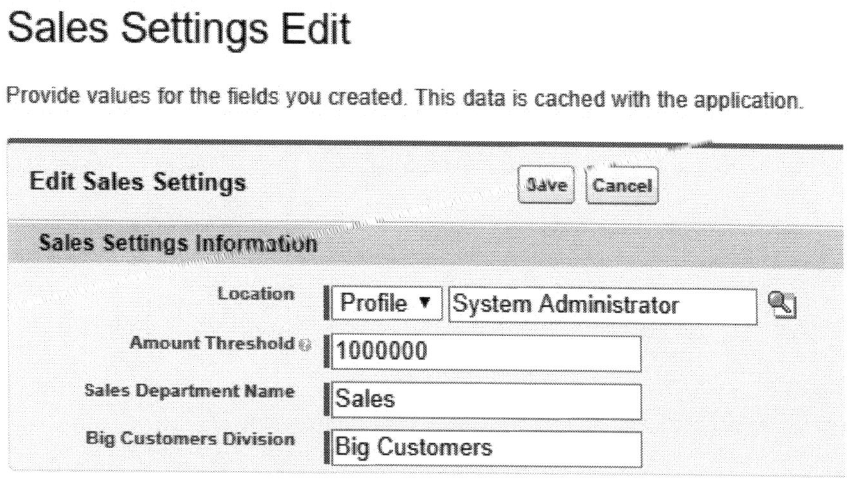

Sales Settings Edit

Provide values for the fields you created. This data is cached with the application.

Edit Sales Settings   Save   Cancel

Sales Settings Information

Location	Profile ▼ │System Administrator
Amount Threshold ⊚	1000000
Sales Department Name	Sales
Big Customers Division	Big Customers

Figure 5.10 – Defining a custom setting value for a specific profile

In this configuration, we are explicitly telling the platform to set **Amount Threshold** to `1000000`: this means that the validation rule, which we are about to modify, will never trigger for system administrator users if the amount is $1 million.

Finally, we'll set another user-based value for the CEO with no limit (we'll be using a gigantic number like 1 trillion and consider it the highest amount that a user can fill in):

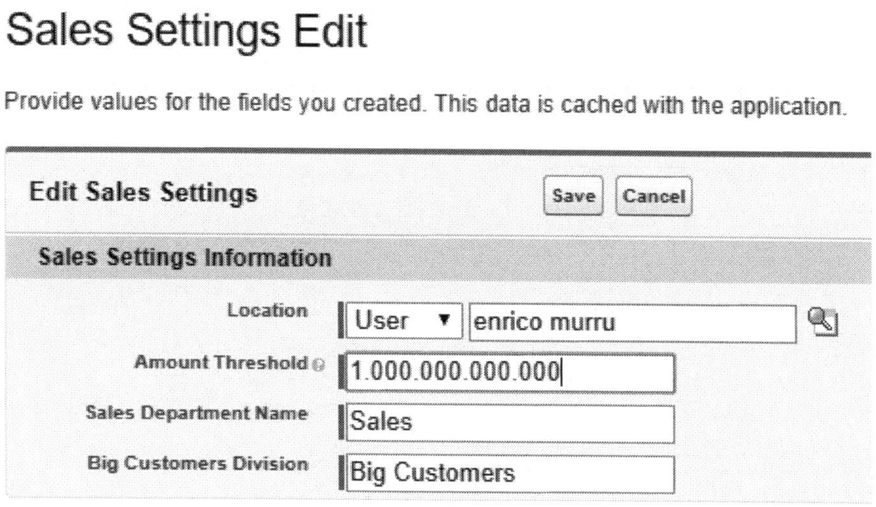

Sales Settings Edit

Provide values for the fields you created. This data is cached with the application.

Edit Sales Settings   Save   Cancel

Sales Settings Information

Location	User ▼ │enrico murru
Amount Threshold ⊚	1.000.000.000.000
Sales Department Name	Sales
Big Customers Division	Big Customers

Figure 5.11 – Defining a custom setting value for a specific user

Next, this is what we'll see for the **Sales Settings** custom setting:

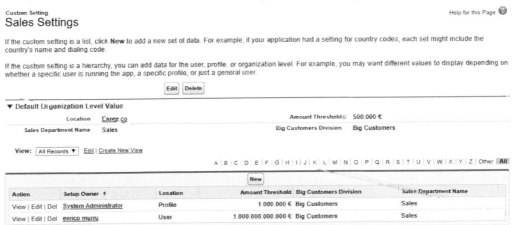

Figure 5.12 – Complete configuration for the Sales Settings custom setting

Next, to show all fields on the user/profile specific records, you need to create a new list view using the **Create New View** link shown as follows (we'll see list views in the next few chapters):

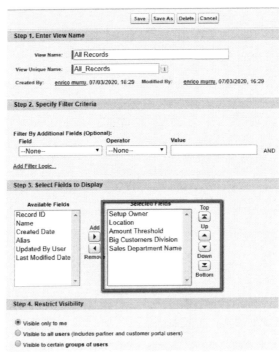

Figure 5.13 – List view configuration on Custom Settings values listing page

We're now ready to update the validation rule's formula. The next section will guide us on how to do it.

Consuming custom settings

Now that you have a valid custom setting configured, the advanced formula editor (review previous chapters for more details) shows a new item on the **Insert Field** screen:

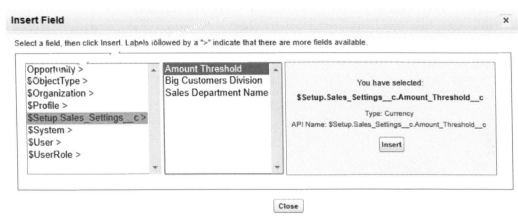

Figure 5.14 – Custom Settings can be referenced from the advanced formula editor

The $Setup variable is used to look for new custom settings on formulas.

The validation rule on **Opportunity** can be rewritten as follows:

```
AND (
  OR (
    $User.Department !=
              $Setup.Sales_Settings__c
                .Sales_Department_Name__c,
    $User.Division !=
              $Setup.Sales_Settings__c
                .Big_Customers_Division__c
  ),
  Amount > $Setup.Sales_Settings__c.Amount_Threshold__c
)
```

From now on, any administrator will be allowed to create any opportunity greater than $1 million without any warning on the department or division, while the CEO can virtually create any opportunity.

With this simple refactoring, we are also able to update any literal found in this formula (which can appear in several other formulas spread all over our metadata) just once from the **Custom Setting** values list page, without directly touching any formula.

Moreover, you are more than likely to implement your customizations on a dedicated testing org (called a *sandbox*). This topic will be covered in *Chapter 17, The Sandbox Model.* You shouldn't ever be allowed to do it in production orgs (to avoid business disruption on your CRM due to unwanted errors).

Bringing metadata from a sandbox to a production org needs time and procedures to be executed (which shouldn't be done by just any user, but only by trusted administrators); using this approach doesn't require moving metadata; only changing custom setting data (you need some testing anyway before changing such configurations, though).

Before concluding Custom Settings, let's review some platform limits and considerations to be considered when using this feature.

Limits and considerations of Custom Settings

One final thought on **Custom Settings** limitations.

We've said that there is an upper limit of 10 MB for **Custom Settings** storage.

- To check how much storage your records are using, go to **Setup | Custom Code | Custom Settings** and click the **Get Usage** button (to get the most refreshed value), and then refer to the **Total Size** column of the **Custom Settings** list:

Figure 5.15 – Custom Settings size

- You can limit the visibility of custom settings to specific profiles by enabling the **Restrict access to custom settings** permission we've seen on the **Schema Settings** page, and then enable **Enhanced Profile User Interface** from **Setup | User Management Settings**.

- Now open any profile (**Setup | Users | Profiles**) or **Permission Set** (we'll look at profiles and permission sets in the next chapter), look for **Custom Setting Definitions**, and then select the custom settings a profile/permission set is enabled to view/edit:

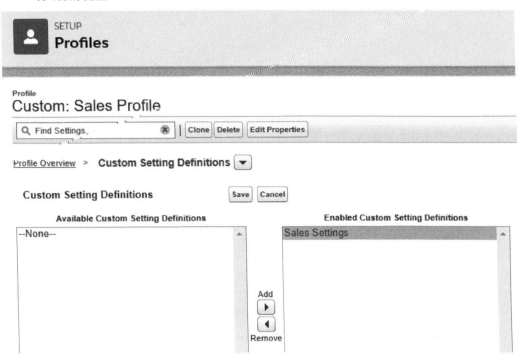

Figure 5.16 – Custom Setting assignment to profiles

Remember that formulas and any other automation will keep working even though the user doesn't have access to **Custom Settings**.

Apart from this, other important limitations are as follows:

- A custom setting is a custom object, so it counts in the total number of custom objects that can be created on an org.

- You can add up to 300 custom fields to a custom setting (this is the maximum amount; if your org allows fewer custom fields per custom object, that limit is applied).

While **Custom Settings** definitions (metadata) can be released from one org to another, their values (data) need to be set up manually (or through a data import tool such as **Data Loader**). Custom metadata types, on the other hand, consider both data definition (metadata) and values (data) part of the metadata itself.

In the next section, we'll see another way of creating dynamic configurations through the use of **custom metadata types**.

Setting up and managing custom metadata types

Custom Metadata Types are the **List Custom Settings** of the next generation. They define fields and create records that can be retrieved from declarative or programmatic configurations.

Unlike **Custom Settings**, which need a second configuration step after the metadata is deployed on the org (applying the values), **Custom Metadata Types** consider both metadata and its data to be all part of the whole metadata. This is particularly useful when building packaged applications that may be delivered to different customers' orgs and it is important to limit the configuration steps:

1. To create a new **Custom Metadata Type**, click **Setup | Custom Code | Custom Metadata Types** and then click the **New Custom Metadata Type** button:

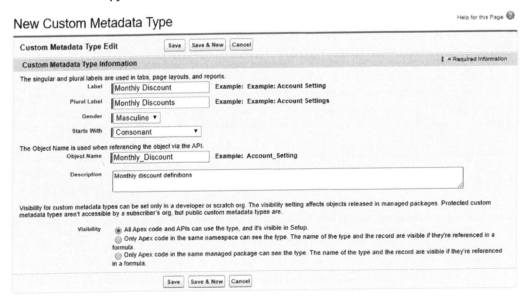

Figure 5.17 – New Custom Metadata Type creation wizard

2. The custom object definition is quite similar to what we saw on **Custom Settings** (there are just some more options regarding an object's label configuration). You have to define the visibility configuration for the new Custom Metadata Type, which should be left to **All Apex Code** and APIs can use the type, which is visible in **Setup** (it's equivalent to the **Public** value for the **Visibility** field of the **Custom Settings** definition). The other values should be left for special behaviors on packaged application development (which you shouldn't take care of now).

3. Click **Save** to land on the **Custom Metadata Type** home page:

Figure 5.18 – Custom Metadata Type configuration home page

4. Unlike Custom Settings, Custom Metadata Types support validation rules and page layouts (layouts were introduced with the *winter 2015* release).

A significant difference between **Custom Settings** and custom objects in general is that the **Custom Metadata Types API** name ends with __mdt and not __c (see that **API Name** has a value of Monthly_Discount__mdt).

Each record is defined by two main standard fields:

- **Custom Metadata Record Name**: This is the API name (or `DeveloperName`) that is used in formulas and code to identify a specific record.

- **Label**: The main label of the record (a readable version of the preceding `DeveloperName`)

This means that, when referencing a custom metadata type in formulas or default values, you need to know its API name to get its values referenced in the formula (we'll see this shortly, in the default value example). This is to say that, if you want to reference the **Monthly Discount** Custom Metadata Type on a custom formula field, for example, you need to remember that the system named it `Monthly_Discount__mdt`.

Like **Custom Settings**, we have **Record Size**, which increases when more fields are added but the minimum size is always 141 bytes and you can have up to 10 MB of stored **Custom Metadata Types**.

The **Monthly Discount Custom Metadata Type** will be used to calculate a different discount on any **Opportunity** amount.

1. Let's create some new fields by clicking on the **New** button in the **Custom Fields** section:

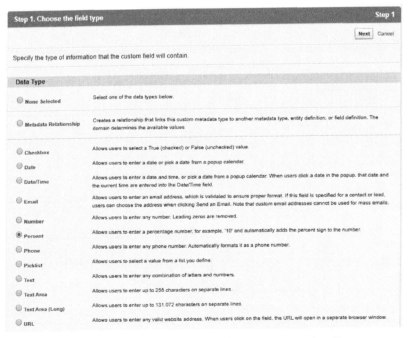

Figure 5.19 – Custom field creation for Custom Metadata Type

2. We can see new types (thinking of **Custom Settings** field creation) such as the **Text Area (Long)** type and a new **Metadata Relationship** (which links a metadata type record to another custom metadata type record or an entity definition or field definition).

> **Further reading**
>
> For more information about **Metadata Relationship** fields, refer to Salesforce Help at `https://help.salesforce.com/articleView?id=custommetadatatypes_relationships_limits.htm&type=5`.

• On the previous screen, let's choose the **Percent** type and click **Next**, which brings us here:

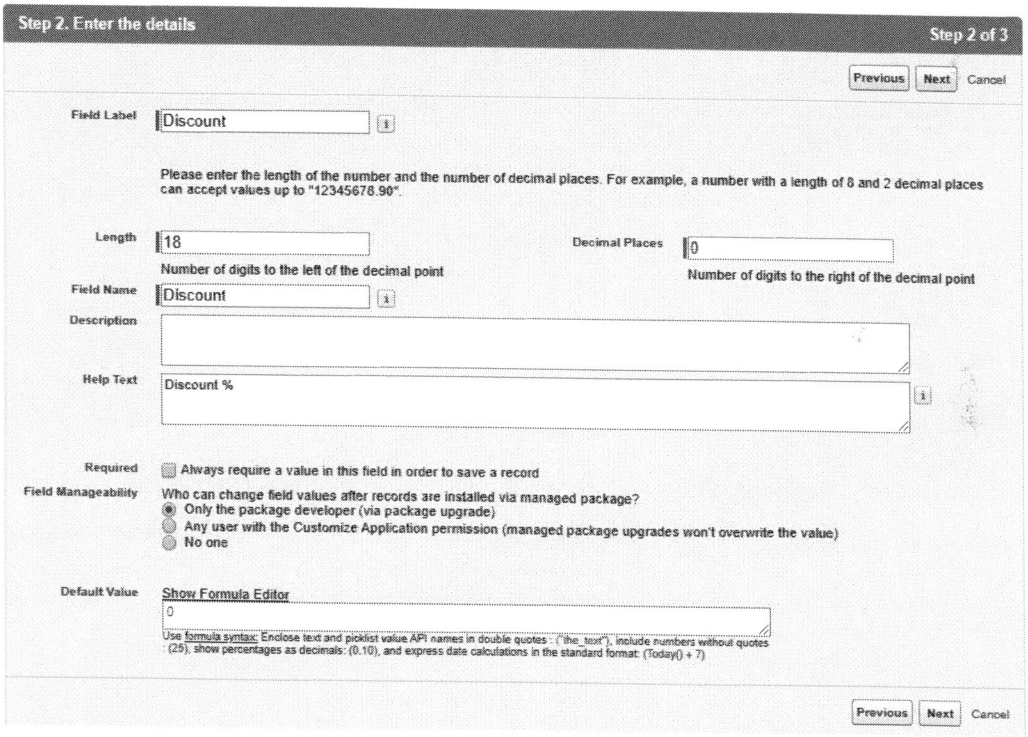

Figure 5.20 – Custom field definition for Custom Metadata Type

We won't cover the **Field Manageability** configuration, as that is related to packaged application development.

- Click **Next** to tell which layout will contain the new field and **Save** again to end the field creation wizard.

- Now we can click the **Manage Monthly Discounts** button to set up the values, and this is the result after creating a different discount for each month:

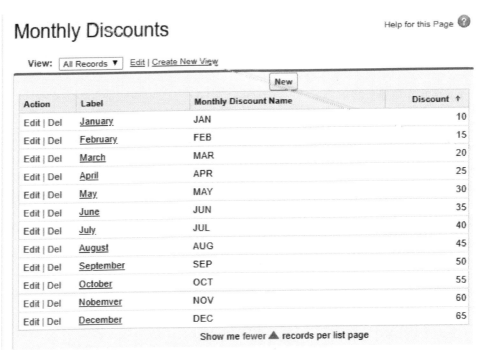

Figure 5.21 – Custom Metadata Type records list

As shown in the preceding screenshot, the **Custom Metadata Type** record list can have custom list views as well.

We're now ready to see the custom metadata setting in practice.

Consuming custom metadata types

Let's now create a new custom field on the Opportunity object called `Discount` with the `Percent` type and let's define this default value using the **Custom Metadata Types** we've just created. Note that while **Custom Settings** need the `$Setup` variable, **Custom Metadata Types** use the `$CustomMetadata` variable to reference a formula.

Let's add the following formula to the **Default Value** field of the **Discount** custom field definition:

```
CASE ( MONTH ( TODAY () ),
    1,  $CustomMetadata.Monthly_Discount__mdt.JAN.Discount__c,
    2,  $CustomMetadata.Monthly_Discount__mdt.FEB.Discount__c,
    3,  $CustomMetadata.Monthly_Discount__mdt.MAR.Discount__c,
    4,  $CustomMetadata.Monthly_Discount__mdt.APR.Discount__c,
    5,  $CustomMetadata.Monthly_Discount__mdt.MAY.Discount__c,
    6,  $CustomMetadata.Monthly_Discount__mdt.JUN.Discount__c,
    7,  $CustomMetadata.Monthly_Discount__mdt.JUL.Discount__c,
    8,  $CustomMetadata.Monthly_Discount__mdt.AUG.Discount__c,
    9,  $CustomMetadata.Monthly_Discount__mdt.SEP.Discount__c,
   10,  $CustomMetadata.Monthly_Discount__mdt.OCT.Discount__c,
   11,  $CustomMetadata.Monthly_Discount__mdt.NOV.Discount__c,
   12,  $CustomMetadata.Monthly_Discount__mdt.DEC.Discount__c,
 0)
```

Given today's month, the algorithm uses the CASE () function to get the proper discount based on the **Monthly Discounts** custom metadata type, and (given that the current month is *March*) this is what you see when creating a new opportunity:

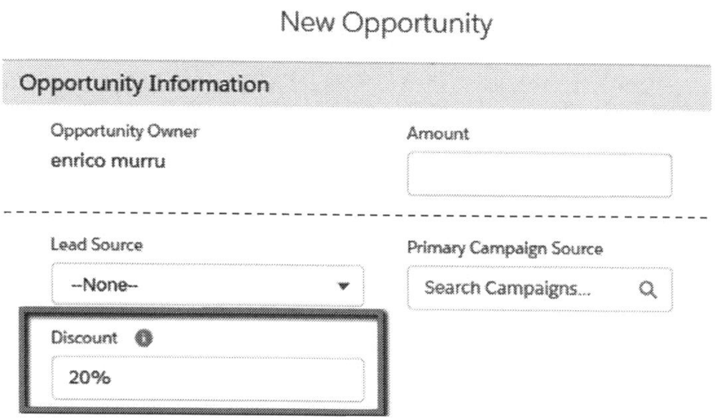

Figure 5.22 – Default value applied to the Discount custom fields if the current month's discount is 20%

Before closing the **Custom Metadata Types** section, let's have a look at some limits and considerations when deploying this feature.

Limits and considerations of Custom Metadata Types

As we saw for **Custom Settings** in the previous sections, you can define **Custom Metadata Types** access at the profile/permission set level by searching on the **Enhanced Profile User Interface** for the permissions for **Custom Metadata Types**:

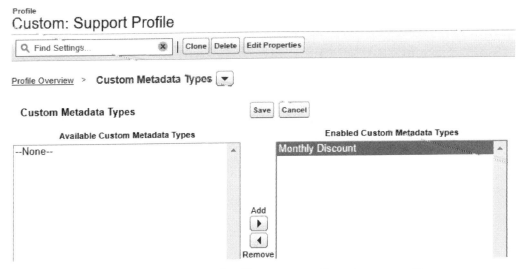

Figure 5.23 – Custom Metadata Type access configuration on a profile

One of the other advantages of using **Custom Metadata Types** is that when they are queried, the query is not counted against the Salesforce transaction limit (there is a specific governor limit regarding the number of SOQL queries that can be issued in a given Apex execution/transaction), unless you are not querying a long text area field. This limit applies to custom Apex coding but also to queries issued in Flows (which you may be a master of – we'll see those in *Chapter 10, Designing Lightning Flows*), so take care of this limitation when using **Custom Metadata Types** when building your automations.

As of *summer 2020*, you can have up to 200 **Custom Metadata Types** definitions per org and each one can have up to 100 custom fields. You can reference up to 15 custom metadata types for Flow definition (Flows will be covered in *Chapter 10, Designing Lightning Flows*). You can use up to 15 different **Custom Metadata Types** in validation rules per object (but you can reference them more than 15 times).

Blaze your trail

Check out the following Trailhead resources to be a master on **Custom Settings** and **Custom Metadata Types**:

- Configuring Your App with Custom Metadata Types: `https://trailhead.salesforce.com/en/content/learn/trails/configure-your-app-with-custom-metadata-types`

- Adding Sound Effects to Your Salesforce Org: `https://trailhead.salesforce.com/en/content/learn/projects/add-sound-effects-to-your-sf-org`

Summary

In this chapter, we've learned the basics of **Custom Settings** and **Custom Metadata Types** management to deliver a customized and effective approach to store configuration parameters.

Putting together everything we've seen about custom object setups, we've understood how to manage these configuration types and use them within formulas such as validation rules or default values, to grant us a way to create dynamic configurations that won't require us to change formulas' algorithms if the referenced constants changes over time.

In the next chapter, we'll close this section by introducing the Salesforce sharing model, to bring an efficient data sharing model in the *"who can see what"* paradigm, unleashing profiles and permission sets, org-wide default sharing, and sharing rules.

6

Security First – The "Who Sees What" Paradigm

The Salesforce platform delivers a wide range of tools and features to enable data access and sharing across users, empowering security, segregation, and effective data management in your org.

Everything is centered on data, and keeping it safe and sound must be your priority. Also, giving users the ability to access only what they need to access is key to enhancing productivity and also avoiding human error (users may access data they should not be allowed to handle). By using permissions on profiles and permission sets, you'll be able to define exactly which data parts are accessible to which users; configuring proper org-wide default sharing, you'll define which records for any object should be accessed by users (for instance, sales reps shouldn't access opportunities created directly by the VP of sales), and you'll also be able to spread out record access with custom rules, thus giving more access power to specific subsets of records to specific subsets of users (for example, giving access to all cases created by Italian customers, disregarding the user who created it, to all service agents for the Italian market).

In this chapter, we'll deal with most aspects related to securing your data, including the following:

- Exploring the security and sharing models
- Configuring permissions with object-level security and field-level security
- Understanding org-wide sharing
- Defining sharing rules to spread out records access

Exploring the Salesforce data security model

Your Salesforce org may contain tens to thousands of users, and being able to control *who sees what* should be an absolute priority for solution architects and administrators for the following reasons:

- **Secures data**: There will be users with more or less power to access data, depending on their company hierarchy's role.
- **Segregates data**: Less confusion for users; they will only be able to access records that they should be aware of.
- **Differentiates duties**: Unless a user can view a record, they'll only be allowed to edit/delete it if their role/profile/sharing configuration allows it.
- **Decreases mistakes**: A user is allowed to manipulate a subset of data, so the likelihood for them to make errors lowers.
- **Speeds up daily routines**: Less data shown to a user means higher speed in daily working tasks.

These are the basic security key points for efficient and reliable data security management across all the users in your Salesforce organization.

> **Note**
> After more than 10 years of experience in Salesforce projects, believe me when I say that setting up a proper data security and sharing model is the best thing you can do for your CRM; if you don't do so or design it late, it'll end up being a big headache to fix this big mistake.

In the following subsections, we'll learn more about how Salesforce helps you set up data visibility and sharing.

Salesforce licensing

Users are at the core of any application as they authenticate on the CRM and, thanks to a specific role and profile, they are allowed to access specific Salesforce features.

When your company or your customers sign a contract with Salesforce, it purchases a set of licenses for its *prospective* users.

This is the concept of **user license**, and you can have a look at what your org supports from **Setup | Company Settings | Company Information** in the **User Licenses** section:

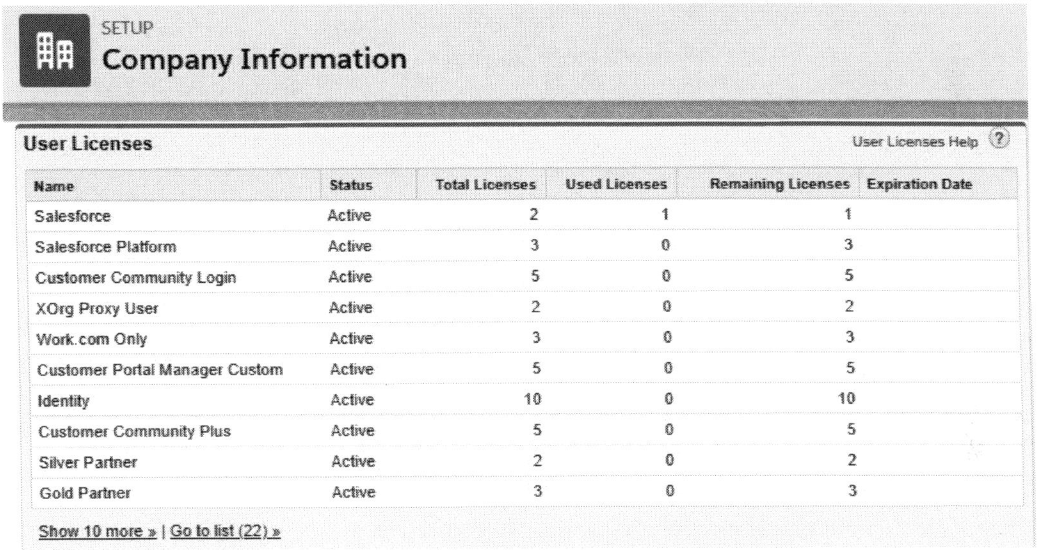

SETUP
Company Information

User Licenses

User Licenses Help ?

Name	Status	Total Licenses	Used Licenses	Remaining Licenses	Expiration Date
Salesforce	Active	2	1	1	
Salesforce Platform	Active	3	0	3	
Customer Community Login	Active	5	0	5	
XOrg Proxy User	Active	2	0	2	
Work.com Only	Active	3	0	3	
Customer Portal Manager Custom	Active	5	0	5	
Identity	Active	10	0	10	
Customer Community Plus	Active	5	0	5	
Silver Partner	Active	2	0	2	
Gold Partner	Active	3	0	3	

Show 10 more » | Go to list (22) »

Figure 6.1 – Available user licenses on a Salesforce org

When creating a new user, the first thing to do on the creation form is to select the proper user license. This is done on the **Setup | Users | New User** page, as follows:

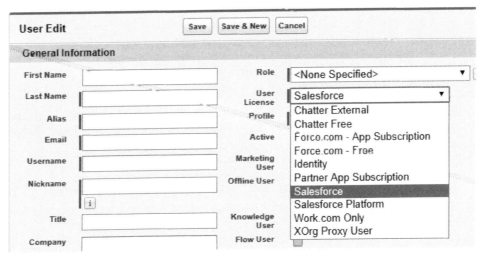

Figure 6.2 – User license selection on the user creation page

We can divide user licensing into three main groups, depending on how data sharing is handled:

- **Full sharing model usage**: These are **internal users** who have full access to the Salesforce sharing model. The various kinds of licensing may differ—for example, on the number of standard Salesforce objects they access.

- **High volume customer portal licenses**: These are **community users** and they don't have access to the Salesforce sharing model. Sharing is done through record relationships with records that the user is related to, using the so-called **sharing sets** (for example, a user is given access to a case record if the case's account is the same as the user's account). With an additional license (for example, the Customer Community Plus license), we can deliver a full sharing model.

- **Chatter-free license**: These users have no access to the sharing model or any other Salesforce business object; users with this license are allowed to access **collaboration** within the CRM, including access to **Chatter**, **Groups**, and people, to name a few.

> **Further reading**
>
> For more details about Salesforce licensing, refer to Salesforce Help at
> `https://help.salesforce.com/articleView?id=users_`
> `licenses_overview.htm&typo=5.`

Now, let's move on to the Salesforce sharing model.

The sharing model

To understand how Salesforce manages data access, let's have a look at the (as I call it) *who sees what* pyramid:

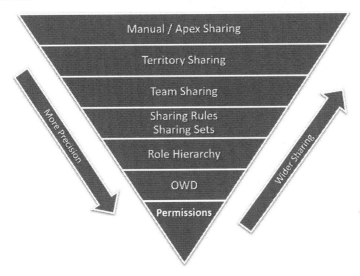

Figure 6.3 – Salesforce sharing architecture

At a glimpse, we can have a look at all the ways that we can define sharing and visibility on Salesforce records; the wider the pyramid gets, the more *people* are able to access records.

Let's see what's inside each pyramid step, and later on, we'll analyze the most important and peculiar features:

- At the lower level (or the *bottom tip* of the pyramid), we find **Permissions**, which are represented by **profiles** and **permission sets**. These define **Object-Level Security (OLS)** and **Field-Level Security (FLS)**—that is, objects and fields that a user is allowed to access. This configuration option allows any administrators to define a fine-grained setup of data access over a specific Salesforce object.

Profiles are mandatory information that must be filled in when creating a user (and a user is related to one and only one profile), while **permission sets** contain more or less the same permissions as profiles and are associated to users (so a user can have more than one permission set related) to extend what their profile allows them to do (for example, a sales user with a **Sales Rep** profile is not allowed to access the case object. However, if they are related to the **Service Manager** permission set, which grants access to case-related objects, they are now able to manage cases).

Exceptions are made for some specific configurations related to data access (for example, the **View All Data/Modify All Data** permissions, which grant access to administrator-like users to all data in view/edit mode). Permissions don't themselves grant access to records, just the possibility to actually see a record or its fields, provided the data has been shared with the user.

- The **Org-Wide Defaults** (**OWD**) field defines how records are basically shared among users, and then the use of the other features on the pyramid opens up access to the user audience. For example, you can define that the **Opportunity** record is **private** by default, which means that unless you are not the owner of an opportunity or you are the manager of the users who is owning the opportunity, you won't be able to access the record.

> Tip
>
> Always set up the most restrictive sharing configurations, and remember that sharing can only be opened if we set **OWD** for a Salesforce object to **Public Read-Only** (that is, anyone in the org can see that kind of record). You cannot use any sharing features to close it, other than the **OWD** configuration itself.
>
> **OWD** is indeed the only configuration able to restrict access to a class of records; this is a base concept of the Salesforce sharing model.

- **Role Hierarchy** is the next step of the pyramid. This hierarchy is mostly used to mirror the company's employee role hierarchy, with managers and subordinates. The higher a user is in the hierarchy, the more records they can have access to, depending on the number of records owned by their subordinates (or people lower than them in the hierarchy).

- **Sharing Rules** are a tool that can be leveraged to expand record access to groups of users that shouldn't be allowed to access a specific set of records because of **OWD** configuration. For example, you can give access to all cases owned by **Service** role people to **Sales** role people, or give access to accounts with the billing country **Italy** to all **Italian Sales** subordinate roles.

Sharing Sets, like **sharing rules**, are a way to expand record access for users whose licensing doesn't allow the sharing model (as we saw earlier with the **High volume customer portal licenses** bullet point).

> **Further reading**
>
> You can get more information about sharing sets from Salesforce Help at `https://help.salesforce.com/articleView?id=networks_setting_light_users.htm&type=5`.

- **Team Sharing** is related to a specific class of objects (**Opportunity**, **Account**, and **Case** only). A record's owner (or a user higher in the hierarchy) can create a specific working team on the record, a team that is immediately granted access to the record in **Read Only** or **Edit** mode, disregarding the actual sharing state of the record.

> **Further reading**
>
> For more info about **Account** teams, refer to `https://help.salesforce.com/articleView?id=accountteam_add.htm&type=5`, for **Opportunity** teams, go to `https://help.salesforce.com/articleView?id=opp_team_manage.htm&type=5`, and for **Case** teams, go to `https://help.salesforce.com/articleView?id=caseteam_setup.htm&type=5`.

- With **Territory Hierarchies**, a feature specific to accounts, opportunities, and their child records of a master-detail relationship, an administrator can give access to records based on a one-dimensional configuration (for instance, country, business unit, or ZIP code). Sharing data is recalculated any time the territory-like field of a record changes (such as when an account's billing country field changes from **Italy** to **USA**).

> **Further reading**
>
> For more info about territory management, refer to Salesforce Help at `https://help.salesforce.com/articleView?id=tm2_territory_mgmt_overview.htm&type=5` and the Territory Management Trailhead module at `https://trailhead.salesforce.com/content/learn/modules/territory-management-basics/get-started-with-enterprise-territory-management`.

- Users can manually give access to their owned records using **Manual Sharing** to other users that don't have access to them.

- Finally, **Apex Sharing** is sharing granted through Apex automation and is provided to give finer-grained access to sharing options when the previous features are not enough for your company's specific sharing model.

Further reading

If you are interested in Apex sharing, refer to Salesforce Developer Help at `https://developer.salesforce.com/docs/atlas.en-us.apexcode.meta/apexcode/apex_bulk_sharing.htm`.

One last thing to be mentioned is **implicit sharing**, which is related to some standard objects and is a baseline feature that cannot be disabled. We have **parent implicit sharing**, which occurs when a user owning a case, opportunity, or contact has implicit sharing of the related account record. **Child implicit sharing** works in the opposite way; if a user owns an account, they are given access to related contacts, opportunities, and cases.

Note

The child implicit sharing level—that is, read, write, or no access—is set up when defining roles.

Let's now explore profiles and permission set configuration to define which part of an entire dataset users can access.

Configuring user permissions with profiles and permission sets

We've seen that a user is related to a specific **license type**, and in the same way, each profile is related to a specific license type. This means that when you select a license type when defining a user, only a subset of all the available profiles is allowed.

This is what you see in your org when clicking on **Setup | Users | Profiles**:

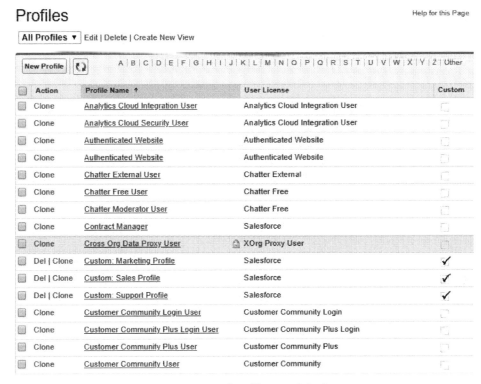

Figure 6.4 – Extract of profiles on a Salesforce org

As you can see, we have standard and custom profiles. Standard profiles come built into your org and their permissions are roughly unchangeable, which is why you should always clone a profile to create a new custom one with the desired permissions.

Remember that you cannot change a profile's license type.

> **Further reading**
>
> If you want to look deeper into profile permissions, jump to Salesforce Help at `https://help.salesforce.com/articleView?id=admin_userprofiles.htm&type=5`.

As we mentioned in the previous section, permission sets are a collection of permissions that can be related to users.

Why do we need permission sets? Can't we just use profiles to set up users' permissions?

I suggest that you use the right combination of profiles and permission sets; if a user has a clear operative need on the CRM (for example, only access to the account object and nothing else), go on with a baseline profile.

If a user should be allowed to access sparse features and objects and it is hard to design a defined set of user classes such as profiles, given the different combinations that your business requires, definitely go on with permission sets. Define some base profiles and then add as many permission sets to your users as they need.

Every permission you can find on permission sets can also found on profiles (but not vice versa).

> **Note**
> Permission sets cannot be used to restrict permissions (if a user's profile has access to a specific object, a permission set cannot restrict it).

Again, you can have standard and custom permission sets that may or may not be related to a specific license (go to **Setup | Users | Permission Sets**):

Permission Sets

On this page you can create, view, and manage permission sets.

In addition, you can use the SalesforceA mobile app to assign permission sets to a user. Download SalesforceA from the App Store or Google Play. iOS | Android

All Permission Sets ▼ Edit | Delete | Create New View

Action	Permission Set Label ↑	Description	License
Clone	CRM User	Denotes that the user is a Sales Cloud or Service Cloud user.	CRM User
Clone	Sales Cloud User	Denotes that the user is a Sales Cloud user.	Sales User
Clone	Salesforce CMS Integration Admin	Gives the admin data access and the permissions to integrate Sales...	Cloud Integration User
Clone	Salesforce Console User	Enable Salesforce Console User	Sales Console User
Clone	Service Cloud User	Denotes that the user is a Service Cloud user.	Service User
Clone	Standard Einstein Activity Capture	Access to Standard Einstein Activity Capture	Standard Einstein Activity Capture User

Figure 6.5 – The Permission Sets list on the setup

Recently (the *Spring '20* platform release), Salesforce delivered a new feature called **Permission Set Groups**. This feature lets you combine multiple permission sets to assign a combination of permissions to a single user. In this scenario, you can create a **service permission set group** that can include a permission set to handle standard service objects (such as cases, accounts, or service console access), a permission set to handle Knowledge articles, and another permission set to access survey creation. This way, you can create classes of permission sets and apply different combinations of permission sets with one click. Another cool feature of **Permission Set Groups** is that you can create **muting permission sets**, which allows you to use a permission set group but mute some of the permissions included. This prevents the proliferation of permission sets and permission set groups.

> **Further reading**
>
> To find out more about permission set groups, refer to Salesforce Help at `https://help.salesforce.com/articleView?id=perm set_groups.htm&type=5` or complete the following module at `https://trailhead.salesforce.com/content/learn/modules/administrator-certification-maintenance-spring-20/get-handson-with-permission-set-groups`.

Now that we have understood what profiles and permission sets are, we can start configuring them to define data access at the object-level and field-level.

Object-Level Security (OLS)

OLS is a set of permissions at the profile or permission set level that is used to state whether a user is able to access a specific data type (Salesforce object).

So, when you create a new permission set or edit a custom profile and look for the **Accounts** settings (if the **Enhanced User Profile** view is not enabled), you'll see a slightly different UI, but with the same configuration options:

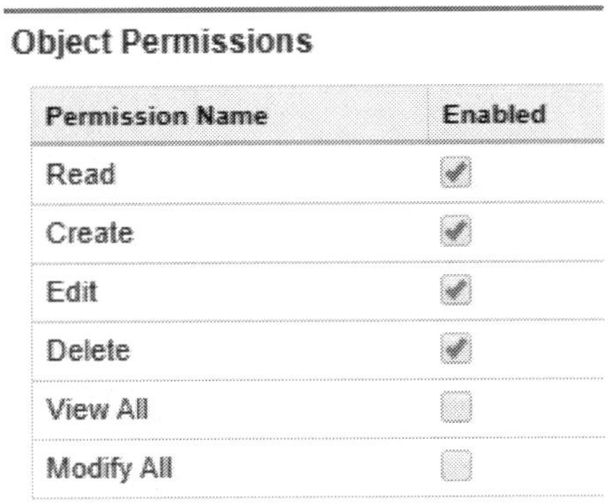

Object Permissions

Permission Name	Enabled
Read	✔
Create	✔
Edit	✔
Delete	✔
View All	☐
Modify All	☐

Figure 6.6 – OLS configuration

These operations are usually referred to as **CRUD operations**:

- **Create**
- **Read**
- **Update** (or Edit)
- **Delete**

The following permissions respect the sharing settings—that is, if a user is enabled to read on the case object but if a specific case record is not shared, they won't be able to actually read it:

- **Read**: Users can read a specific object.

- **Create**: Users can read and create records of this type; you cannot have **Create** flagged without **Read**.

- **Edit**: Users can edit (update) and read records; again there can be no **Edit** without **Read**.

- **Delete**: Users can read, edit, and delete records (once flagged as **Delete**, **Edit** and **Read** are flagged automatically).

All of these configurations are applied to records that the user has access to—that is, if the sharing configuration on the **Account** object is not allowing a user to see a specific record because of org-wide sharing configuration (which we'll see shortly ahead), although the user could, in theory, read the object, the record is not accessible anyway.

The other two object-level permissions, on the other hand, are not constrained by the sharing model:

- **View All**: Users can view all records of a given object.

- **Modify All**: Users can view, edit, and delete all records for a given object.

These configurations are similar to the **View All Data** and **Modify All Data** permissions at the profile/permission set level among the system permissions:

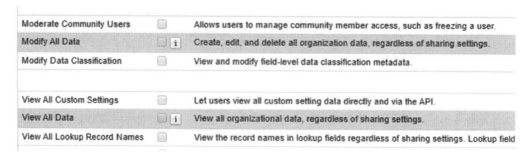

Figure 6.7 – The View All Data and Modify All Data permissions

---

Tip

View All Data and **Modify All Data** should be granted to trusted administrators only, as admins should be the only users who can grant such powerful permissions.

The next level of security we have is the field level one. Let's see how this works.

Field-Level Security (FLS)

To understand FLS, we need to have a look at how this permission setting is configured on a profile or permission set. For example, search for **Accounts** on a profile configuration page, as follows:

Field Permissions

Field Name	☐ Read Access	☐ Edit Access
Account Name	✔	✔
Account Number	✔	✔
Account Owner	✔	✔
Account Site	✔	✔
Account Source	✔	✔
Active	✔	✔
Annual Revenue	✔	✔
Billing Address	✔	✔
Clean Status	✔	☐
Created By	✔	☐
Customer Priority	✔	✔
D&B Company	✔	☐
Data.com Key	✔	✔
Description	✔	✔
D-U-N-S Number	✔	☐
Employees	✔	✔
Fax	✔	✔
Industry	✔	✔
Last Modified By	✔	☐
NAICS Code	✔	☐

Figure 6.8 – FLS configuration

It's as easy as it seems; you can define which fields are marked as read-only (**Read Access**) and which are editable (**Edit Access**). As expected, the **Edit Access** permission requires the **Read Access** permission (being able to edit a field but not read it makes no sense at all).

If the field is on the object's layout but the user doesn't have read access on it, the field won't be visible at all (the same applies for edit mode).

Some fields are marked as readable and editable by default (for example, master-detail and required fields), and some others are read-only (such as **Created By**).

If you want to have a wider look of profiles versus FLS configuration, then do the following:

1. Click on **Setup | Object Manager**, then choose a Salesforce object (for instance, **Case**).

2. Click **Fields & Relationships**, then choose any field (standard or custom).

3. Click the **View Field Accessibility** button. This is what we get:

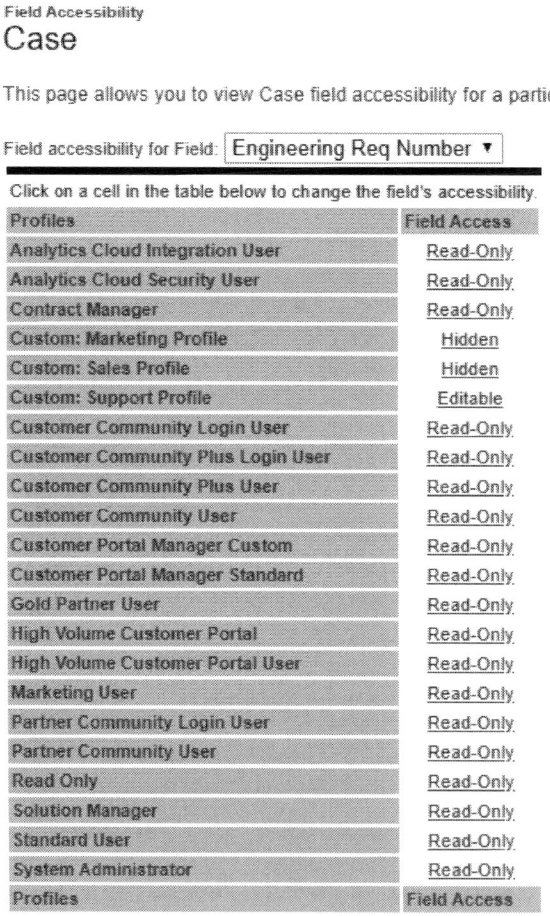

Field Accessibility
Case

This page allows you to view Case field accessibility for a particular field.

Field accessibility for Field: Engineering Req Number ▼

Click on a cell in the table below to change the field's accessibility.

Profiles	Field Access
Analytics Cloud Integration User	Read-Only
Analytics Cloud Security User	Read-Only
Contract Manager	Read-Only
Custom: Marketing Profile	Hidden
Custom: Sales Profile	Hidden
Custom: Support Profile	Editable
Customer Community Login User	Read-Only
Customer Community Plus Login User	Read-Only
Customer Community Plus User	Read-Only
Customer Community User	Read-Only
Customer Portal Manager Custom	Read-Only
Customer Portal Manager Standard	Read-Only
Gold Partner User	Read-Only
High Volume Customer Portal	Read-Only
High Volume Customer Portal User	Read-Only
Marketing User	Read-Only
Partner Community Login User	Read-Only
Partner Community User	Read-Only
Read Only	Read-Only
Solution Manager	Read-Only
Standard User	Read-Only
System Administrator	Read-Only
Profiles	Field Access

Figure 6.9 – Field Accessibility overview

This view is determined by the following:

- Page layout configuration (where fields can be visible, required, or not required)
- FLS (which defines which fields a specific profile is allowed to access in read or edit mode and overrides page layout configurations).
- Specific user permissions (they override both page layouts and FLS configurations. To give an example, users with the **Edit Read Only Fields** permission can always edit read-only fields regardless of any other settings).
- Universally required fields (this overrides any less-restrictive settings on page layouts, so any universally required field is always displayed as required and writable).

Now that you know how to set up granular access to specific pieces of data, we can analyze how to set up record sharing.

Exploring org-wide sharing

In the previous sections, we learned how to configure user permissions so that they can be configured to access objects and fields, using OLS and FLS security options.

In this section, we'll be presenting a more advanced option that works at the record level and that lets users see only a subset of the records in the database.

This means that, even if a user has access to the **Account** object and all related fields, a proper sharing setting can let them access only the accounts that they have created or only the accounts based on European countries, for example.

To define sharing, you generally will set up org-wide sharing (telling Salesforce whether Salesforce object records should or should not be seen by anyone), and if you choose to restrict general access, you can open up access to a class of records or users using sharing rules. In this scenario, org-wide sharing defines the strictest access possible to an object's record.

To configure OWD, click on **Setup | Security | Sharing Settings**. This is where we land:

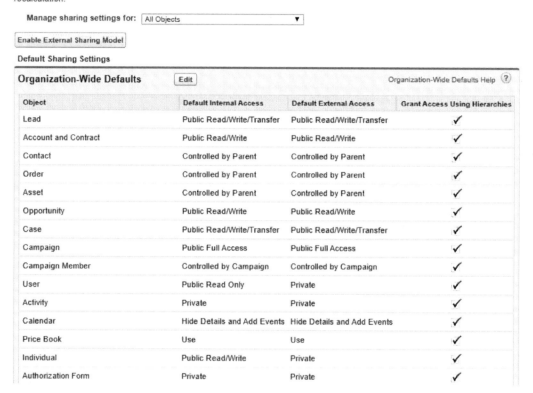

Figure 6.10 – OWD settings configuration

As wec mentioned, this page sets the most restrictive access to records, and any other sharing configuration will only be able to expand sharing and not restrict it more.

In the **Organization-Wide Defaults** section, you can set up the OWD configuration, as follows:

1. Identify an object type.

2. Set the default internal access.

3. Set the default external access (if required, this is needed for external users such as community users).

4. Check or uncheck **Grant Access Using Hierarchies** if enabled and flaggable.

As per the second step, the default access can be as follows:

- **Controlled by Parent**: If a record is a child of another record (for example, **Contact** is a child of **Account**), then if OWD is set to this value, the account owner will be able to access the contact with the same access level. This applies to some standard objects and to custom objects that are the children of master-detail relationships. In this specific case, **Controlled by Parent** will be the only available value.

- **Private**: Only the record's owner and the users above their role hierarchy can view, edit, and report on the record.

- **Public Read Only**: The record is accessible in read-only mode and reportable by any user, but it can only be edited by owners and users above in the hierarchy.

- **Public Read/Write**: The record is *free for all*; anyone can view and edit it. Only the owner will be able to delete and share the record manually.

- **Public Read/Write/Transfer**: This is available on **Case** and **Lead** objects, where the **Transfer** option allows anyone to transfer the record ownership. Only the owner will be able to delete and manually share the record.

- **Public Full Access**: This is available on **Campaign** objects only. It allows anyone to view, edit, and delete a campaign.

> **More information**
>
> For more details on specific objects' default sharing values, refer to Salesforce Help at `https://help.salesforce.com/articleView?id=sharing_model_fields.htm&type=5`.

As seen in *Figure 6.10*, we can configure both internal and external OWD. **External access** is available for external users (for example, customer portal users, partner portal users, and Customer Community Plus users, among others) and their OWD configuration is aligned to the corresponding **internal access**, unless you enable the external sharing model with the **Enable External Sharing Model** button; in this case, the external access OWD configuration must be stricter or equal to internal access.

> **Tip**
>
> Remember that if you update the OWD for an object with a wider setting, the change is applied immediately, but if you set a stricter value, the change can take up to hours to complete, so be careful when planning this change in production orgs.

Now, let's configure the sharing of our custom objects:

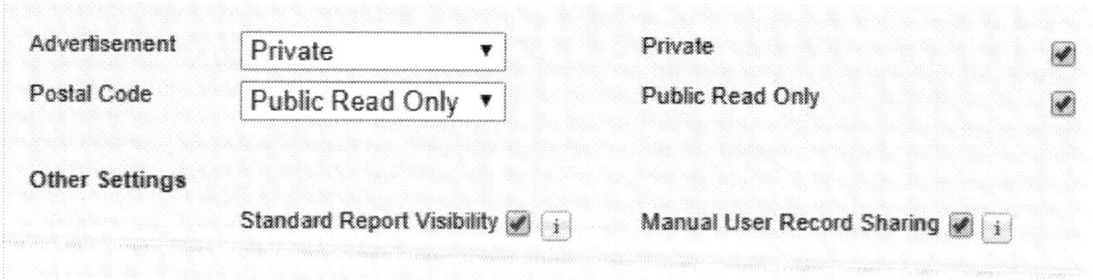

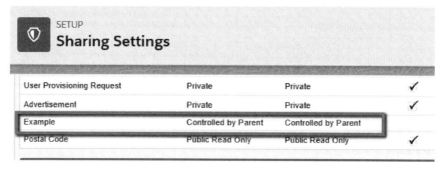

Figure 6.11 – Setting up custom objects' default sharing access

We've set up the following values:

- The **Advertisement** object as **Private** because it is considered as sensitive information and should only be managed by specific users (owners and their managers in the role hierarchy).

- The **Postal Code** object as **Public Read Only** because it is used in a validation rule and should be readable by any user (it's not critical information that must be hidden from a certain type of user, but we still don't want common users to update these values, thus keeping the records read-only to anyone).

If you have followed the previous chapters' configurations, you will have ended up with the **Example** custom object, which has been designed with a master-detail relationship with the **Account** object:

SETUP
Sharing Settings

User Provisioning Request	Private	Private	✓
Advertisement	Private	Private	✓
Example	Controlled by Parent	Controlled by Parent	
Postal Code	Public Read Only	Public Read Only	✓

Figure 6.12 – Sharing settings for custom objects

As expected, you won't be able to edit this object's default access, as it is listed as **Controlled by Parent**.

Let's now briefly see how users' role hierarchies are used to lead record sharing.

Understanding role hierarchies

Salesforce uses role hierarchies to grant access to records by default. This means that if a user owns a record (whose **OWD** is **Private**), it will automatically be shared with users that have a higher role in the company's hierarchy.

The **Grant Access Using Hierarchies** flag seen earlier applies only if the default access is set to **Private** or **Read Only**; otherwise, access is not restricted and it wouldn't need any hierarchy access at all.

Note

The **Grant Access Using Hierarchies** flag can be disabled for custom objects only.

Here is a screenshot of a sample role hierarchy configuration (jump here from **Setup** | **Users** | **Roles**):

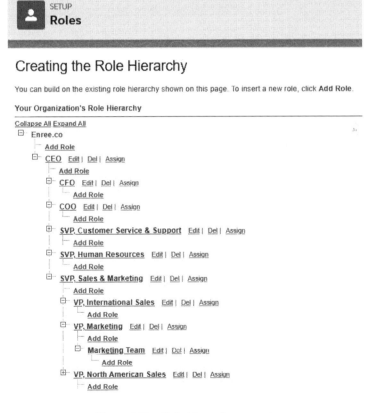

Figure 6.13 – Role hierarchy example

It's good practice to add a role to a user because it simplifies record sharing management; you can still have no role on your user object, but in the case of reporting, this could not be a good thing, especially if your user owns records, because they won't be listed on reports based on role filters.

Now that we have defined the basic org-wide sharing configuration for our most valuable business objects, we can move on by creating sharing rules to extend the default behavior, in order to spread up record sharing under specific criteria.

Sharing rules

So far, all users have the same sharing configuration on records:

- They can read and edit all records from objects with a **Public Read/Write** OWD.

- They can read (but not edit) all records from objects with a **Public Read-only** OWD.

- They are not allowed to access any records they don't own if those records are under a **Private** OWD.

If the user owns a record that is **Private** or **Public read-only**, they'll always be allowed to read and edit the record and, if access is granted through hierarchies, the user's managers will be allowed to access the record as well.

What if we need to spread up sharing to users that are outside an owner's hierarchy?

To give an example, let's say we have a case with an OWD set to **Private**; this means that all cases created by any service agent won't be accessible to the sales SVP, as service agent roles lay on a parallel branch of the sales SVP hierarchy, which is lead by the service SVP (in *Figure 6.12*, this is the branch of **SVP Customer, Service, & Support**). If our business requirements ask for full read access for the sales SVP users to all cases, we need to create an *exception* rule to allow sales SVP users to read cases they shouldn't be allowed to read, as for the OWD configuration. This can be done using **sharing rules**, a powerful tool delivered in the Salesforce platform to achieve new levels of sharing.

If you want to expand the OWD settings (in our example, to give edit access to the **Postal Code** records or read access to **Advertisement** records), you need to use sharing rules. Remember that you cannot use sharing rules to restrict access to records.

To create a new sharing rule, click on **Setup | Security | Sharing Settings** and look for the **Sharing Rules** section for a given object (for example, **Postal Code**), and then click **New**:

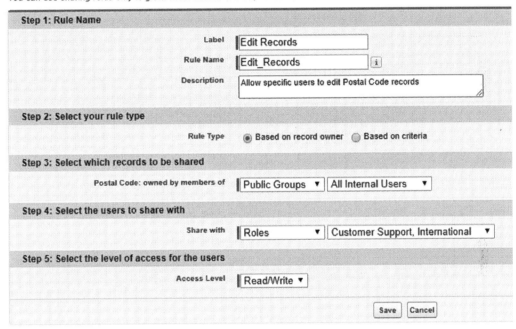

Figure 6.14 – Owner-based sharing rule configuration

Any sharing rule is identified by the following:

- The rule's name
- The type of rule
- Criteria that identify which records will be part of the sharing rule
- Criteria that identify the users to which the sharing is applied
- Setting an access level that the users will obtain on the shared records

The first option to configure in the form to create a new sharing rule (name and label apart, as seen in **Step 2** of *Figure 6.13*) is the rule type:

- **Owner-based**: Records are identified by the kind of users who own them (public groups or roles). For example, select all records owned by the **Service Managers** group or the **Sales Managers** role.

  In the previous example, in *Figure 6.13*, we have selected all **Postal Code** records that are owned by a special group called **All Internal Users**, which identifies all users in the CRM with an internal license, then we selected the **Customer Support, International** role as the users to which the **Postal Code** records will be shared with an access level of **Read/Write**.

  So, we are allowing users, that may not be related to the actual owner of the record, disregarding the role hierarchy, to access in read/write any **Postal Code** record, provided that *any* user will be able to at least read any **Postal Code** record (which was the previous OWD setup).

- **Criteria-based**: Records are identified by specific field values—for example, select all records where the Country field is set to Norway.

  Regarding criteria-based sharing rules, this is what you may come up with for a sharing rule for the **Advertisement** object (we've created a new **Installation Country** picklist):

Setup
Advertisement Sharing Rule

Use sharing rules to make automatic exceptions to your organization-wide sharing settings for defined sets of users.

Note: "Roles and subordinates" includes all users in a role, and the roles below that role.

You can use sharing rules only to grant wider access to data, not to restrict access.

Step 1: Rule Name

Label	Share italian advertisements
Rule Name	Share_italian_advertisement [i]
Description	

Step 2: Select your rule type

Rule Type   ○ Based on record owner   ● Based on criteria

Step 3: Select which records to be shared

Criteria

	Field	Operator	Value	
1.	Is Active ▼	equals ▼	True	🔍
2.	Installation Country ▼	equals ▼	Mexico, USA	🔍
3.	--None-- ▼	--None-- ▼		

Add Row Remove Row

Clear Filter Logic
Filter Logic:

1 AND 2   Tips (?)

Step 4: Select the users to share with

Share with | Roles ▼ | Customer Support, North America ▼ |

Step 5: Select the level of access for the users

Access Level | Read Only ▼ |

Figure 6.15 – Criteria-based sharing rule configuration

The main difference of the owner-based criteria is that we can select specific fields and combine them with a *filter logic* to identify which records should be shared.

In this example, all **Active** advertisements coming from **Mexico, USA** should be shared in **Read Only** mode with all users belonging to the **Customer Support, North America** role. No matter who owns the record, if the advertisement is based in specific countries, it will be shared with the North America support team.

> **Note**
>
> Criteria-based sharing rules are more expensive in terms of performance, and that's why you can have up to **50** criteria-based sharing rules per object and no more than **300** sharing rules per object (owner-based and criteria-based).

Unfortunately, we cannot use custom formulas when defining a criteria-based sharing rule's criteria, so we are pretty limited in the kind of rules we can enable. You can only use the fields on the list, which won't include custom formula fields. This is no surprise, as the sharing engine will execute the sharing rules each time a record is updated, and creating a complex rule can lead to low performances. As a good practice, try limiting the use of criteria-based sharing rules to scenarios where using role hierarchies or owner-based rules cannot lead to what the requirements are asking for. There is an additional limitation regarding criteria configuration on criteria-based sharing rules; only certain field types can be used for criteria definitions, which are listed as follows:

- Auto number
- Checkbox
- Date
- Date/time
- Email
- Formula fields (as already said)
- Lookup relationship (for a user or queue ID)
- Number
- Percent
- Phone
- Picklist
- Text (case sensitive)
- Text area (case sensitive)
- URL

Regarding the level of access configuration on any sharing rule, there is a custom behavior specific to the **Account** object's sharing definition.

When sharing the **Account** object, you'll also have to set up a level of access for related objects, such as **Opportunity Access** and **Case Access**, as shown in the following screenshot:

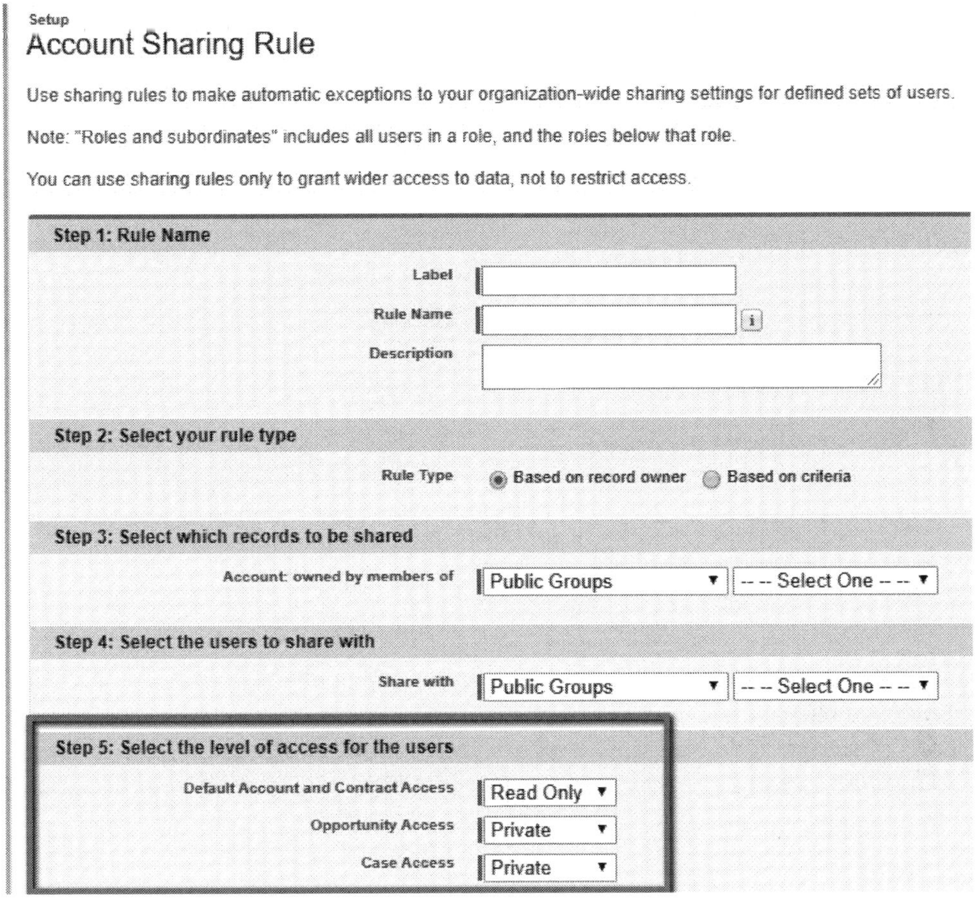

Figure 6.16 – Account sharing rule setup

You can then specify which sharing level is applied to child **Opportunity** and **Case** records.

The following values are supported for the **Default Account and Contract Access** field:

- **Private**: Available only for child opportunities and cases on **Account** sharing rules
- **Read Only**: Available for all three access configurations, giving read-only access
- **Read/Write**: Available for all three access configurations as well, giving full read/write access

Some considerations about sharing rules are as follows:

- In the case of multiple sharing rules on a record, the widest rule is applied.

- Sharing is applied to all records on the CRM (new and old).

Because sharing rule calculations can take a while, the platform puts the calculation in the background and notifies the users with a system email. Finally, if you need users to autonomously share specific records with other users (for example, a service agent can share a case with their colleague in search for help), we can leverage manual sharing. This tool is unfortunately only available in Salesforce Classic at the time of writing, but it will probably be delivered in Lightning Experience as well soon (check out Salesforce's Idea Exchange site to see what's going to be included in future releases at `https://ideas.salesforce.com/s/prioritization`). Let's take a quick ride on this feature.

Manual sharing

Manual sharing grants a user the ability to share a record (that they own) to users who are not necessarily above their role hierarchy (they can actually be anywhere in the hierarchy). This is a *manual* feature that each user is responsible for; this means that, unless a user loses access to the record (for example, because the record is updated and the sharing rules are changed, or because the record is moved to another owner), they'll be able to share access to the record manually.

As said, this kind of sharing can be done by any user to let other users come in to help to solve an issue related to the record, or simply to allow a user that is lower in the hierarchy to access the record and solve a low-level problem; perhaps they want to include a sales rep to handle a case because they sold a product to the customer, and they may be the best person to handle the issue.

> **Note**
> As of the *Spring '20* release, this feature is only available on Salesforce Classic. Take a look at the Salesforce idea at `https://success.salesforce.com/ideaView?id=0873A000000LmluQAC`. Although this idea has a lot of upvotes, it has not yet been delivered, but it's in the development stage at the time of writing. Take the time to upvote it! It is best to handle the issue.

Even if this is not available on Lightning Experience yet, it will probably be delivered soon, so it is more than useful to have a look at it even if it is just in Salesforce Classic.

> **Note**
>
> As my technical reviewer Fabrice Cathala (one of the coolest guys in the Salesforce community; reach out to him at `https://twitter.com/fcathala`) pointed out, and I cannot agree more, do not use Salesforce Classic on your new projects as Lightning Experience is the current standard for Salesforce implementations. Again, stick to Lightning Experience and, if a feature is not available on Lightning Experience yet (but only in Classic), check whether any partners have developed a package on the AppExchange (such as the Lightning Sharing component made by Salesforce Labs, available at `https://appexchange.salesforce.com/appxListingDetail?listingId=a0N3A00000EFp0ZUAT`).

This sharing feature is available only for records whose object's OWD is set to **Private** or **Public Read-Only** and only if the user is the owner or above the owner's hierarchy (and **Grant Access Using Hierarchies** is flagged):

1. Although this book is based on the Lightning Experience UI, we'll quickly switch to *Classic mode* by clicking on the **Switch to Salesforce Classic** link under the profile icon, as shown in the following screenshot:

Figure 6.17 – Switching from Lightning Experience to Classic

2. To access an **Advertisement** record, click on the + tab on the Classic tab set:

Figure 6.18 – Classic mode tab set

3. Then, look for the **Advertisements** tab, click on it, and look for a record:

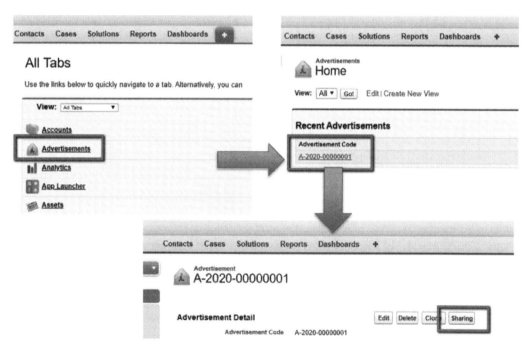

Figure 6.19 – Manually sharing an Advertisement record in Salesforce Classic

4. The new **Sharing** button is enabled only if the previous conditions on the OWD setup are verified (and if the button is added on the page layout). Click it:

Sharing Detail
A-2020-00000001
A-2020-00000001

This page lists the users, groups, roles, and territories that have sharing access to **A-2020-00000001**. Click **Expand List** to view all users who have access to it.

View: [All ▾] Edit | Create New View

A | B | C | D | E | F | G | H | I | J | K | L | M | N | O | P | Q | R | S | T

User and Group Sharing		[Add] [Expand List]		
Action	**Type**	**Name ↑**	**Access Level**	**Reason**
	User	enrico murru	Full Access	Owner

Explanation of Access Levels

- Full Access - User can view, edit, delete, and transfer the record. User can also extend sharing access to other users.
- Read/Write - User can view and edit the record, and add associated records, notes, and attachments to it.
- Read Only - User can view the record, and add associated records to it. They cannot edit the record or add notes or attachments.
- Private - User cannot access the record in any way.

Figure 6.20 – The record's sharing reasons

This page shows all the ways that the record has been shared (with the proper access level), to which users, and the sharing reason (ownership, sharing rule, manual sharing, and so on). In this example, we only have the ownership reason.

5. Then, we click on the **Add** button, which brings up the following screen:

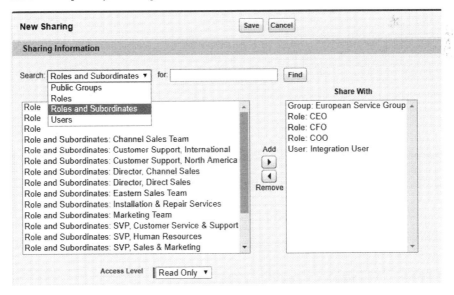

Figure 6.21 – Configuring manual sharing on a record

On this page, we can configure the users, roles, and groups to which the record will be shared and the level of access (**Read Only** or **Read/Write**).

6.   Once saved, the **Sharing Detail** page is updated, as follows:

Figure 6.22 – The sharing details updated after manual sharing

Remember that you cannot share a record with a user whose permissions don't allow them to actually view the object (object-level security) or if the actual owner is an inactive user (switch ownership before manual sharing).

> **Note**
>
> If the owner changes, all manual sharing is removed.

So far, you have acquired all the *not-so-basic* concepts related to record access and sharing in the Salesforce platform. This is a key chapter that you can use as a starting point to understand this subject and gradually enhance your knowledge of Salesforce security configuration.

Blaze your trail

Check out the following Trailhead modules:

- Data security: `https://trailhead.salesforce.com/en/content/learn/modules/data_security`

- Share CRM Data with your partners: `https://trailhead.salesforce.com/en/content/learn/projects/communities_share_crm_data`

- Protect Your Data in Salesforce: `https://trailhead.salesforce.com/en/content/learn/projects/protect-your-data-in-salesforce`

- Keep Data Secure in a Recruiting App: `https://trailhead.salesforce.com/en/content/learn/projects/keep-data-secure-in-a-recruiting-app`

- User Management: `https://trailhead.salesforce.com/en/content/learn/modules/lex_implementation_user_setup_mgmt`

Summary

In this chapter, we've seen how we can enhance security by using the features listed in the *who sees what* pyramid. At first, we defined the permissions each user needs to be allowed to access objects and their fields, using profiles and permission sets.

Then, we leveraged the sharing model, configuring the baseline sharing level with the OWD sharing settings, and then we learned how role hierarchy, sharing rules, and manual sharing can spread record access through our CRM's user base. We saw that role hierarchies allow records to be automatically shared to the record owner's managers, sharing rules allow us to expand record access to groups of users based on the current owner (owner-based rule) or based on record fields (criteria-based rule), and how manual sharing allows any user to share a record with any other user, thus increasing the number of users that can help manage the record.

All these features combine to deliver safer and more efficient access to data, increasing overall user and business processes efficiency.

In the next chapter, we'll get into some action by taking a deep look into all the declarative automation features that the Salesforce platform delivers, starting with workflow rules.

Section 3: Automation Tools

In this section, we will automate our processes with powerful tools such as workflows, approval, process builder, and flows. We will also learn how to deliver actions to enhance user interaction with data.

This section comprises the following chapters:

7
Be a Workflow Champion

With this chapter, we are starting the process automation section of the book. We will begin by talking about the first ever automation feature that the Salesforce platform introduced many years ago (I wasn't part of the Salesforce universe at that time!), called *workflow rules*.

We will learn all about configuring Workflow Rules to create simple, yet powerful, automated actions based on record creation and update. We'll be dealing with available automated actions to perform operations on records or simply send an email to specific users. We'll also learn about the limitations of this technology, following some useful examples to break the subject down.

In this chapter, we'll learn the following:

- What automation is and what Workflow Rules are
- Configuring automated actions
- Considerations regarding the technology

Process automation in Salesforce

If you are working with the Salesforce platform now, it is because your company or customer chose the platform for its promise to enhance the sales and service needs of the company/customer. It also helps to simplify business processes, thereby making the company responses to market quicker and stronger. And what is better than making sales reps or service agents happier by limiting the number of clicks and things to type in during their daily work? This is called **automation**.

Humans have an innate inclination to make mistakes, and when a company uses data to develop its business and that data is incorrect or incomplete, this can lead to wrong business decisions.

Process automation is a feature that reduces the time a CRM user has to spend on clicking and typing stuff, giving agents more time to dedicate to *brain-intensive* actions.

We've seen in *Chapter 3, Mastering Formulas*, something that can be considered process automation; that is, the definition of default values in custom fields. This way, users can avoid unnecessary typing for fields that, for the majority of their working day, they should not have to deal with.

For most scenarios, automation tools are used to *automate* an action, such as the following:

- Setting the **Priority** field on a **Case** record when the customer requests some billing help

- Sending an email to the customer when their **Case** has been closed

- Notifying an external billing system when an opportunity's **Stage** is **Closed Won**

- Guiding a user to compile a wizard to collect different kinds of customer-related data (in the right order)

- Approving an **Expense** record created by an employee

The Salesforce platform supports different flavors of process automation tools (in order of complexity):

- **Workflow Rules**: Given a record, a workflow executes actions on the record itself (or its parent record, if a master-detail relationship exists) based on criteria created from record field values.

- **Approval processes**: Like workflows, an approval is based on a record's data to automate the record approval by the current user's managers (such as an expense or discount).

- **Lightning Process Builder**: This tool is an evolution of Workflow Rules and delivers a more complex decisional criteria composition and a wider number of performable actions.

- **Flows**: This is a complex point-and-click tool, designed to deliver multi-step *user-interacting* wizards and also complex business automated actions (without requiring any user interaction).

- **Custom coding**: With Apex triggers, Visualforce pages, and Lightning Web Components, the Salesforce platform supports a wide variety of code-based frameworks (this is the developers' realm) to deliver server-side and client-side automation for the most complex and challenging needs.

Given that many automation tasks can be designed using all the preceding tools, as a professional, you should choose the best and most performant tool. Your choice will be related to what you want to accomplish and to other key variables such as simplicity, limitations, scale, and user interaction.

> **Further reading**
>
> David Liu, Salesforce MVP, Google engineer, and creator of **Salesforce Coding Lessons for the 99%**, wrote a fantastic article about how to choose a Salesforce automation tool, available at `https://www.sfdc99.com/2018/01/22/workflow-process-builder-flow-apex/`.

Generally speaking, the following applies:

- If you need to get a record approved, an approval process is the right choice.

- If you need to execute an action when a record is updated or created, the platform delivers the Workflow Rules, Process Builder, and Flows features (which we'll be covering in this and subsequent chapters). Salesforce best practices suggest using Process Builder instead of Workflow Rules (given the wider possibilities the tool delivers) and then going with Flows when the kind of automation required involves more complex logic (for example, you require unrelated record data to choose your process' next move or need to iterate through children records). A recent tweet by Adam Olshansky, a famous Salesforce MVP, clearly suggested that flows are the future (refer to `https://twitter.com/adam17amo/status/1276266774187536384`).

- If you need to get data from users and then execute actions with that data, a short way to tell that you need a wizard that gathers data that can be further elaborated and automated can be done through Flows.

> **Further reading**
>
> For an overall view of all the features each tool delivers, have a read of the *Automation Tool Features* section available on Salesforce Help at `https://help.salesforce.com/articleView?id=process_which_tool.htm&type=5`. This highlights each tool based on *complexity, designer tool availability, starting condition, time-based action support, user interaction support*, and also according to the kind of supported actions.
>
> It is suggested that you imprint the table referenced here in your mind!

We are now ready to go in depth with Workflow Rules and all the way to deliver automation with this simple, yet powerful, tool.

Building Workflow Rules

We are about to see (almost) everything about Workflow Rules – how they are shaped, how they can be configured, and what you can actually do with them to deliver Salesforce automation, using point and click and no code.

Workflow Rules are the *oldest* automation tool available on the Salesforce platform and I assume, if these are not your first steps on the platform, that you have certainly already stepped into them.

This is a so-called **IFTTT** tool (meaning **If This Then That**), which means that if a specific condition is met (the *If* part), an action is executed (the *That* part). While a condition is always related to a record that is being created or edited, actions can be related to the record itself or to the parent record (if we have a master-detail relationship in place).

Refer to the following diagram of a Workflow Rule:

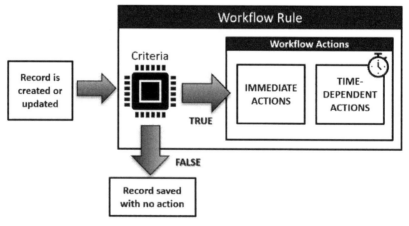

Figure 7.1 – Workflow Rules' basic structure

> **Note**
>
> Salesforce people usually refer to Workflow Rules simply as workflows for brevity.

Workflow Rules are composed of the following:

- **Entry criteria**: These represent the Salesforce object that the rule is related to and a set of criteria or a formula that identifies the conditions after which the actions should take place.

- **Workflow actions**: These are a set of actions that can be performed immediately or with a time dependency.

Looking at Figure 7.1, we see that whenever a record is created or updated (and a workflow rule has been created), the workflow criteria is evaluated and if the result matches the record status, the workflow engine executes some immediate actions (such as updating other fields or sending an email to a user) and/or, depending on a time-based trigger, puts some time-dependent actions in a queue so that they can be executed when configured (such as sending an email to a record owner if the record is not updated within a week). This is automation, guys!

To start our workflow journey, we want to create a workflow on the **Opportunity** object to execute a number of automated actions when a big deal is closed. This is what we picture happens when a sales agent completes the management of a deal (opportunity record) for a key customer or involving a really high amount (this means more money for the company).

To create a workflow, click on **Setup | Process Automation | Workflow Rules**, as shown here:

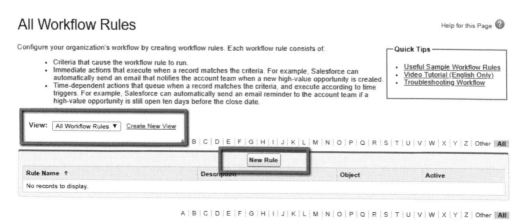

Figure 7.2 – Workflow Rules home page

From the Workflow Rules home page, you can create a new list view (for example, to show **Opportunity**-related rules only) but also create a new workflow rule from scratch with the **New Rule** button, which opens up the **New Workflow Rule** creation wizard.

These first steps ask for a Salesforce object (basically all standard and custom objects are supported); we'll create an **Opportunity**-related workflow. Click **Next** to jump to the second step.

The second step of the wizard is meant to define the workflow rule's name (fill in with **Big_Deal_Closed**) and the criteria involved in the rule. The aim of this workflow is to intercept a big deal (opportunity) being closed successfully (that's how we filled the name and description).

The **Evaluation Criteria** section defines when a workflow is evaluated in terms of record status (we can refer to it as the *evaluation trigger*) and can be compiled with the following values:

- **Created**: The rule is evaluated only when a record (**Opportunity**) is created, ensuring that the rule is evaluated only once in any (opportunity) record lifespan (the rule is ignoring any update operation on the record).

- **Created, and every time it's edited**: The rule is evaluated on creation and when updated, and it is evaluated (and its actions executed) any time the update is performed and the criteria are still valid. This means that if the rule is evaluated on creation, and if the criteria are still met, any subsequent update triggers the actions (even though you perform an update without changing any value). This setup won't let you create *time-dependent* actions (we'll see these in subsequent sections).

- **Created, and any time it's edited to subsequently meet criteria**: This condition is a smarter condition than the previous configuration because it lets the rule trigger on record creation and on update only if the record fields' values are changing from not meeting the criteria to then meeting them. This configuration allows *time-dependent* actions. With this configuration, if we update the record many times without changing any fields involved in the rule's criteria, the workflow is not executed at all (even though conditions are met). This prevents the actions from executing over and over.

Select the second option.

In the last section of the workflow creation page, we can configure the actual conditions of the criteria using a `Field/Operator/Value` form (with the related **Filter Logic** to properly combine field conditions) or a formula editor (as we did in *Chapter 3, Mastering Formulas*).

In our scenario, a big deal is any deal that has an **Amount** greater than or equal to $1 million or whose related account has a **Hot** rating (this is just an example). This condition can be written as shown in the following screenshot:

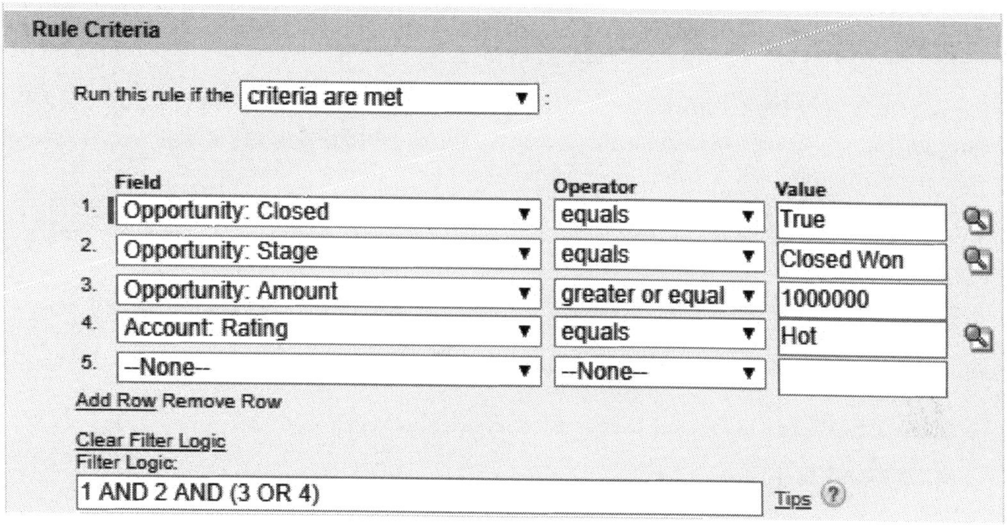

Figure 7.3 – Defining criteria with Field/Operator/Value picklists and Filter Logic

Take a moment to understand the following:

- A **Field** is related to the current object (**Opportunity**), but some other objects are available (**Account, Pricebook,** current **User**), and any parent object is allowed (you just need a master-detail relationship)

- Filter Logic is used to put together the criteria's conditions.

We could have written the following criteria using a plain formula by selecting **formula evaluates to true** on the **Rule Criteria** picklist:

```
AND (
   IsClosed,
   ISPICKVAL( StageName, 'Closed Won' ),
   OR (
      Amount >= 1000000,
      ISPICKVAL( Account.Rating, 'Hot' )
   )
)
```

Click **Save & Next** to close the Workflow creation wizard and to land on the workflow rule recap page.

The workflow is not active yet. This means that the automation won't run even if an opportunity with that field value is closed. We'll be activating the workflow once actions are added, which we'll configure in the next section.

Configuring automated actions

When a criterion is met, a workflow rule's actions (remember, the *That* part of the *IFTTT* acronym) are executed, immediately or with a time-dependent rule (such as 5 days after the record created date or 1 hour after the last update event).

The framework delivers the following kind of actions (all available for Workflow Rules and approval processes, which we'll cover in the next chapter):

- **Field update**
- **Task**
- **Email alert** (available on Process Builder and Flows as well)
- **Outbound message**

We'll describe every kind of automated action with our example opportunity workflow rule in the following sections.

Field update action

The first automated action we'll see is the field update action, which is used to update a record field (for example, to increase a case's priority if a certain customer is important).

To create a new field update action in the **Immediate Workflow Actions** section (refer to Figure 7.4), click on **Add Workflow Action** and select **New Field Update**:

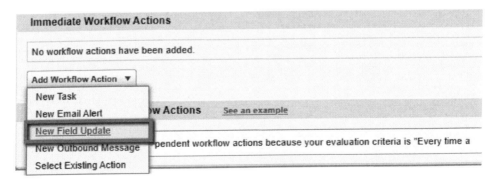

Figure 7.4 – Creating a new field update action

The wizard lets you configure the new action as follows:

- **Name** (let the form choose the unique name): **Update Opp.ty Close Date**
- **Object**: **Opportunity**
- **Field to update**: **Opportunity**, **Close Date**
- **Date options**: **Use a Formula to set the new value**
- **Value**: TODAY ()

> **Tip**
>
> Remember that each automated action is not limited to a specific workflow but can be shared between automation tools. In this case, the action we just created can be used on another workflow rule (**Opportunity**-related) or an approval process.

The **Re-evaluate Workflow Rules after Field Change** checkbox on the **Field Update** creation form is needed if the field you are about to update is key to another workflow rule that you want to be evaluated, otherwise no other workflow is called after this update.

Click **Save & New** to create a new **Field Update** action, and configure the following new values:

- **Name** (let the form choose the unique name): **Update Opp.ty Description**
- **Object**: **Opportunity**
- **Field to update**: **Opportunity**, **Description**
- **Text options**: **Use a Formula to set the new value**
- **Value**: (add this code)

```
IF(
  AND(
    IsClosed,
    ISPICKVAL(StageName, 'Closed Won'),
    OR( Amount >= 1000000, ISPICKVAL(Account.Rating,
'Hot'))
  ),
    'ALERT: this is a *HOT DEAL* with' +
    IF(Amount >= 1000000,
      'an Amount higher than $1M!',
      'a *Hot* customer!'
    ),
    Description
)
```

Again, this field update can be used anywhere (even for workflow rules that are not checking whether the opportunity is closed with an actual big deal). In fact, the formula checks **Closed Status**, **Stage**, and **Amount**, or the customer's **Rating**, leaving the **Description** field as it is if the *big-deal* conditions are not met.

In case of a *Hot Deal*, it will output **ALERT: this is a *HOT DEAL* with an Amount higher than $1M!**" or, in the case of a *Hot Customer*, it will output **ALERT: this is a *HOT DEAL* with a *Hot* customer!**.

Click the **Save** button, which will take us back to the Workflow Rules recap page:

Figure 7.5 – Recap on Workflow Rules with two new field update actions

We will look at the tasks of this action in the following sections.

Activating the workflow to test the automation

To test it out, we need to activate the workflow first. Remember, an inactive workflow won't be of much help.

Click the **Done** button at *step 3* of the workflow creation wizard (thus leaving the edit wizard) and then click the **Activate** button on the workflow recap page's header.

Now, the workflow is ready to be *activated* or *triggered* by an opportunity record with the selected criteria.

Let's now create a new opportunity record by opening the **Sales App | Opportunities tab | New** button with the following values (provided that **Close Date** is set to a date in the past):

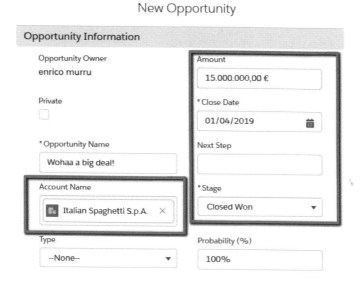

Figure 7.6 – Creating a new big deal

Fill in the **Description** field with a random value and create the new opportunity. We expect that the **Description** and **Close Date** fields will be updated with a description of the big deal and current date (which is 5/4/2020).

Click **Save** to see the workflow in action:

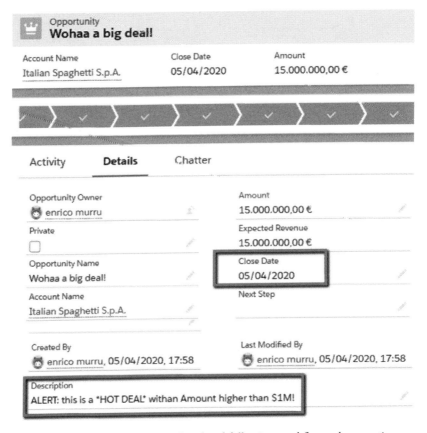

Figure 7.7 – Opportunity record updated following workflow rule execution

That is exactly what we expected.

But wait, there's more!

Let's update the **Description** field, reduce the amount to $ 1k, change the **Description** to **Nothing to declare**, and then click the **Save** button again. What happens?

Absolutely nothing, provided that the **Account** does not have a **Hot** rating and, even if the **Opportunity** is **Closed Won**, the **Amount** is way less than $ 1M, so no action is executed at all.

Now, change the **Rating** field of the **Account** to update using the following details:

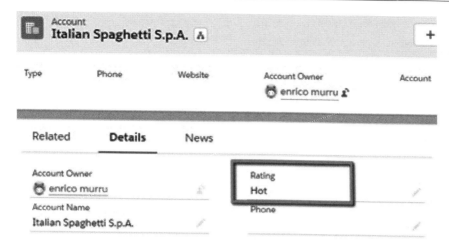

Figure 7.8 – Updating the Rating value of the account, referenced in the Opportunity workflow rule

Do you believe the workflow triggered now?

No, this is only because the triggering object is the **Opportunity** object and not the **Account** object, even though the workflow's condition refers to the related **Account** fields.

Let's click the **Edit** button on the **Opportunity** record created earlier and do not change any field on it; simply click the **Save** button. What do you expect?

The **Description** field on the **Opportunity** record gets updated because the workflow trigger criteria are actually met, as the related account is **Hot** rated. This means that the workflow ran on the opportunity update event and not on the account record update. The proof is in the following screenshot, which shows the new opportunity field values:

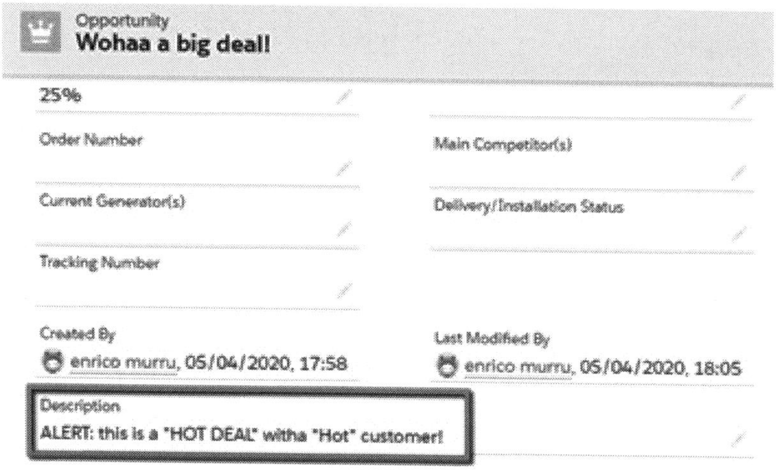

Figure 7.9 – Workflow rule triggered based on a related record field

Now, do you remember the **Created, and every time it's edited** option when we defined the workflow entry criteria? If you try to update the **Description** field, what happens?

The value is replaced with the **Field Update** of our workflow rule. As we said, this option allows the workflow rule to be triggered over and over even if the condition is met, and even if no field changes during the update.

If the criteria were set with **Created, and any time it's edited to subsequently meet criteria**, the workflow wouldn't have triggered again.

So, overall, remember the following regarding **Field Update**:

- **Field Update** actions are executed before email alerts, task, and outbound messages actions.
- They can update any field disregarding any **Field Level Security**.
- **Field Update** effects are shown in **History Tracking** (if enabled).
- Validation rules execute prior to workflow rules, so it is possible to update a record that may not validate against a rule.
- If a field is required, it cannot be set to a blank value.

A cool thing about a field update action is that it is not restricted to a current object type only, but it can update fields on a so-called *parent-record* (if you don't remember what a parent record is, read *Chapter 2, Building the Data Model*, again). We'll see cross-object field updates in the next section.

Cross-object field updates

As we've seen, when an object has a master-detail relationship, a workflow rule's criteria can contain a parent object's fields.

In the same way, it is possible to update a field of a parent object. This works on custom-to-custom and custom-to-standard relationships and for some selected standard-to-standard master details.

Only a few standard objects are supported as parent objects in custom-to-standard master-detail relationships: Account, Asset, Campaign, Case, Contact, Contract, Contract Line Item, Entitlement, Opportunity, Order, Question, Quote, Service Contract, and Solution.

Only the following standard-to-standard master details are supported:

- **Case Comments** updating a **Case**
- **Email** updating a **Case**

- **Opportunity Product** updating an **Opportunity**
- **Opportunity** updating an **Account**

> **Tip**
> It is possible to update a parent record via a workflow action even if the current user is unable to access it due to sharing.

The Task action

The **Task** action is used to create a task related to the current record.

To create a **Task** action, click on the **Edit** button on **Workflow Actions** on the workflow rule home page and select **New Task** to show the action creation form with the following fields:

- **Assigned to**: This is the task's owner and can be assigned one of the following values: **User** (any user on the org), **Role** (any internal or external role), **Owner** (the record's owner or the parent owner; for **Opportunity** it can be set to the owner of **Account**), **Creator** (the same as **Owner**, but for the record's creator), and for **Subject**, the task's subject line or title.

- **Due Date**: A date taken from the current record or the parent records or from the *trigger date* (that is, the date when the rule is executed, that is, *today* for immediate actions or a past date for time-dependent actions). We can even set a due date **plus/minus** a specific number of days.

- **Status**: This is the task's status field (identifies the task's completion status).

- **Priority**: This is just the task's priority field (it indicates the importance of the task).

- **Comments**: What the task owner should deal with (simple comments on the task, such as things to do or things to remember).

Fill in the following fields as follows:

- **Object: Opportunity**
- **Assigned to: CEO**
- **Status: In Progress**
- **Priority: High**
- **Subject: New Big Deal!**
- **Unique Name**: Leave as autocompleted

- **Due Date**: **Opportunity**: **Close Date plus 5 days**

- **Comments**: **Hey boss, a new big deal has just been created!**

Save the action and simply update the opportunity we were playing with (take care to have at least the **Amount** or **Rating** condition met), and a new task magically appears on the **Activity** tab:

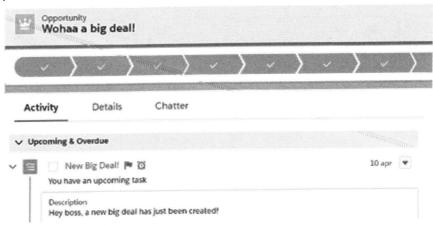

Figure 7.10 – A new task created in the Opportunity record

Creating a task automatically could be a good way to organize the daily work of the CRM users, but we can also use a quicker and more intuitive way to communicate with dear old emails.

The Email Alert action

It's no surprise that the **Email Alert** action is used to send email notifications.

Emails require a template to be sent, which can be done by going to **Setup | Email | Classic Email Templates**. Refer to the following screenshot:

Figure 7.11 – Creating a classic email template

> **Further reading**
>
> Creating an **Email Template** is beyond the scope of this chapter. For further details, refer to Salesforce Help at `https://help.salesforce.com/articleView?id=admin_emailtemplates.htm&type=5`.

To create a new **Email Alert**, just select the **New Email Alert** option when creating a new workflow action:

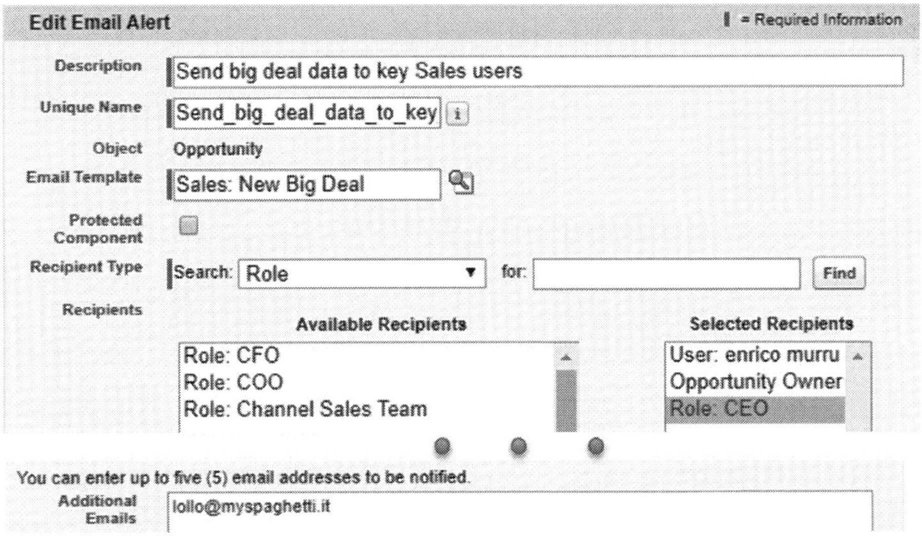

Figure 7.12 – Configuring a new Email Alert action

The following fields are needed:

- **Email Template** (created earlier)
- **Recipients** (chosen from separate fields and related objects)
- *Hardcoded* **Additional Email** addresses

Save it and test it. This is what you will receive on your email client:

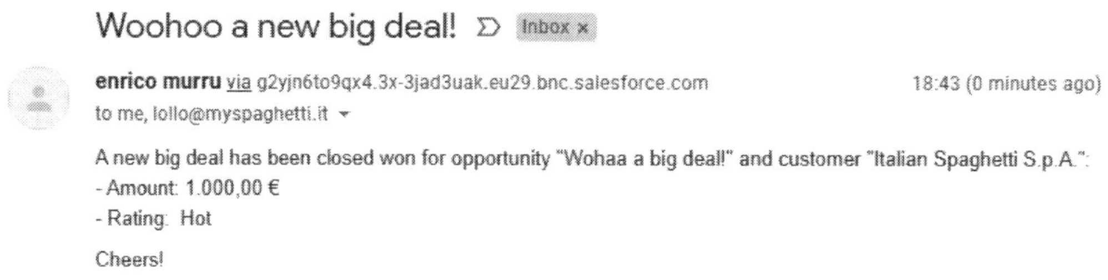

Woohoo a new big deal! ∑ Inbox x

enrico murru via g2yjn6to9qx4.3x-3jad3uak.eu29.bnc.salesforce.com   18:43 (0 minutes ago)
to me, lollo@myspaghetti.it ▾

A new big deal has been closed won for opportunity "Wohaa a big deal!" and customer "Italian Spaghetti S.p.A.":
- Amount: 1.000,00 €
- Rating: Hot

Cheers!

Figure 7.13 – Email received after Email Alert action execution

> **Note**
> When testing your **Email Alert** action, remember that Developer Edition and Trial orgs can send up to 15 email notifications to external email addresses per day: exceeding this limit will prevent any email from being sent.

The Outbound Message action

Outbound messages are used to communicate with external systems in the so-called *machine-to-machine* way, meaning that no user intervention is needed to make this communication complete (an exception is made for the triggering condition that makes this communication start).

In our scenario, the target system may be an order management system, which our CRM should contact if a deal is closed, to start the billing process.

This feature requires some *developer* work on the destination system, because it needs to deal with a specific messaging protocol (called **SOAP protocol**) to conform with this kind of action (after all, there should be an *interface* on the target system ready to receive this kind of message).

To configure a new outbound message, click on **New Outbound Message** on the workflow actions section of the workflow configuration page (like we did for the **Field Update**, **Task**, and **Email Alert** actions), which leads to the following configuration screen:

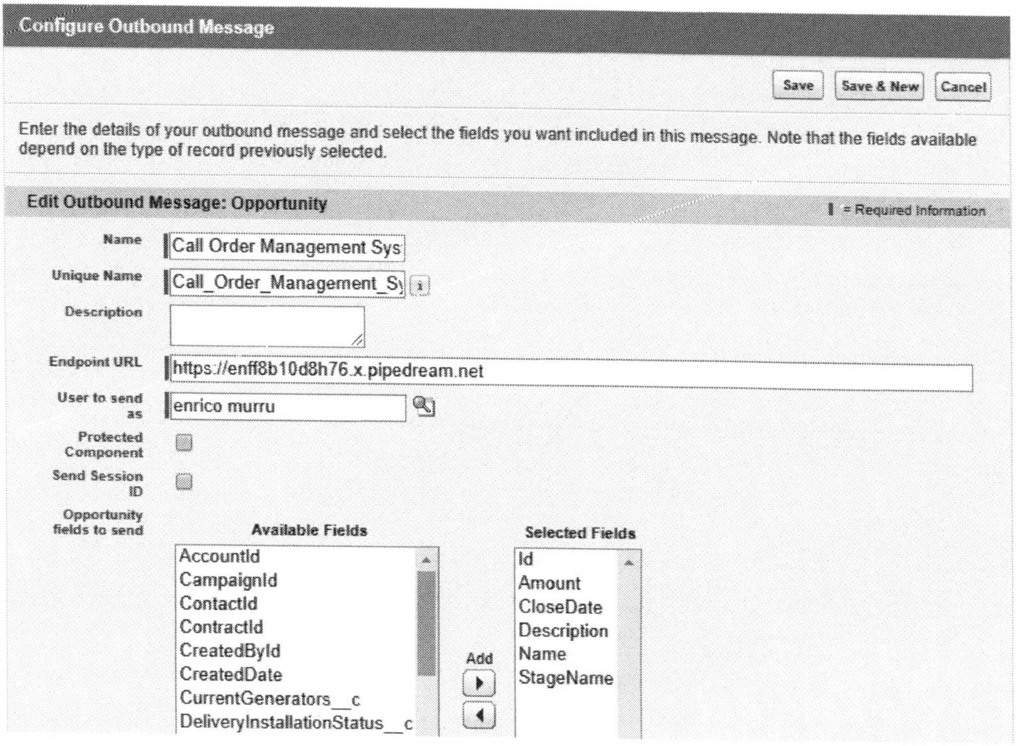

Figure 7.14 – Configuring a new Outbound Message action

The message can send all object-related fields (but no related parent fields) plus the Salesforce Session ID (**Send session ID** options), which can be used to reply to Salesforce so that the target system has a way to send data using Salesforce APIs (this is pretty much all *developer* stuff).

Just for the sake of being aware, the following is the kind of message the system will receive when the workflow executes the action:

```
<soapenv:Envelope . . .>
 <soapenv:Body>
  <notifications . . .>
   <OrganizationId>00D3X000003JaD3UAK</OrganizationId>
   <ActionId>04k3X000000bmMgQAI</ActionId>
   <SessionId xsi:nil="true"/>
   <Notification>
    <Id>04l3X00001I2QhoQAF</Id>
    <sObject xsi:type="sf:Opportunity">
     <sf:Id>0063X000013PWWrQAO</sf:Id>
     <sf:Amount>1000.0</sf:Amount>
```

```
        <sf:CloseDate>2020-04-05</sf:CloseDate>
        <sf:Description>ALERT: this is a. . .</sf:Description>
        <sf:Name>Wohaa a big deal!</sf:Name>
        <sf:StageName>Closed Won</sf:StageName>
      </sObject>
    </Notification>
  </notifications>
  </soapenv:Body>
</soapenv:Envelope>
```

As you can see in the preceding code, the message is not intended for human interaction (even if it is *human-readable*, some details have been removed to facilitate the representation of the message). The highlighted part is the part of the message that contains all the fields we have selected in the configuration of the action.

> **Further reading**
>
> For more details on outbound messaging, refer to Salesforce Developers Help at `https://developer.salesforce.com/docs/atlas.en-us.api.meta/api/sforce_api_om_outboundmessaging.htm`.

Defining time-dependent actions

So far, we've configured *immediate* actions, actions that are executed *contextually* to the workflow criteria evaluation.

What if we need to execute actions hours or even days after the workflow is evaluated?

We would opt for **Time-Dependent actions**, which are actions executed with a calculated delay:

1. To create such actions, we need to create a new workflow rule setting the evaluation criteria option to **created, and any time it's edited to subsequently meet criteria**, as in the following example:

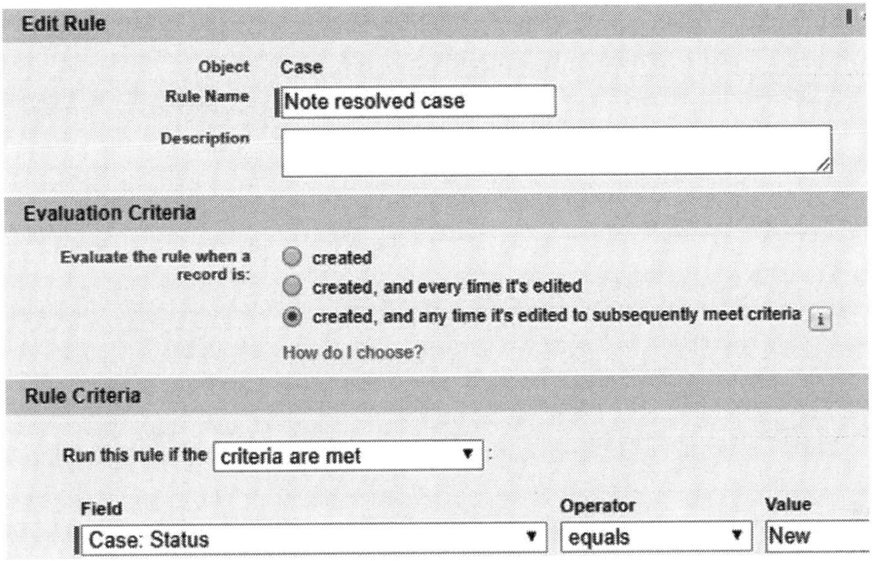

Figure 7.15 – Workflow rule in Case

Here, we can see that the workflow is triggered by the case being created/updated with **Case: Status equals** to **New**. Typically, **Status** set to **New** means that the case has not been worked on yet (so we should alert someone if time passes by).

2.   We can also add a new time-dependent action by clicking the **Add Time Trigger** button on the workflow recap page:

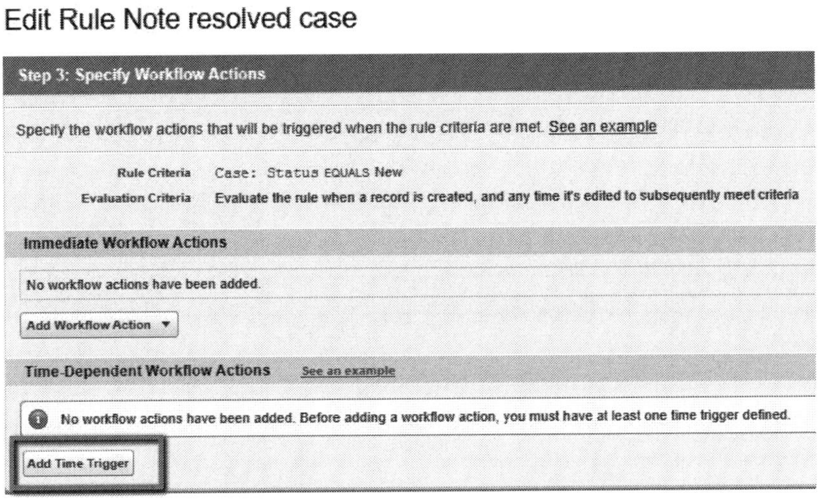

Figure 7.16 – Creating a new time-dependent action

There is also a means for us to define a time delay of hours or days based on a record's date field or from the execution date:

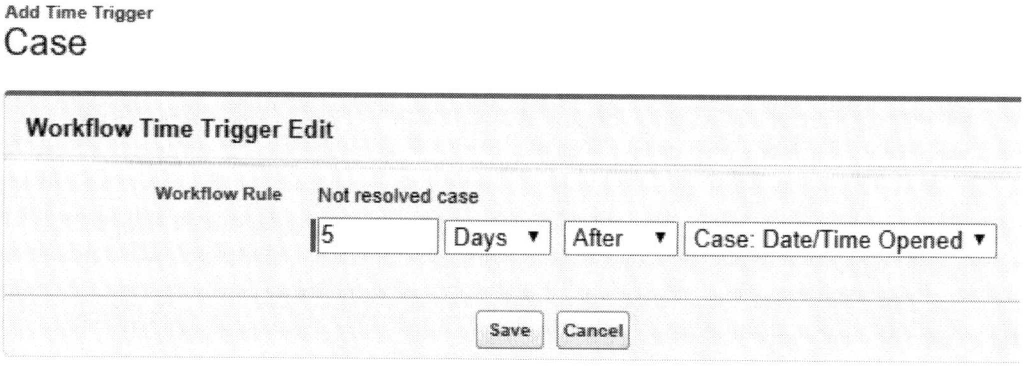

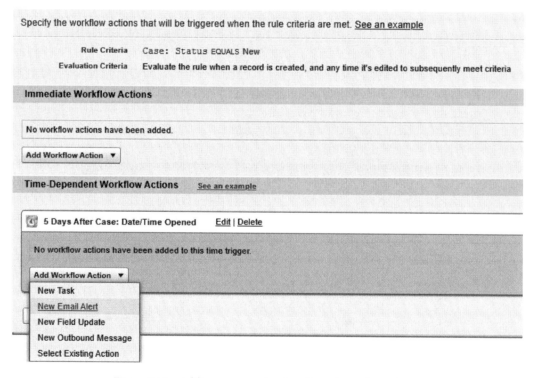

Figure 7.17 – Defining a triggering delay

3. Click **Save** to go back to the recap page and to select a new action creation:

Figure 7.18 – Adding a new action to a time-dependent trigger

Now that we have configured a time trigger, we can add some automated actions that will be executed when the trigger fires (in this example, 5 days after case creation). If a case has not been taken in hand for 5 days, its priority is increased to signal urgency.

To do this, we add a new **Field Update** action to increase the case's **Priority** to **High**:

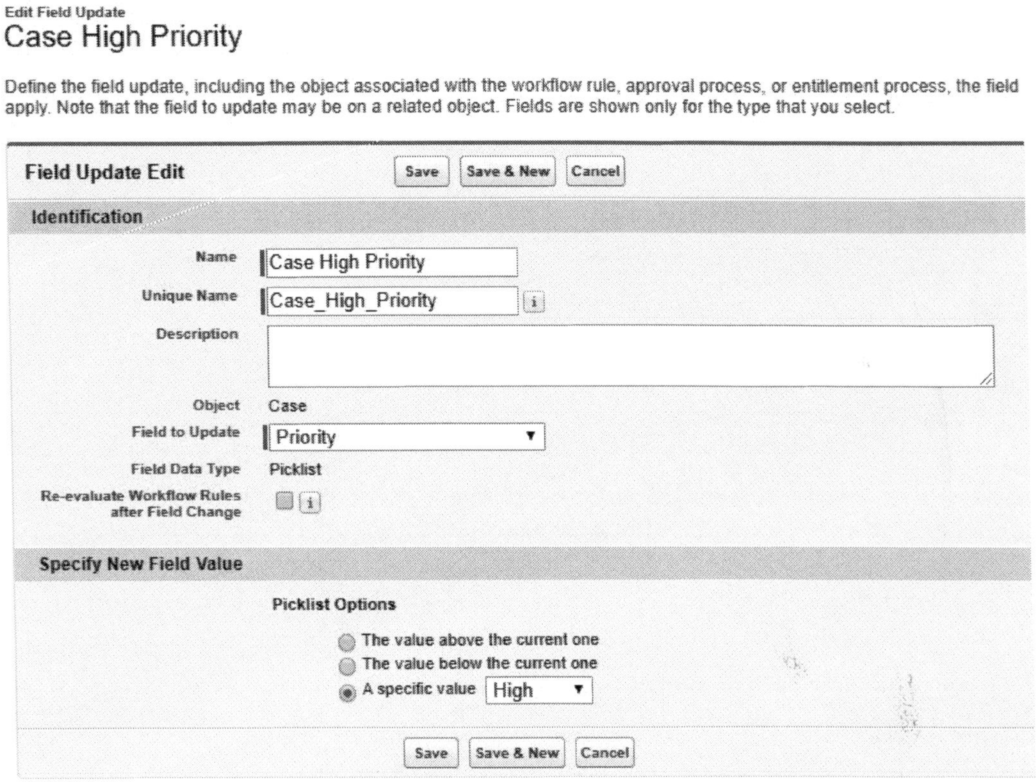

Figure 7.19 – Adding a field update to increase a case's priority

Click **Save**, **Done**, and **Activate** (as we did earlier) to activate the new workflow rule, which is summarized as follows:

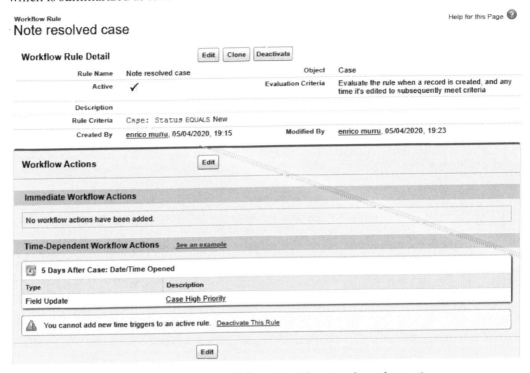

Figure 7.20 – Activating a workflow rule with a time-dependent action

Once the workflow is active, we can check whether it is working as expected.

Testing time-based actions

To test this time-dependent action out, jump to the **Service** application and create a new **Case** with **Status** set to **New** and **Priority** set to **Low**.

As you can see, nothing appears to have happened, but it is quite obvious: the action should take place in 5 days.

So, for this, there is a way to monitor time-dependent actions from **Setup | Environments | Monitoring | Time-Based Workflows**:

Time-Based Workflow

When salesforce.com triggers a workflow rule, its time-dependent actions are placed in the workflow queue. Use the criteria below to monitor the queue.

	Record Name	Object	Workflow Rule Name	Scheduled Date	Created By	Created Date
☐	00001026	Case	Note resolved case	10/04/2020, 19:25	murru, enrico	05/04/2020, 19:25

Figure 7.21 – Monitoring time-dependent actions

What happens if the case is taken in hand and its status changes to **Working** or **Closed**? The workflow evaluation criteria are no longer met, and the action is removed from the queue, so it will no longer trigger in 5 days.

It is important to remember that there is a hardcoded limit of 1,000 time-dependent actions executed per hour. If this limit is reached, the remaining actions are executed in the next available hour.

> **Further reading**
>
> For further considerations on time-based actions, refer to Salesforce Help at `https://help.salesforce.com/articleView?id=workflow_time_action_considerations.htm&type=5`.

Considerations and limits on workflow rules

Like most automation tools, workflow rules have some important limitations you should consider when designing Salesforce automation (as of the *spring 2020 Salesforce release*):

- The total number of rules (inactive or not) across all Salesforce objects must not exceed 2,000.
- The total number of rules (inactive or not) per single object must not exceed 500.
- The total number of active rules per object must not exceed 50.

- You can have up to 40 immediate actions per workflow (up to 10 per action type).

- You can have up to 10 time-based actions per workflow (up to 10 per action type).

Further reading

For a detailed list of limits, refer to Salesforce Help at `https://help.salesforce.com/articleView?id=workflow_limits.htm&type=5`.

Further considerations in terms of using workflow rules can be found at `https://help.salesforce.com/articleView?id=workflow_rules_considerations.htm&type=5`.

Summary

In this chapter, we have introduced the concept of Salesforce automation and how it can be delivered to implement your business processes.

We've seen how workflow rules are shaped and how to create them, using all the available actions in the automation library (including field updates, task creation, email alerting, and outbound messaging), defining immediate or time-based execution, to trigger actions with a time-based delay. With workflows, you now have the power to create automations based on a user's interaction with the CRM, easing their daily workload and handling more complex or *hard to remember* tasks on their behalf.

In the next chapter, we'll deal with approval processes, which we will use to handle record approvals across your users.

8
Setting Up Approval Processes

A close sibling of workflow rule automation is the approval process. This automation tool is meant to allow users to ask their managers/users higher in the company's hierarchy for approval for access to key business records under specific conditions.

In this chapter, we'll be using an example as a base use case to understand the following:

- Designing an approval
- Creating an approval process
- Consuming the approval process

By the end of this chapter, you will have learned how to build an approval process and how to add steps and actions to customize the approval flow.

Designing an approval

In this chapter, we'll be learning about approval processes using a complex example that will involve the **Advertisement** custom object, which we've built in previous chapters.

Approval processes (shortened to **Approvals**) can be used in countless scenarios that can include the following:

- Opportunity approval during the contracting status so that records over a certain amount threshold need explicit approval by the company's CEO before closure

- A case opened by a hot customer that has a pending status and needs explicit approval by the service manager

- A new product has been created by the marketing team but should be approved by the sales VP before it can be marked as sellable

- Employee expense approval by their managers and an additional approval step by the employee's division head if the expense amount is greater than a defined amount (this allows managers to identify "big spenders")

Our business users require that when a new **Advertisement** record is created on the CRM by any user and if the user set up a value in the **Discount** field, the record should be approved by their manager if the discount is greater than 10%, and also by the CEO if the discount exceeds 30%.

Furthermore, the advertisement cannot be activated until it's been approved, and a discount of less than or equal to10% should automatically be approved without the manager's consent.

When deciding to build a new approval, try to answer the following questions (which we'll be answering inline):

- *Which is the Salesforce object that should be approved and in which conditions?* We are talking about the **Advertisement** object and its records should be approved only if the **Discount** and **Price** fields are filled in.

- *Who is allowed to submit the record approval?* In our scenario, business users replied that the owner of the record (which generally will be the creator of the record) must submit the record for approval before activating it (the **Is Active** field is set to **true**).

- *How many approvers are needed and in which conditions?* If the **Discount value** is greater than 10%, the advertisement must be submitted by record owners to their manager, and if it exceeds 30% to the company's CEO.

- *What must happen when a record is approved or rejected?* In the case of approval or rejection, an email must be sent to the submitting user to inform them about the success or the reasons for the rejection. Also, if the **Discount** value is changed after approval to a greater value, the record should be submitted for approval again and cannot be activated.

- *Do we need email templates to alert the users involved in the approval process?* For sure: one to notify approving users, one for approval notification, and one for rejection notification.

- *Should the record be kept locked during approval?* Business users replied that the record must remain untouched until approval or rejection.

Our use case cannot be fully implemented using only **Approval Process** as our CRM requires some more configuration.

Preparing for the approval implementation

To develop our examples, we need some preliminary configurations using the features we've already covered so far in the previous chapters.

Creating new custom fields

We are going to work with the **Advertisement** object, using the **Price** and **Discount** custom fields; while the first field is already on our object, **Discount** should be created from scratch with a **Percent** type: you know how to create a brand new custom field from what we've seen in the previous chapters.

Remember to add the **Discount** field to the **Advertisement Page Layout** and select the proper field-level security for every profile. Another requirement is that an advertisement record should not be activated if the discount has not been **approved**. To implement this configuration, first, we need a new custom field on the **Advertisement** object: create a new picklist field called **Discount_Approval_c** with the values **Approved**, **Not Approved**, and **Approval Requested**.

Leave the default value blank, add the field to the **Advertisement** page layout, and configure **Field Level Security** to **read only** for all profiles: this field will be updated by the **Approval Process** flow only.

Creating a new validation rule

To avoid activating a record when the approval has not run, let's create a validation rule:

- **Name**: Check_Approval_Status_On_Activation

- **Error Condition Formula**:

```
AND( ISCHANGED(Is_Active__c),
    Is_Active__c = true,
    Discount__c > 0,
    Price__c > 0,
```

```
NOT(ISPICKVAL(Discount_Approved__c, 'Approved'))
)
```

- **Error message: You cannot activate the advertisement if the record has not been submitted for approval and approved**
- **Error location: Top of Page**

We've already seen these kinds of formula functions, in *Chapter 4*, *Cleaning Data with Validation Rules*. The validation rule is triggered if the **Is Active** flag is checked but the **Discount Status** field is not set to **Approved** and other checks.

Creating a new workflow

Another requirement is that the approval process should be rerun if the **Discount** field is changed to a higher value. This is done with a workflow rule with the following configurations:

- **Rule name: Reset Approval Status**
- **Object: Advertisement**
- **Evaluate the rule when a record is: created, and every time it's edited**
- **Rule criteria**:

```
AND(
    Discount__c > 0,
    Price__c > 0,
    ISCHANGED(Discount__c),
    PRIORVALUE(Discount__c) < Discount__c
)
```

The workflow will trigger under the following conditions:

- The **Discount** and **Price** fields are filled in
- The **Discount** value changes
- The new value of **Discount** is higher than the previous value

This workflow rule will trigger the following simple field update action:

- **Name: Reset Discount Status**
- **Object: Advertisement**

- **Field to Update**: **Discount Status**
- **Picklist Options**: **A specific value --None--**

Creating some key users

Finally, we talked about three key users:

- Record owner
- Record owner's manager
- CEO

Considering that you'll be testing this configuration in a Salesforce Developer Edition org (which we prepared in the *Chapter 1, A Brief Introduction on Salesforce*) where we have only two standard licenses to use (we need three users), we'll be using the following users and profiles:

- **Record owner**: **Salesforce Platform** licensed user
- **Record owner's manager**: **Salesforce** licensed user
- **CEO**: Your administrator user (with a **Salesforce** license)

In the following screenshot, these are depicted:

Action	Active ↑	Full Name	User License	Profile	Role	Manager
☐	Edit	✓	Murru, Enrico	Salesforce	System Administrator	CEO	
☐	Edit | Login	✓	Lavori, Stefano	Salesforce	Custom Standard User	SVP, Sales & Marketing	Murru, Enrico
☐	Edit | Login	✓	Portoni, Guglielmo	Salesforce Platform	Custom: Sales Platform User	VP, International Sales	Lavori, Stefano

Figure 8.1 – Key users configured on DE org

As you can see in the **Profile** column, we need to create two new custom profiles that we'll clone from the **Standard User** and **Platform User** standard profiles.

> **Tip**
> This is not mandatory, but it's a best practice not to use standard profiles when configuring your users.

For each of the new profiles, take care to configure access to the **Advertisement** object as follows (from **Setup | Profiles**):

- **Object Permissions**: **Read, Create, Edit and Delete**
- **Field Permissions**: **Read Access** for all allowed fields and **Edit Access** for all fields, with an exception made for the **Discount Status** field (which users shouldn't be able to update manually)

Creating a new application

Now, let's create a new custom Lightning application to handle **Advertisement**-related work tasks.

Click on **Setup | Apps | App Manager** and then the **New Lightning App** button, then set up the app with the following main info, including a name, tabs, and allowed profiles:

- **App Name**: **Adv. Division**
- **Navigation Selected Items**: **Home, Advertisements, Accounts, Contacts**
- **User Selected Profiles**: **System Administrator, Custom: Sales Platform User, Custom Standard User**

Updating the Advertisement page layout

To finalize our preliminary configuration, let's enhance the **Advertisement** page layout to better show all key fields as shown in the following screenshot (we'll cover page layout configuration in *12, All about Layout*):

Figure 8.2 – Enhanced page layout for the Advertisement object

For the next step, in the preceding screenshot, you can see the **Submit for Approval** standard button (available from the **Buttons** section on the page layout toolbar): this is the button that users will use to start the approval process.

Creating an approval process

So far, we have all the ingredients to build our new approval process and make our company's business users happy. Now, let's see how to create it:

1. To create a new approval, click **Setup | Process Automation | Approval Processes**, select the proper Salesforce object on the **Manager Approval Processes For:** picklist, click the **Create New Approval Process** button, and select **Use Standard Setup Wizard**.

2. The first step of the wizard asks for **Process Name (Advertisement Discount Approval)**, **Unique Name (Advertisement_Discount_Approval)**, and a **description**.

3. In this step, we need to enter the **entry criteria**, which identifies the **Advertisement** records that should enter the approval process.
   Select **formula evaluates to true** in the **Use this approval process if the following:** picklist and fill in the following criteria:

   ```
   AND( Price__c > 0, Discount__c > 0 )
   ```

   We can use criteria or formula (as we aim to become the best declarative Salesforce programmers in the world, we choose the formula-based configuration).

   The formula is quite simple: any advertisement record with **Price** and **Discount** **greater than 0** will be allowed to enter the process.

   > Tip:
   > If you try to submit a record for approval but the entry criteria do not match any approval processes, you'll get an error and won't be allowed to submit the record.

4. The next step configures the approver user and the *editability* property. The **Next Automated Approver Determined By** picklist is needed to select the user who'll be receiving the submission and it can be set to the standard **Manager** lookup field for the user or any custom hierarchical lookup on the **User** object. The **User Approver Field of Advertisement Owner** checkbox identifies the base user record as the record's owner (if flagged) or the current submitting user (if unflagged, any user that can edit the record will actually be able to submit it for approval, not only the owner).

We'll see this shortly, but when a record is submitted for approval, we can lock the record to avoid modifications during the approval process. Using the **Record Editability Properties** section, we can tell the approval engine to allow **ONLY** administrators to edit the record during the lock phase **OR** administrators and the approver.

This configuration depends on your needs. In our scenario, the business users asked us not to let anyone change the record, so we'll go with the first configuration.

5. The next step configures the email template used to notify approvers of incoming approval actions.

We've chosen to use a custom email template, as described here (you are free to use the defaulted standard one; custom email templates were covered briefly in the previous chapter):

- **Folder**: **Unfiled Public Classic Email Templates**
- **Email Template Name**: **Adv. Discount Approvals**
- **Available For Use**: **true**
- **Subject**: **New Advertisement Discount Approval**
- **Email template**:

```
Advertisement "{!Advertisement__c.Name}" requires
Discount approval.
Click here: {!ApprovalRequest.Internal_URL}
```

Select the previous email template on *step 4* of the approval creation wizard, in the **Email Template** section.

6.   The next step configures the approval page layout as seen by the approvers.

The **Selected Fields** selection list lists the advertisement fields displayed to approvers when they have to decide on record approval or rejection; the **Approval Page Fields** section allows you to also show the approval history (so you know what happened in the past and who the involved users were and their comments).

Security Settings allows a record to only be approved by authenticated users or from outside Salesforce (not recommended).

7.   The final step contains the last configurations of the approval process.

From this step, we can choose who's allowed to submit a record for approval and we can choose among the record's creator, the record's owner, roles, groups, and specific users.

We've been told that the initial submitter must be the record's owner, so we choose **Advertisement Owner** in the **Allowed Submitters** multi picklist in the **Initial Submitters** section.

The **Page Layout Settings** checkbox adds the **Submit for Approval** button and the **Approval History** related list on the **Advertisement** page layout after the approval is created.

Finally, **Submission Settings** grants submitters the power to recall an approval request (so that the record can be submitted again with new field values – this may be because the user mistakenly submitted the record): this is something that is not required in our use case.

Click **Save** to complete the wizard and select the **Take me to the approval detail page to review what I've just created** option. You'll be redirected to the approval record page, which will show the details we've just configured in the creation wizard.

Let's now add some approval steps to our process, so we can handle different levels of record approval across the company's hierarchy of managers (our key users).

Configuring steps and actions

We've not completed the automation setup yet; we still need to configure the *branches* that the approval process will be following, depending on the **Discount** field value and the approval or rejection actions on the record as required by our use case.

The approval process home page, right after the section containing the main approval details, shows a list of steps and actions that we'll use to finalize our automation configuration. Let's cover them one by one.

Initial submission actions

This section contains any automation action that we intend to do when the record is successfully submitted.

A default **Record Lock** action is already there: we'll leave it as it is because in our scenario, the record should be kept locked during submission.

We also want to update the **Discount Status** field to show that the record has been submitted, so click the **Add New** button in the **Initial Submission Actions** section and select the **Field Update** option.

We've already seen how to create a new **Field Update** action: simply create a new **Field Update** action on the **Discount Status** field of the **Advertisement** object, selecting the **Approval Requested** value.

This way, when a record enters the approval process, **Discount Status** is set to **Approval Requested**, telling everyone that the record is going to be approved (or not!).

> Remember:
> The **Discount Status** field shouldn't be updated by any *human user*.

Final approval and rejection actions

Just like **Initial Submission Actions**, we can define actions on record approval or rejection.

We'll be adding an update to the **Discount Status** field, creating two new field updates that will update the field with the following values:

- **Approved** as **Final Approval Action**
- **Not Approved** as **Final Rejection Action**

Moreover, by default, the **Final Approval Actions** section contains a **Record Lock** configuration that automatically locks the record after approval, which is something that our business didn't ask us for, so we'll go with updating that property:

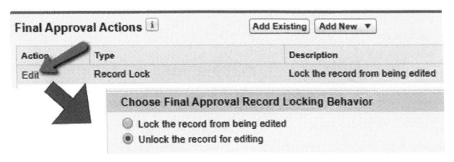

Figure 8.3 – Record unlock configuration

We also want to add two email notifications:

- To notify the submitter about successful record approval
- To notify the submitter about rejection with the provided comments

Let's create two new email templates (as already done earlier) – one for record approval:

- **Email Template Name**: **Adv. Discount Approved**
- **Subject**: **New Advertisement Discount Approved**
- **Email template**:

```
Advertisement "{!Advertisement__c.Name}"has been
approved!
Click here: {!ApprovalRequest.Internal_URL}
```

And one for record rejection:

- **Email Template Name**: **Adv. Discount Rejected**
- **Subject**: **New Advertisement Discount Rejected**
- **Email template**:

```
Advertisement "{!Advertisement__c.Name}"has been rejected
with the following comments:
{!ApprovalRequest.Comments}
Click here: {!ApprovalRequest.Internal_URL}
```

Use these templates to create new **Email Alert** actions – one for **Final Approval Actions** and one for **Final Rejection Actions**:

- **Description**: **Alert Submitter for Approval** | **Alert Submitter for Rejection**
- **Email Template**: **Adv. Discount Approved** | **Adv. Discount Rejected**
- **Recipients**: **Advertisement Owner**

This is what you end up with after all these configurations:

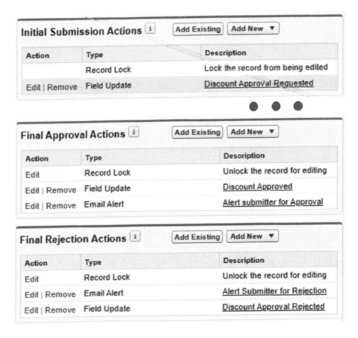

Figure 8.4 – Initial Submission Actions, Final Approval Actions,
and Final Rejection Actions configurations

Creating approval steps

In the **Approval Steps** section, we'll be adding the levels of approval we want to implement for our approval.

We have two clear steps in our use case:

- The record owner's manager approves the record with a discount of greater than 10%.
- The company's CEO is required to approve a record with at least a 30% discount.

Let's see how we can do this:

1. To create a new approval step, click **New Approval Step** in the **Approval Steps** section. In the first step of the step creation wizard, fill in the **Name** field with **Low Discounts** and **Step Number** with **1**. Click **Next**.

2. The second step configures the entry criteria, and is identified by a discount of greater than 10%, as shown here:

| Step 2. Specify Step Criteria | | | | Step 2 of 3 |

Specify whether a record must meet certain criteria before entering this approval step. If these criteria are not met, the approval process can skip to the next step, if one exists. Learn more

Specify Step Criteria

○ All records should enter this step.
● Enter this step if the following [criteria are met ▼], else [approve record ▼] :

Field	Operator	Value	
Advertisement: Discount ▼	greater than ▼	10	AND

Figure 8.5 – Step criteria configuration

In this step, we can define the criteria that are used to match this step (using criteria or formula mode) or simply tell the approval engine that **All records should enter the step** (no criteria required).

Being as this is the first step, if the criteria are not matched, we can choose to approve the record, reject the record, or go to the next step (if any).

Our requirement is to automatically approve records with a discount of less than or equal to 10%.

3. Click **Next** to jump to the approver selection configuration.

    From this step, we can **let the submitter choose the approver manually**, automatically assign the **User** field selected in the Approval Process configuration (the **Manager** field is only available if the approval has been configured so earlier), automatically assign a specific queue (only if the current Salesforce object supports queues), automatically assign specific users (and you can specify that all users must approve the record or just one of them), or we can let approvers delegate approving this step (the **Delegated Approver** field can be set up on the **User** object). Our scenario needs the **Manager** option.

4. Click **Save** to complete the step configuration and let's add the second and last step we need for our implementation, which should trigger CEO approval if **Discount** is set to 30% or more.

This step's configuration is quite straightforward; the main differences are in the criteria configuration, where we select the following criteria: **Advertisement Discount Greater or Equal to 30**.

As this is not the first condition, the **else** picklist is not shown.

The next step's configuration is also slightly different:

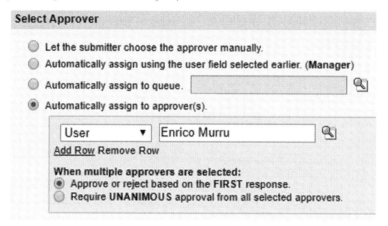

Figure 8.6 – Second approval step's approver configuration

This time, we'll be selecting a specific user (my user is the actual CEO in the DE org).

The last section, **Reject Behavior**, is used to decide whether the record should finally be rejected or should go back to the previous step, requiring the first-step approver to elaborate the approval again: the final rejection implies the execution of **Final Rejection Actions**, which we saw earlier.

In the following screenshot, we are seeing what's happened so far with the **Approval Steps** configuration:

Action	Step Number	Name	Description	Criteria	Assigned Approver	Reject Behavior
Hide Actions	Edit	Del	1	Low Discounts	Discount <= 10% will be automatically approved	Advertisement: Discount GREATER THAN 0.1 , else Approve	Manager	Final Rejection
Hide Actions	Edit	Del	2	High Discounts	Discounts greater then 30% should be explicitly approved by CEO	Advertisement: Discount GREATER OR EQUAL 0.3	User enrico murru	Final Rejection

Figure 8.7 – Approval Steps configuration

As you can see from the preceding screenshot, we can even add actions on each step's approval/rejection – our scenario does not require such additional configurations.

To complete our work, we need to activate the approval process by clicking the **Activate** button.

> **Tip:**
>
> Remember that once an approval process has been activated, no further new steps can be added. You'd need to clone the current approval and create a new one to add more steps.

We are now ready to test the approval process with some advertisement records.

Consuming the approval process

Let's test our new approval process:

1. You need to log in with all users identified, including your administrator user (the CEO), the submitting user, and the first step approver: I suggest you use three different browsers or use the same browser with different *personas* (Chrome, Firefox, Opera, and Microsoft Edge allow it), or the same browser in incognito mode (which allows you to use two different users) and another browser for the third user. You can even use the same browser, but you'd need to go back and forth by logging out from one user to the other.

   A quick way to switch between users is to enable the **Login As** feature, which can be configured from **Setup | Security | Login Access Policies** and by selecting the **Administrator can Log in on Any User** checkbox.

2. Now, with your admin user, you can log in as any other user using the **Login** link or button on the user list view or user details page.

   Using the submitter user (we selected the user **Guglielmo Portoni**, the **Salesforce Platform** licensed user), open the **Adv. Division** app, click on the **Advertisement** tab, create a new **Advertisement** record with a discount lower than our first approval step (5% in the following example), and click the **Submit for Approval** button on the record's button group.

3. The CRM asks for a comment (which is any info the current user wants to give to justify the record approval) but, as expected, the record gets automatically approved:

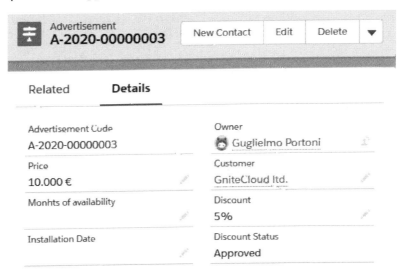

Figure 8.8 – Record automatically approved

Discount Status is automatically set to **Approved** (this is done by **Final Approval Actions**) and no further action is needed (the first step is configured to automatically approve any record whose discount is less than or equal to 10%).

4. For the sake of knowledge, click the **Related** tab to see the approval history:

Figure 8.9 – Approval history for automatic record approval

Remember the validation rule for record activation?

If you try to check the **Is Active** field, you won't get an error.

Let's create a new advertisement record, setting the **Discount** field to 20%, then try to activate it:

1. You should get the validation rule error that follows:

Figure 8.10 – Validation rule triggered before approval submission

This is what we expected: the record has not been approved yet and so we cannot activate it.

2. Now let's click the **Submit for Approval** button again and, after the confirmation of the submissions (the green badge that pops up on your screen), try to update any field. You won't be allowed to, thanks to **Initial Approval Actions**, as shown here:

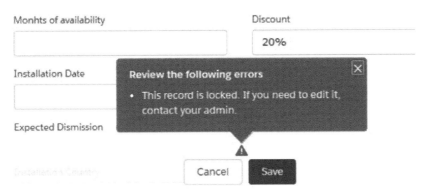

Figure 8.11 – Record locked before approval

This is expected; indeed, the record is still in the approving phase. You should also see the **Discount Status** field set to **Approval Requested**.

3. Now, we need to switch to the first-step approver, a new user we called **Stefano Lavori** (with a **Salesforce** license). This user should have received an email notification like the following:

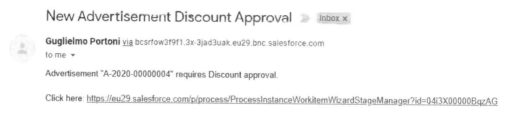

Figure 8.12 – Approval notification mail

This is the email template we configured in the first steps of the approval creation wizard.

4. Now, log in as the first-step approver and click on the link provided in the email to get to the approval page:

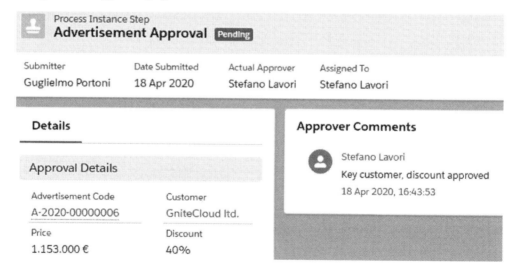

Figure 8.13 – Record approval page

5. On this page, the approver can see the record details (set up in the approval creation wizard), all approval comments, and the status of the current approval (this is *pending*). They can use the **Approve**, **Reject**, and **Reassign** buttons to change the approval status.

6. By clicking the **Approve** button, the record's **Discount Status** automatically changes to **Approved** and an email is sent to the submitter telling them that the record has finally been approved (following the **Final Approval Actions** configured so far).

Take a look at what happened so far on the **Approval History** related list.

If you pressed the **Reject** button, the submitter will have received a rejection email and **Discount Status** will have been set to **Not Approved**. This is the email template we configured with the approval's rejection comments shown:

Figure 8.14 – Rejection notification email

The submitter is now free to update the record again, for example, by setting a lower discount value, and the record can now be resubmitted and, hopefully, will be re-approved by the first-step approver, as shown in the following history list:

Advertisements > A-2020-00000005
Approval History
4 items · Sorted by Is Pending, Date · Updated a few seconds ago

	Step Name	Date ↓	Status	Assigned To	Actual Appr...	Comments	
1	Low Discounts	18/04/2020, 16:40	Approved	Stefano Lavori	Stefano Lavori	Discount ok	▾
2	Approval Request Submit...	18/04/2020, 16:40	Submitted	Guglielmo Portoni	Guglielmo Portoni	Discount set to 25%	▾
3	Low Discounts	18/04/2020, 16:39	Rejected	Stefano Lavori	Stefano Lavori	Discount cannot exceed ...	▾
4	Approval Request Submit...	18/04/2020, 16:38	Submitted	Guglielmo Portoni	Guglielmo Portoni	Request for 30% discount	▾

Figure 8.15 – Approval history after two subsequent submissions and 1 rejection

Now, create a new record with a value higher than 30% (our second approval step) as follows, and submit it for approval.

The first-step approver (in our example, **Guglielmo Portoni**) will be notified about the record and they will be able to approve it. After this first-step approval, the record is directly sent to the CEO who will be able to **Approve** or **Reject** again, as shown in the following **Approval History** list:

Figure 8.16 – Example record approval with multi-step

From this view, we can easily see all the different approval steps the record entered, the approver, the status, and the comment they posted.

You can search for the **Approval Requests** page from **App Launcher** to access the list of all incoming approvals.

So far, you are now a master of approval processes: take care of designing your approval requests and deliver a great user experience.

You can have more than one approval process active at the same time on the same Salesforce object; that's why each approval process has a unique **Process Order number**:

Figure 8.17 – Multiple active approvals on the same Salesforce object

Before closing this chapter, let's list some of the most important Salesforce limits regarding approval process implementation.

Limits and considerations

Here is a list of useful-to-know limits about using approval processes (as of the *Spring 2020 release*):

- **Total active approval processes per org**: 1,000
- **Total approval processes per org**: 2,000
- **Total approval processes per object**: 300
- **Steps per process**: 30
- **Actions per section (initial submission, final approval, final rejection, recall)**: 40
- **Max number of approvers per step**: 25
- **Max number of characters in approval comments**: 4,000

Approval submission is a manual operation (users have to manually click the **Submit for Approval** button to start the approval process) but you can automate this using Lightning Flow or Process Builder.

Blaze your trail

For further learning, jump to Salesforce Trailhead and the following modules:

- Build a discount approval process: `https://trailhead.salesforce.com/en/content/learn/projects/build-a-discount-approval-process`
- Automate business processes for a recruiting app: `https://trailhead.salesforce.com/content/learn/projects/automate-business-processes-recruiting-app`

Summary

Approval process is a key automation feature that can be the core of critical business processes in your org that require explicit record approval among the company's user hierarchy.

In this chapter, through a complex yet real-life example, we've learned how to design a new approval process, linking together all the Salesforce features we've seen so far.

Then, we covered how to bring the design to life by configuring the new approval process and its steps and actions, providing a detailed and granular level of approval for the use case.

After process activation, we saw how the approval process can be used by key users that may be involved in the process.

In the next chapter, we'll talk about Process Builder and the evolution of workflow rules.

9
Process Builder – Workflow Evolution

With the *Spring 2015* platform release, the Salesforce platform released Process Builder to enhance a useful yet old process automation tool that was (and is actually still) widely used among Salesforce *devmins*, Workflow Rules.

With a process, you could do everything with Workflow Rules (seen in previous chapters), such as executing actions based on triggering conditions on a given Salesforce object instantly or with a time dependency, but with a more appealing and modern UI and many more available action types.

In this chapter, we'll learn about the following topics:

- How to define and manage Process Builder
- How to define actions

What is Process Builder?

Process Builder is a modern way to implement state machines using the **If This Then That (IFTTT)** paradigm, with a rich user interface that allows any *devmin* to exactly understand how the automated process is shaped at a glance.

Just as we did with Workflow Rules, select a Salesforce object, define the trigger criteria, and set up the actions you want to execute in order to create a brand new automation.

Unlike Workflow Rules, you can define the order in which actions are executed, while in workflows, you cannot predict which action will be executed first.

Another difference is that Process Builder can deliver automation not only for Salesforce objects but also for Platform Events (which are a special kind of Salesforce object used to send events back and forth inside and outside the platform that we won't cover in this book).

> **Further reading**
>
> For more info about Platform Events, have a look at the **Platform Events Basics** Trailhead module at `https://trailhead.salesforce.com/en/content/learn/modules/platform_events_basics`.

Moreover, you can define a process that can be called by another parent process, which allows you to define *reusable unit* processes that can be used throughout your automations, thus reducing the time needed for implementation and maintenance (one process to rule them all).

Process Builder comes with a lot more actions than Workflow Rules; indeed, Workflow Rules actions enable you to do a field update (of the same object or the parent object), create a task, send an email, and send an outbound message.

An exception is made for the outbound message, which is not supported by Process Builder: with Process Builder, you can define many more actions, such as creating a generic record (not just a task), updating fields on a related record (not only the parent record from a master-child relationship), launching a quick action (refer to *Chapter 11, Interacting with Actions*), posting to Salesforce Chatter, launching a Lightning Flow (refer to *Chapter 10, Designing Lightning Flows*), submitting a record for approval, invoking another process, sending an email, sending a custom notification, and executing some custom Apex code.

A huge difference, isn't it?

> **Tip**
>
> Workflow Rules won't be enhanced anymore: this doesn't mean that Salesforce will discontinue workflows (figure out how many workflow rules are live as of today across all the thousands of Salesforce orgs worldwide), but that no more features will be added to the tool. Process Builder will thus become the preferred process automation tool (have a look at the Trailhead module *Say Goodbye to Workflow and Hello to Process Builder* at `https://trailhead.salesforce.com/en/content/learn/modules/workflow_migration/workflow_migration_intro` in the *Process Builder is the future* section.

Another great addition is that Process Builder can be versioned, meaning that you can have different versions of a process (with only one of them active at a time) and so you can switch from one to another to better implement your business needs (or simply fix a bug).

Finally, remember not to mix workflow rules and processes because you won't be able to predict the exact behavior of the combination, but instead try to migrate old workflows into new processes, as described in the previous tip box.

Besides, configure only one process per object, otherwise, you won't be able to control what's happening as actions can interfere with each other (the same update on fields of a record can happen with a different value, for instance).

> **Tip**
>
> If you are planning a strong and complex automation implementation with an urgent need for performance (for instance, thousands or millions of records updated daily), I suggest evaluating custom Apex code development, which, at this time, delivers better performance.

Now that we have seen which of the main features of processes are built with Process Builder, let's create our first process.

Shaping a process

In our chapter-wide example, we'll be creating a process that will handle an opportunity closure that triggers different kinds of actions, covering almost all of the actions available with this tool.

As we are dealing with opportunities and we don't want too many automations on the same object (best practice is to limit the use of different Salesforce automations to a given Salesforce object), let's deactivate the opportunity-related workflow rules we created in the previous example (the **Big Deal Closed** workflow). To do this, simply go to **Setup | Process Automation | Workflow Rules** and click on the **Deactivate** link next to the **Big Deal Closed** workflow that we created in *Chapter 7, Be a Workflow Champion*.

We'll implement a process on the Opportunity object that triggers when the opportunity is closed and won, which will do the following:

1. Create a new advertisement record with the details coming from the opportunity record and related objects.

2. Update the **Account** record if the deal amount is greater than $1 million, setting the **Rating** field to Hot, and all related open cases should be set to High priority.

3. Create a chatter notification on the **Opportunity** record – a recap of the closure.

4. Send a custom notification to the CEO user notifying them of the closed opportunity only if the amount is greater than $1 million.

5. Send an email notification to the owner of the opportunity 7 days after the execution date, to check whether the **Advertisement** has been activated (only if it is a big deal, that is, with an amount greater than $1 million).

Let's see how to create such a process using Process Builder.

Creating a new process

To create a new process, go to **Setup | Process Automation | Process Builder** and click the **New** button:

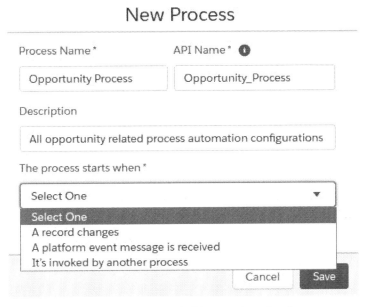

Figure 9.1 – Process Builder creation wizard

The **The process starts when** * picklist defines the target of the new process, which can be the following:

- **A record changes**: The target is a Salesforce object that is created/updated.

- **A platform event message is received**: The target is a **Platform Event** that is received by the Salesforce platform (it can be originated from within the CRM or from an external system).

- **It's invoked by another process**: The triggering event is another process; you are creating a so-called **Invocable Process**.

We want to deal with the Opportunity object, so select **A record changes**; click **Save** to jump to the Process Builder editing app:

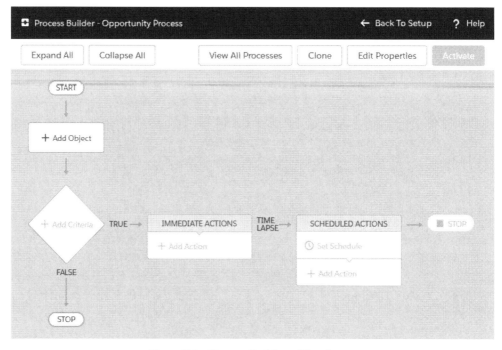

Figure 9.2 – Process Builder editing frame

The previous screenshot shows how a process is shaped, and it contains the following:

- **Trigger** shaped with the **+ Add Object** button, which defines the kind of Salesforce object we want to deal with (available only if we selected the **A record changes** value when creating the process). If you selected **A platform event message is received**, you would have selected a specific Platform Event, otherwise, for **Invocable Processes**, this configuration is not shown.

- **Criteria**, aka the conditions that will execute all actions (you can add more than one criterion with the **+ Add Criteria** button). You can configure criteria to the only criteria evaluated or, after a set of actions are executed, you can *jump* to the next criteria defined.

- **Immediate Actions**: as we've seen with Workflow Rules, you can attach actions that can be executed immediately, configured with the **+ Add Action** button.

- **Scheduled Actions**, which, like workflow rules, are actions executed based on a time-dependent trigger (given a specific date/time field).

Let's define when the process is fired.

Defining the trigger

1. To define the triggering entity (in our scenario, a Salesforce object), click on the +
   Add Object button:

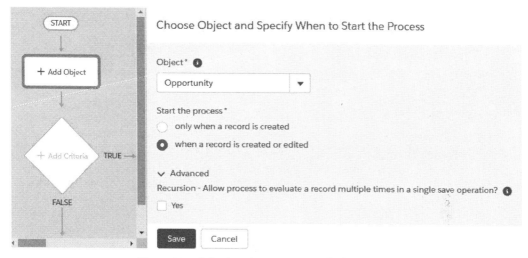

Figure 9.3 – Selecting the triggering Salesforce object

2. Select the **Opportunity** object in the **Object** * picklist and select **when a record
   is created or edited** from the **Start the process** * radio group (select **only when a
   record is created** if you only want to trigger the process when the record is created).

3. In addition, you can select the **Advanced/Recursion** option if you want the process
   to be evaluated more than once (up to 5 times) per save operation: this can be useful
   if you plan to update the same record in the process' actions and, after this update,
   you still want to re-evaluate the process criteria to execute some more actions (this
   can be quite useful in the eventuality that you are correctly configuring only one
   process per object).

> **Tip**
> Each time a *recursive* process is executed, the record is evaluated with the new
> values coming from the previous process execution.

Remember that once the trigger box is set up, you won't be able to change it.

> **Further reading**
>
> We won't cover processes created on Platform Events: refer to Salesforce Help
> at `https://developer.salesforce.com/docs/atlas.en-`
> `us.platform_events.meta/platform_events/platform_`
> `events_subscribe_process.htm`.

Now that we know how to define the different triggering conditions, let's go back to our example and define the criteria.

Defining the criteria

The process is quite simple:

1. Click the + **Add Criteria** button and select the following configuration:

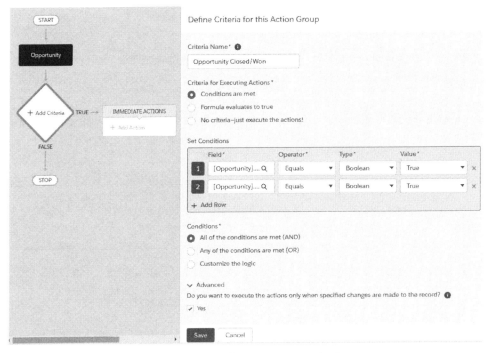

Figure 9.4 – Configuring process criteria

2. The criteria can be set up (as in the previous screenshot) with a list of conditions by selecting **Conditions are met** for the **Criteria for Executing Actions*** radio group or using a formula with **Formula evaluates to true** or with no conditions at all (selecting **No criteria–just execute the actions**).

3. On the **Set Conditions** tab, select the fields we want to add to the criteria. We want to identify the opportunity that we are closing won:

    Unlike workflow rules, you can reference any related object field, as shown in the following screenshot:

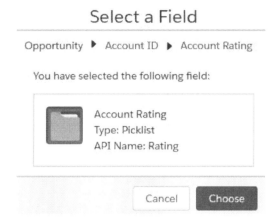

Figure 9.5 – Selecting any related object's field on the process criteria conditions

4. For each field, select an **Operator** (such as Equals, Does not Equal, Is Null, Is changed, and many more depending on the field type), a **Type** (Boolean in our scenario or any other type based on the selected field, or Field Reference if you want to check a value against another field of the **Opportunity** or any other related object's field, or Formula if you want to check against a formula that you create by yourself).

In our example, we can also select whether the items in **Set Conditions** that compose the criteria must be evaluated in **AND**, **OR**, or with custom logic. The previous condition could be written using formulas as shown here (the decision is up to you):

Figure 9.6 – Defining criteria with a formula

Formulas in Process Builder are slightly different from what you are used to, but you'll get used to them quite quickly (use the **Insert:** section to help you learn the new syntax).

5. Finally, the **Advanced** section, if checked, is used to allow action execution only if the fields referred to in the criteria have changed (this is needed to avoid recurrent actions being executed on subsequent record updates).

In our scenario, the actions will be executed only the first time the Opportunity is **closed and won** (so **Do you want to execute the actions only when specified changes are made to the record?** is checked). This way, if the opportunity is saved again, the corresponding actions won't fire again unless the fields used in the conditions change their values and match the criteria.

6. Let's add another criterion (use the same **+ Add Criteria** button) that we will be relating to the opportunity amount also.

    Name it **Big Deal** and use the following formula to set its criteria:

```
AND (
    [Opportunity].Amount >= 1000000,
    [Opportunity].IsWon = true,
    [Opportunity].IsClosed = true
)
```

Click **Save** to save the new criteria. This is what you get as of this step:

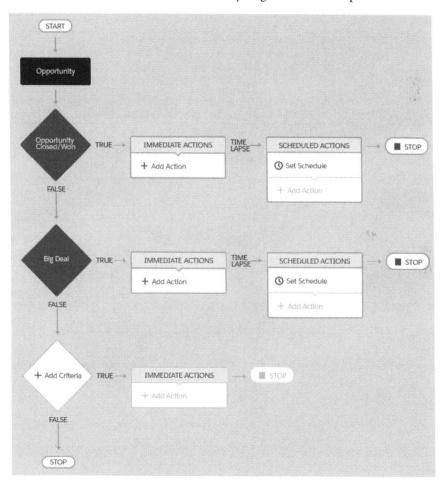

Figure 9.7 – Process with criteria configured

So far, neither criterion will execute any actions. We'll set up actions in the next section.

Another configuration that's useful to note is that you can configure each criteria branch to continue to the next criteria evaluation. This is available only when you have more than one criterion defined and only on branches that have criteria siblings, such as our **Opportunity Closed/Won** branch. Simply click the **Stop** button to open up the set:

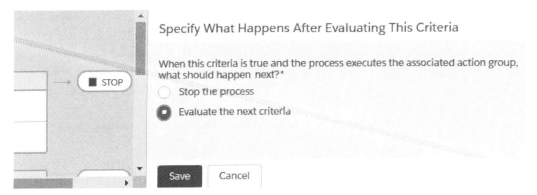

Figure 9.8 – Configuring what happens after a criteria evaluation is completed

Once saved, the branch changes like this:

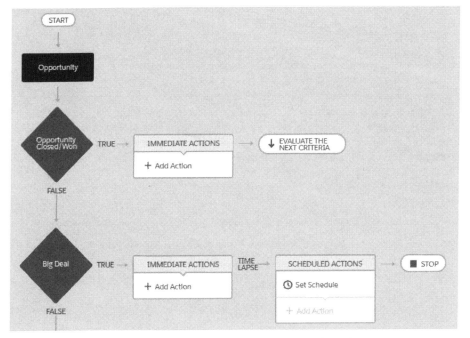

Figure 9.9 – Chaining up subsequent criteria branches

As you can see, the **Scheduled Actions** box has just disappeared, so with this configuration, you won't be able to define time-dependent actions for that branch.

Let's now define some actions.

Defining action groups

So far, the process we have created only evaluates two different criteria, but nothing is done if either of them is matched.

Action groups are nothing more than a group of actions executed in sequence in a given time frame and from given criteria.

We've seen that we can have **Immediate** and **Scheduled** actions, where the first group is executed immediately while the latter is executed after a given amount of time.

In the next sections, we'll see how to configure our actions and add some of them in our example. We'll briefly also see scheduled actions in the last section.

To create a new action, click on the **+ Add Action** button and select one of the available actions. Let's see all of them in the following sections, and start with the **Create a record** action.

Creating a record

To create a new record, choose the **Opportunity Closed/Won** branch and follow these steps:

1. Select the **Create a record** action type.

2. Set up an action name (`Create a new advertisement`).

3. Select the Salesforce object (`Advertisement`).

4. Select all the fields you want to set up on the new object (the mandatory fields will be automatically shown):

- **Customer | Field Reference | [Opportunity].AccountId**

- **Deal | Field Reference | [Opportunity].Id**

- **Installation Country | Field Reference | [Opportunity].Account. ShippingCountry**

- **Installation Address | Formula | [Opportunity].Account.ShippingStreet + ', '
  + [Opportunity].Account.ShippingCity + BR()
  + [Opportunity].Account.ShippingPostalCode
  + ' (' +[Opportunity].Account.ShippingState +')'**

- **Is Active | Boolean | false**

- **Owner ID | Field Reference | [Opportunity].OwnerId**

- **Price | Field Reference | [Opportunity].Amount**

- **Discount | Number | 0**

This is shown in the following screenshot:

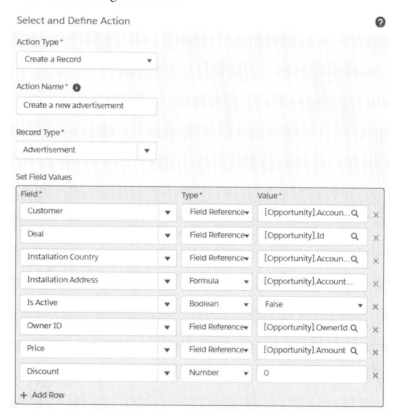

Figure 9.10 – Creating a new Create a record action

With this configuration, when a new deal is closed/won, a new advertisement record is created with fields coming from the **Opportunity** record and the related **Account** record.

Let's see how to update records.

Updating records

With this special kind of action, we can update the following:

- The same record that triggered the process (Opportunity)

- Any parent record related to a lookup or a master detail (for example, the Account related to the Opportunity)

- Any child record of the current object or any related parent object (for example, **Opportunity Products** or a **Contact** of the **Opportunity's Account**)

Now let's follow these steps:

1. Choose the **Big Deal** branch and select the **Update records** type.

2. Provide an action name (`Mark "Hot" Account`).

3. Click on the **Record Type** * search box and select the **Select a record related to the Opportunity** option and look for the **Account ID** relationship to select the Account record:

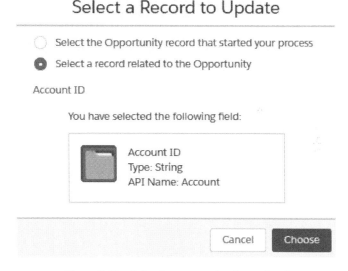

Figure 9.11 – Selecting a record to be updated

4. In the **Criteria for Updating Records** * section, leave it as **No criteria–just update the records!**.

5. Select the fields you want to update – **Account Rating | Picklist |Hot**:

Figure 9.12 – Setting up the Update records action

6. We can use the **Update records** action to update more than one record, such as all the cases related to an account (which is related to the **Opportunity**).

7. Create a new action on the **Big Deal** branch and select [Opportunity].
    Account.Cases on the **Record Type**, as shown here:

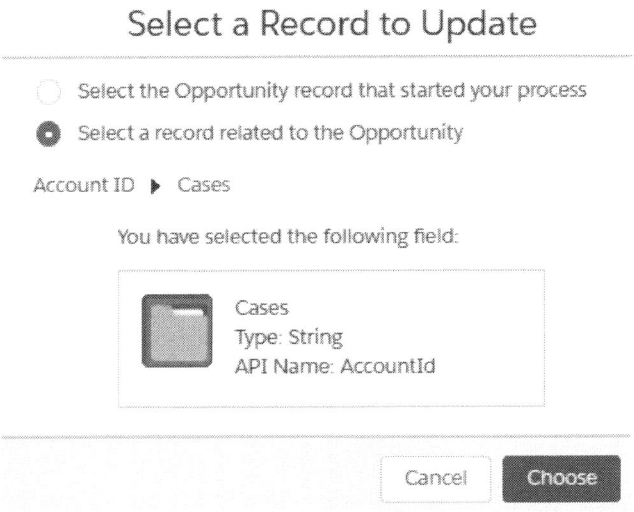

Select a Record to Update

○ Select the Opportunity record that started your process

● Select a record related to the Opportunity

Account ID ▶ Cases

You have selected the following field:

Cases
Type: String
API Name: AccountId

Cancel   Choose

Figure 9.13 – Selecting related children records to be updated

8. As we don't want to update all cases related to the Account record (related to the triggering Opportunity record), click **Updated records meet all conditions** on the **Criteria for Updating Records** * group and indicate that you want all open cases: **Closed | Equals | Boolean | False**.

9. Then, in the **Set new field values for the records you update** section, select the new field values for the cases: **Priority | Picklist | High**.

All should be set up as in the following screenshot:

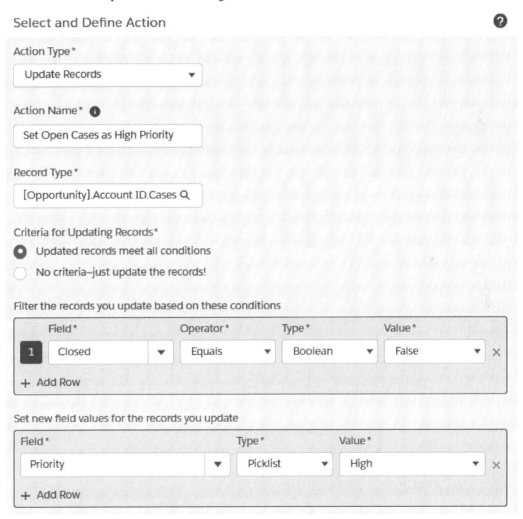

Figure 9.14 – Setting up a multi-record update

So far, this is what you should see in Process Builder:

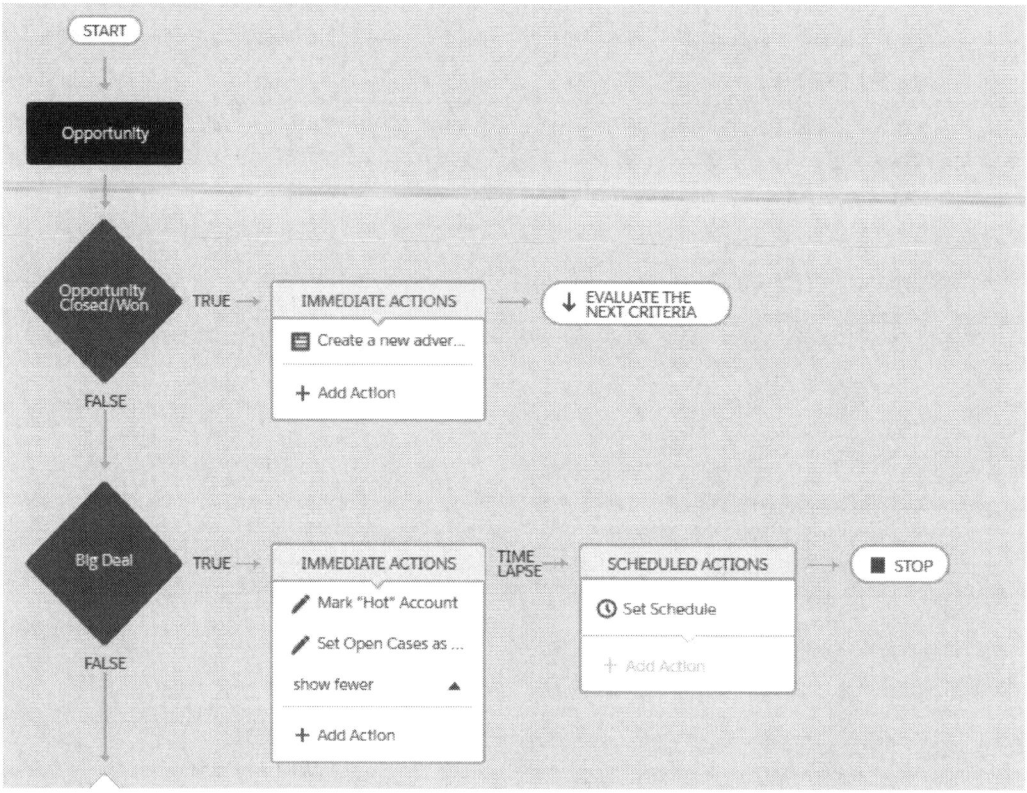

Figure 9.15 – Process Builder configuration after the creation of three actions

Let's now see how to call a process from within a process.

Process

You can define a process to invoke an invocable process (it is a child process).

The actions we have in the **Big Deal** criteria so far can be put in an **Invocable Process** with the following configuration:

- **Process Type**: **It's invoked by another process**
- **Trigger object**: **Account**
- **Criteria**: One simple criterion called **All Accounts** with no actual criteria (select the **No criteria—just execute the actions!** criteria type)
- **Actions**: The same **Mark "Hot" Account** and **Set Open Cases as High Priority** options we configured in the **Big Deal** brand.

This should be what you end up with:

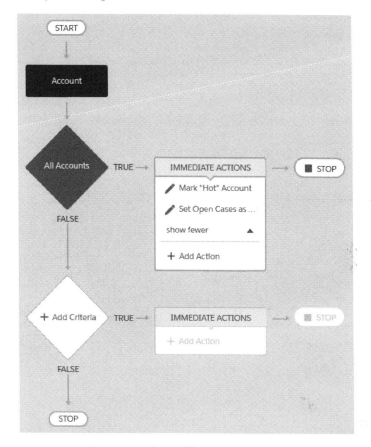

Figure 9.16 – Invocable process definition

We can then transform our *master* process to accommodate our new invocable process:

1. Click the **Activate** button and **Confirm** to *freeze* the new invocable process (every configuration is now grayed out until you deactivate it again).

    This process is now available to be called from another process.

2. Let's remove the immediate actions on the **Big Deal** branch (simply select an action and click the bottom **Delete** button on the action editor).

3. Click again on the + **Add Action** on the immediate actions box of the **Big Deal** branch.

4. Select **Processes** from the **Action Type** picklist.

5. Fill in **Action Name** (`Update Hot Account`).

6. Select the **Hot Account Process** process.

7. Select the related Account object you want to start the invocable process with (`[Opportunity.AccountId]`):

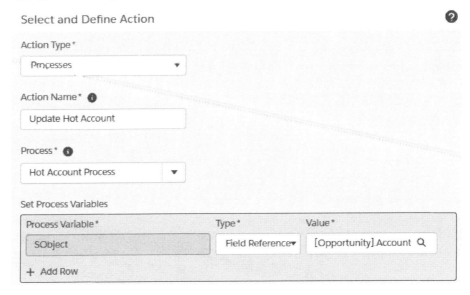

Figure 9.17 – Configuring an invocable process action

In the next section, we'll see the Chatter action to post to Chatter using processes.

Posting to Chatter

Chatter is the Salesforce collaboration tool built into the platform, where all users can collaborate while working on the dataset of your CRM. Chatter is automatically enabled on your org if created after June 10, 2010.

> **Further reading**
>
> Find out what Chatter is and how it can enhance your users' daily jobs on Salesforce Help at `https://help.salesforce.com/articleView?id=collab_setting_up.htm&type=5`.
>
> Trailhead can be found at `https://trailhead.salesforce.com/en/content/learn/modules/lex_implementation_chatter`.

We'll be posting a message on the Account record to Chatter, saying that the current user has just closed a deal.

On the **Opportunity Closed/Won** branch, create a new action:

1. Select the **Post to Chatter** action type.

2. Fill in the name field (`Post on Opportunity`).

3. Set the **Post To*** field to `This Record` (you can choose to post to a specific user or a Chatter group).

4. Write the message (you can use merge fields or tagging using the @ character) as in the following example:

```
The opportunity with amount {![Opportunity].Amount} has
been closed on {![Opportunity].LastModifiedDate} by @[ {!
[Opportunity].OwnerId} ]
fyi @[Stefano Lavori]
```

In this example, we have put two merge fields (the amount and the last modified date of the opportunity object) and two user tags (one explicit for `Stefano Lavori` and one dynamic based on the owner of the opportunity, using the `@[ {!fieldReference} ]` format).

Let's now have a look at custom notification triggering using an action.

Custom notifications

Custom notifications are a new way to set notifications on the CRM introduced in the *Summer 2019 release*. To create a new custom notification, jump to **Setup | Notification Builder | Custom Notifications**, and then click the **New** button:

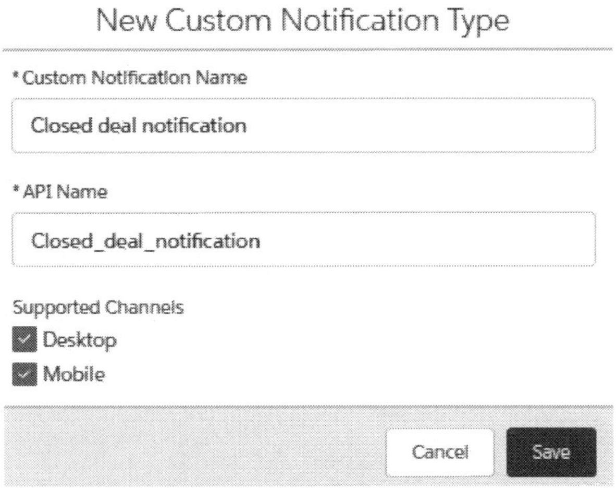

New Custom Notification Type

*Custom Notification Name

Closed deal notification

*API Name

Closed_deal_notification

Supported Channels

☑ Desktop

☑ Mobile

Cancel   Save

Figure 9.18 – Setting up a new custom notification

You can enable mobile or desktop channels so the notification can be shared across channels.

The notification should be sent to the CEO user when a big deal (that is, an amount greater than $1 million) is closed.

Click **+ Add Action** on the **Big Deal** branch and follow these steps:

1. Select **Send Custom Notification** as **Action Type**.

2. Provide an action name (`Notify CEO`).

3. Select the notification type (`Closed Deal Notification`, created earlier).

4. Select a recipient (`User`, but you can even select groups, queues, or the record's owner) and set it to a specific user (the CEO user).

5. Finally, set up a title and body using merge fields as in the following example:

Figure 9.19 – Configuring a custom notification action

We'll see the output of this notification shortly, but before that, we'll dig into scheduled actions.

This time-dependent option is available only when the **Start the Process** configuration is set to the following:

- **Only when a record is created**

- **When a record is created or edited** and the criteria advanced option **Do you want to execute the actions only when specified changes are made to the record?** are checked

In our example, we have a requirement to send an email notification to the owner of the opportunity (with an amount greater than $1 million) *after 7 days* of the execution date.

Click on the **Set Schedule** button on the **Scheduled Actions** box on the **Big Deal** branch and configure it as follows:

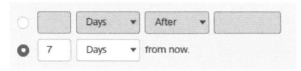

Figure 9.20 – Setting up a scheduled action group

You could have used the first option, using a specific field to calculate the scheduled run, or used hours instead of days: remember that you cannot run in the past.

> **Note**
>
> If the scheduled time is less than now – so it is set in the past, the action is executed as soon as possible.

The Process Builder display has changed:

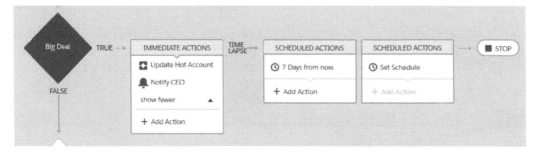

Figure 9.21 – SCHEDULED ACTION group multiple configurations

Indeed, you can add other scheduled actions in the same branch, providing different schedules for the same action.

> **Further reading**
>
> For more info about scheduled actions and their limits, refer to Salesforce Help at `https://help.salesforce.com/articleView?id=process_limits_scheduled_processing.htm&type=5`.

Let's now see how to send emails using Process Builder.

Email alerts

Just like workflow rules, we can add an email notification to a process.

As per our example, we want to send an email notification to the owner of the opportunity (the big deal) *after 7 days* of the execution date, to check whether the **Advertisement** has been activated.

Click + **Add Action** on the **Big Deal** branch on the first **Scheduled Actions** box:

1. Select **Email Alerts** for the action type.

2. Fill in the name (`Advertisement Activation Email`).

3. Select an email alert (we created a simple email alert called **Advertisement Activation Email** with a reference to the **Opportunity**, just as we did in *Chapter 7, Be a Workflow Champion*).

This is what your figuration would be:

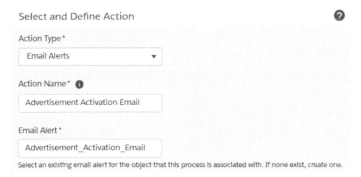

Figure 9.22 – Email alert configuration

With Process Builder, we can activate actions to trigger approval processes.

Submitting for approval

As we saw in the previous chapter about approvals, you can use a process to automatically submit a record for approval.

While our example doesn't take into account approvals, as an exercise, we can build a simple process to automate **Advertisement Discounts** approval, so that it's not up to the user to submit a record for approval.

Create a new process with the following configurations:

1. Add a **Trigger** on the **Advertisement** object.

2. Add a criterion based on the **Discount** field change.

> **Tip**
> Check only discounts that are greater than 0 operators in the **Set Conditions** section and select the **Advanced** checkbox.

3. Add a new **Submit for Approval** action named **Submit Discount Approval** with the following setup:

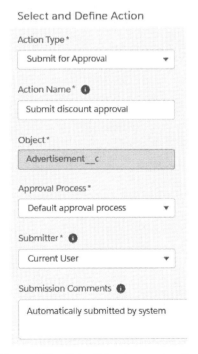

Figure 9.23 – Submit for Approval action

4. Now activate the process with the **Activate** button and create a new advertisement with a big discount (for example, 40%) using one of your test users (mine was **Guglielmo Portoni**): upon record save, it should be automatically submitted for approval.

You can see in **Discount Status** that it is automatically set to **Approval Requested** (as per our approval configuration) and, in the **Advertisements Approval History**, you can see the approval history items with the prior submission comment:

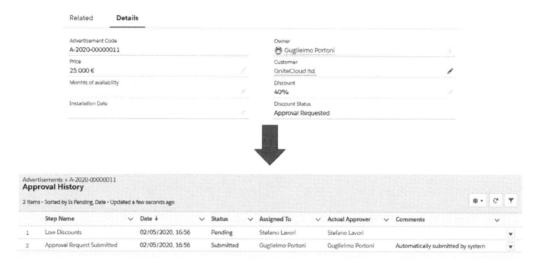

Figure 9.24 – Submit for Approval action after running

Let's briefly see the last available actions with Process Builder.

Flow, Quick Action, and Apex actions

A process can execute the following actions:

*   **Flow**: A feature we'll be covering in the next chapter, flows are used to deliver potentially complex automations. Just as we've seen with processes, a process can trigger a flow of the *auto-launched* type.

*   **Quick Action**: We'll see quick actions in *Chapter 11*, *Interacting with Actions* of the *Automation Tools* section of the book; a process can trigger a quick action (that creates or updates a record only), more or less how it is done with an update record action. The main difference is that the quick action defines the fields (and their default values) that should be filled in the creating/updating record.

- **Quip**: Interact with the Quip document collaboration service (`www.quip.com`) using your Salesforce data (for example, create a new document, chat with quip users).

> **Further reading**
>
> For more info about using Quip, refer to Salesforce Help at `https://help.salesforce.com/articleView?id=process_action_quip.htm&type=5`.

- **Apex**: When you need stronger automation, you can count on Apex code.

> **Further reading**
>
> For more information about calling Apex from a process, refer to Salesforce Help at `https://help.salesforce.com/articleView?id=process_action_apex.htm&type=5`.

Let's now wrap up everything we have shown so far with a cool example.

Wrapping up the example

Throughout our learning, we've put in place our requirements for the **Opportunity** automation, reported as follows. When an Opportunity record is closed and won, it must do the following:

1. Create a new advertisement record with the details coming from the Opportunity record and related objects (*create a record action*).

2. Update the Account record if the deal amount is greater than $1 million, setting the **Rating** field to Hot and all related open cases should be set to High priority (*update records actions*).

3. Create a Chatter notification on the Opportunity record to recap the closure (*post to chatter action*).

4. Send a custom notification to the CEO user notifying them of a closed opportunity only if the amount is greater than $1 million (**Post to chatter Action**).

5. Send an email notification to the owner of the opportunity 7 days after the execution date to check whether the Advertisement has been activated (only if it is a big deal, that is, with an amount greater than $1 million). (*Email alert action with scheduled action.*)

If you haven't done so yet, activate the opportunity process with the **Activate** button. This is how your process' final configuration should look:

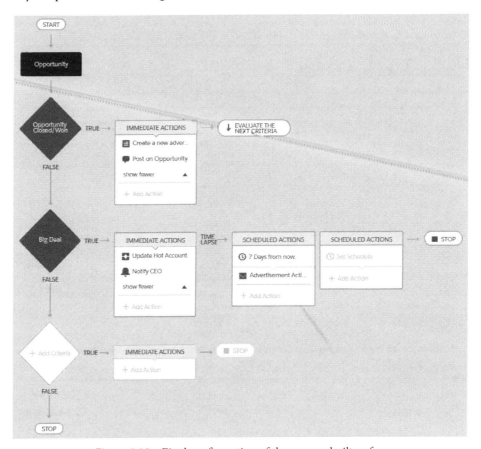

Figure 9.25 – Final configuration of the process built so far

Now, choose an Account record whose **Rating** field is not set to Hot and that has at least one open case with low or medium **Priority**, as shown here:

Account
Burlington Textiles Corp of America
Type
Customer - Direct
Phone
(336) 222-7000
Website
www.burlington.com
Account Owner
Enrico ...
Account Site
Industry
Apparel
Related
Details
News
Account Owner
Enrico Murru
Rating
Warm
Account Name
Burlington Textiles Corp of America
(336) 222-7000
Cases (2)
New
00001019
Contact Name: Jack Rogers
Subject: Structural failure of generator base
Priority: Low
00001020
Contact Name: Jack Rogers
Subject: Power generation below stated level
Priority: Medium
View All

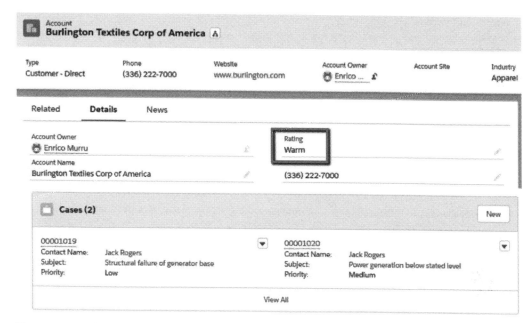

Figure 9.26 – Selecting an Account with a Warm rating and two open cases without priority set to High

Make sure that the account has a compiled shipping address.

Now create a brand new opportunity with an amount greater than $1 million on that account (but don't close it yet):

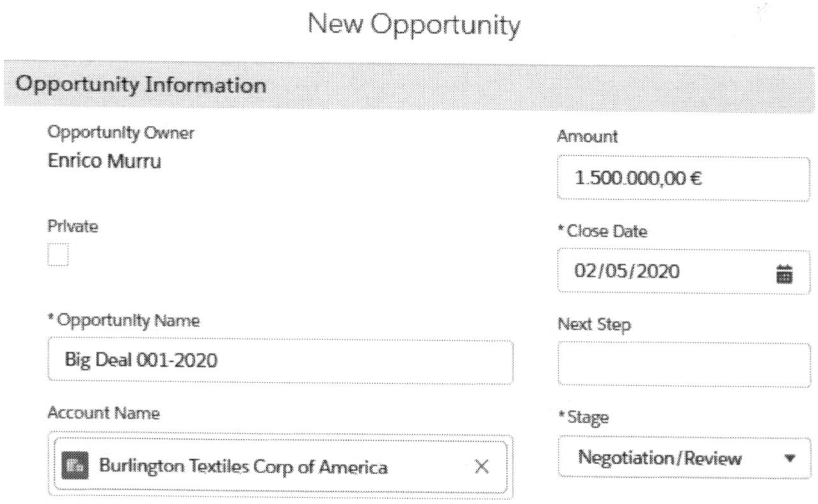

New Opportunity
Opportunity Information
Opportunity Owner
Enrico Murru
Amount
1.500.000,00 €
Private
*Close Date
02/05/2020
*Opportunity Name
Big Deal 001-2020
Next Step
Account Name
Burlington Textiles Corp of America
*Stage
Negotiation/Review

Figure 9.27 – Creating a new opportunity that will trigger the process

If you didn't choose the **Closed Won** stage name, the process won't have run (remember the criteria about **Closed** and **Is Won** on the opportunity).

Now close the opportunity (update the **Stage** field to Closed Won). Chances are that you will be getting an error because of the **Advertisement Approval** process we created earlier: this may be caused by the fact that you are using the CEO user, which doesn't have a manager and the approval process fails. Simply deactivate the Advertisement Approval process or add more criteria definitions on that process to avoid this error (it is up to you to take the challenge!).

If everything went as expected, you should see the following:

1. A new advertisement record on the related list of the **Opportunity** with the fields we set up:

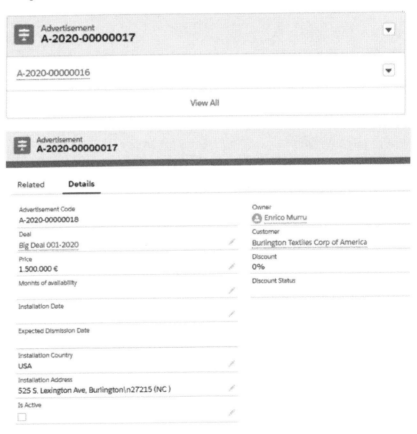

Figure 9.28 – The new advertisement record on the opportunity's related list

2. A Chatter message on the Opportunity record:

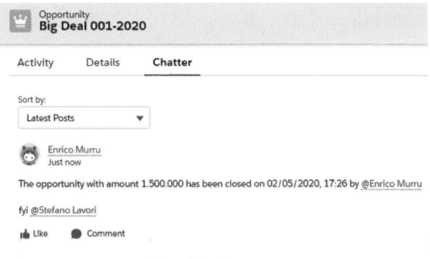

Figure 9.29 – Chatter pot

3. The account set to the **Hot** rating:

Figure 9.30 – Account Rating updated

4. All related cases set to **High** priority:

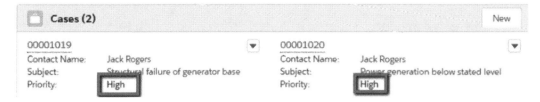

Figure 9.31 – Open child cases' Priority updated

5. A custom notification is shown to the CO user in the upper-right corner:

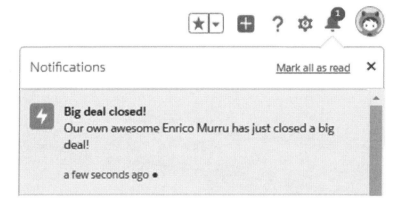

Figure 9.32 – Custom notification sent to the CEO user

What about the email notification 7 days after process execution?

You'll receive the notification email in 7 days as promised (unless the conditions on the criteria change). You'll be able to have a look at all the pending processes from **Setup | Process Automation | Paused Flow Interviews**, as pictured here:

Figure 9.33 – Queue of processes waiting for scheduled action execution

Before closing the chapter, let's talk about basic process management features.

Managing processes

A process can have two different statuses:

- Inactive

- Active

If you find a bug on an active process or simply need to add/change an action or criteria, you need to clone it to update any part of it using the **Clone** button on the Process Builder main window, and then activate it again to make it run.

When you clone a new process, you can create a brand new process or simply create a new version of the process, like here:

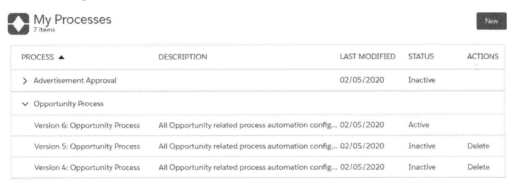

Figure 9.34 – Process version listing

> **Tip**
> You can have up to 50 versions of a given process but only 1 version active at a time.

For more of a deep dive into Process Builder considerations and limits, refer to Salesforce Help at `https://help.salesforce.com/articleView?id=process_considerations.htm&type=5`.

Blaze your trail

To enhance your knowledge, check the following Trailhead modules:

- Lightning Flow: `https://trailhead.salesforce.com/en/content/learn/modules/business_process_automation`

- Workflow Rule Migration: `https://trailhead.salesforce.com/en/content/learn/modules/workflow_migration`

- Quick Start – Process Builder: `https://trailhead.salesforce.com/en/content/learn/projects/quickstart-process-builder`

- Automate Business Processes for a Recruiting App: `https://trailhead.salesforce.com/en/content/learn/projects/automate-business-processes-recruiting-app`

- Improve Data Quality for Your Sales and Support Teams: `https://trailhead.salesforce.com/en/content/learn/projects/improve-data-quality-for-a-cleaning-supply-app`

- Lightning Flow for Service: `https://trailhead.salesforce.com/en/content/learn/modules/service_lightning_flow_for_service`

Summary

In this chapter, we've learned all about Process Builder and how to build flows to enhance our business process automations with more possibilities than the ones provided by workflow rules, such as cross-object criteria definitions, record creation, different ways to send notifications with email alerts, Chatter posts and custom notifications, automatic approval process execution, parent and child record updates, and even triggering invocable processes to simplify our process management.

Except for Lightning Flows, which we'll be covering in the next chapter, Process Builder grants advanced automation features have been explained in this chapter. With Process Builder, you should be able to implement most process automation scenarios. Experience and deep knowledge of all available tools will make you aware of the best uses for Process Builder in your daily work as a Salesforce *devmin*. In the next chapter, we'll have a look at another tool to build even more complex automation scenarios, thanks to Flows.

10
Designing Lightning Flows

If you need complex automation and you are out of developers, Lightning Flow is what you need.

In this chapter, we will see how, with flows, you can build wizards with a click of your mouse, getting data from users and executing all sorts of database operations. You can also use flows to create automated algorithms (that don't require user interaction) to add more possibilities and enhance your Process Builder configurations.

In this chapter, we'll learn the following:

- How a flow is shaped and how to use Flow Builder
- How to build a screen flow with a complex example
- How to build a simple auto-launched flow to be executed from Process Builder
- How to manage flows

Shaping a flow

With great power comes great responsibilities! We are not superheroes (even if we can be trailblazers), but powerful point and click tools such as Lightning Flow can lead you to madness if you don't take your time to design them properly.

The following diagram shows an example flow that we are going to build:

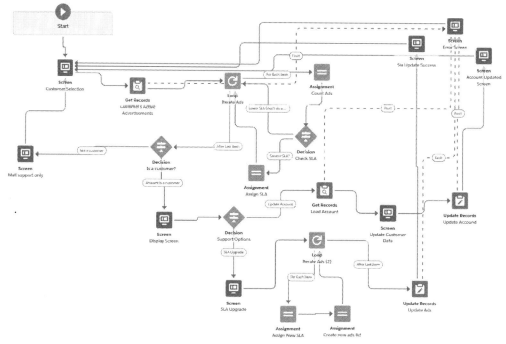

Figure 10.1 – Example flow complexity

What is the use case covered in this complex flow definition?

This flow is used to cover some basic customer service management by performing the following actions, which gives an overall idea of the diagram:

1.   Search for a customer's account.

2.   Check whether it has related advertisement records.

3.   Calculate the customer's **Service Level Agreement** (**SLA**) depending on all advertisement SLA definitions (a new custom field added to the Advertisement object used to state the SLA for the specific advertisement installment).

4.   If the customer doesn't have active ads, they are only given email support.

5.   If the customer has active ads, the user can do two different service actions, either upgrade SLAs on all advertisements or update address and phone data on the Account record.

The five steps are covered in more or less 20 flow blocks. Even now that I have built this example, if I have to change some of its parts, I may get something wrong.

This is the power of flows—so much automation power with such potentially high complexity.

Let's start building our flow, as we have all of the requirements in the previous list:

1. Before starting, create a new custom field named `SLA__c` of the picklist type on the **Advertisement__c** custom object and give it the following values:

*   **Gold**
*   **Silver**
*   **Copper**

2. Then, create some active Advertisement records and assign a value to the SLA field, shown as follows:

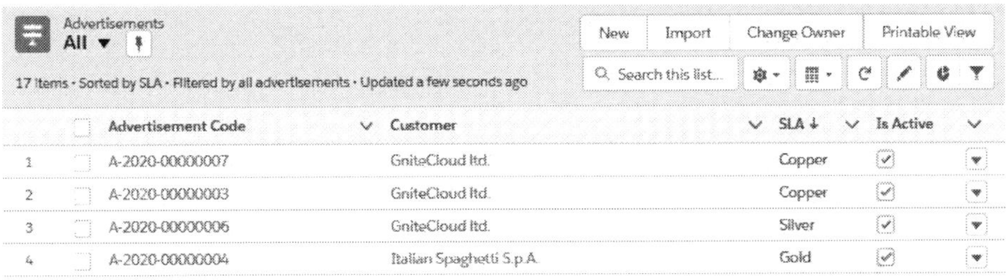

Figure 10.2 – List of Advertisement records with the SLA field filled in

The idea is to create a quick support component to be added on the Home tab of the Adv. Division Lightning app, where the user can do some quick customer-related support on the fly, shown as follows:

Figure 10.3 – The Flow included in the Home tab of a Lightning app

> **Note**
>
> You won't master Flows with this chapter—you'll need some more reading and a lot of trial and error. Review all available guides on the Salesforce Help starting from: `https://help.salesforce.com/articleView?id=flow.htm&type=0`.

Now that we know what we are going to build, let's build it!

Building a flow

To create a new Flow, we need to click on **Setup | Process Automation | Flows** and then the **New Flow** button to jump to Flow Builder—the live point and click Editor to build flows. The New Flow wizard starts with flow type selection:

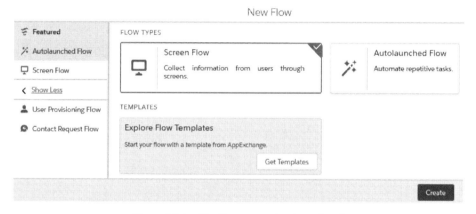

Figure 10.4 – The flow type selection wizard

As briefly shown in the preceding screenshot, we can use the following different kinds of flows:

- **Screen Flow**: Users can interact with forms so the automation can grab data from them.

- **Autolaunched Flow**: No user interaction is required; these flows are used to create complex automation that is not possible using other automation tools such as Process Builder or Workflows.

There are other kinds of flow types available, but there is a 99% chance you'll need these two only in your developments (at least until things don't become a lot more advanced).

Further reading

For a detailed list of flow types, refer to Salesforce Help at `https://help.salesforce.com/articleView?id=flow_concepts_type.htm&type=0`.

You can also install Flows from the AppExchange by clicking the **Get Templates** button on the flow creation wizard or by jumping to `https://appexchange.salesforce.com/appxStore?type=Flow`.

For now, let's choose the Screen Flow type and click the Create button to land on Flow Builder:

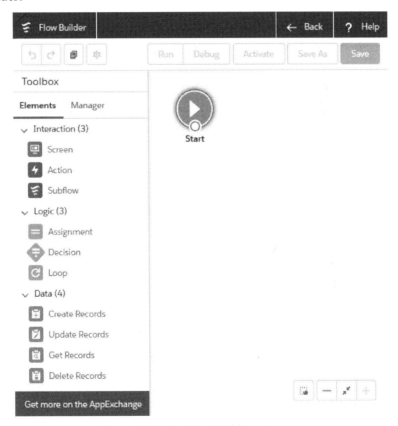

Figure 10.5 – The Flow Builder main page

The Toolbox contains all the things that make up a flow, which is segregated into Elements and Manager.

Elements are all available boxes that can be added to create the automation.

As you can see in *Figure 10.5*, under **Elements**, we have the following:

- **Interaction** elements: They are used to interact with the user with a form (**Screen**), execute an **Action** (such as sending an email or a custom notification or even creating a record with **Quick Actions**, just like we've seen in Process Builder), or call a **Subflow** (like in Process Builder, you can build a flow to be called by another flow).

- **Logic** elements: These items are used to create a **Decisional** node (an IF box), to iterate through items (the **Loop** element can iterate through a collection of records) or **Assignment** of a specific value (changing the address of the **Account** or **Advertisement** SLA needs an Assignment box).

- **Data** elements: These execute all sort of database operations to query, create, update, or delete Salesforce records.

Now we move to **Manager**.

In the following screenshot, we can see the Manager tab with all sorts of resources:

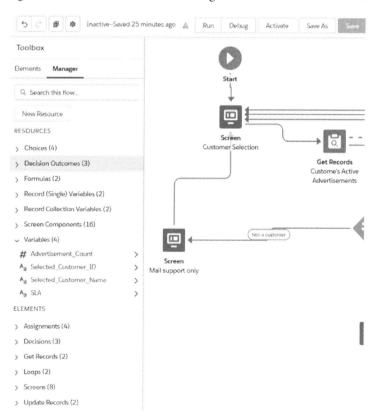

Figure 10.6 – Flow Builder's Manager tab

This tab shows all of the variables that have been defined in the flow, which contain used or calculated data. Everything in a flow is a variable, from a label on a screen element to a list of records retrieved with a query.

From this tab, you'll be able to access anything that is being crafted and configured in the flow, whether they are formulas, constant text values, or labels.

Creating a flow

The first thing we want to do is create a screen for the user to select an account.

Let's drag, from the **Elements** tab, a **Screen** element and drop it on the canvas next to the Start element, then double-click it:

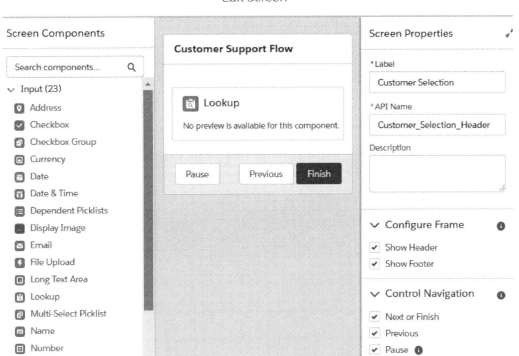

Figure 10.7 – Creating a screen element

A Screen element can contain all sorts of components (take your time to see what's inside the Screen Components list) to interact with the user. Remember to start by setting Label and API Name values for your screen as shown in the previous screenshot.

> **Note**
> It is possible to create custom Lightning components and add them into a flow: so if you need a complex functionality that cannot be supported by standard components, ask your developers to build it. For further reading, jump in to Salesforce Developer Help at `https://developer.salesforce.com/docs/atlas.en-us.lightning.meta/lightning/components_using_flow.htm`.

Each screen component can be configured to show or hide the header (containing the flow title) or the footer (containing the navigation buttons) and to allow some, all, or none of the navigation buttons, as follows:

- **Next** or **Finish**: This is used to continue the flow (this option can be used if your flow is a one-step flow, for example, a flow used to show a list of values coming from different records, but no other action is needed).

- **Previous**: This is used to go back on the previous step (in some cases, it may not be possible or allowed to jump back).

- **Pause**: You can even pause a flow in the middle (for example, the user doesn't have all of the information needed to go on with the process, so they can just put the flow on pause to revive it later on).

The first thing we want to do is give the user a way to quickly search for Accounts, and a lookup field is the best way. Search for **Lookup** from the Screen components and drop it under the Screen header:

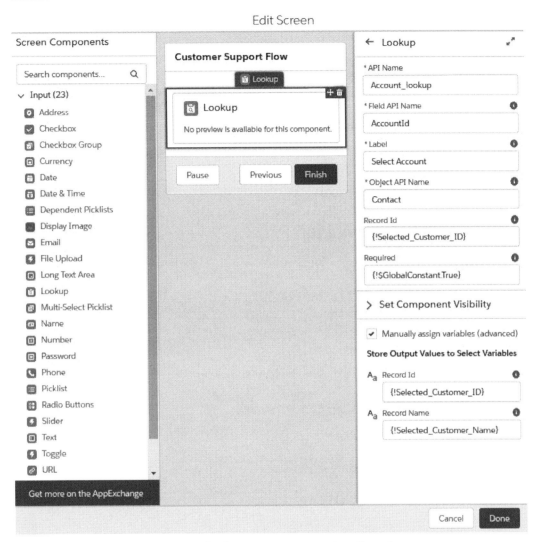

Figure 10.8 – Lookup screen component configuration

The drawback of using this kind of component is that it won't return a record but rather its Salesforce ID. This happens because it should be used to populate an ID field on a lookup/master detail field. That's why, here, we are considering having a fake Contact object with an AccountId field that points to an Account object (as configured on the Field API Name and Object API Name component fields). Simply put, we are using the Contact. AccountId lookup field to get the Salesforce ID of any account on the CRM.

The **Record Id** field is used to give a source value for the lookup (when I open up the screen, you may want to see the lookup already filled in) and if you see the **Record Id** on the **Store Output Values to Select Variables** section, they are configured to match the same variable. That's because we want the lookup to store the Account ID on the same variable that is used to load the Account ID when the screen loads (do you remember the **Previous** button? If we jump back to the **Customer Selection** screen, we'll see the lookup already compiled with the value selected earlier). It is up to you to fill in the **Record Id** field as it is not required.

{!Selected_Customer_ID} and **{!Selected_Customer_Name}** are two resources (variables) that have been created to host the **Account ID** and **Name** values got by the lookup.

Let's see how to build a new resource.

Creating a new resource

To create a new resource on the fly, you can click on the **+ New Resource** option shown when clicking on (almost) any component's configuration field, shown as follows:

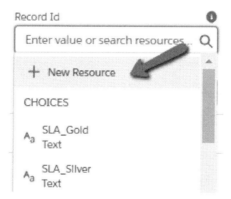

Figure 10.9 – Creating a new resource on the fly

Otherwise, you can click on the **Manager** tab and click the **New Resource** button to create a new variable to store the account's ID and name. Either way, the resource creation wizard is started.

The first thing to select is the variable type:

- **Variable**: This is a value that can be read or written by any flow component (be aware that this value may or may not be tied to an actual Salesforce object, that is, it can be a simple text value).

- **Constant**: This is an invariant value that can be referenced in any flow component (for example, to set a specific default value on a field).

- **Formula**: This builds a formula calculation based on other flow's resources.

- **Text Template**: This is the formatted text.

- Choice: This is an item used when you need to present choices to users (such as with radio buttons or picklists).

- **Record Choice Set**: This is a list of choices coming from a list of Salesforce records (a query is performed).

- **Picklist Choice Set**: This is a list of choices coming from an object's picklist field.

- **Stage**: This defines a user's process throughout the flow execution.

> **Further reading**
>
> For more details about each kind of resource, refer to Salesforce Help at `https://help.salesforce.com/articleView?id=flow_ref_resources.htm&type=5`.

Select **Variable** and compile the fields as shown in the following screenshot:

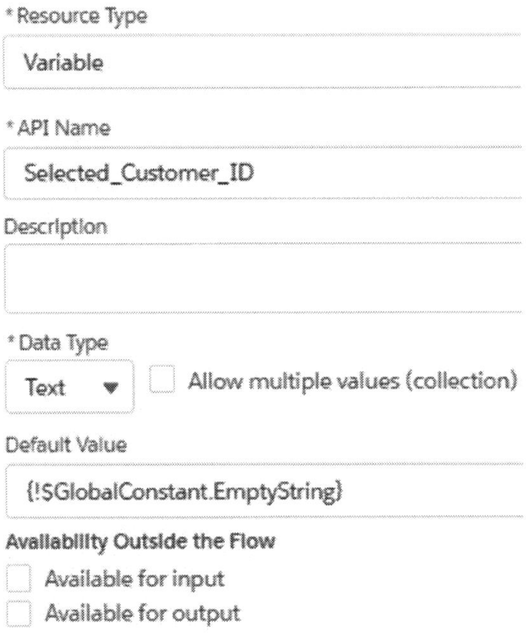

Figure 10.10 – Configuring a text variable

Given the API Name (that we'll be using on the Lookup component), select the **Data Type** (choose **Text**) and give a **Default Value**, selecting **{!$GlobalConstant.EmptyString}** to set the initial value to empty value (there are only three constants, EmptyString and True and False for Boolean values).

> **Tip**
>
> It's always a good practice to default variables with a value, even if it is a blank value; this gives you predictable outcomes when running an automation.

The **Available for input** and **Available for output** checkboxes can be used to expose variables outside of a flow. This is particularly useful when putting flows inside object layouts (so you can configure an ID reference), when using subflows to pass a variable from one flow to another, or when triggering a flow from Process Builder (in case of auto-launched flows), where you need to pass the process' context to the flow.

Save the resource and create another one with the same configuration called **Selected_Customer_Name** to get the account's **Name** value from the Lookup component.

> **Further reading**
>
> We won't cover all kinds of Screen components—check them out on Salesforce Help at `https://help.salesforce.com/articleView?id=flow_ref_elements_screencmp.htm&type=5`.

Save the Screen and let's find out how to connect the new element.

Connecting the elements

To connect the new element so it'll be shown the user when running the flow, drag the Start element to the new screen element to set up your first flow's step:

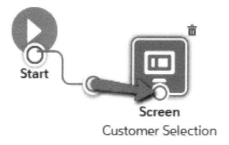

Figure 10.11 – Connect elements by dragging the connection circle

There are different kinds of connectors (we'll see some of them shortly).

> **Further reading**
>
> For a complete list of connectors, refer to Salesforce Help at `https://help.salesforce.com/articleView?id=flow_ref_connectors.htm&type=5`.

Let's keep building the flow by adding some more available elements, such as the **Get Records** element to access records.

Accessing the database with the Get Records element

Take the **Get Records** element from the **Elements** tab and drop it on the canvas. Now that we have a customer, we can check whether it is an active customer (that is, it has active advertisements—remember that the Advertisement object has a lookup to the Account object). Configure the element as follows:

- **Label**: `Customer's Active Advertisement`
- **API Name**: `Customer_Advertisements`
- **Object**: `Advertisement`
- **Conditions Requirements**: `Conditions are met`
- **Field**: `Customer__c`
- **Operator**: `Equals`
- **Value**: `{!Selected_Customer_ID}`

Click the + Add Condition and fill in as follows:

- **Field**: `Is_Active__c`
- **Operator**: `Equals`
- **Value**: `{!$GlobalConstant.True}`

Don't mind the sorting options and be sure to select the following:

- **How Many Records to Store**: `All Records`
- **How to Store Record Data**: **Automatically store all fields**

This is depicted as follows:

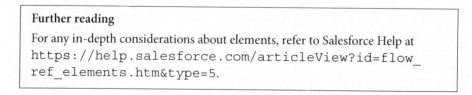

Figure 10.12 – Configuring a Get Records element

This element is simply querying all records of the Advertisement type where the customer lookup is valued with the account selected in the previous step and where the **Is Active** custom field is checked.

> **Further reading**
>
> For any in-depth considerations about elements, refer to Salesforce Help at
> `https://help.salesforce.com/articleView?id=flow_ref_elements.htm&type=5`.

Save the preceding element and link the previous Customer Selection screen element with the Customer's Active Advertisements element, just like we did with the Start element in the previous section.

Now that we have the advertisement records, we need to deduce the following:

- Whether the account is an active customer (that is, it has active advertisements)
- Which is the greater level of SLA between all active advertisements (where Copper < Silver < Gold)

To do this, we can perform the following:

- Iterate through all records (Loop element).
- Count all advertisements by increasing a numeric variable for every advertisement found (Assignment element).
- Store the advertisement SLA on a variable (Assignment) only if the current value is greater than the previous iteration (Decision element).

After this, let's see how to create a **Loop** element.

Adding a Loop element to iterate through records

Let's add the **Loop** element from the **Elements** tab and fill in the following values:

- **Label**: Add `Iterate Ads`.
- **API Name**: Add `Iterate_Ads`.
- **Direction**: This retains the default value (First item to last item).
- **Collection Variable**: Select the **{!Customer_Advertisements}** variable created by the previous Get Records element (its API Name).
- **Loop Variable**: Create a new variable resource called `{!Advertisement_record}` (this is a variable with Data Type valued to Record and Object valued with Advertisement, multiple values not allowed).

Save the element and connect it with the **Customer's Active Advertisements** element. You can see that the **Get Records** connection circle has not disappeared (like it didn't for the previous Screen element):

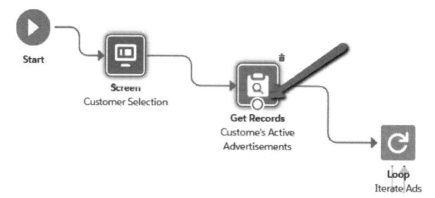

Figure 10.13 – More connections available on the Get Records element

This happens because this element (like all database elements) supports a fault connection if the database operation fails (for example, for an invalid query using bad filtering values or a validation rule that triggers when you try to insert a record using the Create Records element). Let's add a new screen element to support faults.

Adding a default error screen element

We'll be using a simple Screen element to show the error message coming from the faulting flow operation (and that we'll share with the other elements we are about to create) and that is connected with the first screen, so the user can decide to go back from the start:

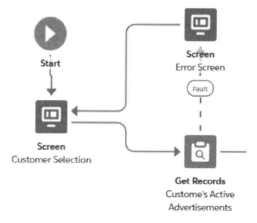

Figure 10.14 – Creating a screen element to show a fault

The screen should simply contain a Display Text component with the following message:

```
Something bad happened:
{!$Flow.FaultMessage}
```

Let's see how to assign variables dynamically inside the Loop element.

Using the Assignment element

Now that we can loop through records, we can do some math by creating a variable and increasing it by a value of 1 for every record found (there is no count element available, unfortunately, that could do this automatically), using a special kind of element called Assignment.

Let's create a new variable resource from the **Manager** tab, filling in the following fields:

- **API Name**: Advertisement_Count
- **Data Type**: Number (no multiple values)
- **Decimal Places**: 0
- **Default Value**: 0

Now that we have the counter variable, let's create a new Assignment element with the following values:

- **Label**: Count Ads
- **API Name**: Count_Ads
- **Variable**: {!Advertisement_Count}
- **Operator**: Add
- **Value**: 1

Yes, we are simply adding 1 to the base value of the Advertisement_Count variable (that we initialized with 0).

Let's connect the **Count Ads** element with the **Iterate Ads** element selecting, when requested, the **For Each Item** connector type (the Loop element delivers two connectors, one for the iteration by passing the iterating element to the flow, and one used when the iteration has completed, called After Last Item).

While iterating, we also want to calculate the highest SLA found on all active advertisements.

First, let's create a new text variable resource where we can store the definitive SLA value:

- **API Name**: SLA
- **Data Type**: Text
- **Default Value**: {!$GlobalConstant.EmptyString}

What we want to do while iterating through the advertisements is to check whether the current value assigned to the SLA variable is lower to the **SLA__c** field value of the current Advertisement record, and if so, then the SLA variable should be set to this value.

Let's say we have four **Advertisement** records on our CRM with the following values for the **SLA__c** field:

- AD0001: **Copper**
- AD0002: **Silver**
- AD0003: **Gold**
- AD0004: **Copper**

Simulating the execution of the loop element through the preceding records, we want to have the following behavior:

- **Loop Element: AD0001, SLA variable: empty, Adv. SLA: Copper, Result: The SLA variable is set to Copper because the empty value is lower than Copper**
- **Loop Element: AD0002, SLA variable: Copper, Adv. SLA: Silver, Result: The SLA variable is set to Silver because the Copper value is lower than Silver**
- **Loop Element: AD0003, SLA variable: Silver, Adv. SLA: Gold, Result: The SLA variable is set to Gold because the Silver value is lower than Gold**
- **Loop Element: AD0004, SLA variable: Gold, Adv. SLA: Copper, Result: The SLA variable is left to Gold because the Gold value is higher than Copper**

We need an easy way to compare the SLA variable and the iterating record **SLA__c** field, which is able to bring values back to a number.

Creating a Formula variable

To compare values on the fly, we can create a Formula resource to map SLA variable values and Advertisement__c.SLA__c values to numbers.

Let's create two Formula resources.

The first resource will have the following values:

- **API Name**: `SLAValue`
- **Data Type**: `Number`
- **Decimal Places**: 0
- **Formula**: `CASE( {!SLA}, 'Gold', 3, 'Silver', 2, 'Copper', 1, 0)`

The second resource will have the following values:

- **API Name**: `TemporaryAdvertisementSLAValue`
- **Data Type**: `Number`
- **Decimal Places**: 0
- **Formula**: `CASE( {!Advertisement_record.SLA__c}, 'Gold', 3, 'Silver', 2, 'Copper', 1, 0)`

Basically, we are giving a number to the SLA values so we can make a decision and decide whether the current looping advertisement has an SLA greater than the one stored on the SLA variable.

Now, we have to create the logic to compare the current advertisement record that we are iterating (saved in the TemporaryAdvertisementSLAValue variable) against the overall variable (SLAValue) that will handle the final SLA value.

Using the Decision element

To implement the compare algorithm, we'll use the Decision element.

Create a **Decision** element by picking it from the **Elements** tab and filling in the following values:

- **Label**: `Check SLA`
- **API Name**: `Check_SLA`

Select the **New Outcome** link and set up the following:

- **Label**: `Greater SLA?`
- **Outcome API Name**: `Greater_SLA`
- **When to Execute Outcome**: **All Conditions Are Met**

- **Resource**: {!TemporaryAdvertisementSLAValue}
- **Operator**: Greater than
- **Value**: {!SLAValue}

Select the **Default Outcome** link and rename it Lower SLA (don't do anything).

What this element does is check whether the TemporaryAdvertisementSLAValue resource (which is a formula based on the current iterating advertisement record) is greater than the SLAValue formula (which is based on the SLA variable where we want to store the highest value of all SLAs).

We are almost there, so don't worry.

Let's create a new **Assignment** element that we need to actually assign the new higher value found, setting the following fields on the element:

- **Label**: Assign SLA
- **API Name**: Assign_SLA
- **Variable**: {!SLA}
- **Operator**: Equals
- **Value**: {!Advertisement_record.SLA__c}

Now, let's join the dots:

1. Connect the Iterate Ads element to the Count Ads element (you should have already done this) using the For Each Item connection.
2. Connect the Count Ads element to the Check SLA element.
3. Connect the Check SLA element to the Assign SLA element using the Greater SLA? connection.
4. Connect the Check SLA element to the Iterate Ads element using the Lower SLA (don't do anything) connection (to continue the iteration).
5. Connect the Assign SLA element to the Iterate Ads element (to continue the iteration).

This is what you should have ended up with so far:

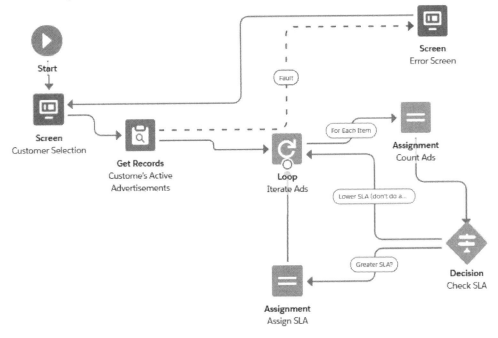

Figure 10.15 – The flow status after the SLA calculation elements are in place

At this point, the flow has calculated the following:

- Whether the customer is an active customer (that is, it has active advertisements, counted in the Advertisement_Count variable)
- What the current SLA level in the SLA variable is

So, first, let's see what happens—if the customer is not active, they are not entitled to live support, so we need to redirect them to email support.

We need another Decision element based on the Advertisement_Count variable:

- **Label**: Is a customer?
- **API Name**: Is_a_customer

Click on the New Outcome and add the following:

- **Label**: Account is a customer
- **Outcome** API Name: Account_is_customer
- **When to Execute Outcome**: All Conditions Are Met

- **Resource**: `{!Advertisement_Count}`
- **Operator**: `Greater Than`
- **Value**: 0

Click on the **Default Outcome** and rename it `Not a customer`.

Let's create a new Screen component called `Mail Support Only` with a simple message displayed below (using a Display Text component):

Figure 10.16– A screen to tell the user that the current customer is not entitled to live support

Connect the **Is a customer?** decision element with the Mail support only element using the **Not a customer** connection and the **Mail support only** element to the **Customer Selection** starting element. This is what we get:

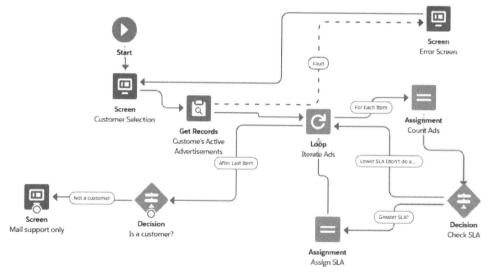

Figure 10.17 – The flow configuration with the customer decisional element

We can now test the flow.

Running a quick flow test

Click on the **Run** button on the upper-left of Flow Builder, and a new tab should open up. Select a customer that you know doesn't have any advertisements and click the **Next** button. You should see the following steps:

Figure 10.18 – Testing out an "inactive" customer

As you can see, the not a customer screen is shown after customer selection and by clicking the **Next** button again, the user is redirected to the first screen with all values already filled in (this is the power of variables).

I guess there is no wow effect here, but this is the power of automation. All of the stuff you needed to configure to make this work is hidden from the user, so their work is way easier!

Remember to hit the **Save** button once in a while. If you see a warning message like the following don't panic, it's just Salesforce telling you that the components and elements you are using may not work when Lightning Experience mode is disabled (Salesforce Classic):

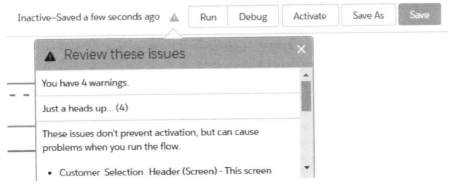

Figure 10.19 – Warning about Lightning Experience only components

Now, let's move a step further.

Adding more steps to support the customer

If the customer is active, we want to provide real live support.

What we want to do is the following:

- Show the customer's name, active advertisements count, and SLA value.
- Display the SLA with three different images (a gold, silver, or copper bar).
- Display a radio group with the following choices: Upgrade SLA and Update customer data.

This is what you'll end up with:

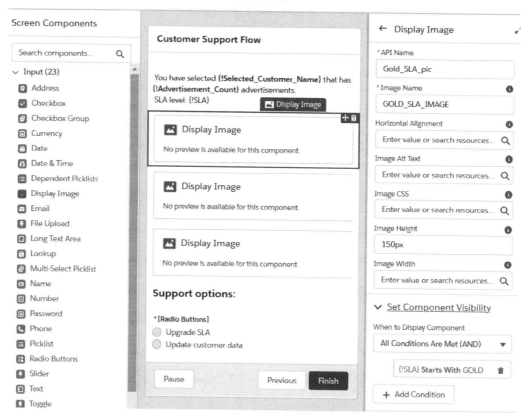

Figure 10.20 – The support screen element

Create a new Screen element named `Customer Support` containing the following components:

- Create one **Display Text** component with the following content:

```
You have selected {!Selected_Customer_Name} that has
{!Advertisement_Count} advertisements.
SLA level: {!SLA}
```

- Create three **Display Image** components.
- Create one **Radio Buttons** component.

Images should be uploaded to your organization from **Setup | Custom Code | Static Resources**. Select three different images that represent the three different SLA values and create three different static resources, like the following ones (their names will be used inside the Display Image components configuration):

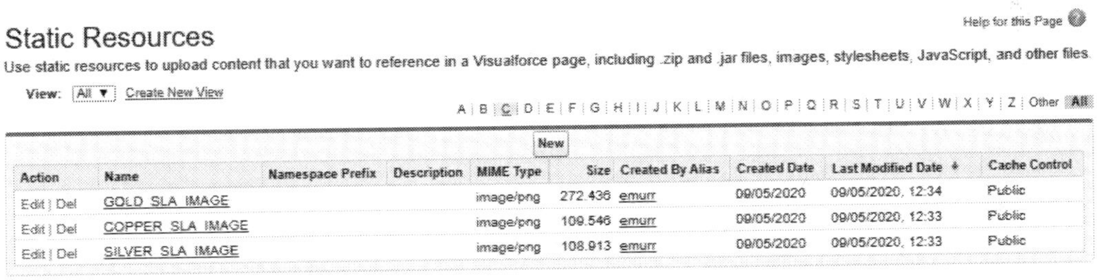

Static Resources

Help for this Page

Use static resources to upload content that you want to reference in a Visualforce page, including .zip and .jar files, images, stylesheets, JavaScript, and other files.

View: All ▼ Create New View

A | B | C | D | E | F | G | H | I | J | K | L | M | N | O | P | Q | R | S | T | U | V | W | X | Y | Z | Other | All

New

Action	Name	Namespace Prefix	Description	MIME Type	Size	Created By Alias	Created Date	Last Modified Date ↓	Cache Control
Edit | Del	GOLD_SLA_IMAGE			image/png	272.436	emurr	09/05/2020	09/05/2020, 12:34	Public
Edit | Del	COPPER_SLA_IMAGE			image/png	109.546	emurr	09/05/2020	09/05/2020, 12:33	Public
Edit | Del	SILVER_SLA_IMAGE			image/png	108.913	emurr	09/05/2020	09/05/2020, 12:33	Public

Figure 10.21 – Static resources for three different images

Add three Display Image components with the following configuration:

- **API Name**: Add **Gold_SLA_pic** (or **Silver/Copper**).
- **Image Name**: Add **GOLD_SLA_IMAGE** (use the corresponding name of the Static Resource).
- **Image Height / Width**: Choose a value for proper image visualization.

Each image should be shown only under the right SLA value. On each component configuration, expand the **Set Component Visibility** section and add a new AND condition using the right SLA value, shown as follows:

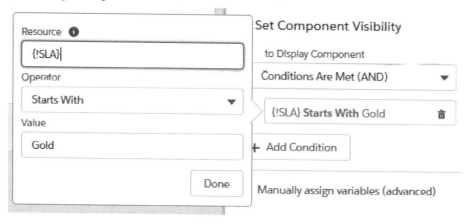

Figure 10.22 – Component visibility configuration

You can configure a specific visibility configuration for any screen component.

Finally, add the **Radio Buttons** component with the following configuration:

- **Label**: Support options
- **API Name**: Support_Options_RadioGroup
- **Require**: Checked
- **Data Type**: Text
- **Default Value**: No Default Value

On the Selected Choices section, create two new resources of the Choice type.

The first resource will have the following values:

- **API Name**: Upgrade_SLA
- **Choice Label**: Upgrade SLA
- **Data Type**: Text
- **Choice Value**: Keep empty

And the second resource will have the following values:

- **API Name**: `Update_Customer_Data`
- **Choice Label**: `Update customer data`
- **Data Type**: `Text`
- **Choice Value**: Keep empty

Be sure you see the new options on the screen canvas:

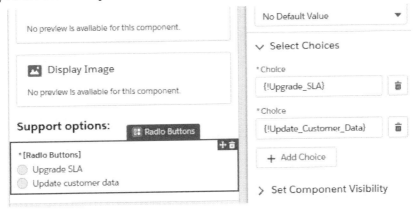

Figure 10.23 – Radio Buttons component configuration

Save this element and connect the **Is a customer?** decision element to it using the **Account is a customer** connection.

This is what you'll see if you try to test the new flow using an account with active advertisements:

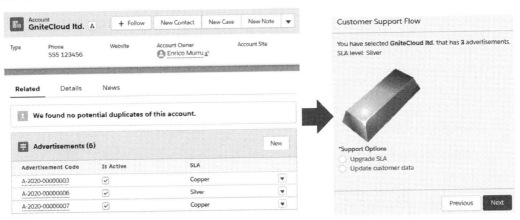

Figure 10.24 – Result of the support screen

Now, let's configure the support part by using almost the same elements we've already used.

A new Decision element will be used to track the user support choice with this configuration:

- **Label**: `Support Options`
- **API Name**: `Support_Options`
- **Outcome Label**: `Update Customer`
- **Outcome API Name**: `Update_Customer`
- **When to Execute Outcome**: `All Conditions Are Met`
- **Resource**: `{!Support_Options_RadioGroup}` (the previous step radio group)
- **Operator**: `Equals`
- **Value**: `{!Update_Customer_Data}` (the previous step choice)
- **Default Outcome label**: `SLA Upgrade` (this is the "else" choice)

Connect the Screen element for customer support with these Support Options elements.

Let's follow the Update Customer branch.

We need to do the following:

- Load the **Account** record: We'll use a **Get Records** element again.
- Show a screen with address and phone input fields: A **Screen** element is OK.
- Update the record: We'll go with an **Update Records** element.
- Show a success screen: This is another Screen element.

To load the Account record, create a new **Get Records** to get the Account record using its ID (which we got from the lookup component in the first screen):

- **Label**: `Load Account`
- **API Name**: `Load_Account`
- **Object**: `Account`
- **Condition Requirements**: `Conditions are Met`
- **Field**: `Id`
- **Operator**: `Equals`
- **Value**: `{!Selected_Customer_ID}`

- **Sort**: None
- **How Many Records to Store**: Only the first record
- **How to Store Record Data**: `Automatically store all fields`

Connect this element to the Support Options decision element using the Update customer connection.

Now, create a new **Screen** element with a Display Text to show the customer's name (using `{!Load_Account.Name}` coming from the previous Get Records element although we may have used the previous `{!Selected_Customer_Name}` variable defined in the first screen).

This screen element must also contain the Address and Phone screen components.

The address component is related to the account's **Shipping Address** fields:

- **API Name**: `Account_Address`
- **Label**: `Billing_Address`
- **City Value**: `{!Load_Account.BillingCity}`
- :
- **Street Value**: `{!Load_Account.BillingStreet}`

And in **Store Output Values to Select Variables**, use the same values:

- City Value: `{!Load_Account.BillingCity}`
- :
- Street Value: `{!Load_Account.BillingStreet}`

The **Phone** element is configured with the following values:

- **API Name**: `Account_Phone`
- **Label**: `Phone`
- **Value**: `{!Load_Account.Phone}`
- **Value (output)**: `{!Load_Account.Phone}`

With this configuration, we are assuring that the components will be loaded with the account's current data, with the following output:

Figure 10.25 – The Screen element showing loaded account data

Connect this element with the previous **Load Account** element.

We now need to update the Account record with the new values coming from the previous form.

Adding an Update Record element

Finally, let's configure a new **Update Records** element to update the account's data, using with the following configuration:

- **Label**: Add Update Account.
- **API Name**: Add Update_Account.

- **How to Find Records to Update and Set Their Values**: Use the IDs and all field values from a record or record collection.

- **Record or Record Collection**: Add `{!Load_Account}`.

It simply updates the record loaded in the Load_Account variable resource: connect this element to the previous one.

Finalizing the flow

Create a final Screen element that states that the account has been updated successfully, connect it back to the **Update Account** element and forward to the **Customer Selection** screen element to allow the user to start another support branch.

In the following diagram, we can see the flow setup so far:

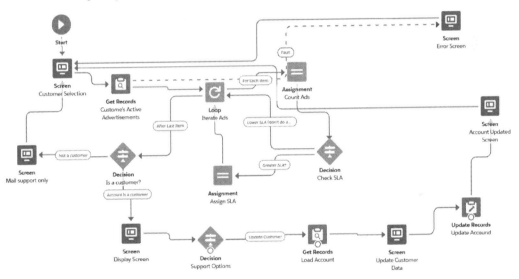

Figure 10.26 – Flow configuration with the Update Customer data branch completed

Let's complete the flow with the final support activity, needed to upgrade the SLA levels for all active advertisements:

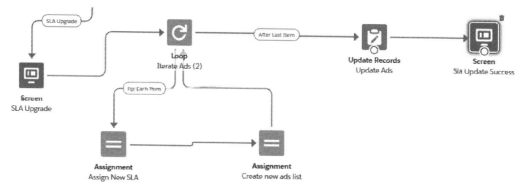

Figure 10.27 – The flow's branch for SLA upgrade support action

This is what you get in the **SLA Upgrade** screen:

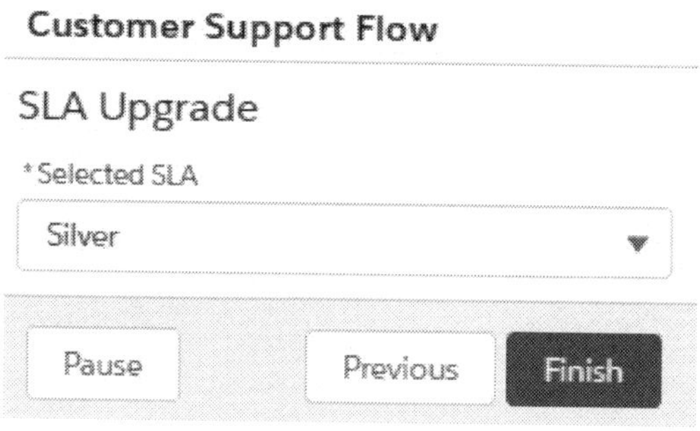

Customer Support Flow

SLA Upgrade

*Selected SLA

Silver ▼

Pause | Previous | Finish

Figure 10.28 – SLA Upgrade screen element setup

I'll leave this configuration to you (you'll be able to use the metadata delivered with this book to check a possible solution), but I'll give you some hints:

- The SLA Upgrade screen is quite easy, and you can use both radio buttons or a picklist with custom choices (that should have the values you see in the SLA__c picklist of the **Advertisement** object).

- You can Loop throughout the same records got from the Customer's Active Advertisements screen.

- You can see a double assignment because the first is used to set the SLA__c value coming from the previous SLA Upgrade screen's picklist and the last one is used to add the iterated record to a new variable of the Data Type Record and `Object Advertisement` with multiple values that will be filled with the records coming from the original list of records. This is needed because you need a new list to perform the following update operation.

- Remember to connect every Data element created so far with the Fault connection to the Error Screen element so the user is always able to see the error and go back to the first step.

If everything went well, this is what you should have come up with:

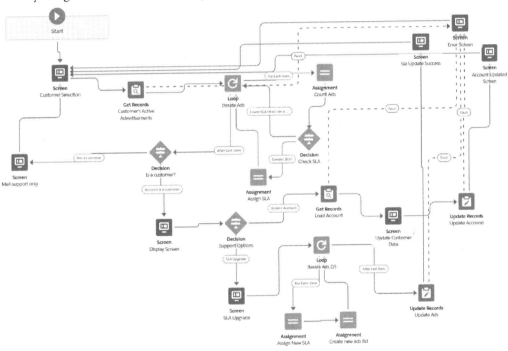

Figure 10.29 – The final result of the flow example

This is quite a complex example for beginners, but it covers most options you can configure with flows.

Check out the code provided with this book to see which solution I adopted. Remember, there can be more than one solution to any automation problem—it is up to you and your experience to figure out how the problem will be solved.

In the next sections, we'll see some other features of Flows.

Running and debugging

We've already seen how to run a flow. You can also use the **Debug** button to run the flow with a debugging panel and see what happens to resources during the flow execution:

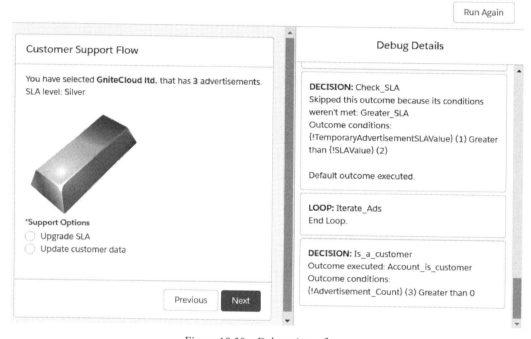

Figure 10.30 – Debugging a flow

If an unexpected error occurs to your flow, you'll receive a mail notification with the details of the error:

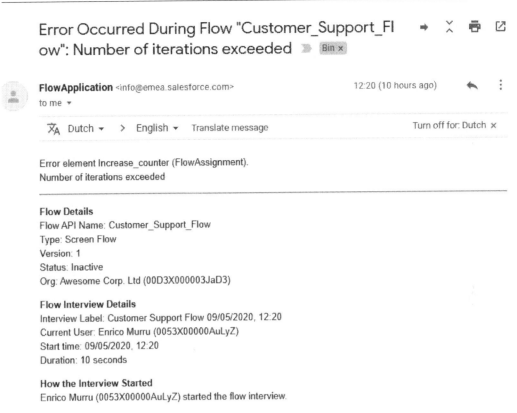

Figure 10.31 – Example of email notification upon flow error

You can configure error email notifications to be sent to specific system users and not to the user who is running the flow (who may not be a technical person). To do so, click on **Setup | Process Automation | Process Automation Settings**:

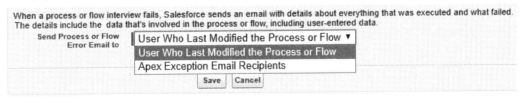

Figure 10.32 – Configuring error email notifications for automation processes

I suggest setting it to **Apex Exception Email Recipients** (which can be configured from **Setup | Email | Apex Exception Email**).

Now that we know how to build and debug a flow, let's understand some management options.

Managing a flow

Just like processes, a flow can be Active or Inactive. Once a flow is activated, it cannot be updated anymore, and to make changes, you need to create a new version of it.

In fact, a flow can be saved with a new version by clicking the **Save As** button on the upper-right corner of Flow Builder. You are able to create a brand new flow or another version of the same, so you can activate it when needed.

This is an example of a flow with more than one version and only one of them active:

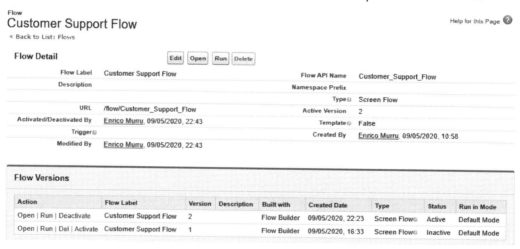

Figure 10.33 – A flow with more available versions

Regarding distribution and places of execution, a flow can be distributed in the following ways:

- A Lightning page using the standard flow component (Lightning App Builder)
- A record quick action using the flow action type

- The Lightning Console

- The Utility bar or any Lightning app

- By URL (see `https://help.salesforce.com/articleView?id=flow_distribute_internal_url.htm&type=5`)

- A Lightning Community

- A Lightning component

- A Visualforce page

- Process Builder (only auto-launched flows)

- Apex or RESTful APIs (only auto-launched flows)

In *Figure 10.35*, we've used the Lightning Home page of the Adv. Division Lightning app to host the flow:

- To set it up, jump to the **Home** tab and click the gear icon on the upper-right corner, then select **Edit Page**—this will open up the Lightning App Builder.

- On the **Components** tab, search for **Flow component** and drop it on the canvas, then select it and configure the **Customer Support Flow** (the flow must be active):

Figure 10.34 – Adding a flow to a Lightning page

- Finally, click the **Activation…** button, select the **Assign as Org Default** button, then **Save** and click **Back** to see your new Home tab:

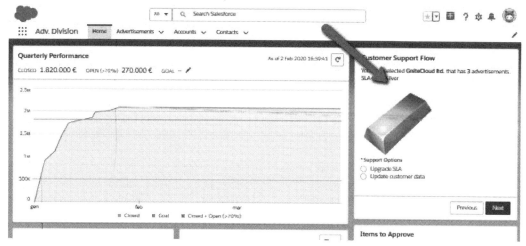

Figure 10.35 – Flow nested into a lightning page

So far, we have seen how to build, run, and manage flows, but we have focused on screen flows that require user interaction from start to end.

Let's now briefly examine another kind of flow, used for deep automation.

Auto-launched Flows

When you don't need user interaction, you can go with auto-launched Flows. They support pretty much the same features as the Screen flows, with exceptions made for the absence of Screen elements and the availability of the Pause element, which is used to pause the flow until a specific event.

> **Further reading**
>
> To understand more about the Pause element, refer to Salesforce Help at https://help.salesforce.com/articleView?id=flow_ref_elements_pause.htm&type=5

The link between an auto-launched flow and the calling flow or calling process is the way you define variable resources. To make a simple example, let's define the following variable resource:

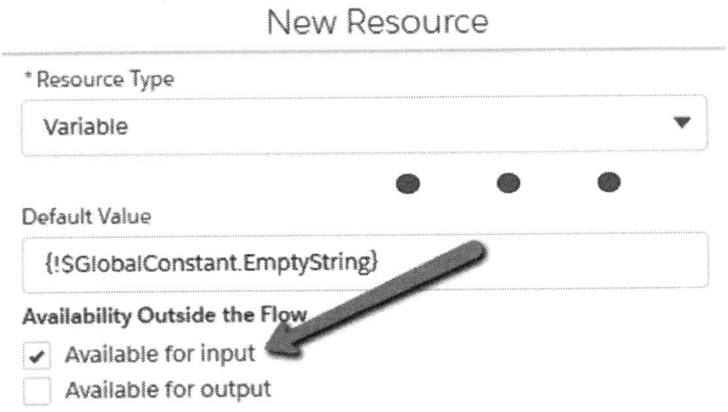

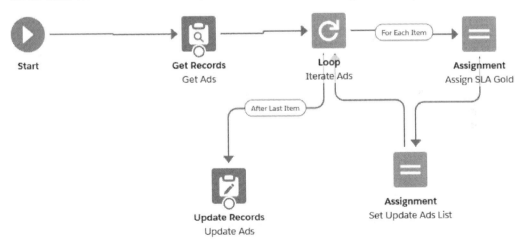

Figure 10.36 – Variable resource defined as available for input

This variable will be passed by the calling process or flow.

Given what we have learned so far, we can build the following flow easily:

Figure 10.37 – A simple auto-launched flow to raise the SLA level for all advertisements

This flow does the following:

- Gets all advertisements related to the account with ID set in the **Account_ID** variable

- Loops throughout the retrieved list

- For each item, sets the **SLA__c** field to **Gold**

- Inserts the record to a new list (for update)

- Updates the generated list of advertisements (because, as we said, we cannot update the same list used from a **Get Records** element)

Use the metadata provided with this book to check out this solution.

Save and activate this flow.

Let's go to Process Builder and select the invocable **Hot Account Process** we created in *Chapter 9, Process Builder – Workflows Evolutions*, and create a new flow based on this named **Hot Account Process (with Flow)**. Now, add a new **IMMEDIATE ACTION** on the **All Accounts** branch of type flows, configured as follows:

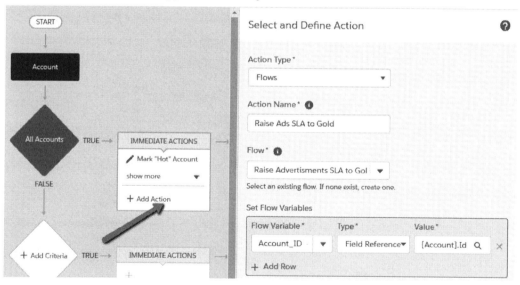

Figure 10.38 – Setting up a new flow action on a process

Account_ID is the only configurable flow variable because it was the only resource on the **Raise Advertisements SLA to Gold** flow to be set to **Available for input**.

The same happens if you include it with the Subflow element on another flow (auto-launched or not):

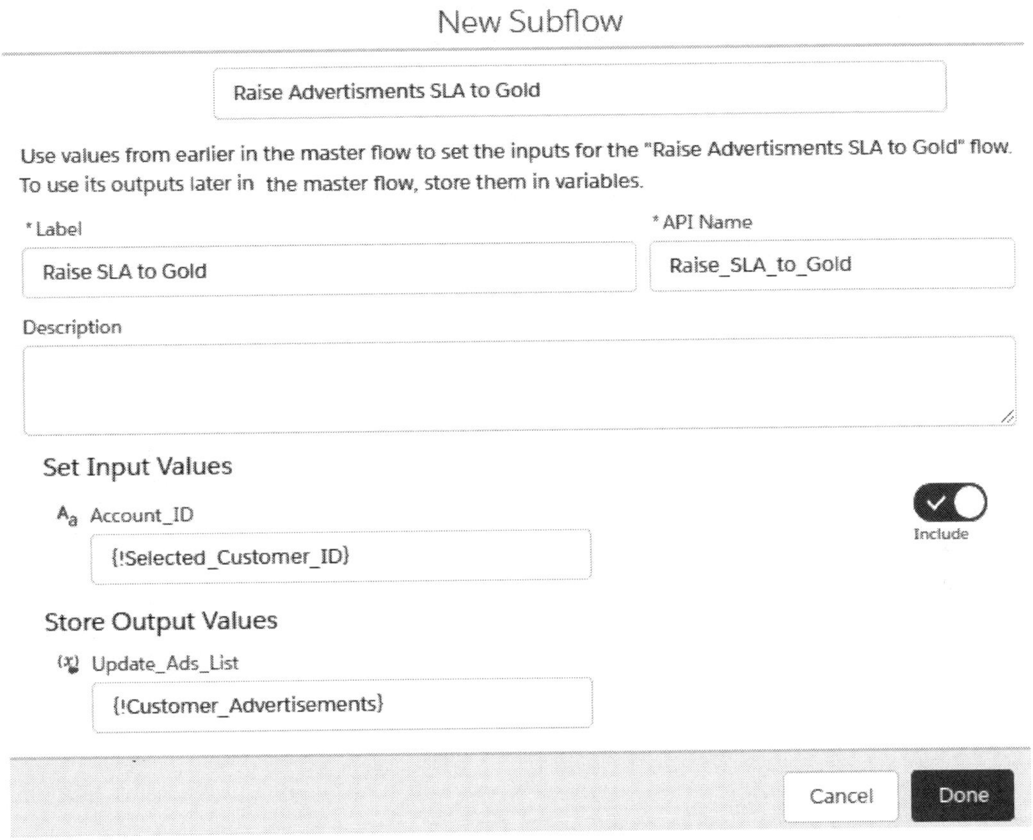

New Subflow

Raise Advertisments SLA to Gold

Use values from earlier in the master flow to set the inputs for the "Raise Advertisments SLA to Gold" flow. To use its outputs later in the master flow, store them in variables.

* Label

Raise SLA to Gold

* API Name

Raise_SLA_to_Gold

Description

Set Input Values

Aₐ Account_ID

{!Selected_Customer_ID}

Include

Store Output Values

Update_Ads_List

{!Customer_Advertisements}

Cancel   Done

Figure 10.39 – Example of a subflow configuration

With auto-launched flows, you are able to build complex automations on the platform and manipulate the dataset in almost any possible way.

In the next section, we'll just point to some online material for flow considerations.

Final considerations

Flow is certainly one of the most complex tools available in the Salesforce CRM and every step we've seen brings way more customization options than we've seen so far.

Also, the potential for great complexity and even flow usage can lead to hitting flow-specific limits.

> **Further reading**
>
> Refer to Salesforce Help to have a look at all of the various limits and considerations related to flow usage at `https://help.salesforce.com/articleView?id=flow_considerations.htm&type=5`. I also suggest having a look at the Flow Core Actions to see how many actions are available that have not been dealt with here, at `https://help.salesforce.com/articleView?id=flow_ref_elements_actions_list.htm&type=5`.

Blaze your trail

Have a look at the following Trailhead trails and modules to learn more about Flows:

- *Build Flows with Flow Builder*: `https://trailhead.salesforce.com/en/content/learn/trails/build-flows-with-flow-builder`

- *Build a Simple Flow*: `https://trailhead.salesforce.com/en/content/learn/projects/build-a-simple-flow`

- *Automate Your Business Processes with Lightning Flow*: `https://trailhead.salesforce.com/en/content/learn/trails/automate_business_processes`

Summary

Even though Lightning Flows are a complex subject that needs time to be mastered, in this chapter, we've seen, with a detailed and complex example, how to combine the building blocks available on the Flow Designer to create a flow to achieve complex automation scenarios.

We've seen how to use all kinds of elements, delivering user interaction, decisional statements, and database operations, all without writing a single line of code. We've learned how to create resources to define the variables that are passed throughout the flow from one element to the other, following the connection between each element to the next. We've finally defined auto-launched flows to deliver pure automated features without user interaction.

In the next chapter, we'll complete the process automation section with Actions to deliver an efficient user experience without the need for coding.

11

Interacting with Actions

So far, we have seen a good number of the available Salesforce automation features, but only flows are allowed to interact with a user.

Actions are another feature that is used to increase daily productivity by defining ready-to-use and customizable actions on records that the user can activate easily within specific Salesforce pages. These actions can range from creating a new object to sending an email to logging a call to executing a Salesforce flow on the fly.

By the end of this chapter, you'll understand what actions are and all the available Actions you can use to customize user interaction with records, focusing on quick actions, which are customizable actions that you can configure to execute quick operations on data.

In this chapter we'll learn about the following topics:

- What actions are and what they are used for
- The different types of actions available on the platform
- How to customize actions to fulfill your business needs

What are actions?

So far, we have talked about the different ways to develop Salesforce automations on Salesforce objects. They were all based on a set of conditions and record fields' values: they trigger certain kinds of action, whether they be workflow actions (for Workflow Rules or Approval Processes), Process Builder Actions, or complex Flow interactions.

In a nutshell, they all have some degree of automatic behavior that implies little to no user interaction—think of workflows, processes, and autolaunched Flows. Screen flows let users interact directly with custom forms, providing a better way to grab data from users; however, they also guide users to a final result, even though the users are unaware of what's happening in the background.

With actions, the users are the key actor, as they decide what, how, and when something has to be performed on the records they own. We obviously have some sort of automation, as an administrator is needed to apply the configuration of actions, but they are easy to understand and easy to use, so users will always know what's happening.

In the following sections, we'll learn how to use standard and custom actions. We'll categorize them and learn how to add more functionality to our apps and deliver users the ability to operate on CRM data with easy-to-use actions that are available on the fly.

Categorizing actions

I have to admit, when I talk about Actions, I get confused because of the different kinds available and the different places in which they can be set on the CRM. Let's classify them to understand their capabilities better.

We can define two macro types of Action:

- **GLOBAL ACTIONS**
- Object-specific actions

No surprise that **GLOBAL ACTIONS** refer to actions that can be used throughout the platform while object-specific actions are related to a specific Salesforce object.

In the following screenshot, we have highlighted some examples of these actions, Global at the top right and Object-Specific on the right:

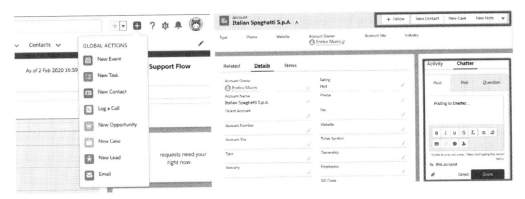

Figure 11.1 – Global versus object-specific Actions

We can further divide Action categories into the following:

- **Standard Chatter Actions**
- **Default Actions**
- **Mobile Smart Actions**
- **Quick Actions**

We'll briefly explain the first three categories, which we can consider as standard actions (that is, provided by the platform as they are and with limited customization options), and then we'll focus on Quick Actions, which are the most customizable kind of Action available on the platform.

Let's begin to understand each of these in the following sections.

Standard Chatter Actions

Salesforce Chatter is the Salesforce platform collaboration tool and has been enabled by default since June 2010.

> **Note**
> If you are dealing with an older organization (created before June 2010) and don't have Chatter enabled, refer to Salesforce Help at `https://help.salesforce.com/articleView?id=collab_setting_up.htm&type=5` to see its activation options.

You can enable Chatter on almost any Salesforce object by enabling the **Feed Tracking** option from **Setup | Feature Settings | Chatter | Feed Tracking**, as shown here:

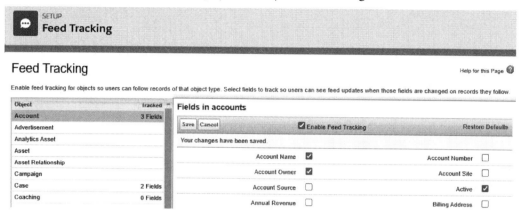

Figure 11.2 – Enabling Feed Tracking in the Account object

By checking the **Enable Feed Tracking** checkbox, you are enabling **Chatter** on the selected Salesforce object, and the **Chatter** panel will appear on the right side of the Salesforce object, as shown in the following screenshot:

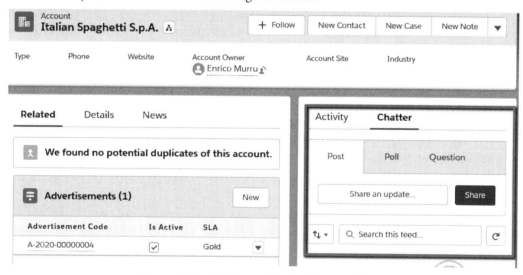

Figure 11.3 – Chatter panel in the Account object

You can also configure fields to be tracked and shown on the Chatter feed if they change in value, as shown in the following screenshot (the record has changed its owner and the **Active** field value):

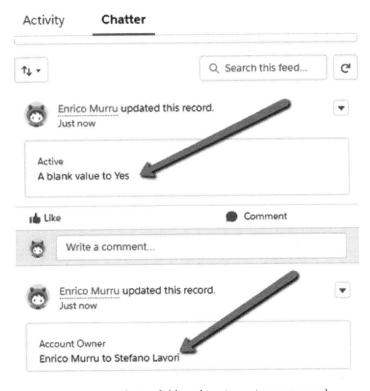

Figure 11.4 – Chatter field tracking in an Account record

The standard Chatter Actions provided by default are as follows:

- **Post**: This posts a message on the record's Chatter feed using a rich text interface, allowing it to post images and attachments or tag people/groups:

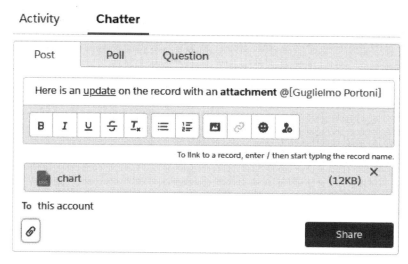

Figure 11.5 – Post Chatter Action

Poll: This creates a poll so that each user can put their own answer, as shown in the following screenshot:

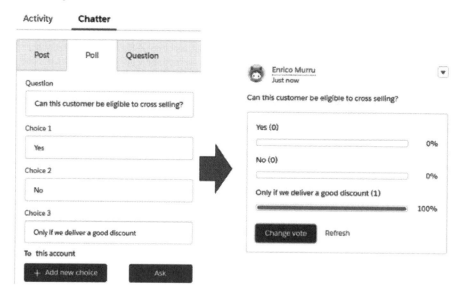

Figure 11.6 – Poll Chatter Action

- **Question**: This posts a question so that users can answer and deliver their opinion, as shown in the following screenshot:

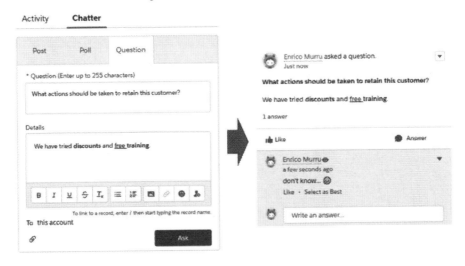

Figure 11.7 – Answer Chatter Action

- **Announcement**: Available on a Chatter group object only, this is used to create group announcements, as shown in the following screenshot:

Figure 11.8 – Announcement Chatter post Action

These actions cannot be customized but you can change their position and/or visibility by going to **Setup | Object Manager** and then selecting an object (for instance, **Account**), clicking **Page Layouts**, and selecting a page layout.

Look at the **Salesforce Mobile and Lightning Experience Actions** and you'll see tens of available actions, some of which are the Chatter standard actions:

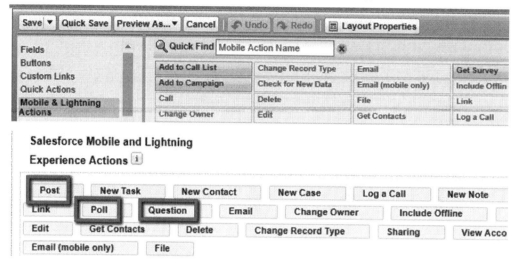

Figure 11.9 – Chatter Actions configuration in the object page layout

Chatter Actions are also available on the Salesforce App whether Chatter is enabled or not.

Default Actions

Default actions are Global Actions that are available on the Salesforce desktop site or on the mobile app, and provide quick ways to create core sales or service records.

To see which actions are available, check out **Global Actions** from **Setup | User Interface | Global Actions | Global Actions** as shown in the following screenshot:

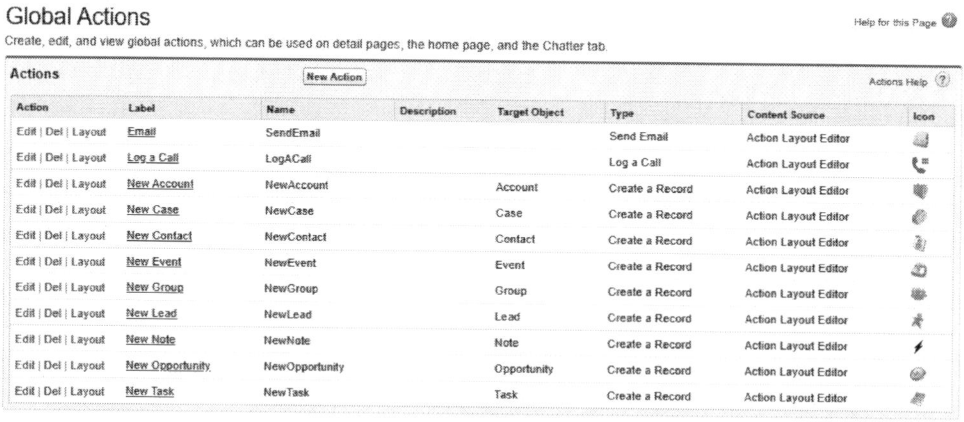

Figure 11.10 – Global Actions list

From this list, we can see that Salesforce brought us some prebuilt Global Actions that we can use from anywhere in the CRM to, for example, create a new lead or a new opportunity, to send new mail, or simply to quickly log a call (by creating a new **Task** record).

You can change the fields that are displayed using the **Layout** link (as we'll see when we'll talk about Quick Actions), and from **Setup | User Interface | Global Actions | Publisher Layouts**, you can select which actions you want to expose, and to which user, by assigning different layouts depending on the user's profile:

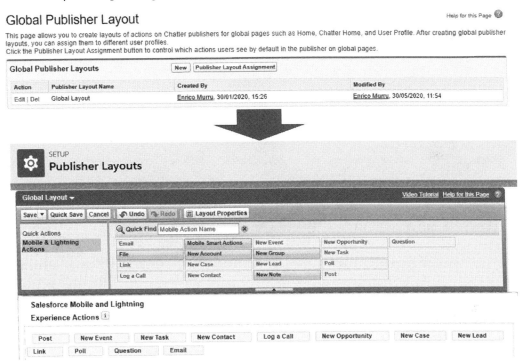

Figure 11.11 – Configuring the publisher's layout

The result is shown in the following screenshot:

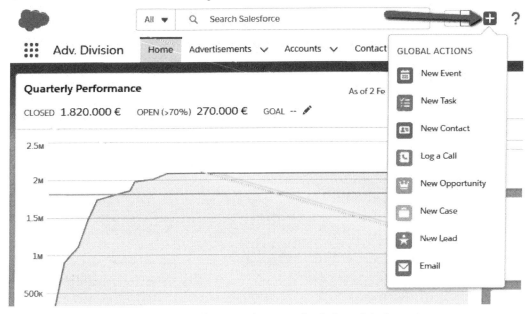

Figure 11.12 – Global Actions shown on the desktop Salesforce site

Each Action is delivered through pop-up windows that appear in the bottom-right part of the screen, as shown in the following screenshot:

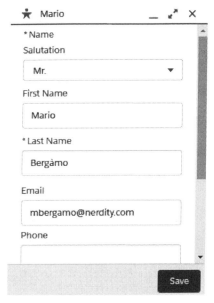

Figure 11.13 – Global Actions shown on the screen

It displays all the fields defined in the Global Action's layout.

> **Further reading**
>
> If you want a list of all the default fields in the Global Action layouts,
> refer to Salesforce Help at `https://help.salesforce.com/`
> `articleView?id=default_actions_fields.htm&type=0.`

Mobile smart actions

Mobile smart actions are a bundle of actions that are available on the Account, Lead, Case, and Opportunity pages, as well as on the Global publisher (which we saw in the previous section).

They basically group some of the most common standard Actions in Salesforce records, and are only available on the Salesforce app.

They appear as a single item in the Publisher layout named **Mobile Smart Actions**; have a look at *Figure 11.11*.

If you add this item to the object or Global publisher layout and access the record/Global Action menu on the Salesforce app, then you'll see different kinds of Action, and for each Action, you will only see the required fields. This means that their layout varies if the number of required fields for the given object changes.

As an example, if you enable **Mobile Smart Actions** on the Global publisher, you'll see the following Actions on the Salesforce app Global Action menu:

- **New Task**
- **New Contact**
- **Log a Call**
- **New Opportunity**
- **New Case**
- **New Lead**

However, if you enable this feature on the **Account** object, you will see these actions:

- **New Task**
- **New Contact**
- **New Case**

- **Log a Call**
- **New Note**
- **New Opportunity**

If you want to change the fields that are displayed on the Action layout or change the bundle composition, remove the **Mobile Smart Actions** item on the record/Global publisher layout and use the single actions shown in the earlier sections.

> **Further reading**
>
> For a detailed list of available actions per Salesforce object, refer to Salesforce Help at `https://help.salesforce.com/articleView?id=smart_actions_overview.htm&type=0`.

Quick Actions

With Quick Actions, the platform delivers a way to customize Global and object actions. They work like the actions we've already seen in the previous sections, but with a higher level of customization. Thanks to **GLOBAL ACTIONS**, we can define user actions that can comply with business needs and thus ease up agents' daily work by creating easy-to-use interaction forms to quickly create records on the fly. If you have some developer powers, you can even use some coding magic to let users interact with complex forms that are built with Visualforce or Lightning components.

There are different kinds of Quick Actions, such as the following:

- **Create a Record**
- **Update a Record**
- **Log a Call**
- **Visualforce**
- **Lightning Component**
- **Flow**
- **Send Email**

If we create a Global Quick Action (from **Setup | User Interface | Global Actions | Global Actions**), then the **Flow** and **Update a Record** actions won't be available, and the Action will not be context aware (we are not on a Salesforce object page and so there is no record page on which the Action is specifically added). **Global Actions** need the **Global Publisher Layout** configuration to be accessible through the + button on the Salesforce desktop site header, as is the case with standard actions.

If we create an Object-Specific Action (by going to **Setup | Object Manager**, selecting an object, and then going to **Buttons, Links, and Actions**), then the Action will be context aware and, for example, the **Log a Call** Action will automatically create a task related to the current object. These actions are only available through the object's page layout.

Let's see how to quickly create a new action.

Creating a record Action

Let's create a new Global Action to create a new **Advertisement** record on the fly using a Quick Action.

Click on **Setup | User Interface | Global Actions | Global Actions** and click the **New** button:

Figure 11.14 – Creating a new Global Action

This configuration indicates the following:

- We want to create a new `Advertisement` object.

- The Action should be automatically named by Salesforce as `New_Advertisement` (the New [Record] standard label is a placeholder for the actual record name).

- It will create a Chatter feed item upon creation and a custom feed too.

- It will display a custom success message upon saving.

- The Action will have the same icon that we selected when we created the custom tab (we can replace it with an image loaded in a static resource, as we saw in *Chapter 10, Designing Lightning Flows*).

Click **Save** to jump to the layout editor for the current Action to configure the fields to be displayed:

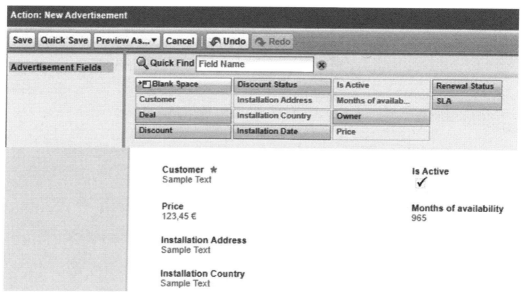

Figure 11.15 – Action layout configuration

Drag and drop the fields you want to display, as shown in the preceding screenshot. You can even double-click on each field in the layout to mark them as required or read-only (we selected the **Customer** field as required in this example).

Click **Save** to complete the configuration and land on the new Action home page:

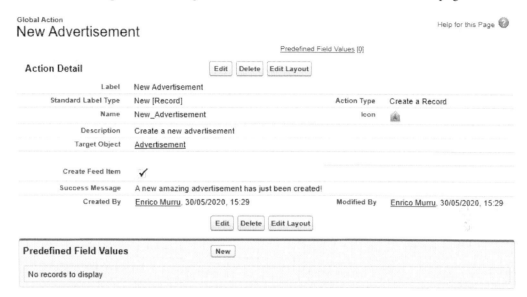

Figure 11.16 – Quick Action home page

There is no limit to the number of fields you can place on an Action layout, but, as it should be a quick and simple form, you should stay within 20 fields; otherwise, you'll impact user efficiency (use default values to limit the number of fields).

When loading an Action layout configuration, all of the required fields will be there, but you can decide to remove them. Just remember to enter a predefined value.

As we are creating a new record on the fly, it would be a good practice to put some default values in fields that we are not exposing (or to reduce their number) or, as we said, to put some default values in required fields that we don't want to show. To do this, click on the **New** button of the **Predefined Field Values** section and set up some default values:

Predefined Field Values		New		
Action	**Field Name**	**API Name**	**Field Type**	**Value**
Edit | Del	Discount	Discount__c	Percent	0
Edit | Del	Months of availability	Months_of_availability__c	Number	12
Edit | Del	Renewal Status	Renewal_Status__c	Picklist	None
Edit | Del	SLA	SLA__c	Picklist	Copper

Figure 11.17 – Predefined values for hidden fields in the create Action

You can set predefined values for both the shown and hidden fields of the Action layout, and the value configuration is pretty much the same as the custom field default value configuration (which we've seen in the previous chapters). This means that you can create simple formulas instead of simple static values.

You can select pretty much any field type except calculated fields (such as formulas, roll-up, autonumber; in fact, as they are calculated, you cannot set a default value) and multipicklists (this is simply a platform limitation; there is no other reason for this limitation). Dependent picklists are also not supported.

If a field has its own default value, but a predefined value is set up, then the predefined value will be used instead.

For picklist fields, we can set both a specific value from picklist-allowed values and a predefined formula. In this situation, the formula value takes precedence over the specific value if only and only if the formula results in a value and doesn't output a blank value.

Now that our Action is configured, we can add it to **Global Publisher Layout** by going to **Setup | User Interface | Global Actions | Publisher Layouts**:

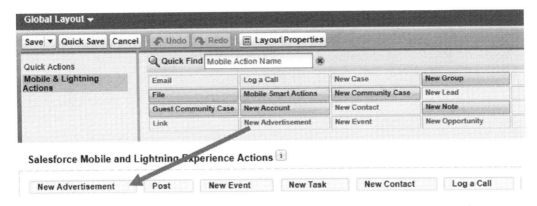

Figure 11.18 – Configuring the publisher's layout to show the newly created Action

Click **Save** and refresh the page, then click on the + Global Action button to see your brand-new Action:

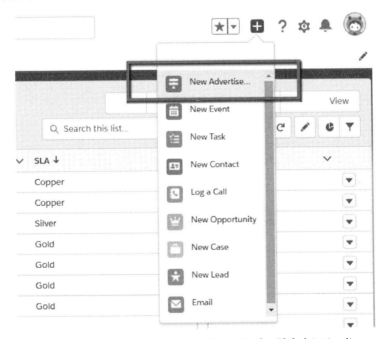

Figure 11.19 – New Advertisement Action in the Global Action list

By clicking the Action, the Action window appears:

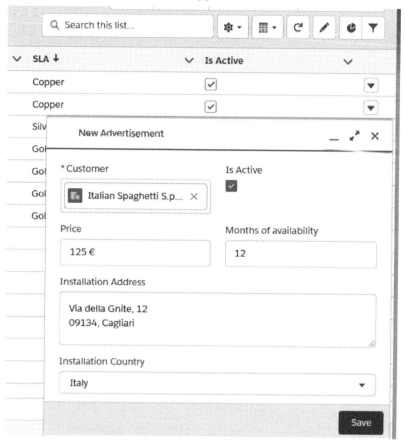

Figure 11.20 – Create a record Action execution

Upon clicking the **Save** button, the custom success message is displayed and the new record, with all user types and predefined values, is created:

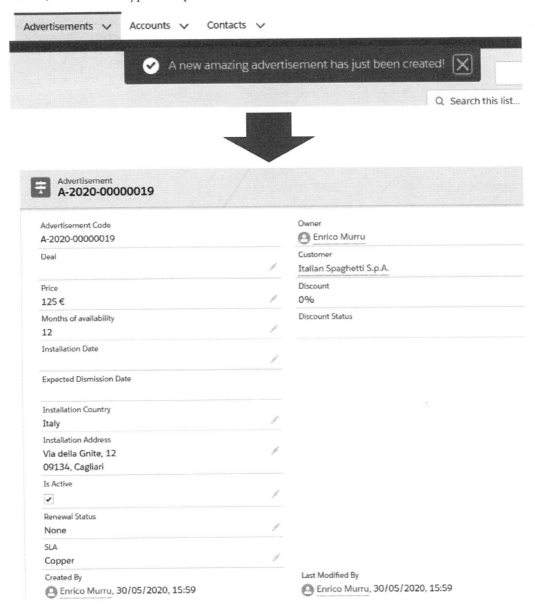

Figure 11.21 – Record creation after action execution

Now let's see how to work with Object-Specific Quick actions.

Object-Specific Quick actions

If you want to create an Object-Specific Quick Action, like the previous one, you need to jump to the Salesforce object home page from **Setup | Object Manager**, click on the **Buttons, Links, and Actions** link, and then click the **New Action** button:

Figure 11.22 – Object-Specific Quick Action creation

We want to create the same quick action we created in the previous section, but starting from the **Account** object:

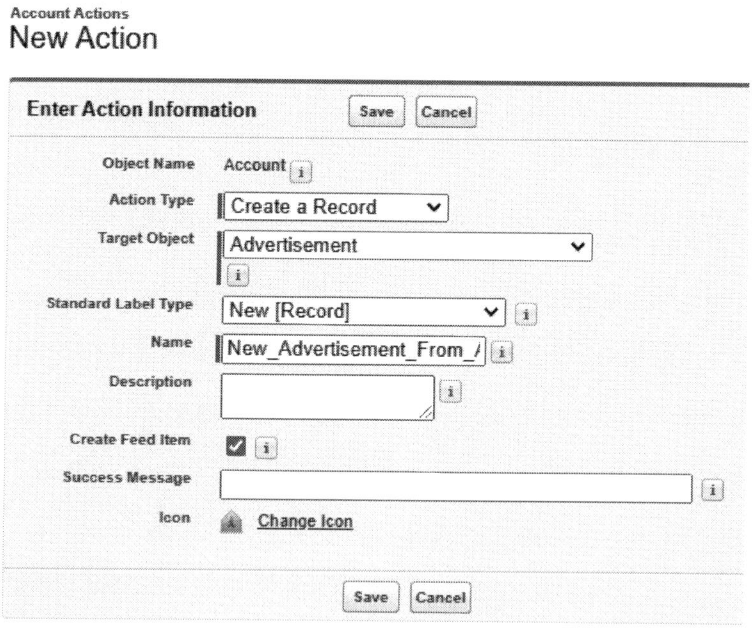

Figure 11.23 – Creating a new Create a Record Action with the Advertisement target object

The configuration is pretty similar; the only difference is that we have a prefilled **Object Name** field set to **Account**. With object-specific actions, the **Target Object** picklist is filled in with the current object's related child objects (for example, here, we can create contacts, cases, accounts, advertisements, and objects that have a lookup field set to the **Account** object, making them child objects).

Click **Save** to set up the Action layout. This is how it will look:

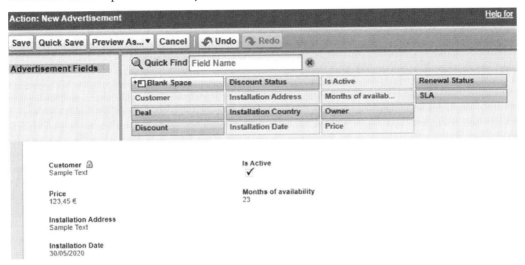

Figure 11.24 – Object-specific layout configuration

As we expect that the customer field (**Account** lookup) will already be populated when the Action is executed, we are setting it to read-only (double-click on the field and click the **Read-only** checkbox). After adding some values (predefined, in our case), the Action will be ready:

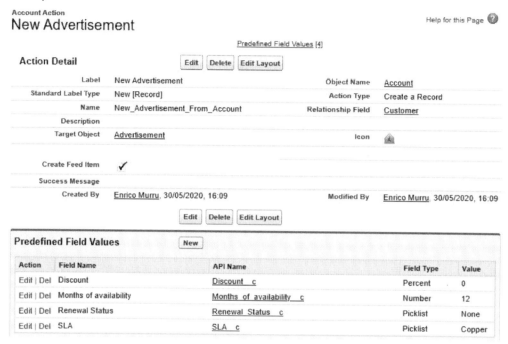

Figure 11.25 – Object-Specific Action all set up

Now select the **Page Layouts** link, edit **Account Layout**, and add the **Mobile and Lightning Actions** item called New Advertisement:

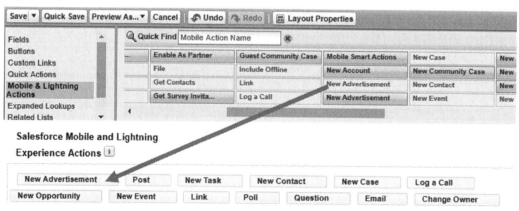

Figure 11.26 – Adding the new Quick Action in the account layout

You may also see the Global Action on the list of available actions (scroll over it with the mouse, as shown in the preceding screenshot, to get the right Action).

Open any account and you'll find the **New Advertisement** Action on the button list:

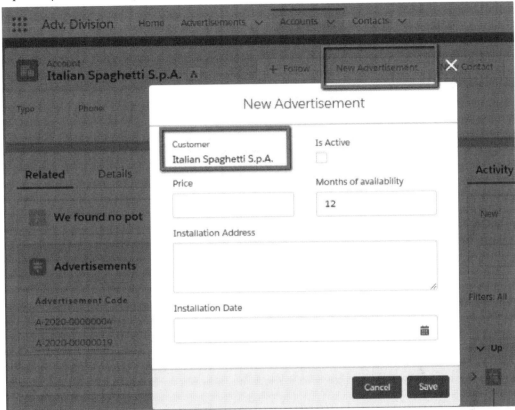

Figure 11.27 – Quick Action in the account layout

Let's see the other available Action types.

Understanding the Update a Record Action

The **Update a Record** Action is used to update specific fields of the current record, and it is only available as an Object-Specific Action.

Jump to the **Contact** object configuration page and create a new Quick Action, as follows:

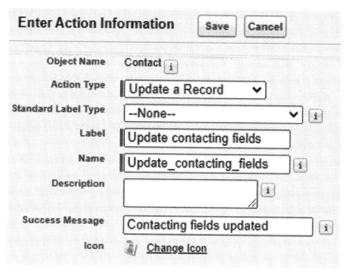

Figure 11.28 – The Update a Record Action in the contact object

If you don't select a value for **Standard Label Type**, then you can set a custom label value.

Our aim is to update only the contacting fields, such as **Email**, **Fax**, and **Phone**, so our layout will have all available fields of this kind:

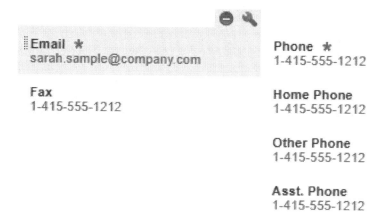

Figure 11.29 – The Update a Record Action layout in the contact object

In our case, we're assuming that we have compiled at least the **Email** and **Phone** fields and we have chosen not to have any predefined values. Add this Action to the **Contact** page layout. The following is the resulting contact record:

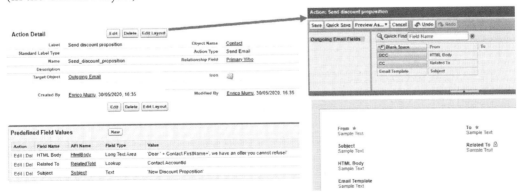

Figure 11.30 – The Update a Record Action executed in a contact record

The Send Email Action

The **Send Email** Action is a pretty simple Action and can be used to speed up email creation, as shown in the following configuration of a **Send Email** Action and its layout (in the **Contact** object):

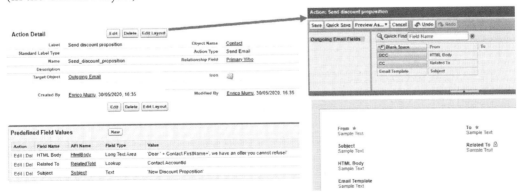

Figure 11.31 – Send Email Action configuration in the contact record

Add the Action to the contact layout and it will be displayed in the **Activity** tab next to the **Chatter** tab, as follows:

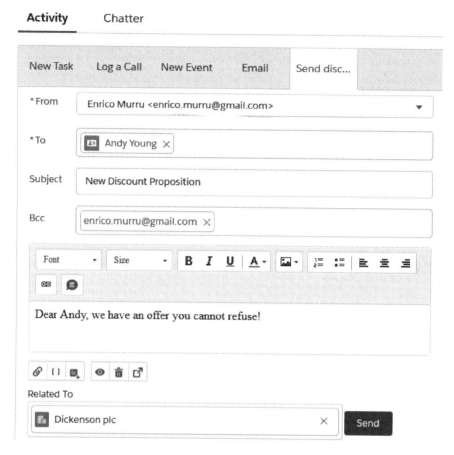

Figure 11.32 – The Send Email Action in execution

Note that the email body and the **Related To** field have been predefined using formulas.

The Log a Call Action

This kind of Action is used to create a quick task in a record.

Here is a sample configuration in the **Contact** object that speeds up note creation after a meeting:

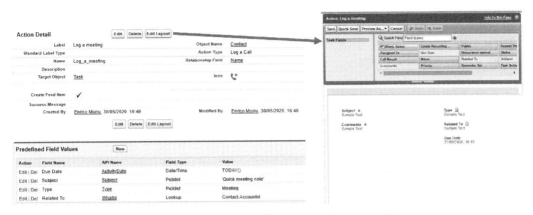

Figure 11.33 – The Log a Call Action in the contact object

The result is a new item in the **Activity** panel:

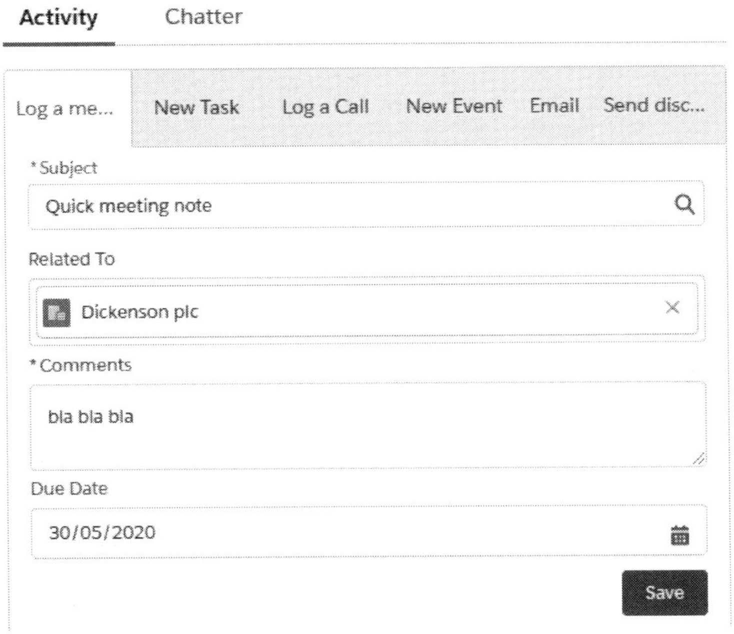

Activity   Chatter

| Log a me... | New Task | Log a Call | New Event | Email | Send disc... |

*Subject

> Quick meeting note   🔍

Related To

> 🏢 Dickenson plc   ✕

*Comments

> bla bla bla

Due Date

> 30/05/2020   📅

Save

Figure 11.34 – The Log a Call Action in execution in a contact record

Customized actions

As we said, we can further customize actions using **Flows** or even custom code with Visualforce pages and Lightning components.

> **Further reading**
>
> Visualforce pages and Lightning components are out of the scope of this book, as they require custom coding skills. To know more about these technologies, refer to Salesforce Help at `https://help.salesforce.com/articleView?id=lightning_component_actions.htm&type=0` for Lightning components with actions and `https://help.salesforce.com/articleView?id=custom_actions_vf_pages_for_object_actions.htm&type=0` for Visualforce pages with actions.

In *Chapter 10, Designing Lightning Flows*, we created a complex example Flow, named Customer Support Flow, which was meant to give different kinds of support to users. We want to allow users to access this Flow right inside an **Account** record.

Let's see how to go about this:

1.   The first thing we need to do is to create a new version of that Flow and define a new variable that must be called `recordId` and is defined as the *input variable* from **Resources Manager**, as follows:

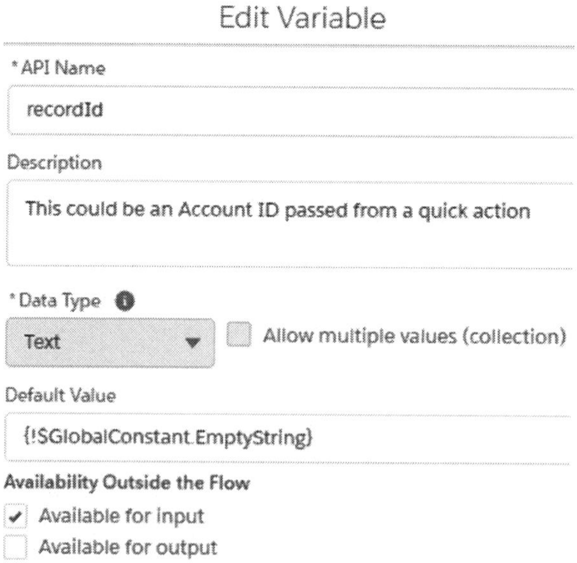

Edit Variable

* API Name

recordId

Description

This could be an Account ID passed from a quick action

* Data Type ⓘ

Text ▾   ☐ Allow multiple values (collection)

Default Value

{!$GlobalConstant.EmptyString}

Availability Outside the Flow

☑ Available for input
☐ Available for output

Figure 11.35 – Defining the recordId variable to host the Quick Action record selection

This is needed because the quick action engine for object-specific actions looks for a Flow input variable called `recordId` and passes the current Salesforce record ID.

2. The other modification is to get the `Selected_Customer_ID`, and change the **Default Value** with `{!recordId}`. This way, the first step of the Flow will begin with the customer lookup already filled in.

   Remember to click the **Save** and **Activate** buttons.

3. Now, create a new **Quick Action** in the **Account** object:

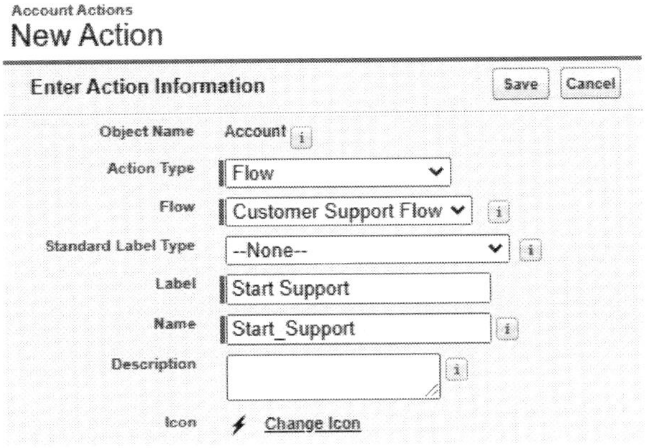

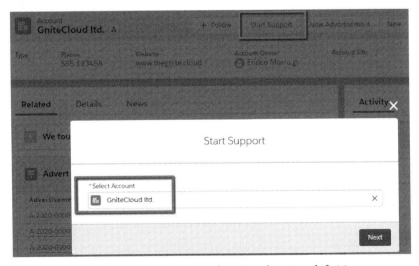

Figure 11.36 – Flow Action in the Account object

4. Add the Action in the page layout of **Account**. It will be displayed in the page level Action menu in the **Highlights** panel:

Figure 11.37 – Flow execution from Quick Action definition

So far, we've seen all available quick actions. We'll close this section with a special kind of Quick Action that can be used to execute an Action on up to 100 records.

Mass quick actions

With mass quick actions, you can execute a Quick Action on more than one record by selecting from a list view (up to 100 records).

This is available for cases, leads, campaigns, contacts, accounts, work orders, opportunities, and custom objects.

> **Note**
>
> Only **Create a Record** and **Update a Record** Action types are available and you cannot use a **Recently Viewed** list to perform a mass quick action execution.

Let's create a new **Update SLA** Quick Action:

1. For this, we go to the **Advertisement** object and select the **SLA** field, as shown in the following screenshot:

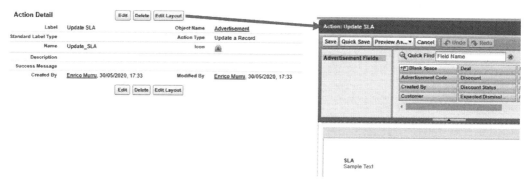

Figure 11.38 – Creating a simple update for a record Action in the Advertisement object

2. Now go to the **Search Layouts for Salesforce Classic** object configuration page and select the **List View** item, then select the **Update SLA** Action in the **List View Actions in Lightning Experience** multipicklist:

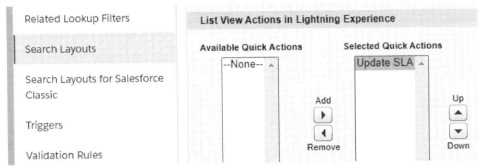

Figure 11.39 – List view of Mass Quick Action configuration

3. Then go to the **Advertisements** tab (select any list view other than **Recently Viewed**) and select all the records you want to update (remember, up to 100) and click the **Update SLA** button:

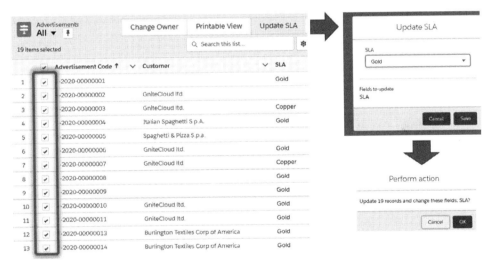

Figure 11.40 – Massive Quick Action execution in Advertisement records

If no errors happen, then the records get updated with the new SLA value.

Actions tips and tricks

Before closing the chapter, here are a few tips on Action creation best practices:

- Use Action names that clearly identify the kind of actions they are going to execute.

- Use short names; if a label is longer than 12 characters, then it gets shortened.

- Fill in the **Description** field of each Action to provide a glimpse of what each Action is meant for, as using short labels can create actions with similar names.

- It is suggested that you use no more than nine actions per layout, as using more actions can slow down the page load.

> **Further reading**
>
> For more considerations about using actions, refer to
> Salesforce Help at `https://help.salesforce.com/`
> `articleView?id=actions_considerations.htm&type=0`.
> For more about Action limits, go to `https://help.salesforce.`
> `com/articleView?id=actions_limitations.htm&type=0`.

Next, we move on to learning about Action creation with buttons and links.

Buttons and links

There is another way to deliver new actions—namely, through custom buttons and links, which are features that can be used to deliver some more Visualforce, JavaScript, and Lightning component stuff to your records.

We can say that **buttons and links** (available before Lightning Experience and quick actions) are the older way of creating some kinds of Quick Action on record pages. We can create a button to be displayed on any object's page layout to redirect the user to an external site (for example, to search for the name of an **Account** on Google) or to a custom and internal Visualforce page to start a wizard or perform custom behavior using the origin record's data.

> **Further reading**
>
> We will not be covering buttons and links in depth, as this configuration
> requires some coding skills. Refer to Salesforce Help at `https://`
> `help.salesforce.com/articleView?id=customize_`
> `enterprise.htm&type=5` for more details on custom buttons and links.

Blazing your trail

Learn more about Salesforce actions from the following links at Trailhead:

- Salesforce Mobile app customization: `https://trailhead.salesforce.com/en/content/learn/modules/salesforce1_mobile app`
- Customize the user interface for a recruiting app: `https://trailhead.salesforce.com/en/content/learn/projects/customize-the-ui-for-a-recruiting-app`
- Lightning Experience customization: `https://trailhead.salesforce.com/en/content/learn/modules/lex_customization`
- Lightning alternatives to JavaScript buttons: `https://trailhead.salesforce.com/en/content/learn/modules/lex_javascript_button_migration`
- App customization lite: `https://trailhead.salesforce.com/en/content/learn/modules/lex_migration_customization`

Summary

With this chapter, we close the process automation section with Salesforce actions to provide a better user experience with quick and smart widgets to speed up CRM operation.

We've seen how to deal with standard Chatter Actions, which deliver accessibility to common collaboration actions, such as **Post**, **Poll**, and **Question**.

Then we analyzed **default Actions**, built-in **GLOBAL ACTIONS** that you can use so that you always have key Actions that can be used on any Salesforce page, and Mobile Smart Actions, to deliver mobile Actions on key CRM objects with no need for you to click for configuration.

Finally, we learned how to customize actions by creating new Global and Object-Specific Quick Actions of all available kinds, from creating or updating Salesforce records, to logging a call or sending an email. We ended by looking at the most complex Actions that use Flows, Visualforce, or Lightning components to deliver an even more customized user experience.

In the next chapter, we'll learn how to customize the user interface to display all kinds of data to provide the best experiences to our users.

Section 4: Composing the User Interface

In this section, we will learn about configuring the layout to display object fields. We will use the Lightning App Builder to customize Lightning pages and unleash Communities to allow external users to reach the CRM.

This section comprises the following chapters:

12
All about Layouts

Throughout this book, we have covered many platform features used to highly customize the CRM without code, using powerful tools. Layouts are no different, yet are easy to master. We've already seen layout concepts when we talked about custom fields, relationships, and when we designed Quick Actions; it's just putting the right elements in the right place so users can access them with ease.

With proper layout configuration, you allow users to see exactly what they need to access, thus increasing their productivity.

In this chapter, we'll learn about the following:

- How to design record layouts
- How to assign layouts to profiles and record types
- How to customize compact layouts and search layouts
- How to create list views

Designing record layouts

We said that data is the core of any business, thus displaying data is equally important for the success of your CRM implementation.

Your users will likely spend most of their time browsing Salesforce records, so designing proper record layouts is key to enhancing their daily work.

Let's explain how we can customize page layouts to help our users to get the right data in the right place at the right time.

Showing the right amount of data

You can control fields' visibility in the following ways:

- At the layout level, including or not including a field in a layout
- At the profile level (using both profiles or permission sets), using the **Field-Level Security (FLS)** options (granting access to a field or not)
- At the profile level, assigning a specific layout to any profile

> **Tip**
>
> Remember that even if a user is assigned a record layout that shows a given field but, due to FLS configuration, they haven't access to the field, the field is not displayed on the record layout.

In this chapter, we'll work on configuring layout composition and assignment to users, to achieve the best data visibility.

Open an **Account** record, which shows the following screen:

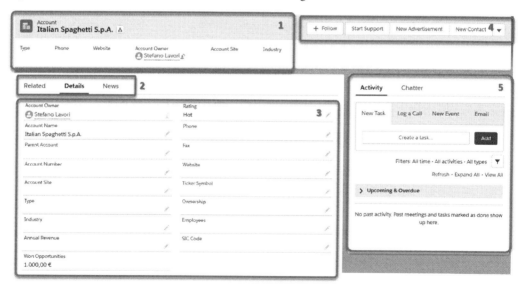

Figure 12.1 – Record layout composition

In this view, you can identify different sections:

1. The first is the record highlight section (called **compact layout**), which contains all of the main record details.

2. Record tabs, with the **Related** and **Details** main tabs (the **News** tab is related to certain objects such as **Account** and **Contact** and shows social news).

3. The content of the record tabs, which can contain all the fields the layout can display or all the related lists for this given record (that is, the related records) or any other content from other tabs (the configuration of those tabs comes from the **App Builder** tool, which we'll see in *Chapter 13, The Lightning App Builder*).

4. A list of available actions (we added them when we used certain types of quick actions).

5. Just like the third section, this section can be configured with the **App Builder** tool and it usually comes with **Activity** and **Chatter** tabs, displaying the main events related to this record: even this section can display quick actions, as seen in *Chapter 11, Interacting with Actions*.

Let's see how to configure these sections.

Record layouts

While in Salesforce Classic record layouts were almost the only thing you had to take care of when designing record pages, with Lightning Experience record layouts are just one of the things you can put on a record page, thanks to the configuration capabilities of the **App Builder** tool.

Let's focus on the record details layout.

With record layouts you can do the following:

- Design how to display fields in the record details section (by configuring a layout).
- Create different layout combinations and assign them to specific profiles.

Let's start by configuring the record layout for the **Advertisement** custom object.

1. This is how its layout appears as of now if you open any **Advertisement** record:

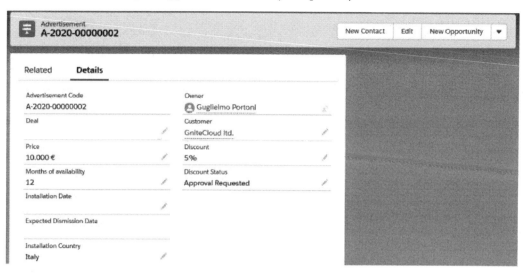

Figure 12.2 – Simple record layout

I can see no **Chatter** or **Activity** section.

2. We can easily enable **Chatter** from **Setup | Feature Settings | Chatter | Feed Tracking**, then select the **Advertisement** record and flag the **Enable Feed Tracking** checkbox (remember to hit the **Save** button). A new **Chatter** panel immediately appears in the right column of your record layout with the common **Chatter** actions:

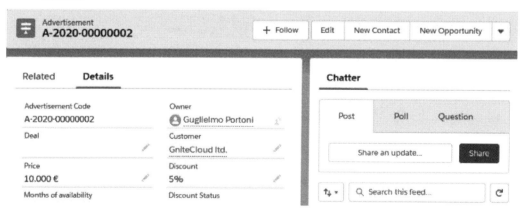

Figure 12.3 – Chatter feed enabled on the Advertisement object

3. To edit the **Details** section and choose what's inside, jump to **Setup | Object Manager**, select the **Advertisement** object, and click **Page Layouts**:

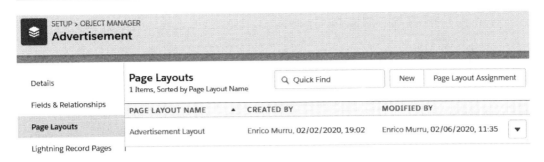

Figure 12.4 – Page Layouts on the Advertisement object

4. We have a page layout only. Click it to show the **Enhanced Page Layout Editor**, displayed as follows:

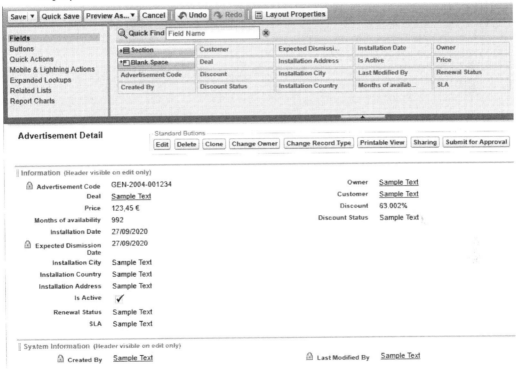

Figure 12.5 – Enhanced Page Layout Editor

From this page, you can drag and drop the following:

- **Fields**: Standard and custom fields, plus **Blank Space** to create a mosaic with blank spaces in each section and **Section** to create brand new sections.

- **Buttons**: Standard and custom buttons (quick actions are usually preferred to buttons in Lightning Experience).

- **Quick Actions**: This lists available quick actions for Salesforce Classic Publisher.

- **Mobile & Lightning Actions**: This lists all available actions for Lightning Experience.

- **Related Lists**: This lists all available related objects that the current object is a parent of (with a lookup or master-detail relationship).

- **Report charts**: Report charting for the given Salesforce object.

The layout will mandatorily display master-detail fields or universally required fields: you won't be able to remove them from the layout.

By hovering over a field, you can see the API name (there can be cases where fields have similar labels):

Figure 12.6 – Item details on the layout designer panel

To better organize the amount of data, we can create new sections, by simply dragging the **Section** item on the page, and adjusting the position and order of all fields:

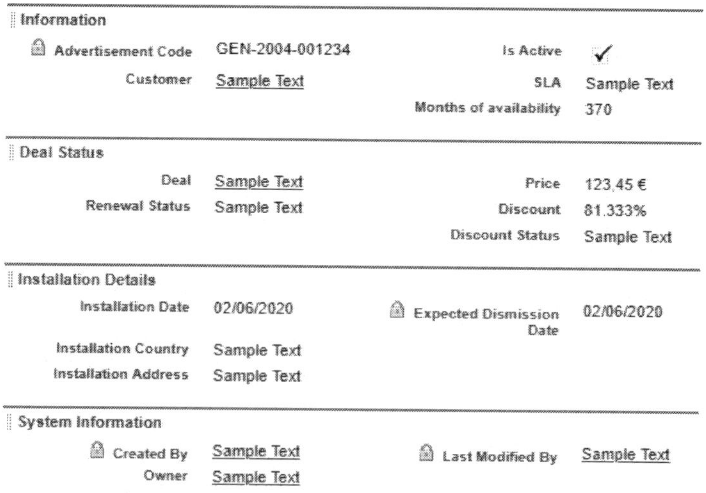

Figure 12.7 – Reshaping the Advertisement record

So after adding a section, this is what we have in the preceding configuration:

- We have created two new sections, **Deal Status** with the info about the deal and **Installation Details** with some installation-related info.

- The **Information** section at the top (which is a standard section) with some general key fields.

- The **System Information** section (standard as well) still contains the **Created By/Last Modified By** info and also the **Owner** info.

Save the layout using the **Quick Save** button (which simply saves but stays on the same page to let you continue with your layout experiments), open an **Account** record in another browser tab, and see how the record layout changes according to our layout configuration:

Figure 12.8 – Record layout modifications

> **Important note**
> Remember that, if you haven't disabled the caching option, it could take up to 15 minutes for the layout to be updated (this is for performance reasons). To recall what we've already said, jump to **Setup | Security | Session Settings** and uncheck **Enable secure and persistent browser caching to improve performance**. Remember not to do it in production.

You can configure each section by double-clicking on its header:

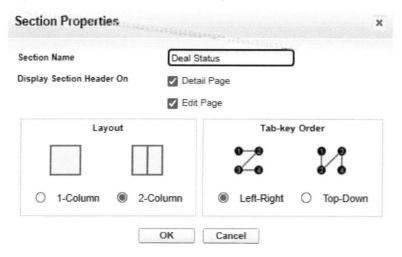

Figure 12.9 – Section properties

Configuring grants you the power to do the following:

- Change the section's name.
- Display the section header in the **View** mode (**Detail** page) or in the **Edit** mode (**Edit** page).
- Change the number of available columns.
- Change the tab behavior.

You can even click **Layout Properties** in the layout editor tool section to change the layout name and show/hide **Highlights Panel** (which is displayed in the Sales/Service Console app as a record recap panel) and **Interaction Log**, which are console-related features of Salesforce Classic (that we won't cover here).

> **Further reading**
>
> We won't cover Salesforce Console apps as they are a specialized kind of
> Salesforce Lightning app with an enhanced browsing experience (which
> lets you use a single browser tab and open multiple sub-tabs to bring
> a complete customer vision), but if you are interested, you can have a
> look at Salesforce Help at `https://help.salesforce.com/`
> `articleView?id=console2_about.htm&type=5`.

Most of the configurations that you find on the **Layout Properties** page (such as the
Custom Console Components, **Mini Page Layout**, and **Mini Console View** links on the
upper header of the editor page) are Salesforce Classic related.

> **Further reading:**
>
> If you want to dig into Salesforce Classic layout customization, start
> from Salesforce Help at `https://help.salesforce.com/`
> `articleView?err=1&id=customize_layoutcustomize_`
> `pd.htm&type=5`.

So far, we have seen how to configure an **Object** page layout to display fields and sections
according to our needs. In the following section, we'll explore the *preview* features, which
let you see a preview of the layout configuration according to a given user's profile and,
finally, how to assign layouts to profiles because not all users should see the same amount
of data (you may need to select only specific fields to be shown to a given user's profile and
hide any other data).

Layout preview and assignment to profiles

We've said that layout fields' visibility depends on how an FLS is configured for each user's
profile/permission sets.

1. As an example, let's take our users:

Action	Active ↑	Full Name	User License	Profile	Role	Manager
☐ | Edit	✓	Murru, Enrico	Salesforce	System Administrator	CEO	
☐ | Edit | Login	✓	Lavori, Stefano	Salesforce	Custom Standard User	SVP, Sales & Marketing	Murru, Enrico
☐ | Edit | Login	✓	Portoni, Guglielmo	Salesforce Platform	Custom: Sales Platform User	VP, International Sales	Lavori, Stefano

Figure 12.10 – Users list on our Developer Edition org

2. As we've seen in previous chapters, let's take the **Custom: Sales Platform User** profile and let's reduce the number of **Advertisements** fields they can have access to:

Figure 12.11 – Profile configuration to lower the number of accessible fields

3. Save this configuration, go back to the layout editor, click the **Preview As...** button, and select the **Custom: Sales Platform User** and also **System Administrator** (which has full permissions):

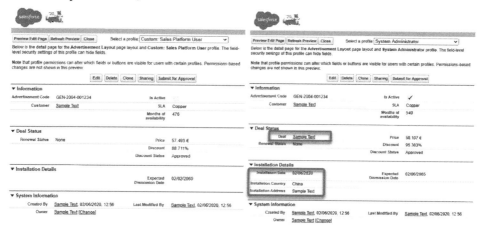

Figure 12.12 – Layout preview with different profiles

4. As expected, we can see in the preceding screenshot that **Custom: Sales Platform User** has limited access to the record.

If we don't want to show the same sections to different profiles, we can create a brand new layout by *cloning* the current layout from the layout editor page by clicking the down-arrow icon next to the **Save** button and selecting **Save As…**.

Let's call this layout `Advertisement Limited Layout` and shape it using only one section:

Figure 12.13 – Brand new layout creation

5. Save it and jump to the **Page Layouts** page for the **Advertisement** object:

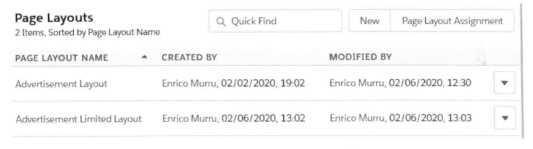

Figure 12.14 – Advertisement Page Layouts home page

6. To assign layouts to different user profiles, click the **Page Layout Assignment** button and make the right configurations:

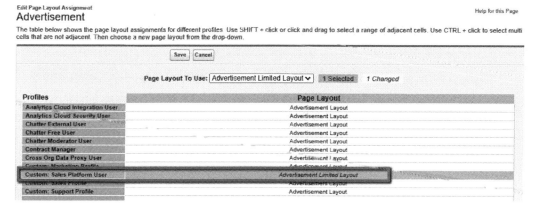

Figure 12.15 – Page Layout Assignment

As we are using only three kinds of profiles, the other profiles don't need to receive a specific configuration, so we'll leave them with the previous configuration (the original layout) and leave the security setup to the FLS configuration.

7. Now if we open the same record with **Custom: Sales Platform User**, this is what we see:

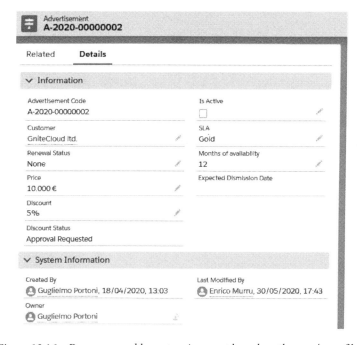

Figure 12.16 – Proper record layout assignment based on the user's profile

So far, you are ready to configure page layouts and assign them to the right profiles, so any kind of user would see the right amount of data, avoiding confusion and improving their daily work.

There is another level of layout assignment that lets you apply different page layouts based on a way to categorize records using a platform feature called **record types**.

Record types assignment

Another important feature related to a Salesforce object is the **record types** definition.

What is a record type? It's a way to differentiate records for the same object that have the *same concept* but a *different execution*.

Let's take the Case object. We can define different record types to differentiate different types of cases, such as **Product Information**, **Installation Support**, or **Activation Request** cases.

Another example could be a custom Salesforce object used to identify vehicles. We can have different kinds of vehicles all with different features, so we can create a vehicle record type named `Motorcycle`, another one called `Car`, and another one called `Truck`. All record types will share the same basic information (the fields), but they may be used differently.

Record types let you define different layouts and picklist values depending on their association with a given record.

An **Activation Request** case may show the **Expected Installation Date** field while **Installation Support** doesn't require it; a `Truck` vehicle can have **Number of wheels** editable and with different values (from 4 to 16) while the `Motorcycle` vehicle only needs 2 wheels and the field would be read-only.

A record type is no more than a standard lookup that is created from the object setup and is used to categorize records.

Let's create a simple `Vehicle` custom object with its own tab (you know how to do it!) with a picklist field that states the number of wheels on the vehicle:

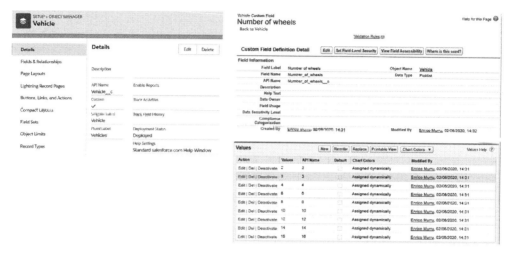

Figure 12.17 – Vehicle definition

Now we can define three record types from the **Record Types** page on the **Vehicle** setup page. At first, the object doesn't have an assigned record type (we can say there is only one record type, called the master record type).

Click the **New** button on the **Record Types** page:

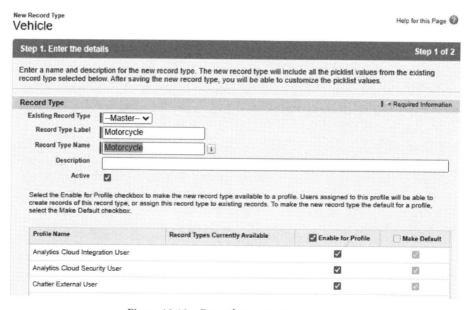

Figure 12.18 – Record type creation, step 1

From the preceding screenshot, we see the following:

- In the first step of the record type creation wizard, select a label and API name for the record type; you can optionally select **Existing Record Type** to inherit a setup, but here we can only inherit from the **Master** record type because we don't have any others yet.

- Mark it as **Active** and enable the record type for the needed profiles (the record type selection will be the first thing a user will type in when creating a new record).

- You can optionally select **Make Default**. This is the first record type, so it will be the default record type: this means that, if you try to create a new **Vehicle** record, the system will automatically assign the **Motorcycle** record type and won't ask you to choose.

- Click **Next** and choose the layout for this kind of record type (leave the default value).

Click **Save & New** and create two other record types following the same flow:

- **Car**: Active, enable for profiles, mark as default, leave default layout selection

- **Truck**: Active, enable for profiles, don't mark as default, leave default layout selection as well

This is how your new **Record Types** page should look:

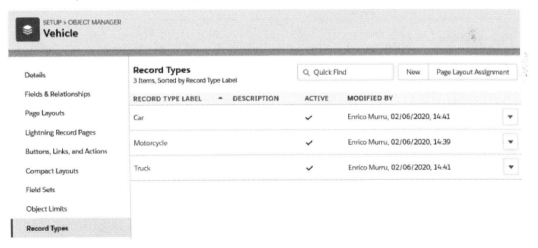

Figure 12.19 – Available record types on the Vehicle object

Now click on the **Car** record type to see the details:

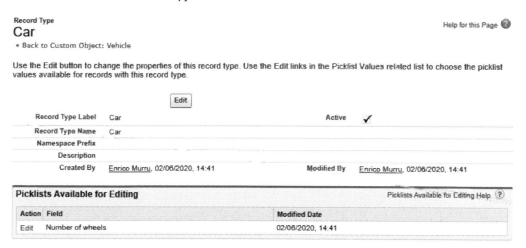

Figure 12.20 – Record type details

From this page, you can configure how the object picklists' values are shown to the user that is creating/editing a record with the current record type. Click the **Edit** link next to the **Number of wheels** picklist and select the values you want to display. It's no surprise that cars will only have four wheels, motorcycles have two, and trucks a selection of possible values. In the following screenshots, we'll see the selected values for all three record types:

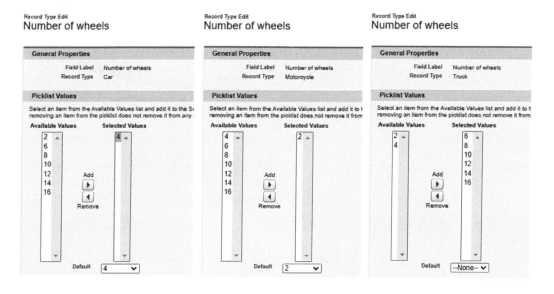

Figure 12.21 – Picklist definition on different record types

Take a close look. We can select all available values and optionally a default value.

If we are to create a new **Vehicle** record (from **All Apps | Vehicles**), this is the flow:

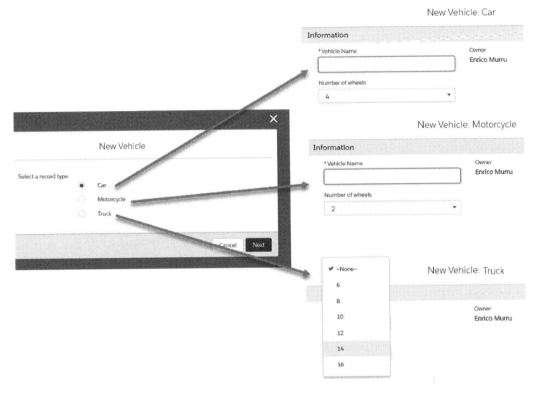

Figure 12.22 – Record type selection on new Vehicle record creation

After creating the first record type, a new **Record Type** lookup field (with the API name `RecordTypeId`) appears among the object fields, which can be used anywhere, such as default values, formulas, or sharing rules.

When record types are enabled, layout-to-profile assignment will gain a new level of configuration, and the **Record Types** column will be as shown in the following screenshot:

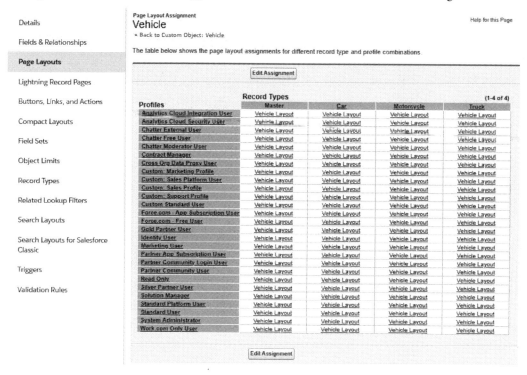

Figure 12.23 – Record types for layout-to-profile assignment

Never use the **Master** record type to do any value assignment or any automation process, because it will never be used once record types are enabled.

> **Further reading**
>
> If you want to enhance your knowledge of record types, refer to Salesforce Help at `https://help.salesforce.com/articleView?id=customize_recordtype.htm&type=5` or have a read of the Salesforce Ben blog at `https://www.salesforceben.com/salesforce-record-type-best-practices-tutorial/`.

Record types let you classify records based on common informative characteristics, and this leads to the option to assign different page layouts, thus exposing them.

Another important part of record layouts is the **Related List** configurations, which give you a wider view of record-related fields: let's explore related lists in the next section.

Related Lists

Another part of record layout configuration is related to **Related Lists**, which are the records related to the current record as child records (with lookup or master-detail relationships with the current record).

Let's take account-related lists, clicking on the **Related** tab on an **Account** record:

Figure 12.24 – An Account record's Related list

On the page layout editor, we can define the following:

- Which related list to show
- Which fields of the related record to show
- Which sort order the child record should be displayed in

Let's jump to the **Account** setup page, select **Page Layout**, and select **Account Layout** and click on the **Related Lists** item on the editor panel to scroll down to the **Related Lists** section.

This is the screen you will see:

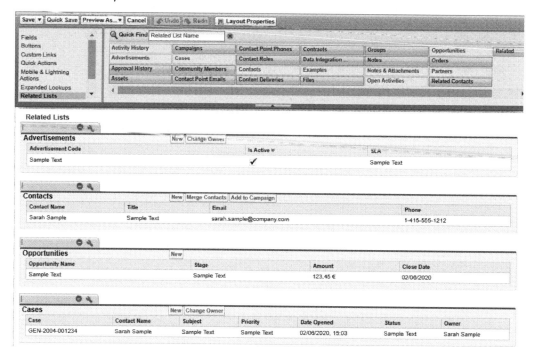

Figure 12.25 – Related Lists configuration

You can add up to 100 related lists by dragging and dropping from the upper panel and each list can be edited using the wrench icon, shown as follows:

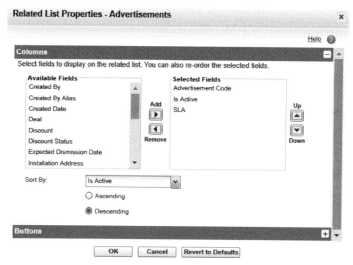

Figure 12.26 – Related Lists options

Define the fields you want to display of the related record and a sort order; optionally, you can even select a button to be displayed (usually list buttons, which can be created from the *Buttons, Links, and Actions* section).

> **Further reading**
>
> As stated in *Chapter 11, Interacting with Actions*, we've not covered buttons and links as this configuration requires some coding skills. Refer to Salesforce Help at `https://help.salesforce.com/articleView?id=customize_enterprise.htm&type=5` for more details on custom buttons and links.

Related lists are an easy way to list related records and expand the amount of data you want to show to your users.

Next, let's have a look at compact layout configuration to highlight key record fields.

Compact Layouts

A cool addition to record layouts is compact layouts, which are used to define a record's key fields in many places, including the Lightning Experience desktop site, the Salesforce mobile app, and the Outlook and Gmail integrations.

> **Further reading**
>
> We're not covering Outlook and Gmail integrations with Salesforce, but if you are curious, refer to Salesforce Help at `https://help.salesforce.com/articleView?id=email_int_overview.htm&type=5`.

Compact layouts are used to show the following:

- Up to seven fields on the record's **Highlights Panel**
- Up to five fields on the expanded lookup panel shown when you put your mouse over a lookup field

To configure a compact layout, simply go to the object's setup page and select **Compact Layouts**; at first, only the **System Default** compact layout is shown (which cannot be modified), so we're going to create a new one:

1.   We begin by clicking the **New** button:

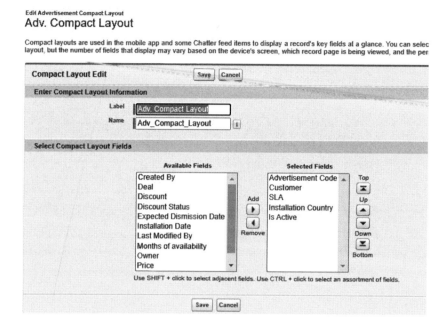

Figure 12.27 – Compact layout configuration

2.   Click on **Compact Layout Assignment** and assign the new compact layout as **Primary Compact Layout**:

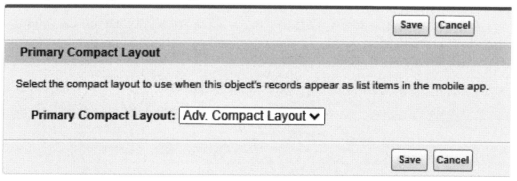

Figure 12.28 – Compact layout assignment

3. Now go to an **Advertisement** record to see the new panel in the upper part with the selected fields in the compact layout:

Figure 12.29 – Record highlights panel

The first field (the **Advertisement** code) is shown below the object name, while the other fields are on the lower line.

The same layout is used when hovering on an **Advertisement** record; to see this in action, click on the **Customer** (**Account**) lookup and browse its **Advertisement** related list, then move the mouse over an **Advertisement** record:

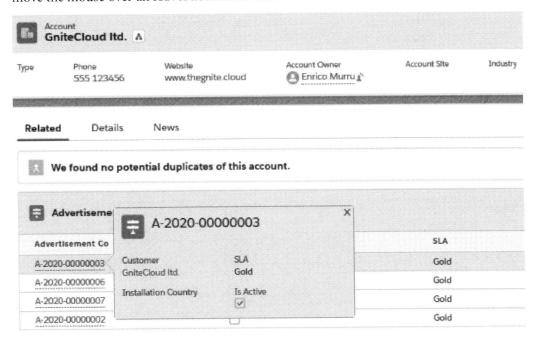

Figure 12.30 – Lookup highlights panel

If you are using record types, you'll be able to select a different Compact Layout for each record type, using the **Compact Layout Assignment** button on the **Compact Layouts** page:

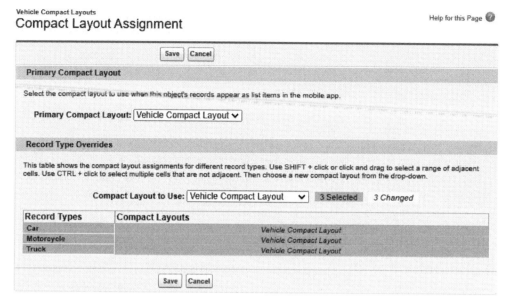

Figure 12.31 – Compact layout assignment with multiple record types

> **Further reading**
>
> For more considerations on compact layouts, refer to
> Salesforce Help at `https://help.salesforce.com/`
> `articleView?id=compact_layout_notes.htm&type=5`.

In the previous sections, we discovered all the main options to set up a Salesforce object's page layout to show the right amount of data to your users, including related list configuration and compact layouts to give a hint of the principal fields that highlight the record.

In the next section, we'll have a quick dive into how to configure search layouts.

Configuring Search Layouts

One more layout option is the **Search Layouts** configuration, which states which fields should be shown when searching for a specific object.

To configure these fields, go to the object's setup page and select **Search Layouts**; then select **Default Layout** or a specific profile layout to set up the fields to be displayed.

In the following example, we select **Default Layout** with **Override the search result column customizations for all users** as we want all user-defined layouts to be reset with this one:

Figure 12.32 – Search layouts configuration

Refresh your tab and simply search for a record (for example, by the content of one of its text fields) using a global search:

Figure 12.33 – Search results displaying selected fields

The results are displayed using the fields configured on the **Search Results** layout.

Let's close the chapter with a quick guide on how to configure list views for easy record listing.

Setting up List Views

One final word on **List Views** is that they are a way to customize the records displayed on the object home page – up to 2,000 records per list.

In the following example, we can see **All** advertisement records:

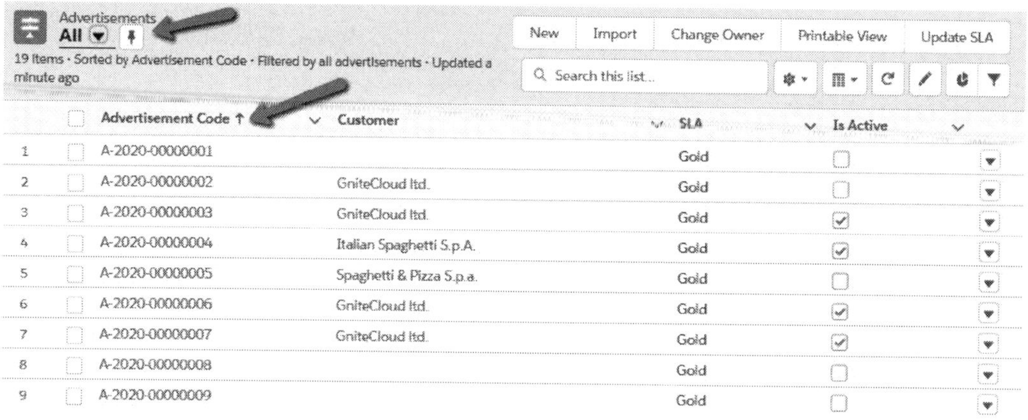

Figure 12.34 – The All list view

The pin icon means that this list view has been pinned, that is, this is the default list view loaded upon landing on the record home page. We can also see that we have the records sorted by **Advertisement Code**.

List views can be customized in terms of the number of fields displayed and the filters applied.

To create a new list view

1.   Click the gear icon next to the **Search this list...** search box and select **New**:

:

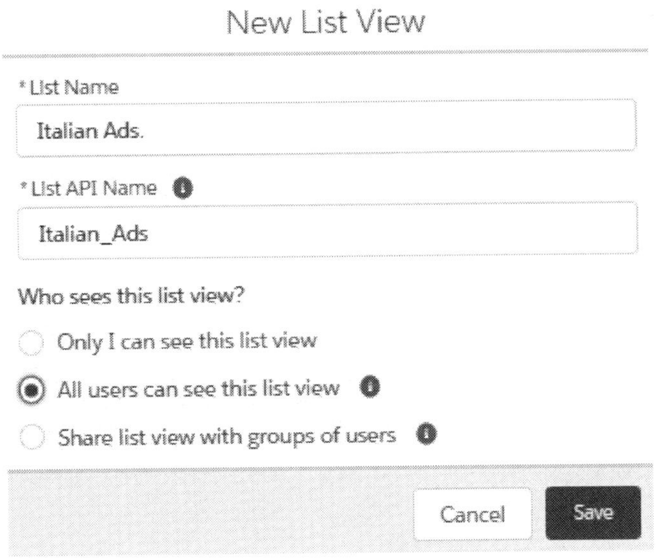

New List View

* List Name

Italian Ads.

* List API Name ⓘ

Italian_Ads

Who sees this list view?

○ Only I can see this list view

◉ All users can see this list view ⓘ

○ Share list view with groups of users ⓘ

Cancel   Save

Figure 12.35 – List view creation

The sharing options allow you to make the list view private, public, or shared only with a group of users.

The result is simple—we have a list view on the **Advertisement** object sorted by **Advertisement Code** and filtered by **My advertisements** (that is, the ads our user is the owner of):

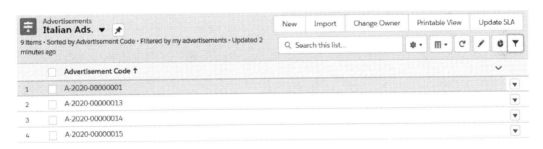

Figure 12.36 – Raw version of a new list view

To change the fields displayed, click on the gear icon, select **Select Fields to Display**, and select all the needed fields:

Select Fields to Display

Available Fields

Visible Fields

Installation Country   Advertisement Code

Installation Date   Customer

Last Modified By   Deal

Last Modified By Alias   Installation Address

Last Modified Date   Is Active

Months of availability

Cancel   Save

Figure 12.37 – Setting up the fields to display in the list view

Now let's update the filters from the **Edit List Filters** option on the gear icon:

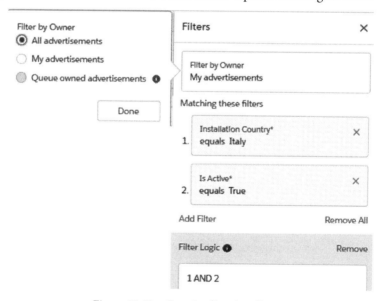

Filter by Owner
◉ All advertisements
○ My advertisements
◯ Queue owned advertisements ❶

Done

Filters   ×

Filter by Owner
My advertisements

Matching these filters

1. Installation Country*
    equals Italy   ×

2. Is Active*
    equals True   ×

Add Filter   Remove All

Filter Logic ❶   Remove

1 AND 2

Figure 12.38 – Creating list view filters

With this utility, you can select the ownership filter (we selected **All advertisements** instead of **My advertisements**), and also two additional filters based on **Installation country** (**Italy**) and on the **Is Active** flag (**True**). You can even create a complex login with all combinations of OR and AND operators.

This list view leads to the following result:

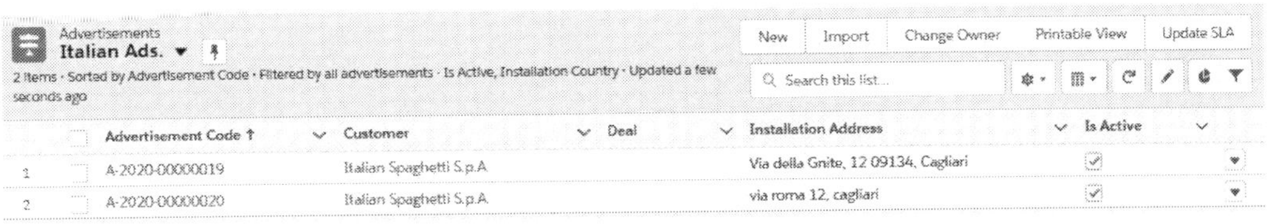

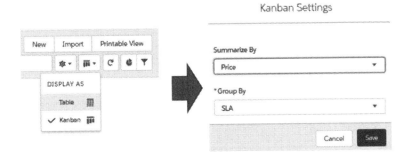

Figure 12.39 – Filtered list view configured

A cool alternative to the common tabular list view is the **Kanban** display, where you can select a field that represents the *lanes* and optionally a summary field:

Figure 12.40 – List view in Kanban mode

This is the result:

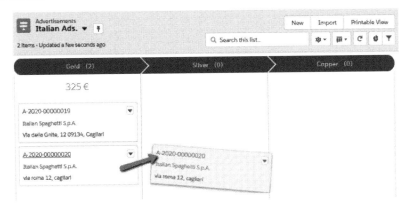

Figure 12.41 – Kanban list view and the drag and drop feature

Using this view, you can easily update the lane field by dragging and dropping the record from one lane to the other.

List views can even be searched using the **Search this list…** search box.

Finally, the **Printable View** button lets you see the list view result in a print-friendly mode:

Figure 12.42 – Print-friendly list view mode

The system opens up a new window that can be quickly printed out.

You'll find yourself creating tens of list views on diverse objects to filter on records and have a quick view of a subset of the dataset, to simply do a check, to identify a potential bug in your automation, or just to have a deeper look at a specific kind of field. We can consider list views as a simplified reporting tool (we'll see reporting in *Chapter 16, Data Reporting*).

Blaze your trail

To enhance your knowledge, refer to the following Trailhead modules:

- Customize the User Interface for a Recruiting App: `https://trailhead.salesforce.com/en/content/learn/projects/customize-the-ui-for-a-recruiting-app`

- App Customization Lite: `https://trailhead.salesforce.com/en/content/learn/modules/lex_migration_customization`

Summary

In this chapter, we discovered the most useful layout options that the Salesforce platform delivers.

We analyzed how to set up a record layout and how it can be customized by adding fields, actions, and new sections. Then we assigned layouts to different profiles. We introduced the concept of record types to further categorize records and give another way to assign different record layouts based on this new categorization. We saw how to add related lists to record layouts to show more records. Compact layouts then helped us to highlight the most important fields for a given object, and with search layouts, we configured which fields to display when searching records with a global search.

Finally, we used List Views with filters to quickly get lists of records to highlight specific conditions that any agent may be required to check on.

In the next chapter, we'll go even further, showing the power of the App Builder to deliver even more custom interfaces.

13
The Lightning App Builder

In *Chapter 12*, *All About Layouts*, we saw how to configure record-related layouts with pure point-and-click actions, and how to assign them to your users. Let's now go a step further.

What if we want to customize a generic page to be added to a Salesforce app or change any record-related page to add more components to increase the amount of data or even to remove components to simplify it?

We can do this with Lightning App Builder, a visual and powerful tool to create and customize Lightning pages and Lightning apps, both for desktop and mobile.

By the end of this chapter, we'll be familiar with the following:

- Using the Lightning App Builder
- Building Lightning pages and apps
- Assigning pages and apps to profiles

Meeting the Lightning App Builder

The Lightning App Builder is a point-and-click tool that lets you create a custom home page, record page, and an app page for the Salesforce Lightning Experience desktop and mobile sites, bringing the power of standard and custom Lightning components into the hands of any Salesforce administrator.

You can customize an **Opportunity** record page to include a custom Lightning component developed by your developers to ask an external shipping system to track a shipment, or customize the service app's home page to include a custom component acquired from the AppExchange.

We've seen in *Chapter 10, Designing Lightning Flows,* that we can nest flows in Salesforce Lightning pages (we used the **customer support flow** in our Lightning app's home page). To do this, we have to use the **Flow** component (one of the many standard components available), configure it to select the Lightning flow we created, and place it where we want it to be shown to the user.

The Lightning App Builder brings the power of coding to user interfaces as well. Indeed, you can add custom Lightning components that your developers have built or even download AppExchange components right into your org and use them where needed.

Let's now see how to create and customize our apps, but before doing this, we need to execute a simple configuration on our org, which is required to let us use custom components (created by our devs or obtained from the AppExchange) on Lightning pages: the **My Domain** activation.

Activating My Domain

The **My Domain** activation gives your org a customized subdomain: if you look at your browser's bar, you can see that the Salesforce URL is something like `https://na5.lightning.force.com` or `https://eu29.lightning.force.com`. Here, the first part of the domain contains the Salesforce instance name where your CRM is located (**NA** stands for **North America**, **EU** for **EMEA**, **AP** for **Asian-Pacific**, and **CS** for **sandbox**-only instances). This means that many customers' orgs can lie on the same Salesforce instance.

You can give your org a personalized subdomain by activating **My Domain** and getting an instance domain such as `https://yourcompanyname.my.salesforce.com`, where `yourcompanyname` can be any valid string that identifies your business (not necessarily your company name).

> **Note**
> Once you activate **My Domain**, you cannot go back: for production environments, you can ask the Salesforce support to change it to another name (this may be needed if the company requires some rebranding or changes its legal name). Try to use the most generic name possible.

To activate **My Domain**, go to **Setup | Company Settings | My Domain**:

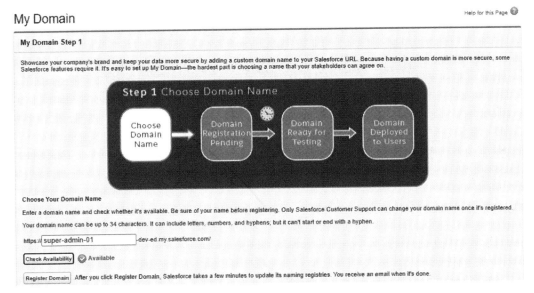

Figure 13.1 – My Domain activation page

From this screenshot, we see that we are performing the following steps:

1. Selecting the subdomain (we chose **super-admin-01**). Developer Edition orgs have an additional `-dev-ed` suffix added automatically to identity that it is a DE org and thereby preventing production orgs from overlapping.

2. Clicking the **Check Availability** button to check whether other admins across the globe have already used the same subdomain.

3. Clicking the **Register Domain** button.

The domain is being registered. This can take a few minutes and you'll receive an email when everything is ready to be deployed. Sometimes, it takes way less than you think and hitting the refresh button on your browser brings up the updated **My Domain** home page, refreshed with the domain ready to be deployed:

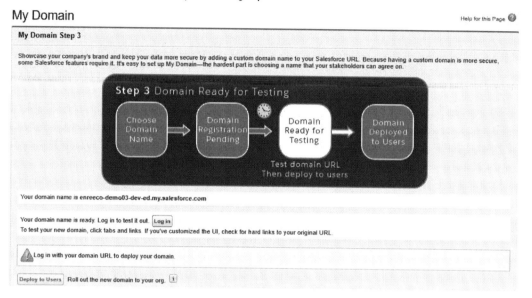

Figure 13.2 – My Domain is ready to be deployed

Next, we perform the following steps for deployment:

1. Click on the **Log in** button.

2. A new tab is opened with the new subdomain (in this example, it should be `https://super-admin-01-dev-ed-lightning.force.com`).

3. Click the **Deploy to Users** button to roll out the new subdomain to any Salesforce user.

This is all done! Close all the old tabs and reopen them with the new subdomain (some may no longer work). Any new tab will be opened with the new subdomain.

To see a cool thing related to **My Domain**, look at the customization of the login page:

1. On the lower part of the **My Domain** configuration page in the **Authentication Configuration** section, click the **Edit** button and change the parameters, shown as follows:

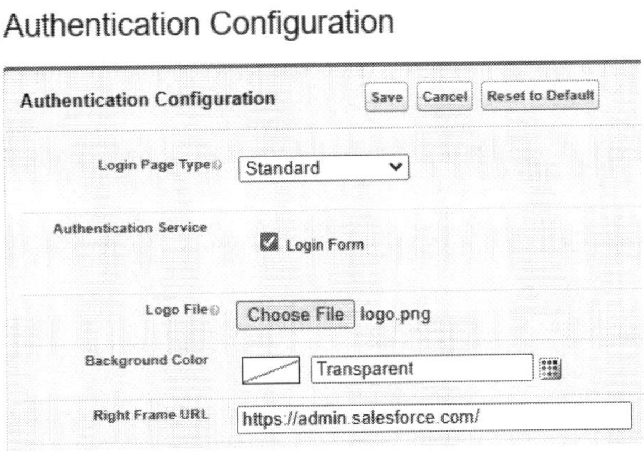

Authentication Configuration

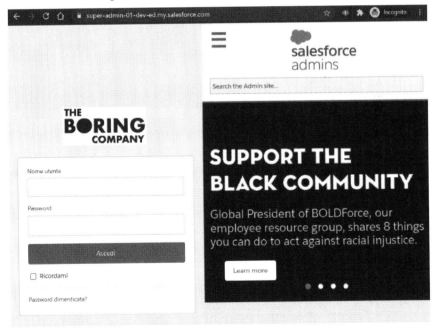

Figure 13.3 – Login page customization from My Domain

- Add a logo image (which should not exceed 100 KB and with a maximum size of 250 x 125 pixels) and a right-frame URL of your favorite size, and then click **Save**.

- Now, open a new incognito window (or another browser different from what you are using now) and enter the **My Domain** URL with the format `https://super-admin-01-dev-ed.my.salesforce.com` (replacing `super-admin-01` with your own subdomain). A customized login form is shown, so that only your users will be allowed to log in:

Figure 13.4 – Customized login page

> **Further reading**
>
> To know more about **My Domain**, refer to Salesforce Help at `https://` `help.salesforce.com/articleView?id=domain_name_` `overview.htm&type=5`.

We are now ready to dig into how the Lightning App Builder works.

Running the Lightning App Builder

We can now edit a simple Lightning page to see what's hidden inside the Lightning App Builder.

To open the Lightning App Builder, you have the following two options:

- Click on **Setup | User Interface | Lightning App Builder** and select the page you want to customize, or the **New** button to create a new Lightning page:

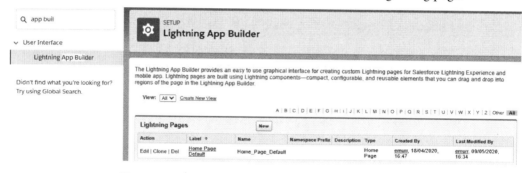

Figure 13.5 – Accessing Lightning App Builder from Setup

- Open any Salesforce Lightning page (for example, our **Adv.Division** custom app's home page), click the gear icon in the top-right corner of the site, and select **Edit Page**:

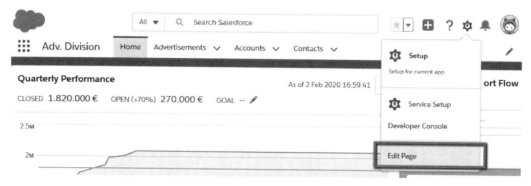

Figure 13.6 – Accessing the Lightning App Builder from any Lightning page

As per our current configuration, we only have one Lightning page and it is used to define the home page of any Salesforce app.

Let's edit this Lightning page. Click on the **Edit** link on the **Lightning App Builder** home page or click **Edit Page** on the gear menu. This is how the Lightning App Builder appears:

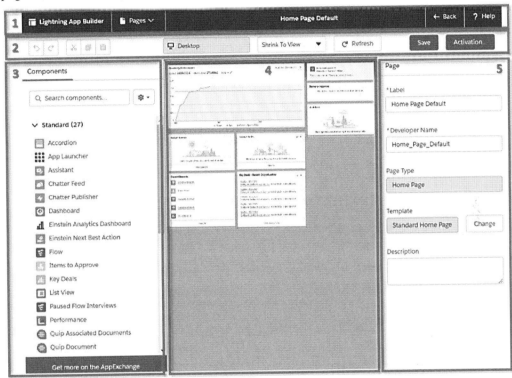

Figure 13.7 – Lightning App Builder configuration page

We can easily identify five main areas:

1. **Header**: From the upper header, you can access the list of available pages to open them and create a new one with the + (**New Page**) link.

   The **Back** button brings you back to the previous page (the **My Domain** home page or the previous page where we clicked the **Edit Page** button).

2. **Edit controls**: The lower part of the builder's header has the following options:

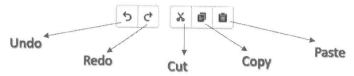

Figure 13.8 – Edit controls on the Lightning App Builder

There is also the **View Mode** settings:

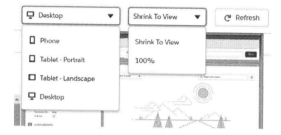

Figure 13.9 – View Mode settings on the Lightning App Builder

You can configure the form factor with which you want to view the preview (**Desktop**, **Phone**, or **Tablet**) and a *zoom* setting that allows you to set all components to the current preview window size using the **Shrink To View** option (so you see all components at a glance) or just a **100%** view with a limited view. This is more or less what you can see in the following screenshot:

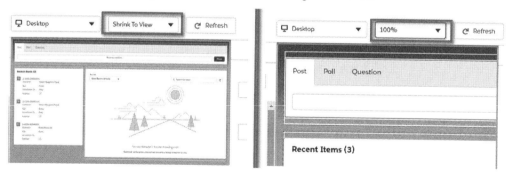

Figure 13.10 – Shrink To View versus 100% view options

This panel also contains the **Save** button and the **Activation...** button (which we'll see in the *Activating Lightning pages* section of this chapter).

3. **Components**: The components section is your toolbar for getting all available components for the kind of page you are creating (app, home, or record Lightning page) and is there so that you can drag and drop components in the preview panel:

Figure 13.11 – Dragging a component to the preview panel

Each component is marked on the right with an icon that defines the supported form factors (for example, the **Chatter Publisher** component is only supported on the **Desktop** form factor):

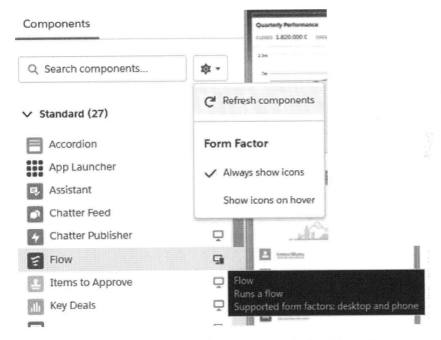

Figure 13.12 – The supported form factor for all components is displayed in the Components panel

In this panel, you'll be able to find the following:

- **Standard Components**: These are components that come built-in with your org.

- **Custom Components**: These are components created within your org (by your devs).

- **Custom – Managed Components**: These are components created by Salesforce partners that can be downloaded from the AppExchange and cannot be modified by your devs.

> **Further reading**
>
> To have a look at all available standard components, refer to Salesforce Help at `https://help.salesforce.com/articleView?id=lightning_page_components.htm&type=0`.

4. **Preview panel**: The preview panel is where the components are merged together to compose the Lightning page. There are different page layouts depending on the template your page is built on (we'll see templates shortly).

    In this panel, you can drop components, as well as select and delete them.

5. **Page and property editor**: The last panel is used to set up the properties of all the components you dropped in the preview panel. It is also used to update the main page settings, shown as follows:

Figure 13.13 – Page editor and property editor panels

To view the page editor, simply click on a *blank* space of the preview panel where no component is placed, while clicking on any component will show the property editor.

Let's now see how to build a new page from scratch.

Creating Lightning pages

To create a new page from scratch, we can click the **+ New Page** link on the **Pages** menu of the Lightning App Builder header or click the **New** button on the Lightning App Builder's **Setup** page.

The Lightning page creation wizard starts by asking which kind of page you want to create:

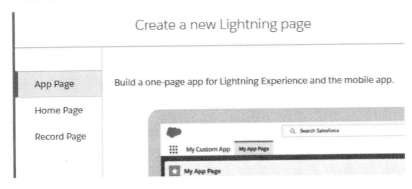

Figure 13.14 – Lightning page type selection

What kind of page do we need?

- **App Page**: This kind of page is supported on both the Lightning Experience desktop site and the Salesforce mobile app. App pages are usually used to create custom home page apps that can be accessed anywhere and offer quick access to the most important features, objects, and actions, Indeed, you can add global actions to the page.

- **Home Page**: This kind of page is supported on the Lightning Experience desktop site only (so not on mobile) and is used as a home page on Salesforce desktop apps. They don't support global action selection (you'll see all global actions available for the current context). You can create different home pages and assign them to different profiles.

- **Record Page**: You can create a customized version of almost any Salesforce object's record page. This kind of page is supported on both mobile and desktop sites. Just like **Home Page**, record pages do not support action selection, meaning that available actions depend on the object configuration.

To create our example, let's choose **App Page** (home and record pages are created in the same way), give it a proper name, and then select a template:

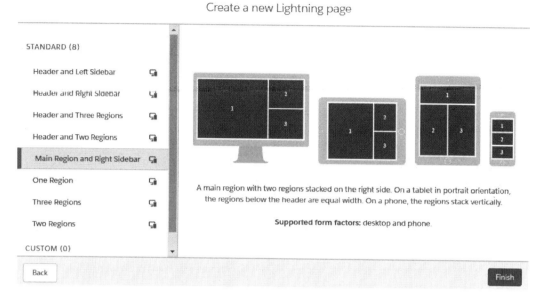

Figure 13.15 – Page template selection

By choosing a template, you are deciding the manner in which components can be dropped on the page and all the different form factors that are available (depending on the fact that the current page type supports different form factors). In the previous screenshot, you can easily see how sections are shown depending on the specific form factor that displays it (desktop, tablet landscape, tablet portrait, and mobile, respectively).

> **Further reading**
>
> If you need a different grid composition, you can build your own page templates using Lightning components. This task requires a developer. Refer to Salesforce Help at `https://developer.salesforce.com/docs/atlas.en-us.226.0.lightning.meta/lightning/components_config_for_app_builder_template_component.htm` for more information.

Click on the **Finish** button to create your new page:

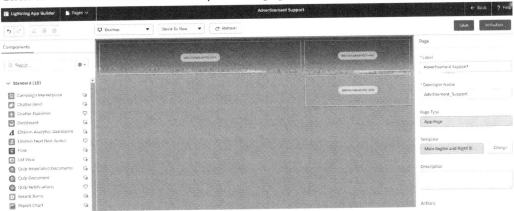

Figure 13.16 – New Lightning app page

On this new page, we have the **Page Editor** panel, where you can do the following:

- Set up the page label and developer name.

- See the current page type (this cannot be updated at this stage).

- Change the template with the **Change** button.

- Select the global actions you want to be shown when the user is on the current page.

If you change the template, after selecting the new template, you are asked to map the regions, so components are automatically moved where you want, shown as follows:

Select a new template

Map template regions

Map the regions of the old template to the regions of the new template. We'll take care of migrating your components. You'll have a chance to refine the layout and placement of your components after switching to the new template.

Current Regions (3)		New Regions (4)
Menu latéral en bas	→	Zone centrale ▼
Zone principale	→	Zone gauche ▼
Menu latéral en haut	→	Zone centrale ▼

Back   Done

Figure 13.17 – Page template change to map old regions to new regions

By clicking the **Select...** button under the **Actions** section, you can select the global actions you want to be displayed:

Figure 13.18 – Global actions selection

From the left sidebar entitled **Components**, perform a drag and drop operation. Let's add some components to the page:

- A **Rich Text** component (left region)
- **Chatter Publisher** (left region)
- **Chatter Feed** (left region)
- **Flow** (upper-right region)
- **List View** (lower-right region)
- **Recent Items** (lower-right region)

This is more or less what you'll see with different form factors:

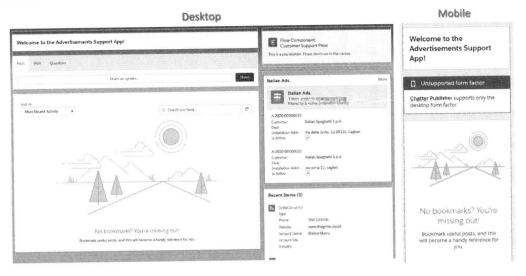

Figure 13.19 – App page preview with different form factors

Let's add some configurations to the **Properties** configuration panel, as shown here:

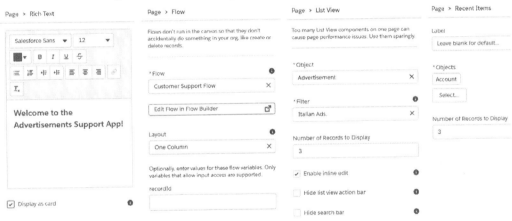

Figure 13.20 – Main component configurations

Chatter Publisher and **Chatter Feed** won't have any specific configuration other than the default one.

Click the **Save** button to save the page, but don't activate it (we'll show page activation in the last section of this chapter, and you'll be able to activate it by yourself with a few clicks).

Let's now see how to create record-related pages in order to customize record home pages.

Record pages

We've seen how to create an app page in the previous section (which is quite similar to the home page, except for the fact that it can be used on both mobile and desktop form factors) and how we create record-related pages, which let you add features and components to dear-old page layouts. When creating a record Lightning page, the wizard will ask for the object type as well:

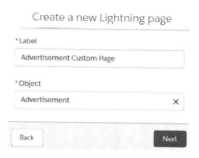

Figure 13.21 – Record Lightning page creation

We perform the following steps:

1. Click **Next** to select the template, as for the home and app page types. You can select **CLONE SALESFORCE DEFAULT PAGE** for the given page type:

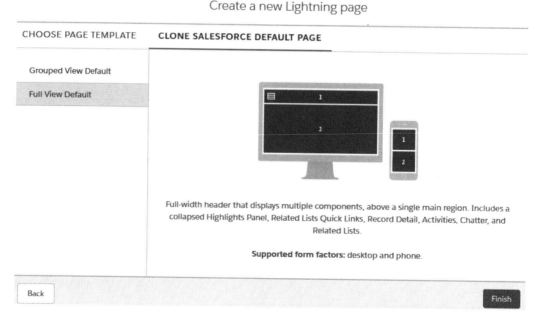

Figure 13.22 – Cloning a default page

This way, we are inheriting the current object's page definition.

2. The first thing we'll customize is the template; we'll add a two-column template:

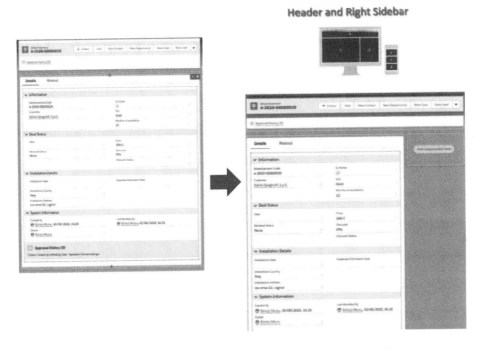

Figure 13.23 – Changing the page template for the Advertisement record Lightning page

3. Add the **Tabs** component to the right sidebar and, above it, the **Related Lists** component.

Now, let's configure the Tabs component on the left sidebar and on the right sidebar, shown as follows:

Figure 13.24 – Customizing the record page's Tabs components

Now, drop the **Chatter Publisher** and **Chatter Feed** components into the **Tabs** component containing the **Feed** tab (on the right sidebar).

This way, we'll see the following:

- In the left sidebar, the record details only

- In the right sidebar, the record's **Chatter Feed** and **Activity** tabs and below these, the related lists (defined in the object's page layout assigned to the current user's profile)

Finally, add the **Related List – Single** component above the **Details** section and set it to the **Approval History**-related list. This way, we'll have a look at how approval is going for the current record:

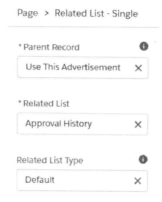

Figure 13.25 – Related List – Single component configuration for Approval History

Save the page without activating it.

The home page-type Lightning page has no special configuration, and their configuration is quite similar to the app and record pages we have covered so far.

There is a cool thing to show in relation to page configuration before concluding this section, and that is page filtering.

Page filters

You can control when a component is displayed on a Lightning page using the **Filters** settings, using filter conditions and logic.

When you select any standard or custom component dropped on the current page, you can add a display logic based on different fields.

Let's take the **Approval History** component of the previous example. We know, from *Chapter 12, All About Layouts*, that if an **Advertisement** object doesn't have any price or discount, no approval should be executed. We can therefore remove the component from the top page if these conditions are not met using **Filters**:

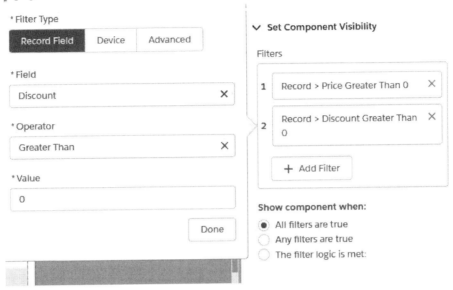

Figure 13.26 – Filters configuration for the Approval History top component

When dealing with a record page, you can select **Record Field** and **Device** (that is the current used form factor), whereas the **Advanced** option allows you to select a number of more *advanced* fields related to a user's permissions, record-related objects (you can get fields coming from any related record), device form factor, or user object (such as profile fields):

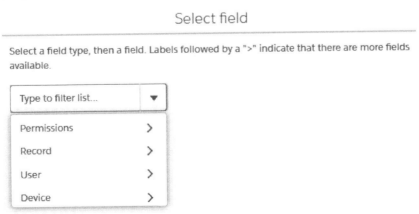

Figure 13.27 – Advanced field selection for a component's filter configuration

Save the page with the new filter and open the previous **Advertisement Support** custom app page (use the **Pages** menu on the builder's header to quickly move from page to page). This kind of page (just like the **Home page** type) is not related to any Salesforce object, so if you plan to use filters, you won't see any record-related filter option. Let's add some filtering to the **Advertisement Support** page and configure the following filters on some of the components:

- **Chatter Publisher**: Doesn't show the component on phone form factors (it isn't supported at all):

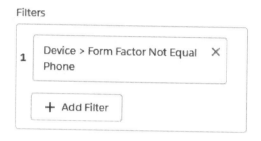

Figure 13.28 – Form factor filter

- **Flow**: Hides the component if the current user is not an administrator:

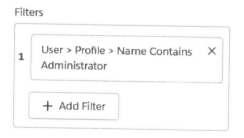

Figure 13.29 – User's profile filter

Further reading

Not all field types are supported. To get more details, refer to Salesforce Help at `https://help.salesforce.com/articleView?id=lightning_page_components_visibility.htm&type=0`.

As we said earlier, we can add custom components to our component library. Let's briefly see how this can be done.

Adding custom components from AppExchange

AppExchange has been built to provide a way to exchange solutions across all Salesforce partners.

> **Further reading**
>
> If you want to go deeper into AppExchange, start from the AppExchange FAQ page at `https://www.salesforce.com/eu/solutions/appexchange/faq/`. Learn how AppExchange was created in this quick post at `https://www.salesforce.com/blog/2019/02/steve-jobs-inspired-appexchange.html`.

From this marketplace, you can get tons of free components, so you don't need to reinvent the wheel.

Let's take a component to show YouTube videos directly in your Salesforce Lightning pages:

1. Go to `http://www.appexchange.com` and search for `Lightning YouTube Container` (`https://appexchange.salesforce.com/appxListingDetail?listingId=a0N3A00000Ecs9zUAB`). This is where you'll land:

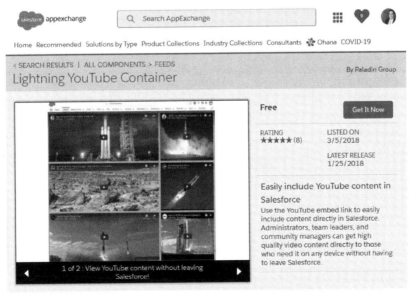

Figure 13.30 – AppExchange listing page

2.   To install this AppExchange listing on your current developer org, make sure this org is linked to your `trailblazer.me` account. Jump to `https://trailblazer.me/settings` and check whether your testing org is connected on the **Connected Account** settings (with the *Winter '20* release, Salesforce has unified logins across many of its portals, including AppExchange, Trailblazer Community, and Help sites).

3.   Click on the **Get It Now** button, select the username of the org where you want this package to be installed, and then click on **Install in Production**, shown as follows:

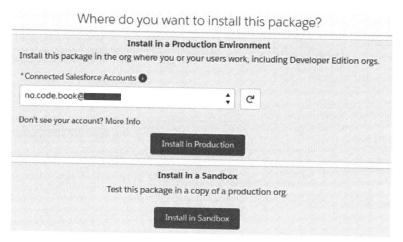

Figure 13.31 – Selecting the org where the listing should be installed

4.   Take care to check whether the org you're going to install the package on is the correct one (you don't want to install unnecessary packages on customer orgs). In the confirmation details popup that appears, click **Confirm and Install**.

     You may be required to log in again.

5.   You are then redirected to the installation page, where you need to decide which users will be allowed to access the package content (select **Install for All Users**):

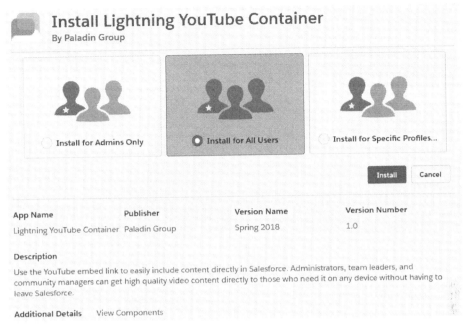

Figure 13.32 – Package installation preparation

6. By clicking **Install**, Salesforce will take care of the installation of the package on your org. Once completed, you'll have the package installed. You can check which packages are installed on your org, as well as find the **Uninstall** command whenever you no longer require the component, in **Setup | Apps | Packaging | Installed Packages**.

7. Now, go back to the Lightning App Builder and select the **Home Page Default** page. Check out the **Components** panel and a new **Custom – Managed** component shows up:

Figure 13.33 – YouTube custom component on the home page default Lightning page

8. Save it and jump back to any home page to see this new component in action:

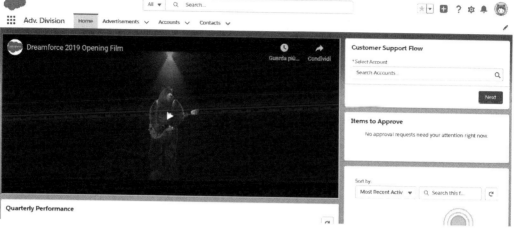

Figure 13.34 – YouTube custom component in action

To conclude this chapter, let's finally see how to activate the pages.

Activating Lightning pages

Before a page can be used, you need to activate it, and you have precisely three kinds of options to activate:

- Make it the default home page across the org.
- Make it the default home page only for specific apps.
- Assign it to specific apps and profiles.

This is true for home Lightning pages, and we choose to select **Home Page Default** as the default org page (this is what we configured in *Chapter 12, All About Layouts*, when configuring the **Flow** component):

ORG DEFAULT   APP DEFAULT   APP AND PROFILE

This page is set as the org default home page.

If you remove this page, the Salesforce system default home page replaces it until you assign a new org default home page.

Remove as Org Default

Figure 13.35 – Home page default set as the org's home default

When dealing with app Lightning pages, the page is a standalone page, meaning it can't be marked as default, as seen on the home type page.

The app is regarded as a custom tab that can be added, if needed, to other Salesforce apps or to the mobile navigation configuration. Any other profile-based configuration must be done via profiles or permission set configuration. This is what you see when activating an app lightning page:

Activation: Advertisement Support

PAGE SETTINGS   LIGHTNING EXPERIENCE   MOBILE NAVIGATION

Give this app page a name, set the page visibility, and choose an icon.

App Name

Enter a name for your app.

Advertisement Support

Icon

Choose an icon to represent your app in Lightning Experience and the mobile app.

Change...

Page Activation

A custom tab was created for this page when it was first activated. Adjust the tab's visibility to users by using Profiles and Permission Sets and by adding page to navigation menus.

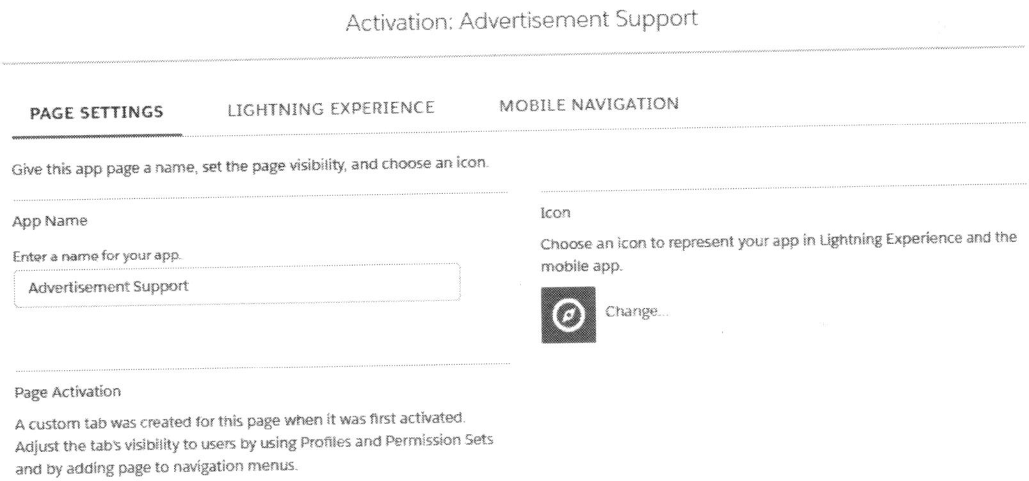

Figure 13.36 – Activating an app Lightning page

Note that this configuration can be done manually by means of the following steps:

- Creating a new tab from **Setup | User Interface | Tabs** (click **New** on **Lightning Page Tabs**).

- Once the tab has been created, enable the tab on the mobile navigation from **Setup | Apps | Mobile Apps | Salesforce | Salesforce Navigation**.

Click **Save** to activate the app Lightning page.

Finally, open **Advertisement Custom Page** (this is a record Lightning page for the **Advertisement** object) and click the **Activation...** button:

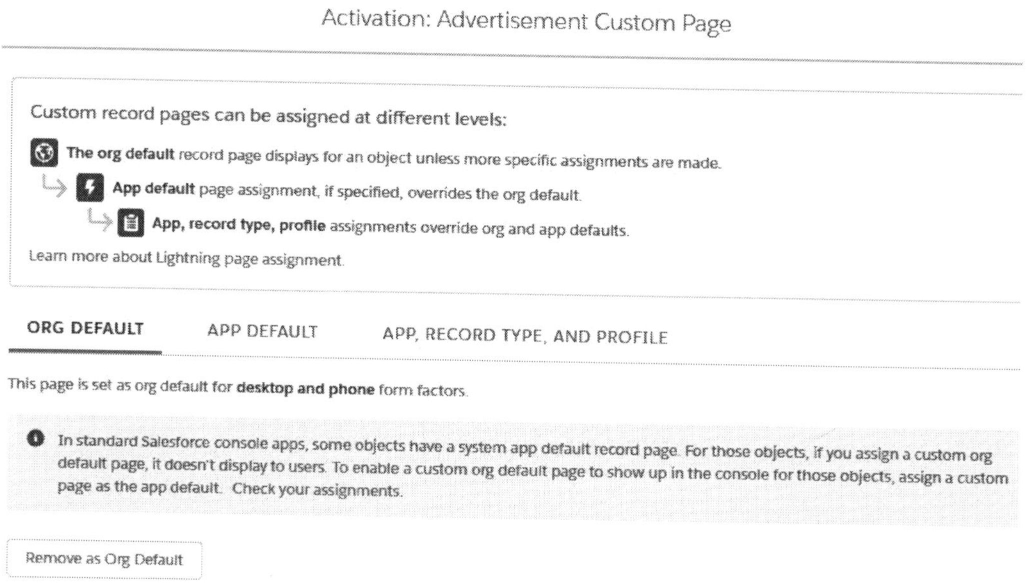

Activation: Advertisement Custom Page

Custom record pages can be assigned at different levels:

The **org default** record page displays for an object unless more specific assignments are made.

App default page assignment, if specified, overrides the org default.

App, record type, profile assignments override org and app defaults.

Learn more about Lightning page assignment.

ORG DEFAULT   APP DEFAULT   APP, RECORD TYPE, AND PROFILE

This page is set as org default for **desktop and phone** form factors.

In standard Salesforce console apps, some objects have a system app default record page. For those objects, if you assign a custom org default page, it doesn't display to users. To enable a custom org default page to show up in the console for those objects, assign a custom page as the app default. Check your assignments.

Remove as Org Default

Figure 13.37 – Record Lightning page activation

It works more or less like the home page, the only difference being that it is related to the **Advertisement** record. Let's mark it as default for mobile and desktop (when requested by the **Mark as Default** wizard).

We have activated all three pages.

We've already seen the default page. If you open any Salesforce app, the same home page with the YouTube video on top is shown (because we marked it as the org default).

Click on the **App Launcher** icon. You can now find the **Advertisement Support** lightning page as a standalone tab, with all components defined in the Lightning Builder:

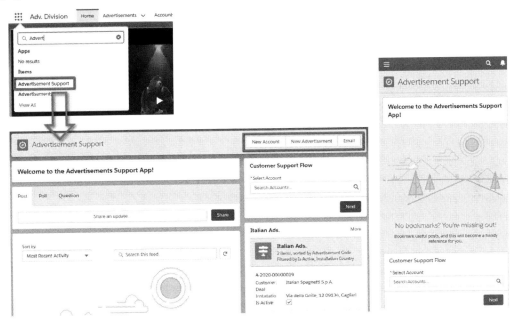

Figure 13.38 – App Lightning page on desktop and mobile

If you look closely, the mobile version on the right side of the previous screenshot doesn't show **Chatter Publisher**, thanks to the filters we have configured.

Finally, let's check the **Advertisement** record page by clicking any **Advertisement** record:

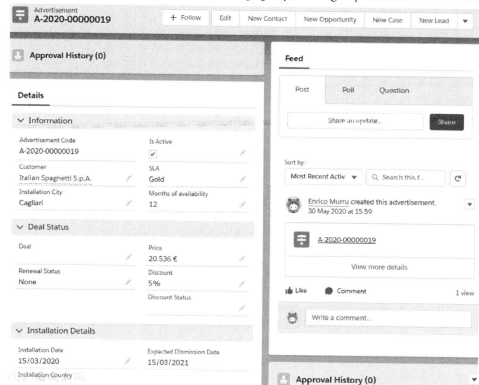

Figure 13.39 – Advertisement record Lightning page

Let's change the price or discount fields to 0, where the upper **Approval History** component disappears, as per filtering configurations.

> **Further reading**
>
> If you want to discover more about using the Lightning App Builder, refer to Salesforce Help at `https://help.salesforce.com/articleView?id=lightning_app_builder_limitations.htm&type=5`.

So far, we've seen how to master the Lightning App Builder tool and how to create wonderful and super-productive Lightning pages. You now have a wide range of choices to customize your Salesforce org.

Blaze your trail

Blaze your you trail on Lightning App Builder with the following Trailhead content:

- Lightning App Builder: `https://trailhead.salesforce.com/en/content/learn/modules/lightning_app_builder`

- Quick Start: Lightning App Builder: `https://trailhead.salesforce.com/en/content/learn/projects/quickstart-app-builder`

Summary

With Lightning App Builder, any Salesforce page can be customized to create a better and more productive view of your data across apps and objects.

We've seen how the tool is shaped and the way it can be used to customize the layout of any Salesforce application's page, by creating home, app, and record Lightning pages.

Each page can then be created from a specific template, which defines the available places (or regions) where components can be placed; once the correct template is selected, the administrator can add standard or custom components to the page and configure their properties to make the page work as needed by the business, user interface, and user experience requirements.

With page filters, it is possible to define the visibility of components within the page, based on permissions, user fields, form factors and, when available, current record fields.

Finally, we saw how to activate a page so that it is available for our users.

In the next chapter, we'll deal with how to expose data to external users by creating amazing communities.

14
Leveraging Customers and Partners Power with Communities

When dealing with customers, there can be different touchpoints that can be activated to manage your customer relationships, such as integrating with **Computer Telephony Integration (CTI)** for phone communication with your call center, delivering an inbound email channel, or a web chat to talk directly with your customers.

If you want to improve your connection with your external stakeholders (customers, partners, or, more generally, external users), **Salesforce Communities** is what you need to use, in order to deliver a 24/7 web-accessible portal that can grant them direct access to Salesforce data, giving them the power to join a business process using most of the Salesforce Automation tools the platform delivers with zero waiting time.

In this chapter, we'll learn the following topics:

- What is a community?
- Creating and managing a community
- Customizing with Experience Builder
- Community creation
- Community management
- Page customization with Experience Builder for Lightning communities

After reading this chapter, you'll have the foundations to understand what a community is and what the available configuration options are that you can use to deliver the best self-service experience to your customers.

What is a community?

In my (more than 10 years) experience in the Salesforce ecosystem, I've been asked "What is a community?" more than once, mostly in the early days when communities were a new tool.

I usually answer by saying that Salesforce Communities allow any company to get in touch with customers, partners, and even employees, creating a *collaborative* place where Salesforce data can be reliably and *securely* accessed.

With Communities, you can create a strong link with your business partners to empower your business (suppliers, resellers, technicians), strengthen customer care with an easy place to find solutions to common issues, and get in touch with your employees to increase Salesforce adoption and collaboration.

A community is a public portal where internal and external users (we've talked about external users in *Chapter 6, Security First – the "Who Sees What" Paradigm*, when talking about **Organization-Wide Default** (**OWD**) sharing) can access Salesforce data directly, without the use of an external connection. This can be achieved using an external portal created in any technology, which connects to the Salesforce platform using Salesforce APIs or with communities.

The main advantage of using Salesforce Communities is that in order to build a community, you don't need to learn new technologies or new programming languages (as it is based on the same **Lightning technology** you deal with in the CRM). A community can be configured both with *point and click*, and code (depending on how much customization effort you need). A community can be accessed by internal and external users to work together for the same goal, be it customer happiness through an efficient service or business empowerment with your partners through sales collaboration.

Salesforce Communities is a whole world inside the Lightning Platform, and it is impossible to cover everything and in depth within a single chapter (there are whole books that cover this subject and that still don't manage to cover all the advanced topics), which is why, in this chapter, you'll be guided through a high-level overview of the main features and options that the platform delivers related to Communities. In my humble opinion, any Salesforce *specialist* must understand the main capabilities of this powerful feature.

Communities works as *public-unauthenticated* portals as well, which means that you can expose Salesforce data to guest users, for example, to create quick help or web-to-lead forms or simply to allow guest users to chat with chat bots or call center agents. This brings some additional limits related to how many *public* resources you can expose (that is, how many public page hits you can have in a month-wide time window).

> **Further reading**
>
> For more information about community usage allocations, refer to Salesforce Help at `https://help.salesforce.com/articleView?id=networks_usage_allocation.htm&type=0`.

Another important feature of Salesforce Communities is the possibility to get pre-built templates, which are an easy way to get all you need in order to create a ready-to-use customer, partner, or employee portal. **Lightning community templates** give us a quicker way to build communities, with an eye to the main features required for the kind of community you are going to build, and the business processes you want to cover.

These templates are strongly based on the Lightning framework and can be customized using the point-and-click **Experience Builder** (which is the Communities' version of the Lightning Application Builder; we learned about this in *Chapter 13, The Lightning App Builder*) or with custom Lightning components that can be easily developed by your developers. If you need a stronger layout and graphical customization, you can even use **Visualforce**-based communities, which requires greater effort in terms of implementation (it doesn't use any template or the Lightning framework) and requires a higher level of coding knowledge.

While using templates, you are somehow limited as regards the kind of user interface and user experience customizations you can achieve. With Visualforce-based communities, you can easily reach a *pixel-perfect* requirement, using almost any frontend graphical framework to adhere to your company's branding guidelines.

Now that you have understood what a community is, in the next section, we'll see how to create a new community from scratch.

Creating and managing a community

This section will cover how to create and manage a community. We will also learn about the different community templates. We will then learn about the self-registration option. We'll see how to configure a community and see a community in action with self-registration.

Before starting to create a community, make sure your org has at least one community license (example on a Developer Edition org, shown as follows):

SETUP

Company Information

Edit   Deactivate Org

User Licenses

User Licenses Help (?)

Name	Status	Total Licenses	Used Licenses	Remaining Licenses	Expiration Date
Salesforce	Active	2	2	0	
Salesforce Platform	Active	3	1	2	
Customer Community Login	Active	5	0	5	
XOrg Proxy User	Active	2	0	2	
Work.com Only	Active	3	0	3	
Customer Portal Manager Custom	Active	5	0	5	
Identity	Active	10	0	10	
Customer Community Plus	Active	5	0	5	
Silver Partner	Active	2	0	2	

Figure 14.1 – Looking for Salesforce community licenses

The previous screenshot shows that the current org has at least two kinds of community licenses, the **Customer Community Login** and **Customer Community Plus** licenses. If you don't have a community user license, you won't be able to create any community at all.

> **Further reading**
>
> For a complete list of all available community user licenses, refer to Salesforce Help at `https://help.salesforce.com/articleView?id=users_license_types_communities.htm&type-5`

To enable Salesforce Communities, click **Setup | Feature Settings | Communities | Communities Settings**, and flag the **Enable communities** option, shown as follows:

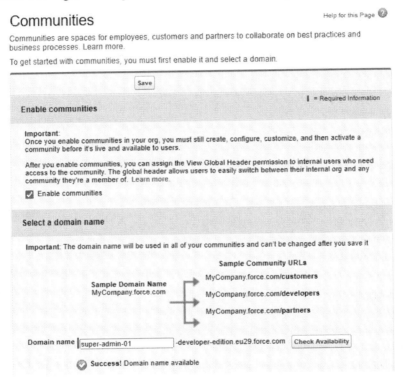

Figure 14.2 – Enabling communities' domains

The preceding screenshot recalls the **My Domain** activation we've seen in *Chapter 13, The Lightning App Builder*. Indeed, Salesforce is asking you to create a brand-new sub-domain, which it will use to serve communities pages. We've chosen **super-admin-01** (pretty much similar to the My Domain sub-domain configuration). As this is a potentially customer-facing portal, you even have the option to link a custom domain to the community, so the customer can see a prettier `http://customers.mycompany.com` instead of `https://mycompany-community.force.com` (Developer Edition orgs or sandboxes will have a slightly different full domain, showing the Salesforce instance and some additional prefixes).

> **Further reading**
>
> Setting up a custom domain is beyond the scope of this chapter, but if you want to learn more, refer to Salesforce Help at `https://help.salesforce.com/articleView?id=000336819&type=1&mode=1`.

Once communities are activated, you cannot revert them, so take your time to choose the right sub-domain and the right time to activate this feature.

Use the **Check Availability** button to check whether the sub-domain is available (that means no other Salesforce org has already taken it), and, when ready, click the **Save** button to complete the activation procedure.

Let's finally create our first community. You should have ended up in the **Setup | Feature Settings | Communities | All Communities** page after communities feature activation, so click on the **New Community** button to start the Community Creation wizard, shown as follows:

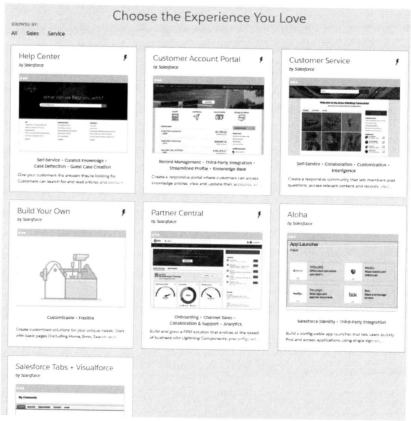

Figure 14.3 – Choosing a community template to create a brand-new template

As you can see in the preceding screenshot, the first step of the wizard shows the available templates you can use to create your new community. This list may vary depending on the time of writing (sometimes Salesforce adds some new templates and discontinues others) or on the number of **Lightning Bolt Solutions** you have installed in your org (a portable package that can be installed in any org to provide industry-specific components such as **Community Templates** or **Lightning Flows**).

Further reading

To get a better understanding of Lightning Bolt Solutions, refer to Salesforce Help at `https://help.salesforce.com/articleView?id=community_builder_export_overview.htm&type=5`. The **AppExchange** portal delivers tens of free Lightning Bolt Solutions, so you can try to avoid reinventing the wheel. Check them out at `https://appexchange.salesforce.com/appxStore?type=BoltTemplate`.

At the time of writing (the *Summer '20* platform release), these are the available community templates, as shown in the preceding screenshot:

- **Help Center** is a public community for accessing common knowledge for basic self-service support.

- **Customer Account Portal** is a private community that lets users interact directly with Salesforce data that they own (such as account information), interact with business processes they are part of, search knowledge bases, and solve straightforward issues with self-service.

- **Customer Service** is a simple self-service customer-faced portal to achieve collaboration for common customer-related issues.

- **Build Your Own** templates provide the main pages a community needs, such as record creation pages (for example, for cases or any other custom object), record lists, search, password check and reset, login, and registration.

- **Partner Central** is a portal dedicated to partners and sales-related business flows (lead, campaign, opportunities), facilitating collaboration to increase revenues.

- **Aloha** is a simple configurable app launcher commonly used to let users (mostly internal users) access applications they access during their daily routine (through *single sign-on* authentication, such as social logins).

- **Salesforce Tabs + Visualforce** is a *classic* themed template that can be customized using Visualforce coding and advanced setup skills. It is possible to create pixel-perfect user interfaces to match a company's customer engagement policies, that is, this template doesn't use the Lightning framework.

When selecting any community, you'll get a preview of the theme and the relevant features built within, as you can see in the following screenshot:

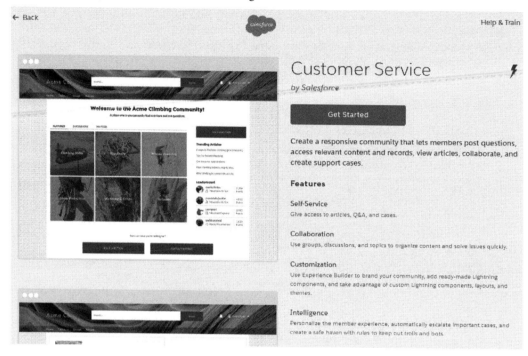

Figure 14.4 – Customer Service template selection

You can change the template following creation from the **Experience Builder** setup options (we'll see Experience Builder later in this chapter).

Once you are done looking at the preview, click on the **Get Started** button to input:

Enter a Name

Not sure what to enter? Don't worry—you can always change it later.

Name

Awesome Self-Service

URL

super-admin-01-developer-edition.eu29.forc...   customers

Create

Figure 14.5 – Naming a community

As you can see in the preceding screenshot, there are two fields, namely, **Name** and **URL**. The community's **Name** field identifies the community on the setup lists, being a simple label. The community's **URL** (optional) is appended at the end of the community sub-domain. In this example, the community will be accessed through the following URL: `https://super-admin-01-developer-edition.eu29.force.com/customers`.

> **Further reading**
>
> Note that the `-developer-edition` part of the community domain is only set on Developer Edition orgs, while the server instance name (called `pod`, in this example, **eu29**) will only be placed on Developer Edition orgs or Sandbox orgs (we'll cover sandboxes in *Chapter 17, The Sandbox Model*).

Then, click the **Create** button to start community creation.

> **Further reading**
>
> Remember that, as of *Summer '20*, you can only build up to 100 communities (this limit is displayed on the **Setup | Feature Settings | Communities | All Communities** page).

Once the community is created, you are redirected to **Experience Workspaces**, as shown in the following screenshot:

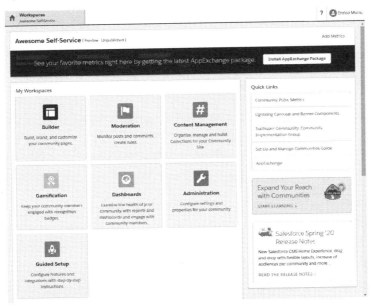

Figure 14.6 – Workspaces page for complete community setup

As you can see in the preceding screenshot, from this page you can configure almost any part of your community:

- **Builder** accesses Experience Builder to customize the branding, user interface, and pages.

- **Moderation** configures community moderation strategies and tools, to ensure that content published is relevant and appropriate. You can refer to `https://help.salesforce.com/articleView?id=networks_moderation_overview.htm&type=0` for **Moderation** setup.

- **Content Management** configures external **Content Management System (CMS)** connections to get content from your website, configure topics and recommendations to create a navigational structure of your community, and organize information. You can refer to `https://help.salesforce.com/articleView?id=networks_topics_overview.htm&type=5` and `https://help.salesforce.com/articleView?id=communities_cms_connect.htm&type=5` for **Content Management** setup.

- **Gamification** provides setup gamification tools, including badges and reputation levels, to keep your members engaged in the community. You can refer to `https://help.salesforce.com/articleView?id=networks_gamification.htm&type=0` for **Gamification** communities advanced configurations.

- **Dashboards** easily accesses reports and dashboards to track user engagement on the community. You can refer to `https://help.salesforce.com/articleView?id=networks_reporting_intro.htm&type=5` for more information about **Dashboards**.

- **Administration** provides the main settings and properties for your community.

In the next section, we'll only analyze the **Administration** configurations, which will cover the majority of your needs, and show how to customize community pages with Experience Builder.

Analyzing community administration

Click on the **Administration** tab to configure the sections shown in the following screenshot:

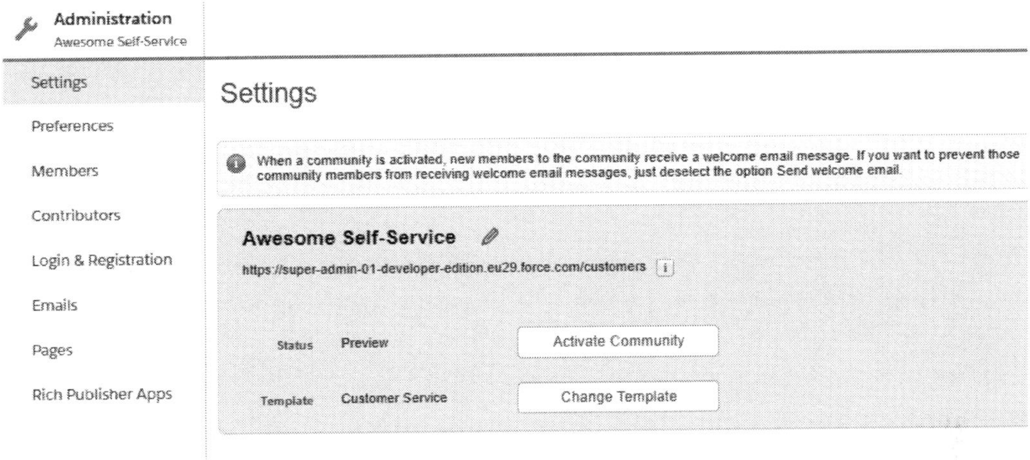

Figure 14.7 – Settings tab on the Administration page

As you can see in the preceding screenshot, these sections need to be configured:

- **Settings**: This tab shows you the activation status and template.

- **Preferences**: This tab shows you general community preferences.

- **Members**: This tab shows you who can access the community.

- **Contributors**: This tab shows you who is capable of what within the community.

- **Login & Registration**: This tab shows you branding options (such as the community logo), login page, logout redirect URL, password-related page configurations, and self-registration options.

- **Emails**: This tab lists email channel configurations, such as the sender's email address, email branding, and email templates for common user interaction.

- **Pages**: This tab shows you home and *out of order* page configurations.

- **Rich Publisher Apps**: This tab shows you custom-made Chatter publisher actions that can be created within your org by your developers or installed from the AppExchange.

Some of the settings, especially on the **Preferences** page, are specific for the template you are using, and some template types (for example, with Visualforce communities) may show more tabs.

Let's see what each configuration delivers in the following sections.

The Settings tab

The **Settings** tab (already shown in *Figure 14.7*) is used to activate a community or deactivate it. You can give the community URL to any stakeholder you need to show a preview to, even if the community is not activated yet.

Remember the following things:

- You need to publish the community from Experience Builder at least once to see it in action.

- Once you activate a community, all current members are notified with a welcome mail (see the **Emails** tab to disable this feature).

This page lets you change the previously selected template in case you change your mind.

The Preferences tab

This page is used to enable some optional behavior within the community. It is divided into **General, Community Management,** and **Files** sections, as displayed in the following screenshot:

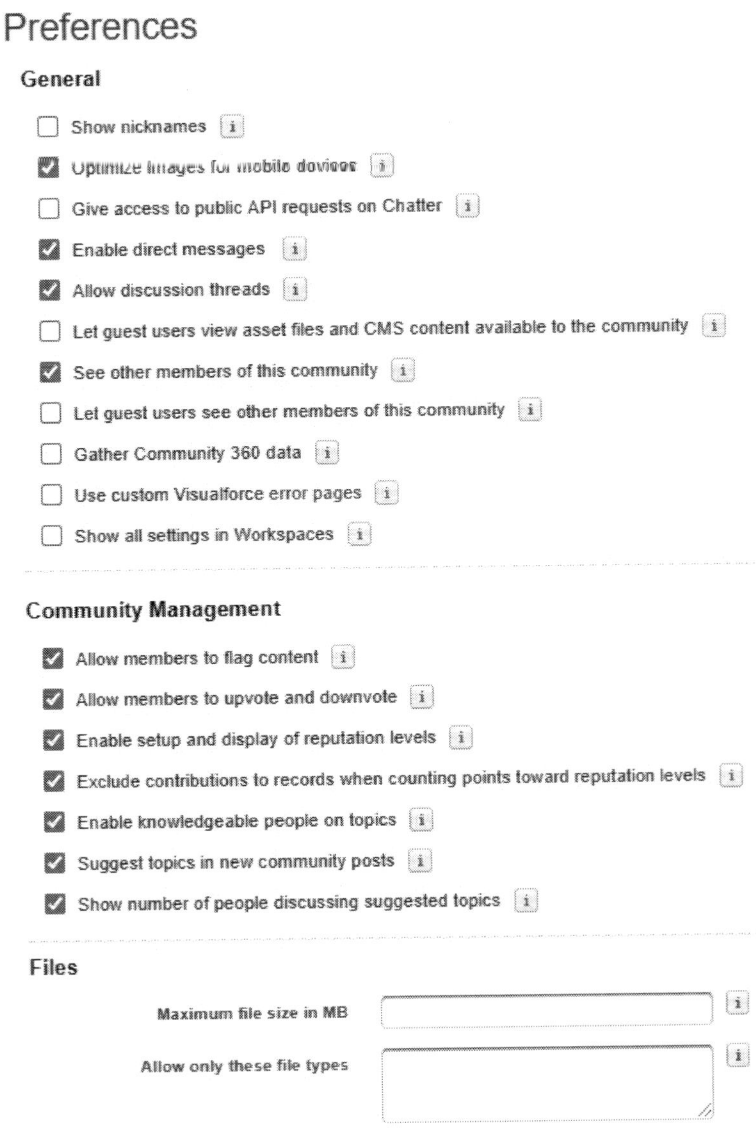

Preferences

General

☐ Show nicknames ⓘ

☑ Optimize images for mobile devices ⓘ

☐ Give access to public API requests on Chatter ⓘ

☑ Enable direct messages ⓘ

☑ Allow discussion threads ⓘ

☐ Let guest users view asset files and CMS content available to the community ⓘ

☑ See other members of this community ⓘ

☐ Let guest users see other members of this community ⓘ

☐ Gather Community 360 data ⓘ

☐ Use custom Visualforce error pages ⓘ

☐ Show all settings in Workspaces ⓘ

Community Management

☑ Allow members to flag content ⓘ

☑ Allow members to upvote and downvote ⓘ

☑ Enable setup and display of reputation levels ⓘ

☑ Exclude contributions to records when counting points toward reputation levels ⓘ

☑ Enable knowledgeable people on topics ⓘ

☑ Suggest topics in new community posts ⓘ

☑ Show number of people discussing suggested topics ⓘ

Files

Maximum file size in MB ⓘ

Allow only these file types ⓘ

Figure 14.8 – The Preferences tab on the Administration page

As you can see from the preceding screenshot, the **General** section has the following most frequently used features:

- **Show nicknames**: This option shows nicknames instead of full names in your community, thereby protecting member identities. This is helpful within a public community where unregistered visitors may access member profiles.

- **Optimize images for mobile devices**: This option scales down images when accessing the community from a mobile device.

- **Enable direct messages**: This option allows community members to send secure private messages to other members when the **Customer Service** template is used.

- **Allow discussion threads**: By using this option, users can reply to answers to generate a thread on the Chatter feed.

- **See other members of this community**: This option allows authenticated users to view other members of the community.

- **Let guest users see other members of this community**: This option allows guest users to view the other members of the community.

- **Show all settings in Workspaces**: This option shows all settings hidden by default based on the community's template. This can be useful to have a coherent view of the settings of all communities in your org.

From the **Community Management** section, here are the most frequently used features:

- **Allow members to flag content**: By using this option, members can flag content as inappropriate, so as to trigger moderation.

- **Allow members to upvote and downvote**: By using this option, the *like* action is replaced with upvote and downvote buttons.

- **Enable setup and display of reputation levels**: This option can configure reputation points and levels depending on the kind of actions a user performs within the community. The **Reputation Levels** and **Reputation Points** tabs are automatically added to the **Administration** page.

- **Enable knowledgeable people on topics**: This option allows community administrators to select users who are knowledgeable on specific topics that can be discussed in the community (we'll learn about this topic in the *Adding navigational topics* subsection).

- **Suggest topics in new community posts**: When a new post is created from the community, this option enables an internal engine to suggest the topics.

- **Show number of people discussing suggested topics**: This option displays the number of people collaborating on a specific topic.

Finally, the **Files** section defines the maximum file size and available extension that can be attached to any post.

> **Further reading**
>
> To have a look at other preferences, refer to Salesforce Help at `https://help.salesforce.com/articleView?id=networks_customize_miscellaneous.htm&type=5`.

Once you have configured the settings, click **Save**.

The Members tab

We use the **Members** tab to select which users are allowed to access the community. Access is granted to users by profile or permission set association:

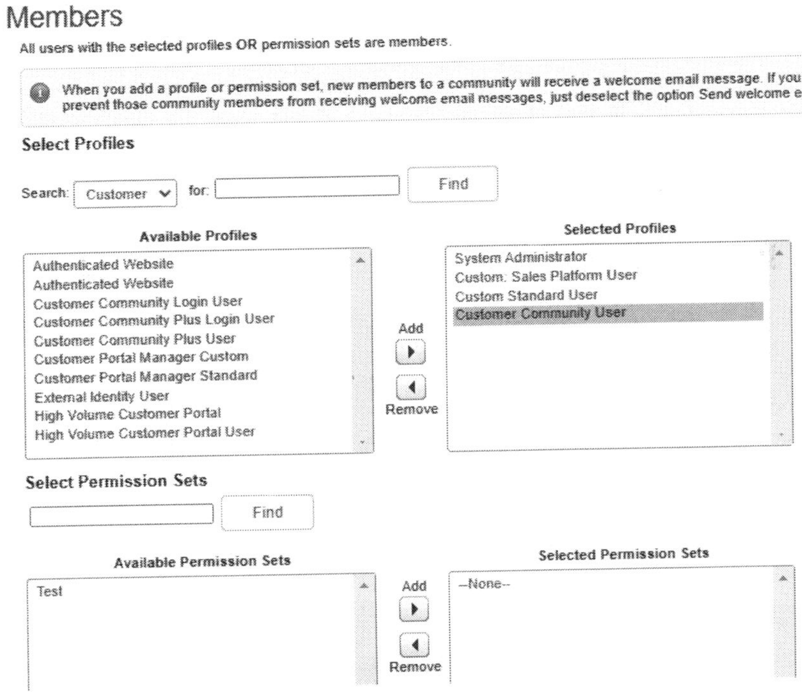

Figure 14.9 – The Members tab on the Administration page

As you can see in the preceding screenshot, we are adding some *internal* profiles, such as **System Administrator**, **Custom: Sales Platform User**, and **Custom Standard User** (which are linked to the users we have used throughout this book), but also the *external* **Customer Community User**, which is a community user licensed profile and which, as of now, isn't related to any user.

Remember, do not remove the administrator user, otherwise you will no longer be able to edit the community (the **Workspaces** link disappears). However, should this happen accidentally, you can manually assign your profile through the user of Data Loader, as shown in this article: `https://help.salesforce.com/articleView?id=000338383&language=en_US&type=1&mode=1`.

Finally, click **Save** when finished.

The Login & Registration tab

In this page, we can configure some pretty important stuff, as shown in the following screenshot:

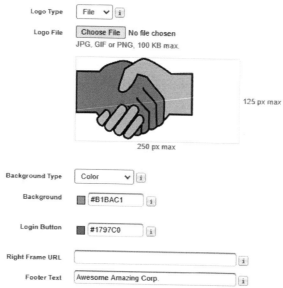

Figure 14.10 – Branding options

As you can see in the preceding screenshot, the following options can be configured:

- The community logo, by choosing from a Salesforce file (that you can upload from this form and should be less than 100 KB in size with a pixel size of 125 x 250) or a generic URL

- The background type (with a color or an image)

- The login button color

- The right-frame URL (if a standard login is used)

- Footer text (if a standard login is used)

We can also configure the following in this page:

- A custom login page chosen from the standard Salesforce login page, an Experience Builder-made Lightning page, or a Visualforce page (leave the default value):

Figure 14.11 – Login page configuration

- A logout URL that should be loaded after the user logs out

- The password-related pages (forgot and reset password fields, both with default settings, Experience Builder customization or Visualforce page types)

- Enablement for self-registration (we'll learn about this in the *Learning about self-registration* section):

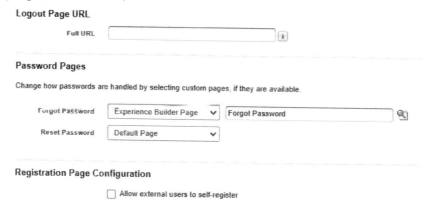

Figure 14.12 – Other login and registration options

Lastly, click on **Save** when done.

The Emails tab

This section is used to configure some email notification-related options, as shown in the following screenshot:

Figure 14.13 – The Emails tab on the Administration page

As you can see in the preceding screenshot, the following options can be configured:

- Sender's name and email address
- Chatter notification email branding (click the **Preview** link to see what the user would see when a new message is received)
- General email templating, including the **Send welcome email** option that I warmly suggest to disable until you are ready to make the community available to the public (when you activate it, all users in the community will receive a notification, something that can become annoying during the development process)

Click on the **Save** button when finished.

The Pages tab

Use this section to configure the **Community Home** landing page (we have used the Lightning page created on Experience Builder) and a **Service Not Available** page (uploaded as an HTML file on a static resource, which is something we won't configure in this community). Here is what you'll see in terms of the setup:

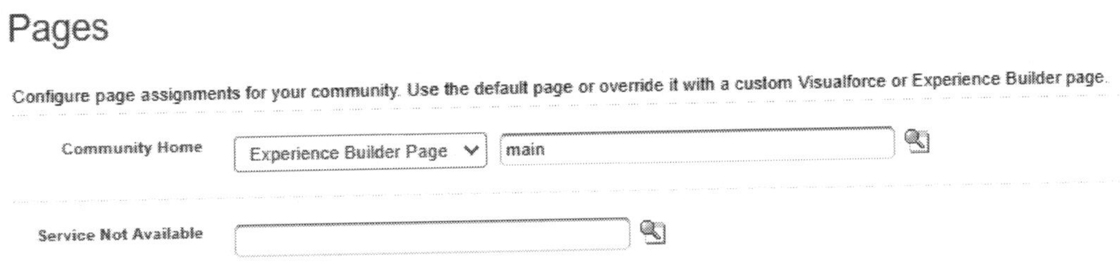

Pages

Configure page assignments for your community. Use the default page or override it with a custom Visualforce or Experience Builder page.

| Community Home | Experience Builder Page ∨ | main | 🔍 |

| Service Not Available | | 🔍 |

Figure 14.14 – Pages tab on the Administrator page

To learn more about service unavailability pages, refer to Salesforce Help at `https://help.salesforce.com/articleView?id=networks_custom_sna_page.htm&type=5`.

The Rich Publisher Apps tab

This configuration is available only on Lightning communities and allows you to see some publisher actions in Chatter Publisher. To create a new Publisher app, you need developer skills (Lightning components need to be built).

Further reading

To get more information about rich publisher apps, complete the **Rich Publisher Apps for Communities** Trailhead module available at `https://trailhead.salesforce.com/content/learn/modules/rpa`.

In this section, we learned about community administration configurations and its various tabs. Before testing the community, let's configure the self-registration option to allow customer self-registration from the community.

Learning about self-registration

Go to the **Administration** page, select the **Login & Registration** tab, scroll down to the **Registration Page Configuration** section, and then enable the **Allow external users to self-register** option. A number of new options are displayed:

Figure 14.15 – Self-registration configuration

First, the community must have a self-registration page (and the **Register** page is already selected), and then we need to select the Salesforce profile (external profile only) that will be automatically related to the new user. **Customer Community User** (which is the only external profile we selected earlier in the **Members** tab) is automatically selected.

But there is another lookup field that is required – the **Account** field. Indeed, each external user must be related to an account and contact record, and while the contact record is created from the *personal* user information obtained from the registration page defined earlier, the **Account** record, which may hold *business*-related data, is not requested to the user during registration. If you want to create a personalized account record for any customer user, you need to go with custom development tasks (using Lightning components and Apex code), or you can change it later manually on the backend.

In our scenario, we created a simple account record named **Customer Account**, which is not holding any relevant information.

> **Further reading**
>
> If you want to manually create a new community user, you need to follow the steps provided in Salesforce Help at `https://help.salesforce.com/articleView?id=networks_create_external_users.htm&type=5`.

If you try to click the **Save** button, an error message will display, stating the following message:

```
To use this profile as the default for self-registration, go to
Setup > Communities Settings and select Allow using standard
external profiles for self-registration and user creation.
```

Since the *Winter '20* release, if you want to use standard community profiles, you need to explicitly allow this from the setup. This is done because the standard profile comes with a default set of permissions and you should create your own custom profiles to adhere to your company's security policies.

Just for the sake of this example, go to **Setup | Feature Settings | Communities | Communities Settings**, flag the **Allow using standard external profiles for self-registration and user creation** checkbox, and then click the **Save** button. Otherwise, create a brand-new custom profile and assign it to the **Members** configuration of your community.

Go back to the **Login & Registration** setting and complete the configuration by hitting the **Save** button (and a green success message should state that everything went as expected).

Before testing, let's add a simple configuration that is needed to create navigational topics to let users post questions on the community.

Adding navigational topics

Navigational topics are a way to organize community information, to let users collaborate by posting questions and answers. Navigational topics are similar to public rooms where users can post related material.

Navigational content is usually displayed on the navigation component at the top of the community site:

Figure 14.16 – Navigational topics example

In the preceding screenshot, we have created two navigational topics, **GENERAL** and **NEW PRODUCTS**, which can be easily navigated through the navigation menu.

To create new navigational topics, click on **Workspaces | Content Management | Topics** and then click on the **Navigational Topics** link on the left sidebar, and create as many topics as you wish:

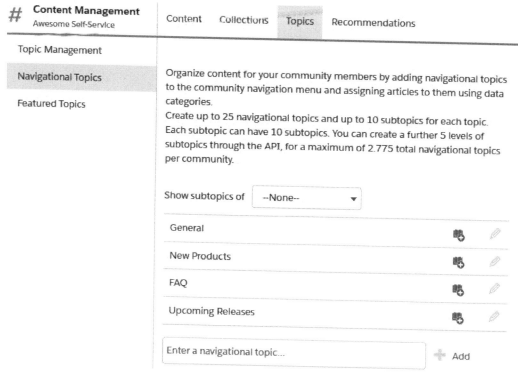

Figure 14.17 – Creating navigational topics for the community

If you want, in the **Featured Topics** tab, you can select some *featured* topics that will be displayed on a specific page component for *hot* topics (generally automatically added to each Lightning template's community landing page by default).

> **Further reading**
>
> For more customization options on topics, refer to Salesforce Help at `https://help.salesforce.com/articleView?id=networks_topics_overview.htm&type=5`.

Let's test the community now.

Let's try it on

So far, simple configurations apart, we haven't done anything on the page customization side, but we can try the community without any issues, as the community's template delivers most of the features you need.

Firstly, you need to open **Experience Builder** (which we'll see in the *Customizing with Experience Builder* section) from **Workspaces | Builder**:

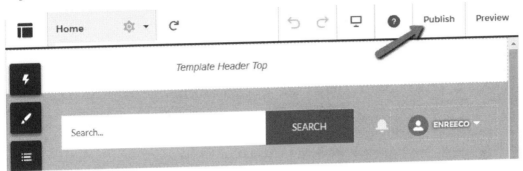

Figure 14.18 – The Publish option in Experience Builder

As you can see in the preceding screenshot, click on the **Publish** button in the top-right corner of the builder to trigger your first community publish. Then, let the engine do its job and wait for a confirmation email.

To allow for complete community functionality, activate the community from **Workspaces | Administration | Settings** and click the **Activate Community** button. This way, all customer-related flows (such as activation and password reset) will work as expected.

We are now ready to test our community. Click back to **Workspaces | Administration | Settings** and open the community's URL with another browser or in incognito mode (do this, otherwise you'll be logged in with your current administrator user, which is not a bad thing, but we want to demonstrate how the community is displayed to a potential customer user).

You will be redirected to the login page with the logo we defined earlier:

Figure 14.19 – Community login page

As you can see in the preceding screenshot, this is an Experience Builder custom page and not the standard Salesforce login page (which you can access, as an internal user, using the **Are you an employee? Login here** link). Customer users must log in from this page, as their username is strictly related to our org, while internal users' usernames are *shared* across orgs (this means that there cannot be two users across all Salesforce clouds with the same username, but there can be two external users, partners, or community users with the same username, but in different orgs).

To create a brand-new user, click on the **Not a member?** link and compile the following form:

Figure 14.20 – Register form

As you can see in the preceding screenshot, this is the register page we configured in the *Learning about self registration* section.

Then, a new email is sent to the user. Remember to enable the **Send welcome email** option on the **Administration | Email** page, otherwise you won't receive a welcome email with the password reset and your only option would be to reset the password manually from the login page.

The reset password page will be the standard one (as we configured earlier, as of the *Summer '20* release, you can also add the Visualforce page option):

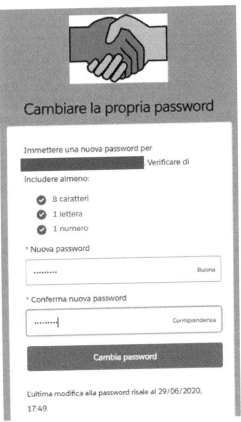

Figure 14.21 – Reset password page

You can see that, if your own mother tongue is not English, the user is automatically presented with the browser's configured language (Italian, in my case). This can be easily updated on the profile settings page when the user logs in.

Once the password is reset, you are redirected to the home page of your brand-new community:

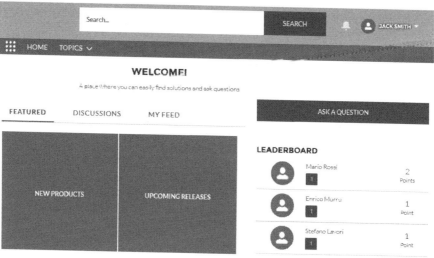

Figure 14.22 – Community's home page

As you can see in the preceding screenshot, from this base configuration, you can do the following:

- **Update user data**: You can change the user's settings, such as name, language, and email, as shown in the following screenshot:

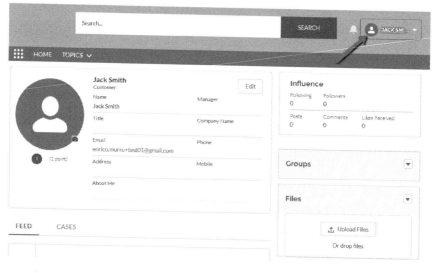

Figure 14.23 – Updating community user data

- **Ask a question on a specific topic**: You can collaborate within the community by posting questions, shown as follows:

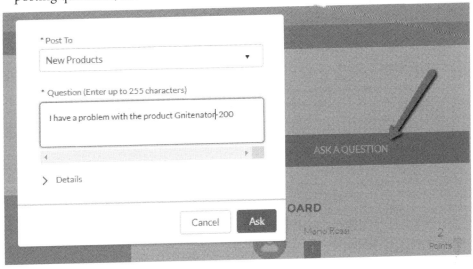

Figure 14.24 – Posting on the community

- **Opening a support case**: You can request support from the service guys, direct from the community (this will automatically create a support case record that can be handled by internal Salesforce users):

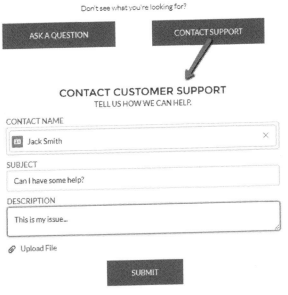

Figure 14.25 – Creating a case from within the community

- **Collaborate on posts**: You can reply, share, and *like* posts. You can see this in the following screenshot:

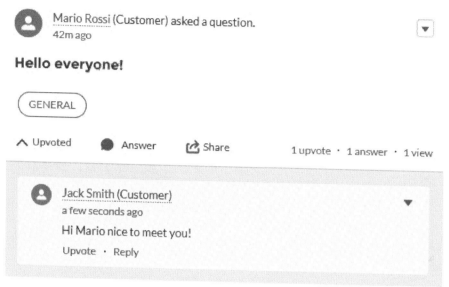

Figure 14.26 – Answering a post

By customizing the community, you can provide way more to your customers, but as we've demonstrated, the community is already up and running with minimal effort. All the base stuff is there; we just need to add our personal touch.

Let's now have a look at Experience Builder, to give our pages some more customization using standard and custom Lightning components, by defining a branding, and adding some more love.

Customizing with Experience Builder

In this section, we are going to learn about Experience Builder. We will also learn about how to add, manage its components, and build amazing pages for our community.

To customize your current community template, you need to access the Experience Builder tool from **Workspaces | Builder**:

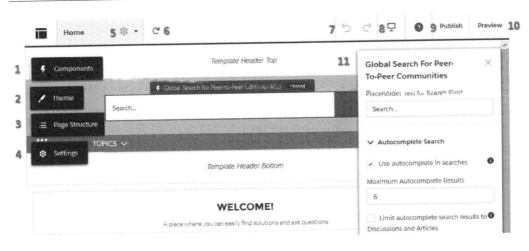

Figure 14.27 – Experience Builder in action

As you can see from the preceding screenshot, these are all your available options:

1. Drag and drop Lightning components on the underlying page, choosing from standard (built-in with your org), custom (built by your devs within your org), or custom from the **AppExchange** (installed from packages).

2. Change the template's theme to match your company's branding rules.

3. Navigate the page structure to see which components have been added.

4. Navigate through the community settings (such as public access, security features, and updates).

5. Access all the pages and their variations.

6. Refresh the current page.

7. Undo/redo shortcuts.

8. Change the device form factor.

9. Publish changes.

10. Preview the community in a browser tab with the selected form factor.

11. Select a component and update its properties.

Now, let's see some of the principal customization options in the following sections.

Adding and managing components

The **Components** panel lists all available components, whether they be standard, custom, or from the AppExchange, while the **Page Structure** panel lists all currently dropped components, as shown in the following screenshot:

Figure 14.28 – Available components panel

In order to add more features to a page, simply drag and drop a component on the current page and put it in any available place, shown as follows:

Figure 14.29 – Dropping a component on the page layout

Each component is then configurable with its own properties panel, pretty much like we did on the Lightning App Builder, seen in *Chapter 13, The Lightning App Builder*.

> **Further reading**
>
> The kind of available standard components vai y from template to template. To see a complete and updated list of such components and a detailed description of all available components and how to configure them, refer to Salesforce Help at `https://help.salesforce.com/articleView?id=rss_component_reference_table.htm&type=5`.

Remember to test your new component with the **Preview** button and publish the changes with the **Publish** button once you are ready and confident.

Branding your community

With the **Theme Settings** button, you can do the following:

- Change the main template theme (that is, the set of colors and layout configuration) through the **Change Theme** button.

- Update colors, images, fonts, and general theme settings (such as the header region display, or the display of the search component, to name a few).

Customizing a theme requires no particular coding skills; it's all just point-and-click configuration from color palettes (which can be automatically generated from an image you are using as background or as a header, or from the company's logo), font names, or page sizes:

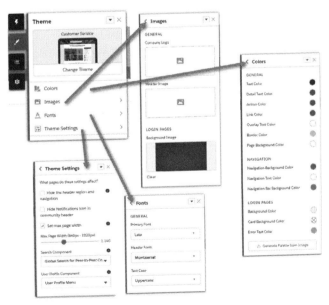

Figure 14.30 – Configuring a theme

> **Further reading**
>
> For more details on theme customization options, refer to Salesforce Help at `https://help.salesforce.com/articleView?id=community_builder_theme_customize.htm&type=5#community_designer_brand`.

Now, let's complete our new community setup.

Finalizing the community setup

Using the **Settings** button, you can work with some general and advanced community configurations (only accessible from the Builder), shown as follows:

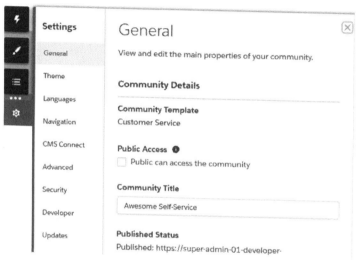

Figure 14.31 – Community setup

As you can see in the preceding screenshot, from this tab, you can configure the following:

- **General**: This allows access to some general information pertaining to the current community, such as which template is used, public community access, title, publish status, and public profile (guest user) configuration.

- **Theme**: This helps in setting up the main template's theme.

- **Languages**: This configures the available languages.

- **Advanced**: Using this option, you can configure the tracking of page views (**Google Analytics** configuration) and the HTML markup of the `<head>` tag for each page.

- **Navigation**: Using this option, you can configure navigation menus (for example, the topics we have added previously).

- **CMS Connect**: This option can be used to add some HTML headers and footers coming from an external CMS.

- **Security**: This option provides advanced configuration security options (check out Salesforce Help for more details at `https://help.salesforce.com/articleView?id=networks_security.htm&type=5#community_builder_general_settings`).

- **Developer**: This option lets you export your current template configuration to *jump start* a new project.

- **Updates**: If Salesforce releases a template update on any release, this is where you'll find the notification, that is, any update can have an impact on your community, so take care to check what's new or deprecated in the new version (check out Salesforce Help for a quick overview of what changed in the most recent releases at `https://help.salesforce.com/articleView?id=communities_update_template.htm&type=5#communities_update_template`).

Now, let's see how to complete community configuration with some page settings.

Managing pages

By clicking the page browser button on Experience Builder, you access a list of all available pages and their basic settings:

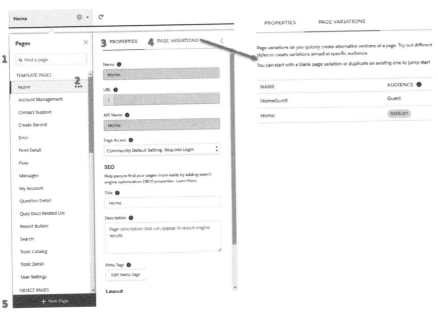

Figure 14.32 – Page configuration setup

As you can see in the preceding screenshot, from this panel we can do the following:

1. Search pages.

2. Open the page properties.

3. Configure page properties such as name, path, type of access (public or not), some SEO fields, such as **Title** and **Description**, additional **Meta Tags**, and the current page layout (you can choose different page layouts depending on the current theme).

4. Configure page variations that are alternative versions of the page to be shown to different audiences.

5. Create brand-new pages.

> **Further reading**
>
> To get a deeper look at page configuration options, check out Salesforce Help at `https://help.salesforce.com/articleView?id=community_builder_manage_pages_overview.htm&type=5#community_builder_manage_pages_overview`.

So far, we have covered almost every main topic in terms of Salesforce Community configuration and customization. As said previously, this is a vast subject that is impossible to cover in a single chapter, but you now have all the basic tools to start an efficient and engaging Salesforce Community enablement.

Blaze your trail

Here is a list of great Trailhead trails to increase your knowledge and expertise:

*   Expand Your Reach with Communities: `https://trailhead.salesforce.com/en/content/learn/trails/communities`

*   Customize Your Community: `https://trailhead.salesforce.com/en/content/learn/trails/customize-your-community`

Summary

Throughout this chapter, we've rolled out a simple Salesforce Community using all the declarative tools available on the platform. We understood what a community is and how it can increase customer and partner happiness with the help of efficient and secure access to Salesforce data.

We started creating our first community by showing all the available configurations to reliably manage it, from creation to publication. Having configured self-registration, you now have the skills to let external users have the option of self-registration in the community, and be able to access all pages of the community template without using a single line of code.

Then, we tested the community and demonstrated that a community can be built and tested with no advanced customization. We then introduced Experience Builder to show what options you have to customize the user experience and user interface for the selected community template, by setting up branding, page layouts, and by adding Lightning components to add some more love to the template.

In the next chapter, we'll start the data management section with data import and export using the tool our beloved platform delivers.

Section 5: Data Management

In this section, we will use built-in tools to import and export data from your org. We will learn the basics of Data Loader for higher data manipulation, and see how to use reporting to highlight your business' KPIs.

This section comprises the following chapters:

- *Chapter 15, Importing and Exporting Data Declaratively*
- *Chapter 16, Learning about Data Reporting*

15
Importing and Exporting Data Declaratively

In the previous chapters, we focused mainly on Salesforce platform customization in order to make our platform behave so that our business requirements fit. It began from user interface customization, went on to process automation development, and finally to security enhancement with strong data sharing and visibility rules. But what about the data itself? How can we manage data within the platform?

We can identify two principal methods for this – data import/export and data reporting.

With reporting, we can make real-time queries on data to monitor data creation/ modification day by day, while with data import/export, we can actually load records into Salesforce object definitions and extract them for later use (for example, for backup purposes or archiving).

In this chapter, we'll blaze a trail through the following:

- The Data Import Wizard
- The Data Export Service
- Data Loader

Importing data into Salesforce

Data Lifecycle Management (**DLM**) is a hot topic when lighting up a new CRM implementation. How would you import the first records to make it fully operational from day one after go-live? How do you cleanse data if there is a bug in the automation you implemented (no human work is bug-free)? How do you cleanse data in the event of human errors?

And how would you extract data periodically to back up your records? How would you extract data to import it into another organization (org)?

The Salesforce platform provides a client application called **Data Loader** that can be used to do all sorts of massive CRUD (create-read-update-delete) operations on records, so you don't have to do them manually.

We'll talk about this great, useful, and well-known app that should always be in your toolbox in the last, dedicated section. In this and the next section, we'll talk about importing and exporting data from within the platform without using any external tools.

The Import wizard

To execute data import, declaratively jump to the **Data Import Wizard**, accessible from **Setup | Integrations | Data Import Wizard**, to land on the following page:

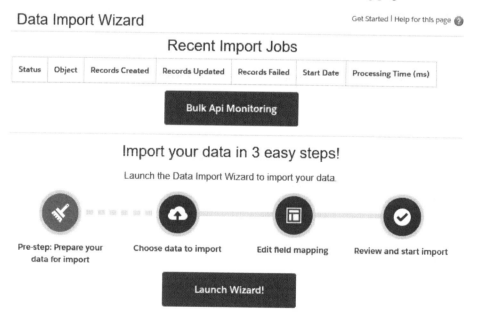

Figure 15.1 – Data Import Wizard main page

The first thing to note about this built-in import tool is an important limitation on the kind of standard Salesforce objects it supports: **Account**, **Contact**, **Lead**, **Campaign Member**, and **Solution**.

It supports any custom object you have implemented in your org (including *Custom Settings*).

This means that, if you want to import other kinds of standard objects such as cases, campaigns, or assets, you must go with **Data Loader** (yes, you have no choice yet!).

One other important limitation is on the number of records that can be imported at a time, which is *50,000*. So, if you need to import 100,000 contacts, you need to run the wizard twice. **Data Loader** isn't affected by this low limit, as we'll see in the last section.

The wizard can be used to create and/or update records but not to delete them. To execute record deletion, you need to switch to Data Loader as well.

Let's work with the wizard to create some brand new records.

Starting the wizard: selecting the target object

To start the Data Import Wizard, click the **Launch Wizard!** button on the page shown in *Figure 15.1*.

The first thing you'll select is the kind of records you want to manage, and you'll choose between standard and custom objects, as shown in the following screenshot:

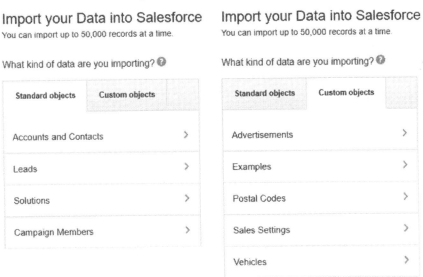

Figure 15.2 – Selecting a target Salesforce object

As you can see, **Accounts and Contacts** is a single choice, as they are created/updated together (a contact would be created with its company's information as well).

In *Chapter 14, Leveraging Customers and Partners Power with Community Builder*, we created some custom objects that we can see on the right side of *Figure 15.2*, as well as the custom setting we created in *Chapter 5, Handling Dynamic Configuration* – the **Sales Settings** custom setting.

Let's select **Accounts and Contacts** and let's highlight the de-duplication configuration settings.

Selecting the matching options

When creating and/or updating records, the system does some background checks to avoid record duplication and ensure matching. It's not good to have duplicate records in your organizations, otherwise, your users will get mad trying to understand which record they should handle during their daily work.

The following screenshot shows the create, update, and upsert options:

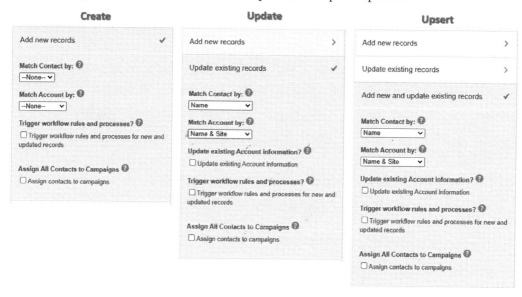

Figure 15.3 – Selecting the operation to execute and the de-duplication options

From the preceding screenshot, we can observe the following:

- Basically, when selecting **Add new records**, the import job tries to create new records and matches **Contact** records by the **Name** and **Email** fields in the record, while **Account** records can be identified by the **Name & Site** fields (together).

  If you have defined custom external ID fields on **Contact** or **Account** objects, you can use them as well (it could be an external customer code of any kind that your external systems use to identify a company or a customer). If a match is found on **Account** or **Contact** records, no update action is done on the system.

- If you choose **Update existing records**, the job will simply update the records (and not create them) and you can use them as matching fields to the `Salesforce.com ID` value (which you should put in the import file that we'll import in the next step).

- By choosing **Add new and update existing records**, you are choosing the *upsert* action, that is, if a match is found, the records are updated, otherwise new records are created. These options support `Salesforce.com ID` as a valid field de-duplication option.

- The create, update, and upsert options have the **Update existing Account information** option to allow **Account** information to be updated. This is available because, as external systems may not be the *owner* of an account's business data, you don't want the system data of the **Account** to be updated if the record is already on the database.

- The **Trigger workflow rules and processes for new and updated records** checkbox is disabled by default for performance reasons, as Salesforce automation such as workflow and processes can slow down record processing.

- Finally, **Assign contacts to campaigns** is used to automatically assign all imported contacts to a specific **Campaign** record, which you can select right before the job runs.

> **Further reading**
>
> Take a look at Salesforce Help at `https://help.salesforce.com/articleView?id=import_which_data_import_tool.htm&type=5` to deepen your knowledge on importing other standard objects such as **Leads**, **Campaign Members**, and **Solutions**.

When dealing with custom objects, we'll have a match by **Name** to create and also `Salesforce.com ID` and any *external ID* field, as seen earlier. The cool thing is that you'll also be able to detect lookup objects, as shown in the following screenshot:

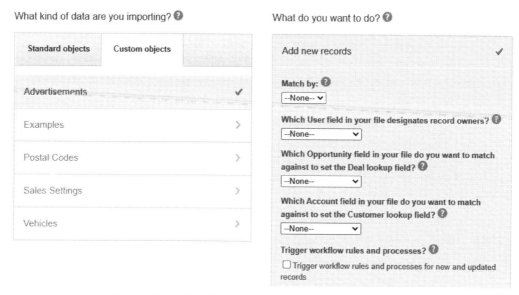

Figure 15.4 – Identifying related records on custom objects

Pretty much as we've seen with the **Accounts and Contacts** import, you can select matching fields for all lookup fields in this example for the **User** record thanks to the **Owner** relationship, or for **Opportunity** and **Account** records because of the respective lookups.

Preparing the import file

After we have selected the proper action for the import process, we need to import an actual file. The supported file format is **CSV** (**comma-separated value** file format), which is a simple text file in the following format (white spaces between commas have been added for formatting purposes but should be avoided):

```
"column 1",        "column 2",        "column 3"
"value 1 row 1" , "value 2 row 1" , "value 3 row 1"
"value 1 row 2" , "value 2 row 2" , "value 3 row 2"
"value 1 row 3" , "value 2 row 3" , "value 3 row 3"
```

The file is expected to be filled in the first row with the column names (aka field names) to be imported and from the second row onward with the values, where each line identifies a record.

You can export CSV files from diverse applications (Salesforce report exports are a good way to get a CSV file). For simplicity, you can create your file by hand in the format shown at the beginning of this section.

While the system will ask you the proper mapping before running the job, if you follow a few simple rules in naming the columns on the CSV file, you'll have the import job done more quickly:

- For **Accounts and Contacts** imports, follow the mapping suggested in Salesforce Help at `https://help.salesforce.com/articleView?id=field_mapping_for_other_data_sources_and_organization_import.htm&type=5`.

- For **Leads** import mapping, refer to Salesforce Help at `https://help.salesforce.com/articleView?id=field_mapping_for_importing_leads.htm&type=5`.

- For other standard and custom objects, use the Salesforce object field's labels.

Here is an example of an **Accounts and Contacts** import file (take care to remove any white spaces between commas, otherwise the file won't be imported correctly; the character is only used to show where the line ends):

```
"Account Name","Account Phone","Industry","First Name","Last
Name","Mobile Phone","E-mail Address"
"Amazing Corp.","555-123456","Telco","Jack","Sparrow","555-123-
123","jsparrow@amazingcorp.com"
"Amazing Corp.","555-123456","Telco","Bracco","Baldo","555-123-
678","bbaldo@amazingcorp.com"
"Italian Plumbers Ltd.","555-999555","Services","Mario","Sup
er", "555-555-555","supermario@plumbers.it"
```

This file should create two accounts (`Amazing Corp.` and `Italian Plumbers Ltd.`) but three contacts (as two of them rely on the same **Account, Amazing Corp.**).

Select **Add new records**, match the contact by **Name** and match the account by **Name & Site** (in the previous CSV, no **Site** field had been added but it's not a problem at all, since the **Name** field will be used).

Now drop the previous CSV file onto **Drag CSV file here to upload**. Make sure the file is correctly parsed and click the **Next** button.

Ready to import

The last step is used to correct any bad mapping (you may have misspelled a field label) with the **Change** edit link and see some examples of the records that are going to be imported, as shown here:

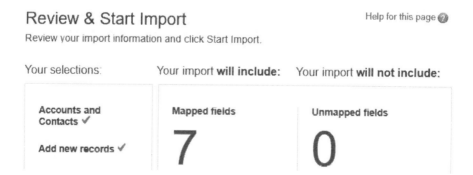

Edit Field Mapping: Accounts and Contacts

Your file has been auto-mapped to existing Salesforce fields, but you can edit the mappings if you wish. Unmapped fields will not be imported.

Help for this page 📀

Edit	Mapped Salesforce Object	CSV Header	Example	Example
Change	Account: Account N...	Account Name	Amazing	Amazing Corp.
Change	Account: Phone	Account Phone	555-123	555-123456
Change	Account: Industry	Industry	Telco	Telco
Change	Contact: First Name	First Name	Jack	Bracco
Change	Contact: Last Name	Last Name	Sparrow	Baldo
Change	Contact: Mobile	Mobile Phone	555-123	555-123-678
Change	Contact: Email	E-mail Address	jsparrow	bbaldo@amazingcorp.com

Figure 15.5 – Check before importing

Click the **Next** button again to see a recap of what you've configured so far:

Review & Start Import

Help for this page 📀

Review your import information and click Start Import.

Your selections:	Your import **will include:**	Your import **will not include:**
Accounts and Contacts ✔	Mapped fields	Unmapped fields
Add new records ✔	7	0

Figure 15.6 – Final recap before importing records

Click the **Start Import** button to start the import job. The import is done using the **Bulk APIs**, which are a set of APIs used to load massive records in the system, and once the job starts, you are redirected to the corresponding job's page with all the related info (such as the start and end time, number of records, and other technical stuff).

You can go back to **Setup | Integrations | Data Import Wizard** in a few seconds to see the **Contact** and **Account** jobs being executed properly:

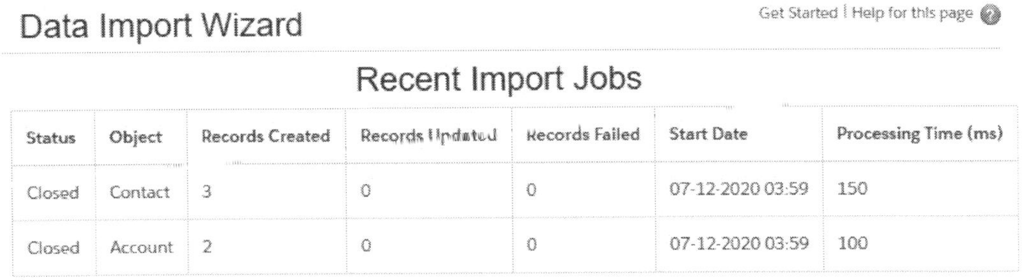

Data Import Wizard

Get Started | Help for this page 📎

Recent Import Jobs

Status	Object	Records Created	Records Updated	Records Failed	Start Date	Processing Time (ms)
Closed	Contact	3	0	0	07-12-2020 03:59	150
Closed	Account	2	0	0	07-12-2020 03:59	100

Figure 15.7 – Import jobs listed

Remember the following additional limitations:

- The CSV file can weigh up to 100 MB

- Each row cannot exceed 100 KB (about 4,000 characters)

- You can have up to 90 fields per record

> **Further reading**
>
> If you want to learn more, refer to Salesforce Help at `https://help.salesforce.com/articleView?id=faq_import_general.htm&type=5` for some quick and dirty FAQs.

Practice creating CSV files to import some other kinds of objects and get your developer edition org populated with tens of records. This way, you'll be ready for the **Data Loader** section, when we'll be using the same kind of files to handle data operations with some more advanced options.

Let's now have a look at Salesforce's standard exportation tool.

Exporting data from Salesforce

Exporting data from Salesforce is something that is usually done using data reporting or the execution of SOQL queries with external tools.

We'll be having a look at reports in *Chapter 16, Learning about Data Reporting*, and will have a quick introduction to SOQL queries in the next section relating to the Data Loader tool.

Salesforce delivers a simple way to extract data from the platform with the **Data Export** feature, accessible from **Setup | Data | Data Export**:

Monthly Export Service

Help for this Page

Data Export lets you prepare a copy of all your data in salesforce.com. From this page you can start the export process manually or schedule it to run automatically. When an export is ready for download you will receive an email containing a link that allows you to download the file(s). The export files are also available on this page for 48 hours, after which time they are deleted.

> **Next scheduled export:**
> None

Export Now   Schedule Export

Figure 15.8 – Data Export feature

This tool lets you extract all or a subset of records from the CRM in the following two ways:

- One-shot export with the **Export Now** button
- Scheduled export with the **Schedule Export** button

Depending on the kind of Salesforce edition you are playing with, you'll be allowed to export data weekly (7 days) or monthly (29 days), and this time limitation applies both to one-shot export and scheduled export. Weekly export is only available in the **Enterprise**, **Performance**, and **Unlimited** editions.

Important note

Let's say we are playing with our Developer Edition org and that a 29-day limit is set up. If you have done an export less than 29 days ago, you won't be able to execute another export job until 29 days, whether it is a one-shot or scheduled export.

This is the reason this feature is used as a *low-cost* backup tool.

Switching to Data Loader or a report export, you'll be able to download (almost) as much data as you want and (almost) as frequently as you want. Remember that Salesforce is a cloud platform and its resources are not unlimited, so the *all you want* phrase can't always be true.

Let's use the tool and click the **Start Export** button to land in the export wizard:

Monthly Export Service

Export File Encoding	ISO-8859-1 (General US & Western European, ISO-LATIN-1) ∨
Include images, documents, and attachments	☐ ⓘ
Include Salesforce Files and Salesforce CRM Content document versions	☐ ⓘ
Replace carriage returns with spaces	☑

[Start Export] [Cancel]

Exported Data

Select what type of information you would like to include in the export. The data types listed below use the Apex API names. If you are not familiar with these names data for your export.

☑ Include all data

☐ Contract	☐ Order	☐ OrderItem
☐ ContractContactRole	☐ RecordType	☐ BusinessProcess
☐ CommSubscriptionTiming	☐ DataPrepServiceLocator	☐ EngagementChannelType
☐ ManagedContentBodyLink	☐ ManagedContentMigration	☐ ManagedContentTypeSearchBlackList
☐ PartyConsent	☐ PaymentIdempotent	☐ StrategyMonthlyStats
☐ Advertisement__c	☐ Example__c	☐ Postal_Code__c
☐ Vehicle__c		

Figure 15.9 – Configuring an export job

From this page, you can select the following:

- The **Export File Encoding** format.

- **Include images, documents, and attachments** and **Include Salesforce Files and Salesforce CRM Content document versions** to create bigger export files with attachments related to the record that is being exported.

- The kind of Salesforce objects you want to export, by selecting **Include all data**. So, you'll be including every Salesforce object.

Now we are ready to run the job. Click the **Start Export** button to run the export job:

Figure 15.10 – Export job queued

Depending on the dataset, the job can take a while to complete. Salesforce will send you an email notification when the job completes:

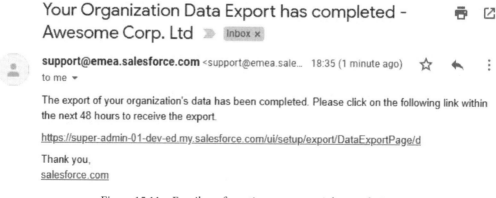

Figure 15.11 – Email confirmation on export job completion

The file is downloadable for 48 hours after its creation, and after this time frame, it is automatically deleted. The exported file is in ZIP format and contains a CSV file for every object selected (in our example, it will contain tens of files because we selected the option to include all data, and so all available standard Salesforce objects are included).

If the data exceeds 512 MB, the system creates a set of files with a weight of up to 512 MB.

This is what you'll see on the **Data Export** page:

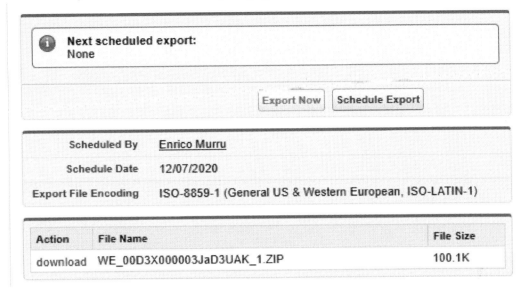

Figure 15.12 – Downloadable files from the Data Export page

If you want to schedule a data export so you are 100% sure that you have a periodic backup (remember that there has to be a *human* who actively jumps to this page and manually downloads the ZIP files once the export is completed), click the **Schedule Export** button to see pretty much what we saw in *Figure 15.8*, with some more options regarding the schedule frequency, as shown in the following screenshot:

Figure 15.13 – Frequency options for a scheduled data export job

This interface will change slightly as a weekly export is enabled on your org.

Set up a day/time when the system is not overloaded. In fact, if the system is way too loaded, the job won't be executed exactly when requested in the schedule frequency, leading to delayed exportation. Remember that the 7-day or 29-day interval is a hard limit, so any other execution will be delayed as well.

What we've seen so far can easily be replicated using Data Loader, an external and free tool that provides easy and massive data access on the Salesforce platform.

Data Loader

If you want to have full control over data imports and exports, the Data Loader app is what you need (and it is what you'll probably be asked to use for some quick data cleansing activities).

Data Loader is a client application available for free where you can insert, update, delete, or export massive Salesforce records, using CSV files to handle input or output files and a direct org connection (you add your Salesforce credentials sometime before running a Data Loader job).

This tool can be used with a user interface so you can interactively configure the database operations, parameters, queries, and field mappings or from a command line (on Windows only) when you want an import/export job to be run automatically without using intervention.

> **Further reading**
>
> We'll be concentrating on the user interface version, but if you want to learn more about the command line or *Batch Mode* version, start from Salesforce Help at `https://help.salesforce.com/articleView?id=loader_batchmode.htm&type=5`.

Data Loader is highly recommended when you have to load between 5,000 and 5,000,000 records (which is a higher limit). If you need more, you can execute more jobs or use external tools (such as dataloader.io by Mulesoft, available at an extra cost) or when you need to import Salesforce standard objects that are not supported by the Data Import Wizard yet.

Let's install Data Loader and run it.

Installing Data Loader

To install Data Loader, jump to **Setup | Integrations | Data Loader** and choose your operating system (at the time of writing, only Windows and macOS are supported – from this page, you'll also be able to have a look at the installation instructions):

- Windows: `https://help.salesforce.com/articleView?id=loader_install_windows.htm&type=5`

- macOS: `https://help.salesforce.com/articleView?id=loader_install_mac.htm&type=5`

We won't report system requirements here as they are likely to change over time, so refer to Salesforce Help at `https://help.salesforce.com/articleView?id=installing_the_data_loader.htm&type=5` for a complete list of requirements, including the OS version and the Java JDK version that should be installed before Data Loader.

You can have different Data Loader installations active at one time, and you'll see a new Data Loader version published after every major Salesforce release.

Let's now learn about all available Data Loader actions.

Running and configuring Data Loader

Double-click on the icon to execute the app. In the following screenshot, we are showing the Windows version:

Figure 15.14 – The Data Loader user interface

The first thing we note is that we have different available actions:

- **Insert**: Create brand new records.

- **Update**: Update records identified by Salesforce ID.

- **Upsert**: Update records identified by Salesforce ID or an external ID field or create a record if no match is found.

- **Delete**: Delete records, putting them in the recycle bin (reachable from **App Launcher | Recycle Bin**).

- **Hard Delete**: Delete records without sending them to the recycle bin. This option is grayed out by default if the **Bulk API** option is not enabled.

- **Export**: Export data given a SOQL query.

- **Export All**: Export data given a SOQL query that runs on the recycle bin dataset as well (so you'll get deleted records too).

To execute any action, you need an active connection to a Salesforce org, which can be created after any button click.

Activating a connection

To activate the running org connection, click on any action. You can choose between **OAuth** and **Password Authentication**. The former is the more secure option as it doesn't require any username/password management by Data Loader (it will only store an authentication token that can be revoked from your org in the event of malicious use).

If you choose the **OAuth** option, you'll be asked by the Salesforce login screen for your credentials and prompted to allow the connection:

Figure 15.15 – Creating a new Data Loader connection using OAuth

If you choose the **Password Authentication** option, you'll simply get asked for your credentials from within a login form:

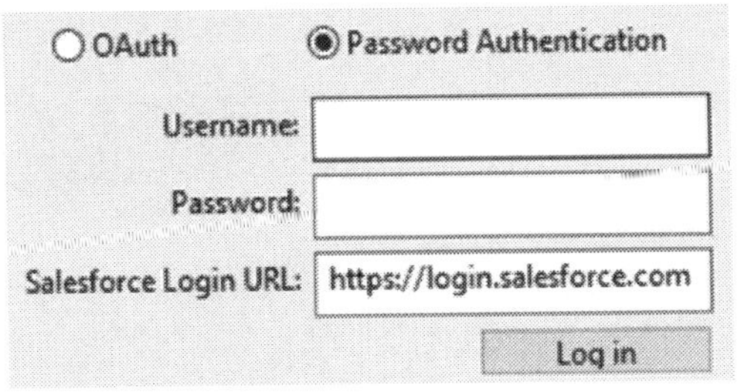

Figure 15.16 – Creating a new Data Loader connection using Password Authentication

If you want to change org and create a brand new connection, click on **File | Logout** so any time you click on an action button, you'll be prompted for a new Salesforce login.

If you close Data Loader and open it again, the previous connection will still be available (unless you are using **OAuth** but an admin has *closed* your session: this way, you'll need to authenticate again).

Now that we have a valid connection, let's try the available action.

The Insert action

Let's create a new CSV file with the following values (remember to remove any blank spaces between commas):

```
"Code","Account Name","Account Phone","Industry","Rating"
"AC00001","Account 1","555-123456","Telco","Hot"
"AC00002","Account 2","555-123457","High Tech","Warm"
"AC00003","Account 3","555-123458","Services","Cold"
"AC00004","Account 4","555-123459","Services","Cold"
"AC00005","Account 5","555-123460","Telco","Hot"
"AC00006","Account 9","555-123461","Energy & Utilities","Warm"
```

The **Code** field is a brand new custom field defined as follows:

- API Name: Code__c
- Label: Code
- Data Type: Text

- Required: `false`
- Unique: `true` (case insensitive)
- External ID: `true`
- Default value: *blank*

Also, enable your user's profile so you are able to read/write it.

> **Tip**
>
> Even if you have an administrator profile, meaning so you can see virtually any object and field even though your profile has not actually been enabled to, when using external tools, a field access check is enforced, and so you may not be able to access the field.

Click the **Insert** button and select the object type you are going to insert (**Account**), as shown in the following screenshot:

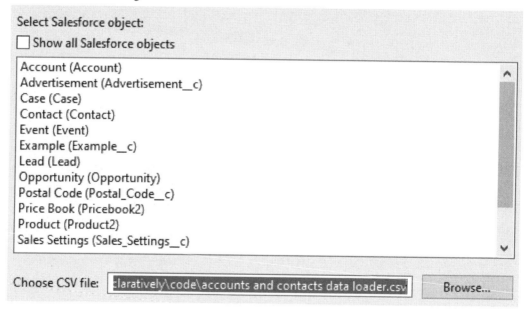

Figure 15.17 – Selecting the object type to insert

Click **Next** so Data Loader can analyze the CSV and infer the number of records (it will say that you are going to operate on six records).

Click **OK** to jump to the mapping step. Despite the Data Import Wizard, you need to manually map all fields or let Data Loader try to infer the field names:

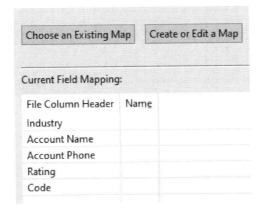

Figure 15.18 – Defining the mapping

Click on **Create or Edit a Map** and then **Auto-Match Fields to Columns** to see Data
Loader try to get the best out of labels and CSV column names:

Match the Salesforce fields to your columns.

Clear Mapping | Auto-Match Fields to Columns

Name	Label	Type
AccountNumber	Account Number	string
AccountSource	Account Source	picklist
Active_c	Active	picklist
AnnualRevenue	Annual Revenue	currency
BillingCity	Billing City	string
BillingCountry	Billing Country	string
BillingGeocodeAccuracy	Billing Geocode Accuracy	picklist

Drag the Salesforce fields down to the column mapping. To remove a mapping, select a row and click Delete.

File Column Header	Name
Account Name	Name
Account Phone	Phone
Code	Code_c
Industry	Industry
Rating	Rating

Figure 15.19 – Mapping CSV fields

If everything goes well, you'll find the tool auto-matching all the fields in the CSV,
otherwise, some manual selection will be required. You can click the **Save Mapping**
button so you can save an XML file containing the selected mapping. This way, you can
import it in future executions.

Now that we have all the mapping we need, we can click **Next** to select a directory where success and error files will be saved. Click **Finish** to run the insert job.

Data Loader will *talk* with Salesforce using standard APIs to insert the records and let you know at which point the job is, showing a popup with a recap when the job is done:

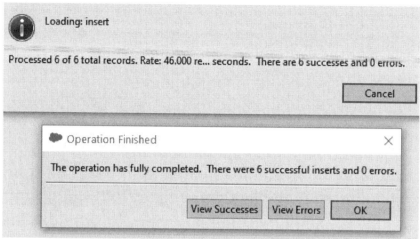

Figure 15.20 – Insert job completed

The tool also created two files containing the success and error records:

ID	CODE	ACCOUNT NAM	ACCOUNT PHO	INDUSTRY	RATING	STATUS
0013X00002pEYntQAG	AC00001	Account 1	555-123456	Telco	Hot	Item Created
0013X00002pEYnuQAG	AC00002	Account 2	555-123457	High Tech	Warm	Item Created
0013X00002pEYnvQAG	AC00003	Account 3	555-123458	Services	Cold	Item Created
0013X00002pEYnwQAG	AC00004	Account 4	555-123459	Services	Cold	Item Created
0013X00002pEZ47QAG	AC00005	Account 5	555-123460	Telco	Hot	Item Created
0013X00002pEZ48QAG	AC00006	Account 9	555-123461	Energy & Utilities	Warm	Item Created

Figure 15.21 – Success CSV result

The success file contains the Salesforce **ID** of the item created and its **STATUS**.

If you create a CSV containing some incorrect values (such as an empty, required **Name** field or a field with too many characters), this is what you'll get in the resulting error file:

CODE	ACCOUNT NAM	ACCOUNT PHO	INDUSTR	RATING	ERROR
AC00001		555-123456	Telco	Hot	Required fields are missing: [Name]
AC12345678!	Account Y	555-123461	Energy & Uti	Warm	Code: data value too large: AC12345678....1234567890 (max length=255)

Figure 15.22 – Error CSV result

In this file, you'll see the record payload plus the details of the error thrown.

Let's now see some other actions.

The Export action

The **Export** action is used to get data from Salesforce. To do this, it is necessary to tell the Data Loader which is the filter or SOQL query that has to be issued to get the necessary records.

This action starts with the object type selection (choose **Account**) and a target directory where the CSV file with the exported data will be placed. Click **Next** to jump to the SOQL query creation step:

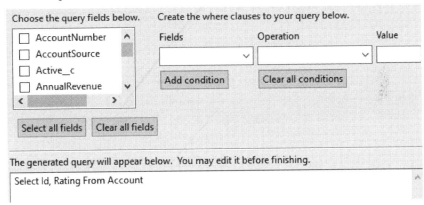

Figure 15.23 – SOQL query creation in the Export action

A simple SOQL query is illustrated here:

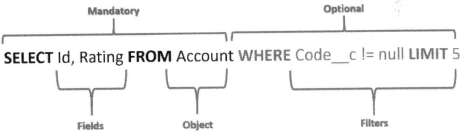

Figure 15.24 – SOQL query basic structure

It is composed of a mandatory part that selects the Salesforce object and its fields to be retrieved, and an optional part where you can define additional filters on the dataset to query, all packed up with some SOQL keywords (in the preceding example, we have SELECT, FROM, WHERE, and LIMIT).

In the preceding example, we are saying that we want to retrieve the Id and Rating fields from all **Account** records that have a Code__c field not *blank* and the result should contain five elements only.

In *Figure 15.22*, we have skipped the WHERE part, so we are simply getting all the accounts with no additional filters. There are some SOQL query best practices and one is not to execute queries with no filters, as this can compromise query performances, but as we know we have few records on the **Account** record, we can continue with no risk.

> **Further reading**
>
> We'll not cover SOQL queries in this book, but I strongly suggest starting over from Trailhead with the **SOQL for Admins** module available at https://
> trailhead.salesforce.com/content/learn/modules/
> soql-for-admins.

Once the query has been completed (this Data Loader step has a listbox that's useful to get the field names and create some filter clauses), click the **Finish** button to make Data Loader do all the work. The result is a CSV file containing all the data we asked for:

ID	RATING
0013X00002pEYkyQAG	
0013X00002pEYkzQAG	
0013X00002noYQKQA2	
0013X00002Yevq9QAB	Cold
0013X00002Yevq7QAB	
0013X00002Yevq8QAB	
0013X00002YevpzQAB	Hot
0013X00002Yevq0QAB	Hot
0013X00002Yevq1QAB	
0013X00002Yevq2QAB	
0013X00002Yevq3QAB	Warm

Figure 15.25 – Export CSV result

We'll be using this file to execute an update action.

The Export All action

This action works exactly like the **Export** action, with the only difference being that its query is executed on the recycle bin as well, allowing you to query on deleted records.

This action is particularly useful when you want to *undo* a previous delete action because of errors or simply want to get deleted records of a special kind that users may have mistakenly deleted.

The Update action

The **Update** action is quite similar to the **Insert** action. Indeed, you select the object type and select a CSV file containing the records to be updated; in this file, you'll mandatorily need to have the Salesforce ID of the record you are going to update.

Let's say that users started to fill in the Rating field on **Account** records recently, so you have a lot of records without that field compiled that should be populated with the Cold value.

So, you can do a simple **Export** action run with a query such as SELECT Id, Rating FROM Account WHERE Rating__c = null and get a CSV containing all *blank-rated* accounts. Then, change the CSV to fill in all void values with the Cold value and use it as an input file for the **Update** action, shown as follows:

ID	RATING
0013X00002pEYkyQAG	Cold
0013X00002pEYkzQAG	Cold
0013X00002noYQKQA2	Cold
0013X00002Yevq9QAB	Cold
0013X00002Yevq7QAB	Cold
0013X00002Yevq8QAB	Cold

Figure 15.26 – CSV input for the Update action

As mentioned, the **ID** field is mandatory, otherwise, no update is possible.

Set the proper mapping (in this case, you'll only need to map to fields), choose the target folders for the results, and click the **Finish** Button. Data Loader will start the update operations, returning success and error files as a result.

The Upsert action

The **Upsert** action puts together the **Insert** and **Update** actions into a single action where records can be created or updated, depending on whether the record, identified by an ID or external ID field, is found.

To use an example, let's create a new CSV similar to the *insert CSV*, where we are using the first two records of the previous file and adding two more records, as shown in the following screenshot:

Code	Account Nan	Account Phor	Industry	Rating
AC00001	Account 1	555-123456	Telco	Hot
AC00002	Account 2	555-123457	High Tech	Warm
AC99999	Account 9999	555-99999	Energy & Utilities	Warm
AC99998	Account 9998	555-99998	Telco	Warm

Figure 15.27 – Upsert CSV input file

We want to use the Code field as a match field for already existing **Accounts**.

The **Upsert** action starts pretty much like the **Insert** and **Update** actions, but in the second step, it asks you to select the field for matching on account:

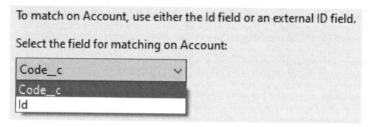

Figure 15.28 – Selecting the matching field on the Upsert action

Data Loader automatically lists potential fields obtained by describing how the currently selected object is shaped and selecting only the external ID fields. For the **Account** object, in our example, the only external ID fields are the Salesforce ID and the brand new **Code** field (which is also on our CSV).

Click **Next** for the parent object selection (if any). This is an option that you can use when you have parent objects and you want to refer to a parent record using an external ID instead of an ID (in our example, a parent record could be a parent **Account** object). Let's leave these options blank and click **Next** again to land on the mapping step, which works, as we've already seen in *Figure 15.18*, on the **Insert** action.

The last step is selecting the target directory for the success and error result files and the **Finish** button will start the **Upsert** job. If everything went OK, this will be the result:

ID	CODE	ACCOUNT NA	ACCOUNT PHO	INDUSTRY	RATING	STATUS
0013X00002pEYntQAG	AC00001	Account 1	555-123456	Telco	Hot	Item Updated
0013X00002pEYnuQAG	AC00002	Account 2	555-123457	High Tech	Warm	Item Updated
0013X00002pEZN0QAO	AC99999	Account 9999	555-99999	Energy & Utilities	Warm	Item Created
0013X00002pEZN1QAO	AC99998	Account 9998	555-99998	Telco	Warm	Item Created

Figure 15.29 – Upsert action success result

As you can see from the `Status` column, we have two updated records (the one we already created with the **Insert** action) and two created records that didn't match with any record by the `Code` field, so, for any of them, Data Loader returns the Salesforce ID field as well.

The Delete and Hard Delete actions

Finally, the **Delete** action is used to delete records that you have previously queried.

Before deleting any records, take your time to back up the records; you'll never know whether you'll need those records again or if you are actually making a great mistake!

The procedure is very similar to insert and update actions, with the only difference being that the mapping step is only able to map the ID field:

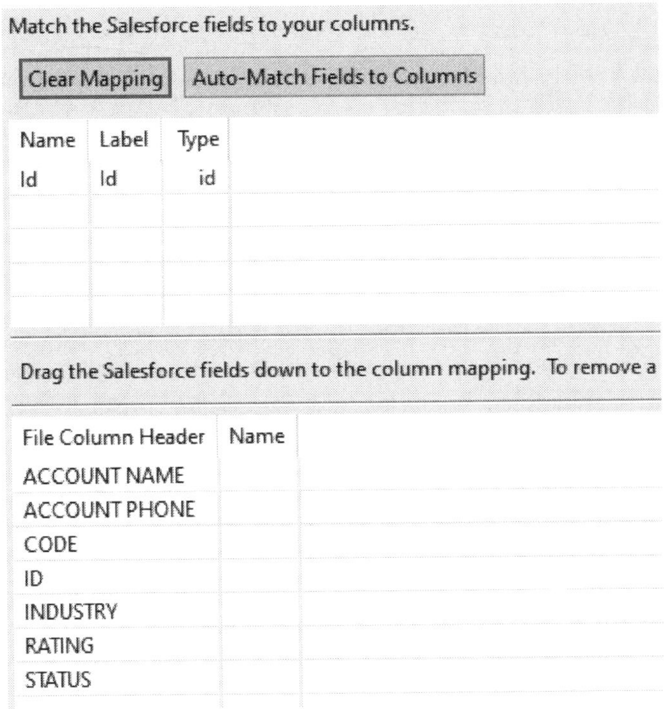

Figure 15.30 – Field mapping on the Delete action

To test this out, you can take any successful results of the previous examples and use them to delete the corresponding records.

While the **Delete** action deletes a record but leaves it in the recycle bin, the **Hard Delete** action, as stated previously, deletes records without any chance of restoring them. This action is disabled by default because it only works if you tell Data Loader to use the **Bulk APIs,** which are a set of APIs that Salesforce provides specifically for massive data management.

To enable this mode, go to the **Settings | Settings** menu item and look for the **Use Bulk API** checkbox. After hitting the **Save** button, you'll see the **Hard Delete** action enabled.

This action works exactly like the regular **Delete** action; it only behaves differently on the database side.

Before closing, let's see some common configuration settings.

Tweaking the settings

From **Settings | Settings**, you can configure some basic to advanced Data Loader settings. Let's look at some of the most common ones:

- **Batch size**: Insert, update, upsert, and delete actions can be executed in batches of up to 200 records. If **Use Bulk API** is checked, this can be set to up to 10,000. The greater the value, the quicker the action, but it can also cause errors if complex automations are implemented.

- **Insert null values**: If checked, any data operation inserts a blank value as a null value in the corresponding field (not available if **Use Bulk API** is enabled).

- **Query request size**: Salesforce can return an export result in batches of up to 2,000 records. The greater the value, the quicker the export – but more memory is used by the client's laptop.

- **Use European date format**: Supports the date and date/time formats of dd/MM/yyyy and dd/mm/yyyy HH:mm:ss.

- **Allow field truncation**: If checked, any field value that exceeds the field's maximum length is truncated, otherwise, it returns an error (not available if **Use Bulk API** is enabled).

> **Further reading**
>
> There are more advanced Data Loader options. To learn more, refer to Salesforce Help at `https://help.salesforce.com/articleView?id=configuring_the_data_loader.htm&type=5`.

This ends the **Data Loader** section and the import and export chapter. You should have acquired all the basic concepts to start getting your hands on data manipulation and run effective data life cycle management throughout your org.

Blaze your trail

Complete the following modules on Trailhead to increase your knowledge:

- Import and Export with Data Management Tools: `https://trailhead.salesforce.com/en/content/learn/projects/import-and-export-with-data-management-tools`

- Data Management: `https://trailhead.salesforce.com/en/content/learn/modules/lex_implementation_data_management?trail_id=manage-your-salesforce-data`

Summary

Throughout this chapter, we have focused on basic concepts of data life cycle management, identifying the tools that the Salesforce platform delivers to grant us a chance to largely extract and import data.

The first tool we saw was the **Data Import Wizard**, used to import up to 50,000 records at a time for a certain selection of standard Salesforce objects and all custom objects, using the tool declaratively to define the kind of action to perform on records (insert, update, or upsert) and the field mapping needed when uploading the CSV file with all the involved records.

The second tool looked at was the **Export Data** service, a simple way to periodically extract all the data from the CRM, but with strict time limits.

The third and final tool was **Data Loader**, an important tool that can be used to execute any kind of data manipulation, including insert, update, upsert, and extract actions (from the recycle bin too), and even delete and hard delete, to delete records without any chance of recovering them from the recycle bin.

From now on, you have all the basic concepts to start your data life cycle management strategy.

In the next chapter, we'll cover another way to extract and visualize data from the database, the data reporting tool, with standard Salesforce reports.

16
Learning about Data Reporting

Reports are a fundamental tool to understand how a business is doing, creating specific views that implement key metrics that let business users understand what is happening in your organization (org). With reporting, you can understand whether there have been cases open for many days with no solution provided for the customer, or you can highlight the best sales representatives by identifying who sells the most. You can also see how many leads are not converted into real customers or take our **Advertisement** example, which we run throughout this book, monitoring the creation of new advertisement deals and aggregating data depending on the country.

In this chapter, we'll learn the basics of reporting:

- Building a report
- Creating a new report
- Customizing a report with calculated fields
- Managing reports
- Further considerations for reporting

By reading this chapter, you will learn about reporting, which will help you understand it and decide where you should steer the wheel if something is affecting your business.

Building a report

What is a report? Easy. Have you ever worked with digital spreadsheets (such as Microsoft Excel, Google Sheets, or OpenDocument spreadsheets) and played with columns to filter out, highlight, or create formulas on your data to get a better view of the thousands (if not millions) of rows? Have you ever used spreadsheet data to trace a graph right into the sheet?

In this section, we will learn about building a report and how to prepare a dataset. We will also learn about creating a new report and shaping it with the Lightning report builder. We will also filter reports and add charts to them.

Here is an example of what you can do with regular spreadsheet tools:

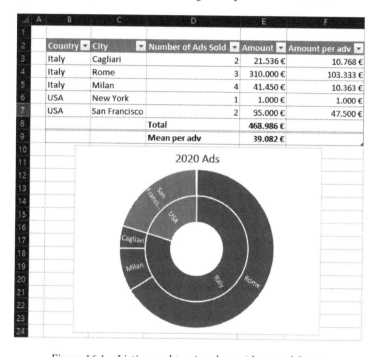

Figure 16.1 – Listing and tracing data with spreadsheets

The Salesforce platform provides different tools for reporting but standard reports, which are the most used and easy to learn for most reporting needs, come for free with your Salesforce license. We can easily create a Salesforce report that matches – more or less – the previous spreadsheet, as you can see in the following screenshot:

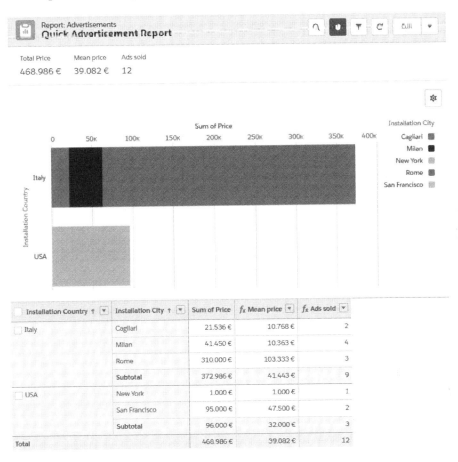

Figure 16.2 – Report example of the Advertisement object

As you can see in the preceding screenshot, the view is quite similar to the spreadsheet one. Indeed, we have the following:

- A table containing all records, with record counts and mean formulas, all grouped by the relevant fields.
- A chart that visually represents data.

So, you may ask, why do I have to learn Salesforce reports if I'm a digital spreadsheet master? A few reasons are as follows:

- You are using a tool that is built into the platform and lets you grab all of the required data in real time.

- Charts are interactive, meaning that if you select a specific part of the chart, the report gets filtered accordingly (for example, by highlighting all *Italy*-related data).

- You can subscribe to reports, so you can automatically get the results from a report every time a specific condition is met (for example, *alert me if there is a case that is not handled within 7 days*).

- Because you are going to become the next Salesforce trailblazer and you need to know anything related to Salesforce.

- Reports are run using the running user's visibility rules; this means that they can only see the data they have access to using sharing rules.

Let's now build the report shown in *Figure 16.2*.

Preparing the dataset

Before creating the new report, let's make sure we have some data on our **Advertisment** object.

We want to highlight advertisements related to a specific country and city. We already have the **Installation Country** picklist on the **Advertisement** object, but no city field so far. Let's create a new **Installation City** field (as we saw in *Chapter 2, Building the Data Model*), of the text type. Remember to add the right *field-level security* to the field and to add it to the **Advertisement** object's layout (as we saw in *Chapter 12, All About Layouts*).

Then create a new list view on the **Advertisement** object to list all *active* advertisements to show country, city, and price, so you can update the values by hand and from the list view itself (remember that there is an *approval* process defined for the **Discount** record, so you need to be sure no discount is applied or that all discounts have already been approved before updating any record). This is more or less what you may come up with:

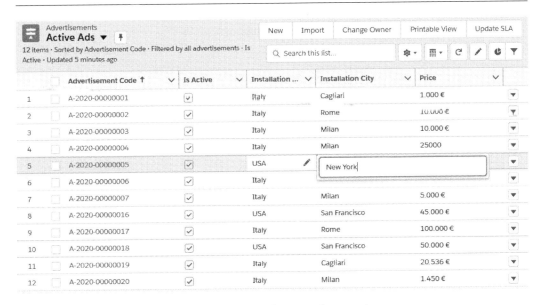

Figure 16.3 – Using list views for records

As you can see in the preceding screenshot, this is an **Advertisement** list view with some records in it.

So, let's create a new report.

Creating a new report

To create a new report, simply jump to **App Launcher | Reports** and click the **New Report** button. Skip the **New Report (Salesforce Classic)** button, as it lets you use the *Classic* report builder interface, which we don't want to cover in this book, as 99% of the features are available in the *Lightning* builder as well.

> **Further reading:**
> If you want to learn more about the differences between the *Classic* and *Lightning* builder, refer to Salesforce Help at `https://help.salesforce.com/articleView?id=reports_build_lex.htm&type=5` and look for the **Note** box in the link.

The first thing you are asked for is the **report type**, which is the kind of report related to a specific object.

If you selected the **Allow Reports** checkbox on the Salesforce object creation wizard, you'll be able to look for the **Advertisements** report type, which is automatically created by Salesforce upon object creation:

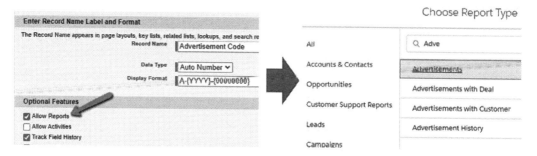

Figure 16.4 – Allow Reports grants immediate access to the Advertisements report type

As you can see in the preceding screenshot, when you select the **Allow Reports** checkbox, Salesforce creates a *standard* report type that you can easily use to build your reports on that object. If the custom object includes a master-detail lookup, the behavior is different, as the system only created a report type that links the parent and the child object (as we'll see in the next section).

> **Further reading:**
> To learn more about automatic standard report type creation for custom objects, refer to Salesforce Help at https://help.salesforce.com/articleView?id=000316872&language=en_US&type=1&mode=1.

So, let's see what a report type is and how it can be created in the next section.

Understanding report types

Report Types are a way to define what a report is based on and which fields it may contain. As we discussed earlier, Salesforce supports standard report types, mostly for standard records and some for custom objects that are enabled for reports. Standard report types cannot be updated in any way.

> **Further reading:**
> To know all the standard report types available on the platform, refer to Salesforce Help at https://help.salesforce.com/articleView?id=standard_report_folders.htm&type=5.

Report types let you define reports based on the related object, such as **Accounts and Contacts**, or **Opportunities**, or **Products**.

Let's create a custom report type that shows all **accounts** that have at least one **Advertisement**. To create a new custom report type, follow these steps:

1. Click on **Setup | Feature Settings | Analytics | Reports & Dashboards | Report Types** and click the **New Custom Report Type** button.

2. Select **Account** on the **Primary Object** picklist.

3. Then fill in **Report Type Label** with **Account & Advertisements** and let the form auto-complete the **Report Type Name** field.

4. Then add a **Description** and select **Opportunities** in the Store in **Category** picklist.

5. Finally, select the **Deployed** radio button for **Deployment Status** (this prevents other users from using this report type while it is being built):

New Custom Report Type

Help for this Page

Step 1. Define the Custom Report Type	Step 1 of 2

Next   Cancel

| = Required Information

Report Type Focus

Specify what type of records (rows) will be the focus of reports generated by this report type.

Example: If reporting on "Contacts with Opportunities with Partners," select "Contacts" as the primary object.

Primary Object | Accounts

Identification

Report Type Label | Account & Advertisements

Report Type Name | Account_Advertisements | i

Note: Description will be visible to users who create reports.

Description | Accounts that have at least one advertisement

Store in Category | Opportunities

Deployment

A report type with deployed status is available for use in the report wizard. While in development, report types are visible only to authorized administrators and their delegates.

Deployment Status   ○ In Development
                     ◉ Deployed

Figure 16.5 – Custom report type main fields form

6. Click **Next** to define the report *record set*, that is, the kind of records involved in the report, provided that the **Account** object is the parent record.

7. Click on the **(Click to relate another object)** link and select **Advertisements** from the picklist shown.

8. Select **Each "A" record must have at least one related "B" record** from the **A to B Relationship** radio group, as shown in the following screenshot:

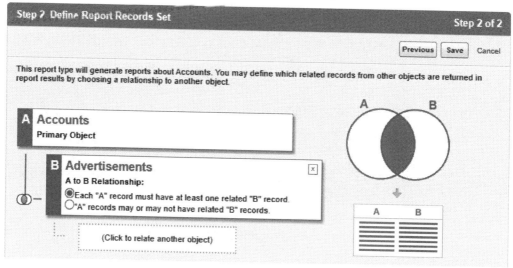

Figure 16.6 – Defining the report type's record set

As you can see in the preceding screenshot, by selecting *the second choice* in the radio group, any report that uses the chosen report type will display any **Account** record, whether it has an advertisement record related or not. By choosing the first choice, our reports will only result in accounts that have at least one advertisement record related.

9. Click the **Save** button to save the new report type, that is, on the report type page, select the fields that can be used when creating a new report from **Fields Available for Reports** using the **Edit Layout** button:

Fields Available for Reports	Edit Layout	Preview Layout	Fields Available for Reports Help (?)
Source		Selected Fields	
Accounts		62	
Advertisements		20	

Figure 16.7 – Defining available fields on the report type

As you can see in the preceding screenshot, this section will contain the count of **selected fields** for every object selected on the report type.

When using standard report types for the custom object, there is no way to update the available fields (standard report types cannot be modified) so you won't need to add available fields if you create new fields on the custom object.

We won't use this custom report type in our example as the standard **Advertisements** report type is enough for our needs.

Let's now see how the Lightning report builder and its features help us in shaping our reports.

Shaping a report with the Lightning report builder

Let's create a new report as shown in *Figure 16.4* by selecting the **Advertisements** standard report type and clicking the **Next** button to land on the Lightning report builder, shown as follows:

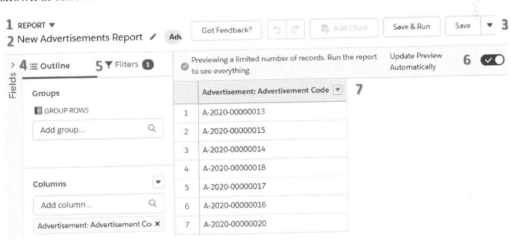

Figure 16.8 – Getting to know the Lightning report builder

As you can see in the preceding screenshot, you can take advantage of different tools and features available in the builder:

1. Report format selection lets you select a *regular* report or a **joined report**, a particular type of report format that we'll see later on, in the *Joined Report* subsection.

2. The report's name editor box (click on the pencil icon to change it).

3. The report action bar, where you can save and run it, or add a chart (the **Add Chart** button is enabled on certain conditions that we'll see shortly).

4. The **Outline** panel lets you identify the fields to display and the fields used to group rows.

5. The **Filters** panel lets you define the filters to add to your report.

6. Check **Update Preview Automatically** to make the preview panel update automatically when you make any changes to the report definition.

7. The builder canvas or preview panel, where you'll see the report preview as you build it.

> **Tip:**
> A report can be modified in almost any part but report type selection is forever, that is, if you need to change the report type, you'll need to create a brand-new report.

Let's start building our report by following these steps:

1. In the **GROUP ROWS** section, search for the **Installation Country** field. Once you select the first grouping field, the **GROUP COLUMNS** section is shown, which will let you define a grouping for a given column (you may need to display the number of advertisements per country grouped by the **Discount Status** picklist or by the **Is Active** checkbox field. We won't choose column grouping in our example).

The following screenshot shows you the **GROUP ROWS** and **GROUP COLUMNS** sections:

Figure 16.9 – Groups and Columns configuration

2. In the **Columns** section, search and select the **Installation City** and **Price** fields, and remove the **Advertisement Code** field (we don't need this level of detail).

> **Tip:**
>
> A report with no grouping is called a **tabular** report and is not allowed to display any charts. A report with at least one grouping field is called a **summary** report because it lets you show summary and subtotal fields. A report with both row and column grouping is called a **matrix** report.

We also want to add a second level of row grouping, using the **Installation City** field. To do this, you can add a second grouping from the **GROUP ROWS** section or simply click on the **Installation City** header's options icon (the down arrow icon) and select **Group Rows by This Field** and de-select the **Detail Rows** flag at the bottom of the preview panel (this will automatically add a **Record Count** column and simplifies the report view):

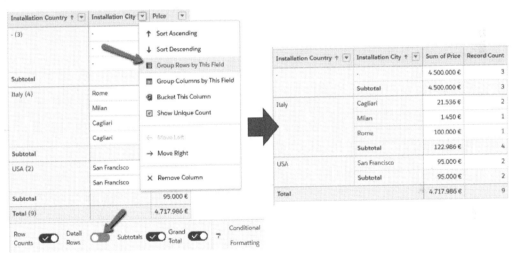

Figure 16.10 – Grouping using the column header and reducing the number of details

Before going on, click on the **Save** button to save your report (choose a name and a description) and leave the **Private Reports** folder selection.

The header can also be used to sort fields and create **bucker fields**, a special kind of calculated column used to group values (which we'll see shortly).

In the **Columns** section's option icon, you'll also have the following options:

- Add a bucket field.
- Add a summary formula (a formula related to a specific grouping, such as the mean value of an amount).
- Add a row-level formula (which is applied to create formulas on each row of the report, such as calculating the real price of an advertisement after discount application).

We'll see buckets in the *Buckets fields* section. For now, let's see how to apply filters to a report in the next section.

Filtering reports

Click on the **Filters** tab to add some filters to your report:

1. First, we want to filter on all records, so click on the **Show Me** section and select all advertisements.

2. We want all records created in the current year so in **Expected Dismission Date** (which should automatically be selected) select the **Advertisement: Created Date** field and from the **Date** picklist, select **Current CY** (under the **Calendar Year** group). If you don't need any time-dependent filters, you can select the **All Time** value.

3. As you can see, the **Show Me** and **Date-based** filters are not removable. To add some more custom filters, in the **Filters** search box, select any field you want to filter the report on. Let's select the **Is Active** field, and select the **true** value, that is, we want to display active advertisements only.

    This is what you get after the **Filters** configuration:

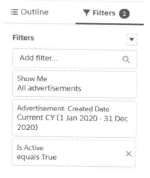

Figure 16.11 – Filters setup

Once you apply the third filter, you'll see a lower record count (although all your records have the **Is Active** field set to true):

Installation Country ↑ ⬝	Installation City ↑ ⬝	Sum of Price	Record Count
Italy	Cagliari	21.536 €	2
	Milan	41.450 €	4
	Rome	310.000 €	3
	Subtotal	372.986 €	9
USA	New York	1.000 €	1
	San Francisco	95.000 €	2
	Subtotal	96.000 €	3
Total		468.986 €	12

Figure 16.12 – Report preview showing all active advertisements

We have almost completed our example. The next thing we want to create is a field that highlights the mean value of the advertisements sold. To do this, we'll need a summary formula.

Before moving on, remember to save the report.

Customizing records with calculated fields

We can further customize reports using calculated fields with the following:

- **Bucket fields**
- **Column summaries**
- **Summary formulas**
- **Row-level formulas**

For our example, we're going to use a single column summary field, but we'll briefly see all the available options in the following sections.

Bucket fields

Bucket fields are used to group fields by values, and they can be created from numeric or text fields.

Let's create two example bucket fields, one on the **Discount Status** field (which is a picklist field, and so a textual field) and one on the **Price** field (which is a currency field, and so a numeric field). To create a bucket field, click on the **Columns** section's options button (the down arrow) and select **Add Bucket Column**:

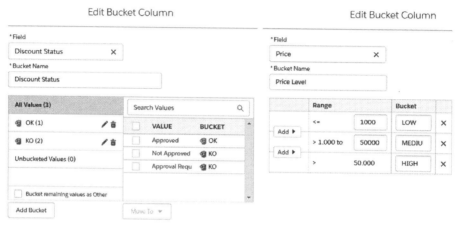

Figure 16.13 – Creating a textual and numeric bucket field

As you can see in the preceding screenshot, the interface is quite trivial and differs on the text and numeric fields:

- On the text fields, you can create different buckets, each one being assigned to one or more text values (as of the *Summer '20* release, unfortunately, you cannot add a *blank* value to the bucket).

- On numeric fields, you can select a range of values.

As each bucket field is related to each record, you'll be able to see the new fields only if you enable the **Detail Rows** flags (which we disabled earlier):

Installation Country ↑ ▼	Installation City ↑ ▼	Price ▼	Discount Status ↓ ▼	Price Level ▼
Italy (9)	Cagliari (2)	20.536 €	-	MEDIUM
		1.000 €	-	LOW
	Subtotal	21.536 € Avg: 10.768 €		
	Milan (4)	25.000 €	OK	MEDIUM
		1.450 €	-	MEDIUM
		5.000 €	-	MEDIUM
		10.000 €	-	MEDIUM
	Subtotal	41.450 € Avg: 10.363 €		
	Rome (3)	10.000 €	OK	MEDIUM
		200.000 €	OK	HIGH

Figure 16.14 – Numeric and text bucket fields displayed

In this example report, we can see that for each city, we have a list of prices and for each price, we can see its price level shown as a text field (which is clearer than reading each price one by one).

Buckets can be used to group rows and columns. Once you have tried testing, de-select the **Detail Rows** flag again at the bottom of the Lightning report builder.

Column summaries

With column summaries, we can create summary formulas on groupings by selecting the kind of summarization you want, choosing between the **sum**, **average**, **max**, and **min** functions.

To create a new column summary, simply click on any field (that is related to a record) in the **Columns** section (or on the field's column option icon on the preview panel) and select the proper summarization function:

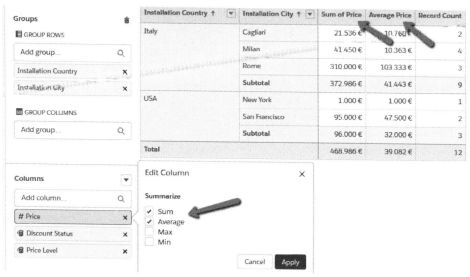

Figure 16.15 – Creating column summaries

We wanted to calculate the total and average value of the advertisement prices throughout countries and cities. The same result could have been obtained using summary formulas.

Summary formulas

With summary formulas, we can apply a formula to group subtotals and grand totals, such as calculating taxes based on the price, given an algorithm.

Let's say the customer will pay taxes depending on the country of installation and the amount is calculated on the country's subtotal.

Click on the **Columns** section's options menu and select **Add Summary Formula**:

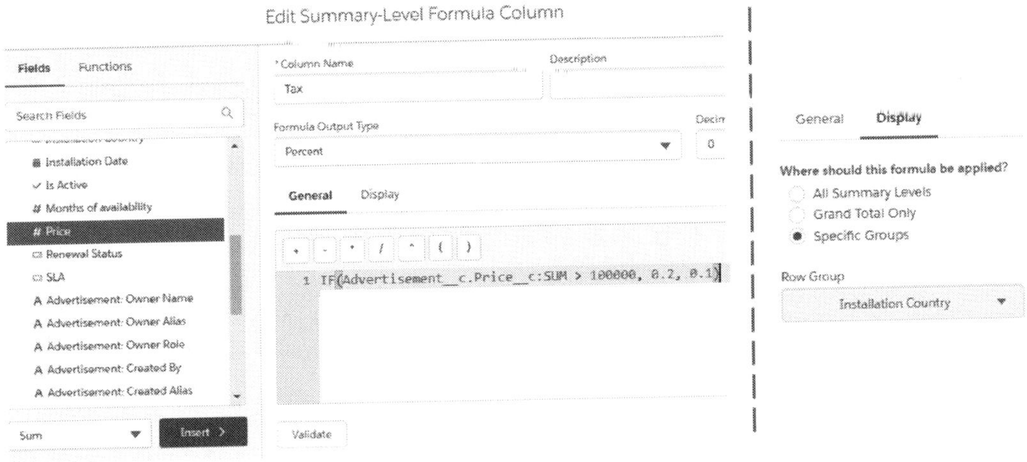

Figure 16.16 – Creating a Summary Formula field

As you can see in the preceding screenshot, in the **Fields** section, you can select almost any field of the report (including buckets and grouping fields) and build your algorithm, using only grouping values (we are working on *total* or *subtotal* values) such as SUM, AVERAGE, MIN, and MAX (choose the specific summary function on the picklist next to the **Insert** > button.

We have built the following algorithm:

```
IF(Advertisement__c.Price__c:SUM > 100000, 0.2, 0.1)
```

The formula has the **Percent** type and returns a tax percentage value based on the fact that the sum of the **Price** field is greater than €100,000.

Finally, click on the **Display** tab and select **Specific Groups** in the **Where should this formula be applied?** section and select the **Installation Country** row group. This way, you'll only see the summary formula calculated for each country, shown as follows:

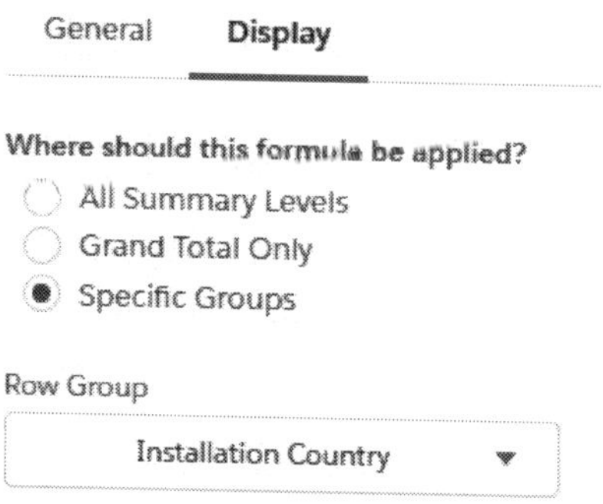

General   **Display**

Where should this formula be applied?
- All Summary Levels
- Grand Total Only
- ● Specific Groups

Row Group

Installation Country ▼

Figure 16.17 – Changing the display configuration of a summary formula

This is the result on the preview panel:

Installation Country ↑ ▼	Installation City ↑ ▼	Sum of Price	Average Price	Record Count	fx Tax ▼
Italy	Cagliari	21.536 €	10.768 €	2	-
	Milan	41.450 €	10.363 €	4	-
	Rome	310.000 €	103.333 €	3	-
	Subtotal	372.986 €	41.443 €	9	20%
USA	New York	1.000 €	1.000 €	1	-
	San Francisco	95.000 €	47.500 €	2	-
	Subtotal	96.000 €	32.000 €	3	10%
Total		468.986 €	39.082 €	12	

Figure 16.18 – Previewing the summary formula

As you can see, for each main grouping (in this case, for each country), the **Tax** summary formula shows a different output, because the **Sum of Price** values differ.

> **Further reading:**
>
> To know more about summary formulas, refer to Salesforce Help at `https://help.salesforce.com/articleView?id=reports_builder_fields_formulas.htm&type=5`.

Finally, let's see how to build a row-level formula that is computed by the report engine for each row of the report.

Row-level formulas

To create a record-level calculation on reports (without the need to create a custom formula field), use a row-level formula. Select **Add Row-Level Formula** in the **Columns** section's options menu.

Let's create a formula that calculates the number of **Installation Days**:

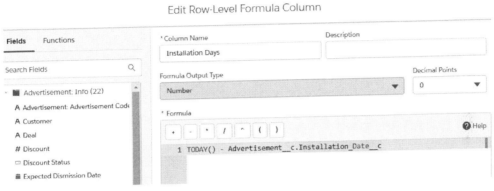

Figure 16.19 – Row-level formula example

As you can see in the preceding screenshot, the formula is quite simple:

```
TODAY() - Advertisement__c.Installation_Date__c
```

As we've seen in the formula fields, the subtract dates field will return the number of days between dates.

Make sure your records have a value for the **Installation Date** field, otherwise the formula returns value 0. This is what you'll end up with:

Installation Country ↑	Installation City ↑	Price	Discount Status ↓	Price Level	fx Installation Days	Installation Date
Italy (9)	Cagliari (2)	20.536 €	-	MEDIUM	139	15/03/2020
		1.000 €	-	LOW	213	01/01/2020
	Subtotal	21.536 € Avg: 10.768 €				
	Milan (4)	25.000 €	OK	MEDIUM	122	01/04/2020
		1.450 €	-	MEDIUM	212	02/01/2020
		5.000 €	-	MEDIUM	31	01/07/2020
		10.000 €	-	MEDIUM	153	01/03/2020

Figure 16.20 – Row-level formula preview

We've added the **Installation Days** column and removed the **Installation Date** column summary option (otherwise the subtotals would have summarized those days, which is not a notable calculation for our example).

> **Further reading:**
>
> To know more about row-level formulas, refer to Salesforce Help at `https://help.salesforce.com/articleView?id=reports_formulas_row_level.htm&type=5`.

Let's close this section with a simple but effective customization to highlight values, the **Conditional Formatting** option.

Conditional Formatting

On the lower-right part of the preview panel, click the **Conditional Formatting** button to define specific formatting (simply the *cell-background color*). You can add rules based on summary formula fields:

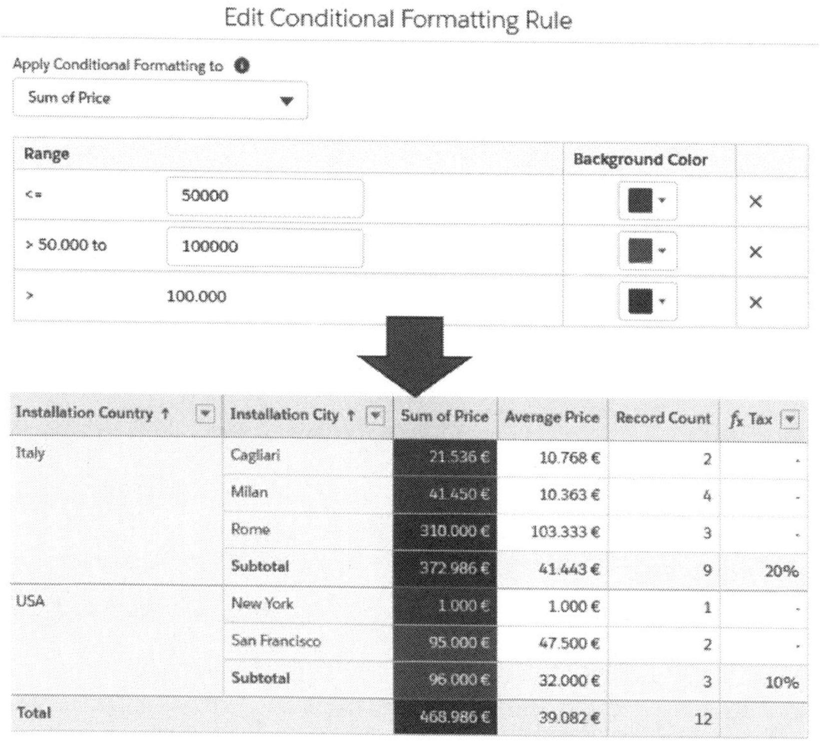

Figure 16.21 – Summary values shown with a different background based on their values

As you can see in the preceding screenshot, in this example, if the price field summarized is lower than €50,000, it is displayed as red; if it's greater than €100,000 as green; and yellow otherwise.

Let's now see how to add charts to visualize data.

Adding charts

In order to add a chart, the report should have at least a grouping (a row or column grouping). Click the **Add Chart** button in the buttons section (next to the **Save & Run** button) to open the charting options:

Figure 16.22 – Charting options

There are different charts available and each of them has its own specific configuration and usage. We'll be using the **Stacked Bar** chart type.

This chart type will display two different bars, each one based on the **Installation Country** value, and inside each bar, you'll see different colored parts based on the **Sum of Price value** for each **installation city**, shown as follows:

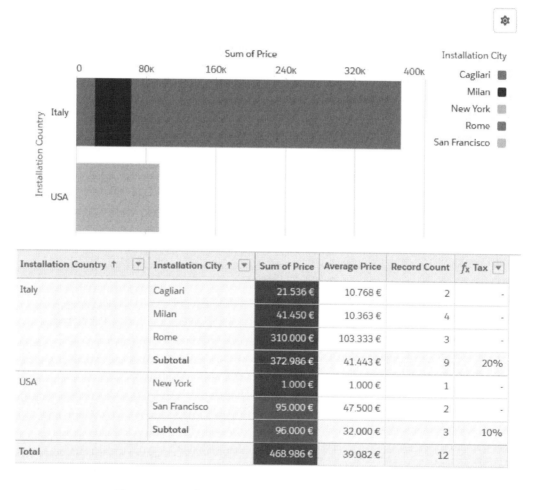

Installation Country ↑ ▼	Installation City ↑ ▼	Sum of Price	Average Price	Record Count	f_x Tax ▼
Italy	Cagliari	21.536 €	10.768 €	2	-
	Milan	41.450 €	10.363 €	4	-
	Rome	310.000 €	103.333 €	3	-
	Subtotal	372.986 €	41.443 €	9	20%
USA	New York	1.000 €	1.000 €	1	-
	San Francisco	95.000 €	47.500 €	2	-
	Subtotal	96.000 €	32.000 €	3	10%
Total		468.986 €	39.082 €	12	

Figure 16.23 – Charting a report with a Stacked Bar chart type

The cool thing about charts is that you can filter the report on the fly by clicking on any item on the chart.

Save the report with the **Show & Run** button to show the report with all the available data (the preview shown is only a small quantity of the available records, to improve the performance during the building phase). Now click on any *colored part* of any bar and you'll see the report *self-filtering*:

Figure 16.24 – Filtering a report using the chart

Before closing the report customization section, let's briefly talk about a special kind of report called a **joined report**.

Joined Report

With joined reports, we can merge together different report types into a single report that combines two or more different record sets (up to 5).

With this kind of report, we can show in a single report all the opportunities coming from a given account and, using the same report type, all opportunities closed and lost – all together. Another example could be matching opportunities and cases given the same account.

Each report part of a *join* is called a **block**. Blocks must have a common field (such as the **Account Name** field), otherwise, it is impossible to match the rows.

Let's create a joined report that matches opportunities and advertisements by the **Account** record:

1. Create a new report and choose the **Opportunities** report type.

2. Then, click the **Report** menu in the upper-right corner of the report builder and select **Joined Report** and click **Apply**.

3. Rename the report in **Opportunities and Advertisements**.

4. Click the **Add Block** button (next to the report name) and select the standard report type, **Advertisements with Customers**.

5. Remove a bunch of the opportunities fields, leaving only the **Opportunity Name**, **Stage**, and **Amount** fields browsing the **Columns** section.

6. On **Group Across Blocks**, select the **Account Name** field (which is based on the **Account** lookup of the **Opportunity** object and on the **Customer** lookup of the **Advertisement** object).

7. Add the **Price** and **Installation Country** fields to the right block browsing the **Columns** section.

8. Jump to the **Filters** section and remove all notable filters (indeed, select all available records in both blocks).

This is more or less what you should end up with:

Figure 16.25 – Configuring a joined report

Note that the linking field, the **Account Name** field, is displayed on the right.

If your org's accounts have both **Opportunities and Advertisements**, you should see the resulting report:

Account Name ↑ ▼	Opportunities Opportunities block 1				Advertisements with Customer Advertisements with Customer block 1		
	Opportunity Name ▼	Stage ▼	Amount ▼		Advertisement... ▼	Price ▼	Instal...
Burlington Textiles Co...	Upgrade Service Gold	Id. Decisio...	150.000,00 €		A-2020-00000016	45.000 €	USA
	Burlington Textiles Weaving Plant Generator	Closed Won	235.000,00 €		A-2020-00000017	100.000 €	Italy
	Burlington Textiles - 10 YEARS SUPPORT	Negotiatio...	1.254.800,00 €		A-2020-00000018	50.000 €	USA
	Big Deal 001-2020	Closed Won	1.500.000,00 €		A-2020-00000014	1.500.000 €	-
	Big Deal 001-2020	Closed Won	1.500.000,00 €		A-2020-00000015	1.500.000 €	-
	Big Deal 001-2020	Closed Won	1.500.000,00 €		A-2020-00000013	1.500.000 €	-
	Big Deal 001-2020	Closed Won	1.500.000,00 €				
	Big Deal 001-2020	Closed Won	1.500.000,00 €				
	Big Deal 001-2020	Closed Won	1.500.000,00 €				
Subtotal	Count: 9				Count: 6	4.695.000 €	
Dickenson plc	Dickenson Mobile Generators	Qualification	15.000,00 €				
Subtotal	Count: 1						

Figure 16.26 – Results of a joined report

Remember that each block of the report may return up to 2,000 records, so filter them accordingly.

In this section, we learned how to create a new report, along with filtering the report. We also learned about customizing the values shown in the report using different formula options. We also learned how to add charts to the reports and how to master joined reports, a specific kind of report.

Now that we know how to create and build a report, let's see some report management options.

Managing reports

Before closing, let's spend some time on report management.

In the previous section, we saw how to create a new report. *But is there a way to share a report with specific users?*

The answer is yes – by using folders. Thanks to report folders, we can perform the same containment actions we perform on files on our laptops; that is, we create a folder, put one or more reports in it, and our reports are well organized. You can even configure sharing for each folder to enable different kinds of users to access the reports.

Managing folders

Reports are saved by default in the `Private Reports` folder, which is accessible to owners only. If you want to make it available to other users, you need to use folders.

To create a new folder, do the following:

1. Click on **App Launcher | Reports**.
2. Click the **New Folder** button.
3. On the form that opens, enter the folder's name.

The new folder will be listed in the **All Folders** section:

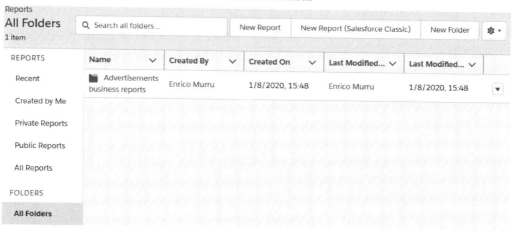

Figure 16.27 – Public report folder listing

To assign a report to a specific folder, jump to the **All Reports** section, search for your report, and, using the right-side options menu (the down-arrow icon), click **Move** and select the new folder.

To share a folder, go back to the **All Folders** section, open the options on the right-hand side of the folder item, and select **Share**:

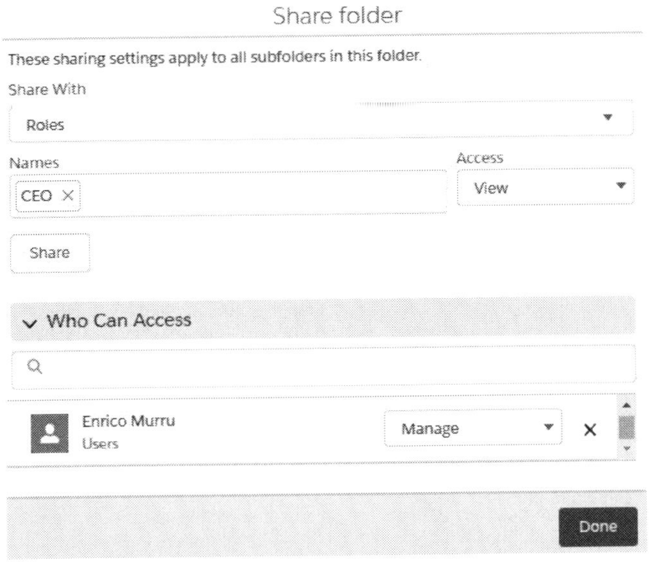

Figure 16.28 – Sharing a folder

As you can see in the preceding screenshot, you can select users, roles, and groups to share the folder with and specify an access level:

- **View**: The user with this access level can see the folder and run the contained reports.

- **Edit**: The user is granted the same access as **View** but also has the power to add reports to the folder and edit its reports.

- **Manage**: This is the same as **Edit**, with the ability to manage folders (update and delete) and manage their sharing, and also to create subfolders.

Another cool option about reports is the subscription feature, which lets you receive a summary of report results via email, executed on a customizable frequency.

Subscribing to reports

To subscribe to a record, simply click the **Subscribe** button in the report's upper buttons section to display the following form:

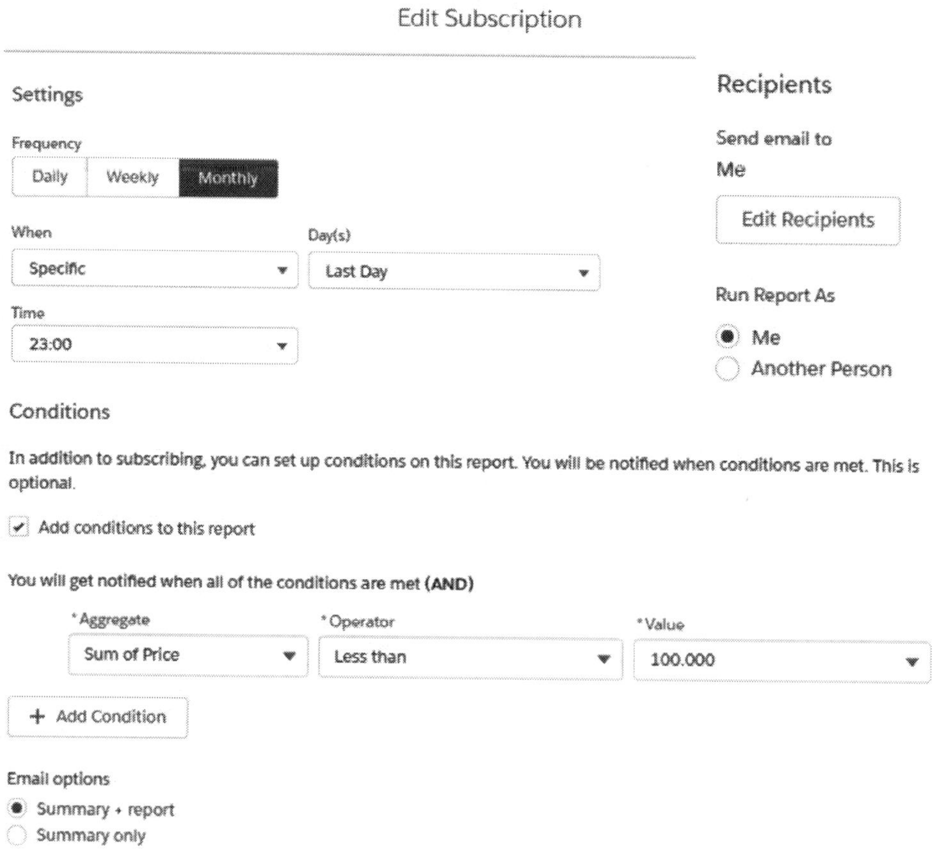

Edit Subscription

Settings

Frequency

| Daily | Weekly | Monthly |

When

Specific ▼

Time

23:00 ▼

Day(s)

Last Day ▼

Recipients

Send email to

Me

Edit Recipients

Run Report As

● Me
○ Another Person

Conditions

In addition to subscribing, you can set up conditions on this report. You will be notified when conditions are met. This is optional.

☑ Add conditions to this report

You will get notified when all of the conditions are met **(AND)**

*Aggregate	*Operator	*Value
Sum of Price ▼	Less than ▼	100.000 ▼

+ Add Condition

Email options
● Summary + report
○ Summary only

Figure 16.29 – Report subscription options for the previous section report

As you can see in the preceding screenshot, we can configure report subscription using the following setups:

- Frequency on automatic record execution with corresponding details (days, months, and time).

- The recipient of the email notification and the option to run the report as another user.

- Additional conditions to trigger the notification (in this case, only if the total sum of the **Price** field doesn't exceed €100,00).

- The notification email format, which may include a report in `.csv` format.

Remember that subscription notifications can contain up to 2,000 result records and that any user can subscribe to up to 5 reports at a time.

In this section, we learned about managing reports along with managing folders and subscribing to reports via email.

Let's close the chapter with some considerations about reports along with some platform limitations that you should be aware of when creating reports.

Further considerations for reporting

Depending on your organization type, reports can have quite different limitations. For example, regarding the number of custom report types, in the Developer Edition, you can build up to 400 custom items, while in an Unlimited Edition org, the limit jumps to 2,000.

There are also some *structural* limits, such as the following (as of the *Summer '20* release):

- The report builder displays up to 20 preview records for summary and matrix reports and up to 50 for tabular reports.

- Reports display up to 2,000 records and we export a report using the **Export** button.

- Reports execution timeouts after 10 minutes by default.

- A joined report can have up to 5 blocks, with 100 columns each.

- A report type can have up to 1,000 fields and up to 60 objects.

- A report can include up to 5 bucket fields and each bucket can have up to 20 buckets, where each bucket can contain up to 20 values.

> **Further reading:**
> Have a look at Salesforce Help for a complete list of reporting limits, at
> `https://help.salesforce.com/articleView?id=faq_`
> `reports_common_limits.htm&type=5`.

Such kinds of limits are subject to change release after release, that's why I haven't shown them here.

Blaze your trail

Have a look at the following Trailhead content to increase your reporting skills:

- Reports & Dashboards for Lightning Experience: `https://trailhead.salesforce.com/en/content/learn/modules/lex_implementation_reports_dashboards`

- Quick Start: Reports & Dashboards: `https://trailhead.salesforce.com/en/content/learn/projects/quickstart-reports`

- Reports & Dashboards for Salesforce Classic: `https://trailhead.salesforce.com/en/content/learn/modules/reports_dashboards`

- Create Reports and Dashboards for Sales and Marketing Managers: `https://trailhead.salesforce.com/en/content/learn/projects/create-reports-and-dashboards-for-sales-and-marketing-managers`

- Sales Reports for Lightning Experience: `https://trailhead.salesforce.com/en/content/learn/modules/sales_admin_sales_reports_for_lex`

- Platform App Builder Certification Prep: Business Logic and Reporting: `https://trailhead.salesforce.com/en/content/learn/modules/platform-app-builder-pt2`

- Embed Dashboards and Report Charts on Lightning Pages: `https://trailhead.salesforce.com/en/content/learn/projects/rd-embed-reports-dashboards`

- Evaluate Report Data with Formulas: `https://trailhead.salesforce.com/en/content/learn/projects/rd-summary-formulas`

- Lightning Experience Reports & Dashboards Specialist: `https://trailhead.salesforce.com/en/content/learn/superbadges/superbadge-lex-rd`

Summary

In this chapter, we have learned how to report data on our CRM to build monitoring views based on business **Key Performance Indicators** (**KPIs**) to match unusual business conditions or simply to have a look at how your sales/service operations are going.

We started by explaining what a report is and what is needed to create one, from standard and custom report types, which define available objects and fields on the report you are going to build. Then, we showed how the report builder is shaped and how it delivers the main tools needed to create an effective report, from columns and grouping selection to filtering options to deliver on your actual business KPIs.

Then, we analyzed different ways of supporting automatic calculations on reports without using custom formula fields, by using bucket fields, column summaries, summary formulas, and row-level formulas.

Now that you have built the report, you have the skills to add some charting options to give a better view of results (a picture is worth a thousand words). We also talked about joined reports to merge different report types into a single report.

Finally, you also now have the skills to handle access and visibility on reports using folders and to subscribe to reports, leaving the last topic for some considerations on reporting limitations.

We have closed the *Data Management* section by looking at reports, and in the next chapter, we'll talk about how to release your implementations from dedicated staging orgs, called **sandboxes**, to production, analyzing the so-called **sandbox model**, and finally, we'll talk about how to release changes from org to org using **change sets**.

Section 6: Ready to Release?

In this section, we will learn how to use sandboxes to test your new developments and unleash change sets to move changes between orgs.

This section comprises the following chapters:

17
The Sandbox Model

Throughout this book, we have played with Salesforce platform features using a Developer Edition org, but you'll likely work as a Salesforce administrator or developer in a more complex context, where a production org contains all business data and current (and stable) platform customization, while all new changes or bug fixes will be done on separate environments to safely develop and test those new metadata changes (we defined the metadata concept in *Chapter 1, A Brief Introduction to Salesforce*, when describing the Salesforce platform architecture).

That's why it's fundamental that you learn all about sandboxes, a special kind of Salesforce org strictly related to your company/customer production org, where you can, as the name implies, play with platform features without harming anyone.

In this chapter, we'll cover the following topics:

- What a sandbox is and what types are available
- Managing sandboxes
- How sandboxes can be used to provide a safe release architecture

What is a sandbox?

When talking about testing, I love to mention a popular meme among developers relating to the *almighty* Chuck Norris that states the following:

Figure 17.1 – A popular and funny meme about testing in production environments

Although this is funny and sometimes it may seem, with the power of inexperience, the easiest choice, this is not a good philosophy at all!

Developing your customizations and testing them in a dedicated and safe org is the key to delivering good software, be it a bugfix or a complex 6-month project.

The main characteristic of a sandbox is that they are a (more or less) complete copy of production, regarding metadata data and data: the level of *similarity* with production depends on the kind of sandbox we choose.

Sandboxes prove to be helpful in a variety of situations, including the following:

- They create an isolated environment where you can develop code, with no risk to production data and business processes, until you are ready to release the changes.

- They create a safe environment where you can test against copies of production data.

- They allow key users to train on new features ahead of the actual production release.

- They preview Salesforce releases before they are released in production orgs.

To deal with sandboxes, you need a production org where sandbox creation can be triggered (as I said, they are strictly linked to production orgs).

There are different kinds of sandboxes and their availability depends on the production org type and additional licenses purchased.

In the following sections, we'll understand what kind of sandboxes are available and what their common uses are, and we'll see how to create a sandbox using a trial edition org and how to manage them. We'll also have a quick look at Salesforce releases and explain how and when they are published.

Creating a new sandbox

Before explaining all sandbox types, let's see how a sandbox can be created.

If you don't have a production org to play with (you likely don't or aren't allowed to), you can create a trial Professional Edition org from `https://www.salesforce.com/form/signup/freetrial-sales-ue/` (this link may change over time; if this happens, simply search on the `www.salesforce.com` site for a **Trial** link or button to access a trial org or jump to `https://www.salesforce.com/editions-pricing/overview/`, choose an edition such as Service or Sales, and click any **Free Trial** button you see on the page).

On the landing form, compile the requested form with sample data and a valid email address:

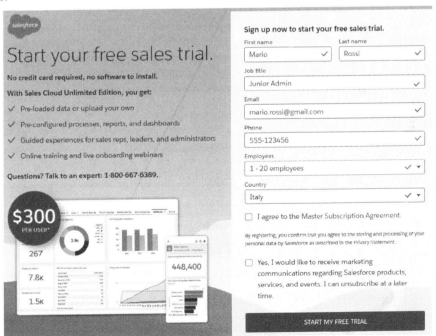

Figure 17.2 – Creating a new trial production org

The process is just like Developer Edition org creation, the only difference being that a Developer Edition org will last until you use it, while a trial lasts for 30 days only (or until you purchase a production license).

You should receive a confirmation email and a prompt to reset your password. You'll end up in a fully featured production org with an upper banner that shows the countdown to org expiration:

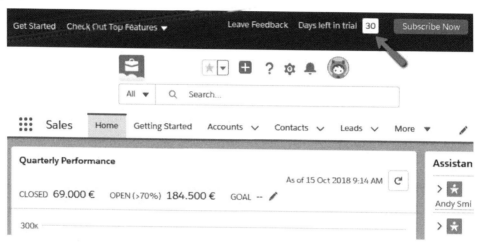

Figure 17.3 – Landing page of a trial org

Now you have a potential production org where you can set up sandboxes.

To create a new sandbox, jump to **Setup | Environments | Sandboxes**, which takes you to the following page:

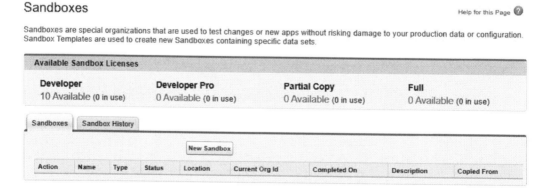

Figure 17.4 – Sandbox management page

Your free trial comes with 10 Developer sandboxes (we'll see different kinds of sandbox types shortly).

To create a new sandbox, click on the **New Sandbox** button and fill in the form (a quick overview of sandbox types is also shown):

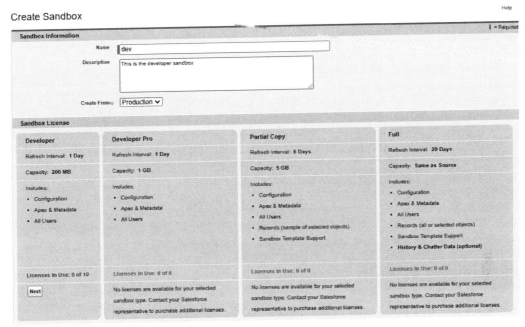

Figure 17.5 – Sandbox creation form

Click the **Next** button on the only available type, and skip the next step that asks for an **Apex Class** (you can define some custom code to be executed after sandbox creation to add additional automated setup) by clicking the **Create** button. The **Sandboxes** page now lists the new **dev** sandbox as being created with a **Processing** status:

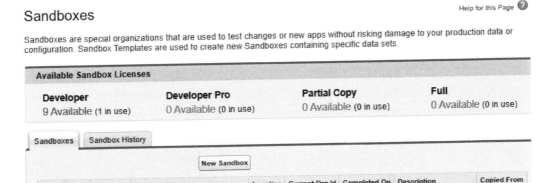

Figure 17.6 – List of available and processing sandboxes

Your sandbox should take 15 minutes to be created (it might even take longer, but as your free trial has few customizations, the *copy* process will require less time). With highly customized production orgs with tons of data, the sandbox copy process can last for days (again, depending on the sandbox type chosen).

Once the sandbox is created and activated, you'll be able to access it from `https://test.salesforce.com` using the following credentials:

- A production username ending with `.sandboxname` (in our case, if the production username is `mario.rossi-wxyz1@gmail.com`, the sandbox username would be `mario.rossi-wxyz1@gmail.com.dev`, with `dev` being the sandbox name).

- The production password.

Once created, we can perform a bunch of actions on sandboxes. Let's see this in the next section.

Managing sandboxes

Once created, you can manage the sandboxes from the production org using a selection of actions available from the sandboxes list page.

On the **Action** column of the sandbox list page, you can do all sort of actions to manage a sandbox with a simple link for each action, aside from creating a new one:

- The first is the **Log In** action, which simply opens up a new tab with the sandbox's login page. This doesn't automatically log in to the org; you need to insert the right credentials (think of it as a shortcut).

- The **Clone** action lets you clone a sandbox, creating a new sandbox with the same sandbox type and all the metadata and data. This is available only if you have enough free sandbox slots available.

- The **Refresh** action is needed if you want to *reset* the sandbox and recreate it from the same source org (that is, production or the parent sandbox, if you created it with the **Clone** action). The current sandbox version is still available during the refreshing process (it is, after all, like a **Create** action) but, when the refresh is completed and the **Activate** action is executed, the new version completely replaces the old one, which is completely deleted (both the data and metadata are no longer available). Be careful when you activate a refreshed sandbox.

- Each sandbox type has its own minimum refresh interval, so this action appears only when the interval is reached. For example, in our scenario, we created a Developer sandbox, which has a one-day refresh interval. This means that once 24 hours have passed since sandbox creation, the **Refresh** action becomes available.

- If you refreshed a sandbox but decide you don't want it to be activated, you can use the **Discard** action.

- Finally, the **Delete** action lets you permanently remove a sandbox, by deleting all metadata and data contained therein. Just like the **Refresh** action, the **Delete** action appears only after the minimum refresh interval is met.

Let's now dig into the different sandbox types and their best use cases.

Types of sandboxes

As of the *Summer '20* release, the platform delivers the following sandbox types:

- Developer
- Developer Pro
- Partial Copy
- Full Copy

Let's look at the details of each one.

Developer sandbox type

This sandbox type is principally used for development. When it is created from production, it contains all production metadata but no records at all (an exception is made for the **User** object, but only internal users are copied).

With no access to production data, administrators and developers can safely execute their customizations without the risk of accessing *inaccessible* data and manipulating it (for example, if actual contact emails were copied, admins may work with real email addresses, meaning they have the opportunity to disturb actual customers, which is absolutely not good!).

This kind of sandbox can be refreshed once every 24 hours and can hold up to 200 MB of data and 200 MB of file storage. As production orgs comes with several Developer sandboxes, this type is usually delivered to single developers or small teams of developers.

Developer Pro sandbox type

This is a *more powerful* Developer sandbox, with a limit of up to 1 GB for data and file storage. This kind of sandbox, refreshable every 24 hours and containing only production metadata and no data as well, is generally used for internal testing and *global* development environments, where the implementations of different developers (in different Developer sandboxes) or different groups of developers are merged together (*does the new process I've just built conflict with the approval process another colleague has just implemented?*). Let's check this out in the internal testing sandbox!

Partial Copy sandbox type

As the name itself indicates, this sandbox includes a partial copy of production data, besides the full metadata copy. With its 5 GB data and file storage and a 5 day refresh interval, it is primarily used for user acceptance tests (if no Full sandbox is available), integration tests (that is, testing with integration to external systems), and training.

To use Partial Copy sandboxes, you need to use **Sandbox Templates** (accessible from the Sandbox list page if you have at least one **Partial Copy** license), which lets you decide which objects you want to copy from production, shown as follows:

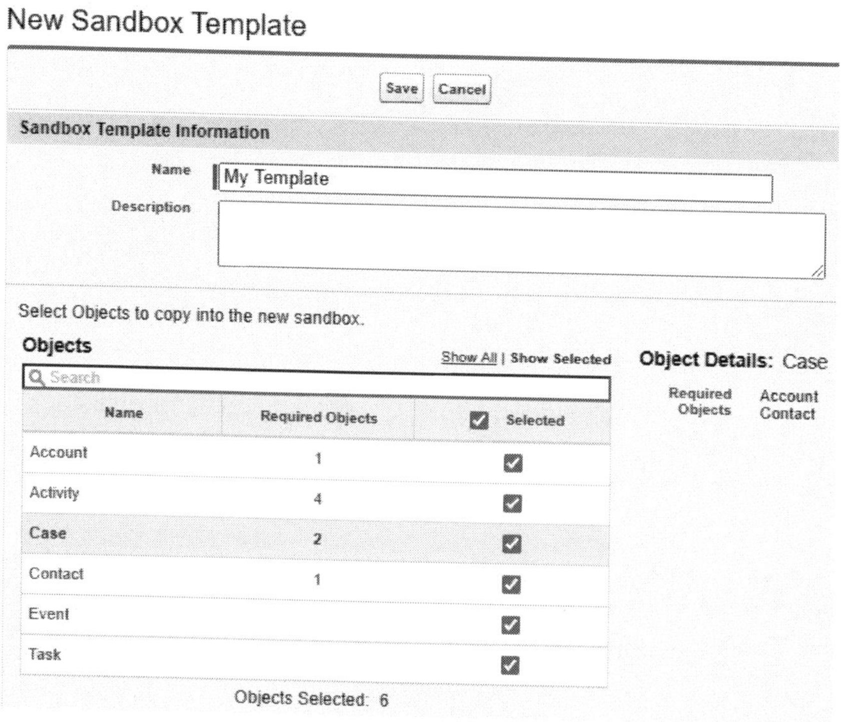

Figure 17.7 – Creating a Sandbox template

When creating a Partial Copy sandbox, the system mandatorily asks for a sandbox template: the sandbox engine thus creates a copy of production filled with up to 5 GB of data, including 10,000 records per object selected (less if reaching the storage limit). There is no way to select and filter the records that are copied.

Full sandbox type

If you need to have a perfect copy of production, the Full copy sandbox is what you need.

A Full sandbox is created with the same storage limits as the production org, a full metadata copy, and a full copy of the records. This makes this sandbox type ideal for user acceptance testing (where real data may be needed) and for performance and load testing, as you'll reach the same production dimensions.

This sandbox has a refresh window of 29 days and, if you want, you can apply a Sandbox template on creation (but it is not mandatory). This would reduce the sandbox creation time that, for this type, can take even days to complete, so the less data you copy, the faster it copies.

Sandbox allocation

Depending on the Salesforce edition, you'll get a certain amount of sandboxes out of the box. For example, if you purchased a Performance Edition org, as of the *Summer '20* release, you'll get 100 Developer, 5 Developer Pro, 1 Partial Copy, and 1 Full sandbox.

> **Further reading**
>
> For more and updated information regarding sandbox type allocations, refer to Salesforce Help at `https://help.salesforce.com/articleView?id=data_sandbox_environments.htm&type=5`.

As has already been mentioned, sandboxes can be used to *preview* Salesforce releases. Let's briefly see what this means.

Salesforce releases

The Salesforce team delivers thee major releases a year on the platform, called Spring, Summer, and Winter for a specific year (where Winter release is related to *next year*, for example, in the year 2022, we'll have *Spring '22, Summer '22*, and *Winter '22* releases).

Thanks to the *multitenant* architecture, all customers' CRMs runs with the same platform code base and upgrades are seamless and automatic and rarely affect live customizations.

Bugs can happen after a release, or simply a new feature makes your customization work differently (and sometimes different means bad in the business processes world), but you can be prepared for this by testing your key features (this is called *regression testing*) on a sandbox in preview mode.

The preview mode simply means that a sandbox receives the new major release before the official production release date (usually about 1 month before). As you can figure out, not all sandboxes can go in preview mode, and it depends on the *instance* the sandbox lives on.

The instance is a big container of countless CRM configurations that stay together in the multitenant architecture where no CRM instance bothers the others (from your CRM, you can only see your data!). You can picture a Salesforce instance as your own laptop, where different programs execute with limited interaction but using the same resources (such as RAM, disk storage, and bandwidth). Salesforce takes care to prevent a situation where a customer may use too many resources, thereby leaving the other customers on the same instance with low performances.

To check which is your org's instance, you can have a look at your browser bar. My trail org has been created in `https://eu27.lightning.force.com`, which means that it relies on the *EU27* instance. If you applied a **My Domain** configuration (we have seen the **My Domain** configuration in *Chapter 13, The Lightning App Builder*), you won't see any instance reference. To check your org's instance (whether it is a production or sandbox instance), simply jump to **Setup | Company Settings | Company Information** and check the **Instance** field, shown as follows:

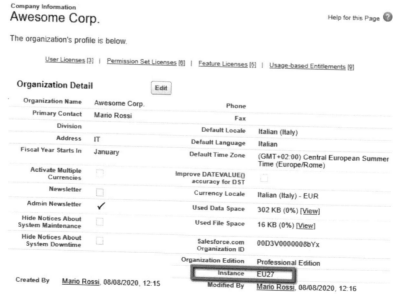

Figure 17.8 – Retrieving an org instance from the Company Information page

If you want to check sandbox instances, you can use the sandbox list page from your production org under the **Location** column, as shown here:

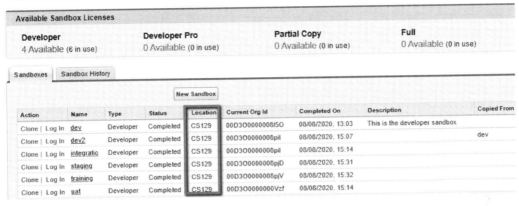

Figure 17.9 – Getting sandbox instances

> **Note**
>
> The sandbox instance name is always in the form of CS*X* (*Customer Sandbox*). Your sandboxes can be created in different instances, not necessarily in the same one.

If you want to know whether you are on a preview instance, simply jump to the *beta* site, `https://sandbox-preview.herokuapp.com`, and enter your instance name and click the **Submit** button:

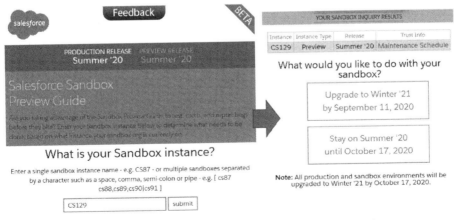

Figure 17.10 – Establishing whether your sandbox is in a preview instance

This tool lets you know whether your org is in a preview instance and, depending on what you want to do (that is, stay with the current release until the next release is deployed in production or get the preview before production), tells you what to do:

- If you are in a non-preview instance, if you want to get a preview, you need to refresh that sandbox before a given date, otherwise it remains with the *old* release version.

- If you are in a preview instance, you'll automatically receive the major upgrade on a given date (no action needed), but if you want to remain with the *old* release version until it is released in production, you need to refresh the sandbox after a given date.

This web app tells you everything you need in order to plan your sandbox preview management on time.

You can find the main maintenance info (including more or less the next three major release dates) at `http://www.trust.salesforce.com`. This is useful when planning the release dates for lengthy projects.

> **Tip**
>
> Never ever plan a production release during the same weekend as a major release. The system gets locked for only 5 minutes, but if you are doing a deploy in those 5 minutes on a nightly release, it will give you some headaches.

Now that sandbox configuration and usage have no secrets for you, let's close the chapter with an example of how sandboxes can be used to run different phases of application life cycle management, that is, your release strategy from development to production.

Understanding sandbox architectures

You can use different sandbox types for different release stages. There is no mandatory configuration setup. You can use a Full type sandbox to execute your development phase, although it makes no sense at all (really high license pricing being one of the main reasons).

Let's picture an example of how you can design the environment strategy within your project's release strategy.

Consider the following sandbox architecture, which can be applied to most projects:

Figure 17.11 – Example org strategy

In this figure, **Production** is the only org that is not a sandbox.

We can start with two sandboxes, **Dev1** and **Dev2**, which can be of the Developer type, and are assigned to two different developers/administrators or for two different implementations that may be unrelated.

Once developers have completed their job (meaning that the implementation is stable), the changes can be brought to the **Integration** sandbox, of the Developer Pro type, where everything is tested to check whether anything from different implementations is interfering with the desired flow. In this sandbox, the technical leads can conduct some implementation quality assurance and any external integration test can also be done to check whether everything is working as expected, even if no real data is in place. If something is wrong, **Dev1** and **Dev2** are used to deliver some fixes to comply with business requirements.

The **Integration** sandbox is also the place where **Dev1** brings in changes made by **Dev2** and vice versa.

Once internal testing has passed successfully, the work of developers and administrators is brought to the UAT sandbox where tests are executed with actual data. This sandbox should be of the Partial Copy type or, even better and suggested, a Full type. This sandbox is usually linked to external systems (if any) with their own *UAT* environment.

When all tests pass, changes are released to the Staging sandbox, which should be the last place where future production behavior is checked. Why do we need another testing environment? We have the UAT after all. While UAT can contain different implementations that may not be released on the same day in production (this is not a good practice but something that actually happens in projects), the Staging org ensures a final test to check whether anything can go wrong in production. This is why, if my customers don't want to define the rule that states that if you bring something in UAT, you won't release anything in production until everything passes the test (and so no partial deploy would be allowed), I usually suggest creating another testing org ahead of production, at the cost of another Partial Copy or Full license.

The Staging org (which should be a Partial Copy sandbox) is used to train users on the new changes. This is an org that is nice to have; indeed, you can train your users on UAT or Staging orgs.

Finally, the **Training** org is used, as the name itself suggests, to teach CRM users on how to use the new features, and this is a key org, especially in CRM transformation projects where users should be familiar with the new Salesforce experience: this sandbox could be a simple Developer Pro version (you'll certainly need some data to be manually loaded) or, if it is one of your available options, a Partial Copy sandbox.

Choose your sandbox architecture strategy according to your needs and depending on your available resources. If you are working on a small project with no code or little automation implementation, you probably don't need the complexity of *Figure 17.11* and end up with only two sandboxes prior to production, with no Full type sandbox, or within a really big project that is started in parallel with several other projects. Hence, that picture can then grow in complexity as more `dev-int-uat` sandboxes may be created for the different releases.

You now have all the knowledge needed to start playing with your sandbox strategy.

Blaze your trail

Check out the following Trailhead content to increase your knowledge of sandboxes:

- Salesforce release readiness strategies: `https://trailhead.salesforce.com/en/content/learn/trails/sf_release_prep`

Summary

If you have read this chapter, you have acquired the principles of Salesforce CRM customization and you are ready to release your first implementation to production. Within this chapter, we have shown how changes in metadata can be safely built and tested on dedicated sandbox orgs. We have seen how to create a sandbox and how to manage it, using clone, refresh, discard, and delete actions. We have discovered the different types of sandbox available on the platform and their features and best uses. We've also understood the principles behind Salesforce releases and how major releases are related to sandbox preview mode.

Finally, we have seen an example of sandbox architecture to cover all the main release process management needs, from development to testing.

From now on, you know the basics of sandbox management and sandbox architecture setup, adapting your project needs to your project's (sometimes unique) release management strategy.

In the next chapter, we'll demonstrate how to release changes from org to org using built-in point and click tools.

18
Deploying Your Solution

As we've seen in *Chapter 17, The Sandbox Model*, you'll be implementing any Salesforce customization inside a dedicated org, called a sandbox, to avoid impacting on the production org directly, where the business runs. Once you are confident that what you have configured complies with the business requirements you've been tasked with, we can employ different ways and strategies to move the changes into the next sandbox (for **user acceptance testing**, or **UAT**) or in production.

You may also be asked to develop a completely separate feature that has no link with your production org, and so you can use a Developer Edition org for the implementation phase, and then move this *package* to a sandbox or even production (this is not suggested at all; test any customization in a sandbox prior to releasing to production!).

In this chapter, we'll focus on the following most common ways to do this job:

- By using change sets to move changes to the *sandbox-to-production* flow
- By using packages to move changes between unrelated orgs
- By using AppExchange packages to reuse solutions built by other vendors

Moving metadata

Moving new or changed customizations from org to org (from your development sandbox to an internal test sandbox, or from the UAT sandbox to production org) can be an easy experience if you know exactly what you are doing and have sufficient experience to anticipate anything that can block the deploy process, or it may prove to be a source of headaches if you are still learning the art.

Tens of things can go bad, from a missing custom field (you forgot to include a small piece of metadata in your *deploy package*), to failing Apex tests (we haven't talked about Apex coding, but let's say that Apex tests are a way for the platform to let you think about what you are doing, by forcing developers to write Apex code to test their Apex code), to mystery error messages that only an in depth Google search or a thousand hours spent doing deployments can hopefully solve.

There are different ways and tools to move changes between orgs:

- **Change sets**: These are used to move metadata between orgs in a *sandbox-to-production* architecture.

- **Packages**: These are used to move metadata between unrelated orgs (but you can use them in a *sandbox-to-production* architecture as well).

- **Metadata APIs**: These are the programming APIs used to generically move metadata from an origin to a destination org with no necessary link. This set of APIs is used by common deployment tools and services such as **Workbench** (`https://workbench.developerforce.com`, which we'll look at briefly later on), or the **ANT Migration Tool** (`https://developer.salesforce.com/docs/atlas.en-us.daas.meta/daas/meta_development.htm`), the Salesforce CLI (`https://developer.salesforce.com/tools/sfdxcli`), or almost any Salesforce **IDE** (which stands for **Integrated Development Environment** – that is, a desktop or cloud app to customize with code and more).

Refer to Salesforce Help at `https://developer.salesforce.com/docs/atlas.en-us.api_meta.meta/api_meta/meta_intro.htm` to know more about the Metadata APIs.

We won't explore the Metadata APIs in this chapter as they are a developer subject, but we'll briefly see how these APIs are *consumed* by the Workbench app, a multi-purpose tool that can provide some help.

Let's now look at a must-know deployment feature that all *devmins* should be aware of, called **change sets**.

Delivering changes with change sets

Although a lot can be done to make change sets more appealing for big customizations, they are a tool highly appreciated by developers and administrators as they easily let metadata be deployed from sandbox to sandbox until production, following the sandbox flow architecture we saw in *Chapter 17, The Sandbox Model*.

To set up and use change sets to deploy changes between orgs under the same production org, here are the requisite steps:

1. Configure a deployment connection between the source and destination orgs (basically, the destination org is enabled to receive change sets coming from a given origin org).

2. Create an *outbound* change set in the source organization.

3. Add changed metadata items to the change set.

4. Upload the outbound change set to the destination org.

5. Validate the *inbound* change set on the destination org.

6. Deploy the change set on the destination org.

7. Monitor the deployment.

8. Repeat *steps 3* to *7* if any error occurs.

Let's focus on all of these steps.

Setting up a connection between sandboxes

The first thing to do when enabling change sets is to create connections between orgs.

Let's recall the sandbox architecture we designed with a trial Salesforce org in *Chapter 17, The Sandbox Model*:

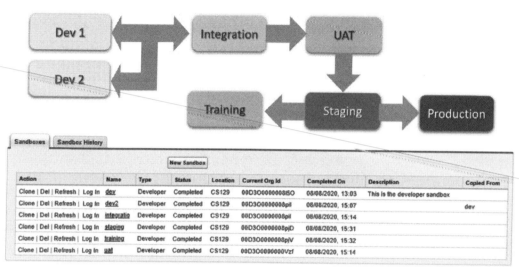

Figure 18.1 – Sandbox example architecture

To simplify the flow, we only have two backward release directions, that is from the *Integration* sandbox to *Dev1* and *Dev2* sandboxes, to bring back any customization that is not covered on other development sandboxes.

Remember that you can only enable connections between orgs that are linked to the same production org, so change sets cannot be used on Developer Edition orgs.

To enable a specific connection, log in to the trial production org and jump to **Setup | Environments | Deploy | Deployment Settings**, shown as follows:

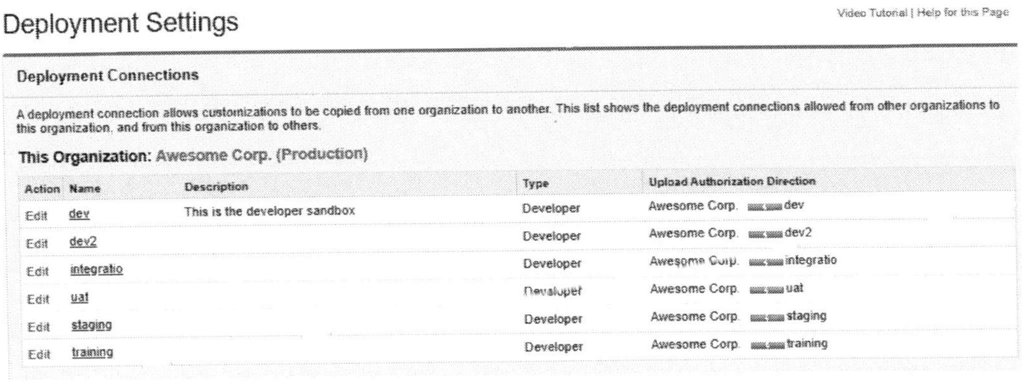

Deployment Settings

Deployment Connections

A deployment connection allows customizations to be copied from one organization to another. This list shows the deployment connections allowed from other organizations to this organization, and from this organization to others.

This Organization: Awesome Corp. (Production)

Action	Name	Description	Type	Upload Authorization Direction
Edit	dev	This is the developer sandbox	Developer	Awesome Corp. ⬛⬛ dev
Edit	dev2		Developer	Awesome Corp. ⬛⬛ dev2
Edit	integratio		Developer	Awesome Corp. ⬛⬛ integratio
Edit	uat		Developer	Awesome Corp. ⬛⬛ uat
Edit	staging		Developer	Awesome Corp. ⬛⬛ staging
Edit	training		Developer	Awesome Corp. ⬛⬛ training

Figure 18.2 – Defining a deployment connection

From *Figure 18.1*, we only want to enable a connection from the *Staging* sandbox, so click on the **Edit** link next to the **Staging** line and flag the **Allow Inbound Changes** flag, as shown here:

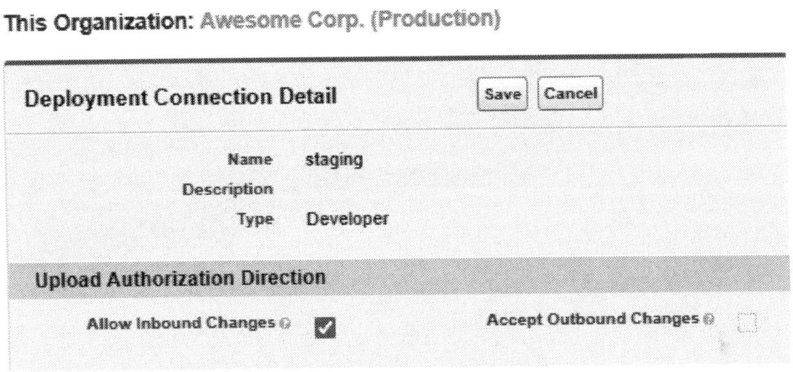

This Organization: Awesome Corp. (Production)

Deployment Connection Detail   Save Cancel

Name	staging
Description	
Type	Developer

Upload Authorization Direction

Allow Inbound Changes ⊙ ☑   Accept Outbound Changes ⊙ ☐

Figure 18.3 – Enabling an inbound connection

By clicking the **Save** button, the connection is enabled and you'll be allowed to move a change set from the **Staging** sandbox to production.

You can, as an exercise, proceed to configure the other sandboxes shown in *Figure 18.1*:

- **dev** from **integration**
- **dev2** from **integration**
- **integration** from **dev**
- **integration** from **dev2**

- **uat** from **integration**

- **staging** from **uat**

- **training** from **staging**

After these configurations, this is what you'll get on the **Deployment Settings** page for the **Integration** sandbox:

This Organization: integratio (Developer Sandbox)

Action	Name	Description	Type	Upload Authorization Direction
Edit	Produzione	Organizzazione di produzione	Produzione	integratio ◄──── Produzione
Edit	dev	This is the developer sandbox	Developer	integratio ◄────► dev
Edit	dev2		Developer	integratio ◄────► dev2
Edit	uat		Developer	integratio ────► uat
Edit	staging		Developer	integratio ◄──── staging
Edit	training		Developer	integratio ◄──── training

Figure 18.4 – Deployment settings for the Integration sandbox

In the preceding screenshot, you can easily see that the Integration sandbox does the following:

- It allows inbound change sets from **dev** and **dev2**.
- It is allowed to deliver outbound change sets to **dev** and **dev2**.
- It is allowed to deliver outbound change sets to **uat**.

Now that we have all the required connections as per our release strategy and sandbox architecture (for our example, we'll just need the **staging** to production connection), let's see how to create a new change set.

Creating a change set

To create a new **Outbound Change Set**, log in to the **Staging** sandbox (remember, this is the same production username plus .**staging** or whatever name you have used, and the same production password using the https://test.salesforce.com login page) and go to **Setup** | **Environments** | **Change Sets** | **Outbound Change Sets** and then click the **New** button, shown as follows:

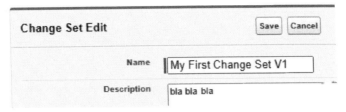

Figure 18.5 – Naming a new change set

> **Tip**
>
> Give your change sets a unique name with a version number. This way, you won't encounter any issues in terms of remembering which change set you have just uploaded.

Click the **Save** button to land on the new **Change Set** page, shown as follows:

Figure 18.6 – Change Set home page

Once the change set is created, it can be populated with metadata items (that will be released in the destination org) by clicking the **Add** button in the **Change Set Components** section:

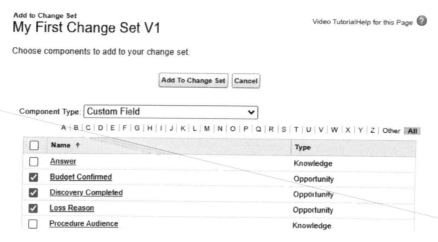

Figure 18.7 – Adding new items to a change set

You can select more than one metadata item at a time but from the same metadata type (we are adding three custom fields to the change set).

By clicking the **Add to Change Set** button, you'll see that the items have been added:

Figure 18.8 – Items added to the change set

> **Tip**
>
> Change set item manipulation doesn't have the best user experience.
> If you have hundreds of custom fields, adding a selection of them to a
> package could be a big headache. There are online tools that help in this
> and other tasks such as the **ORGanizer for Salesforce** (`https://`
> `organizer.enree.co`), a tool I developed in 2016, and which
> is one of the most appreciated Salesforce Chrome Extensions on the
> market, or the **Salesforce Change Set Helper** (`https://chrome.`
> `google.com/webstore/detail/salesforce-change-`
> `set-hel/gdjfanbphogoonpaetebaaoohdcigpoi`), or
> the **Salesforce Change Set Turbo** (`https://chrome.google.`
> `com/webstore/detail/salesforce-change-set-tur/`
> `dlcjllapchpeedkecmhfnpfenpbglioo`). Search for `Change Set`
> `Helper` on the Chrome Web Store to see more available apps.

Not all metadata items are available for deployment with change sets. Refer to
Salesforce Help for a detailed list at `https://help.salesforce.com/`
`articleView?id=changesets_about_components.htm&type=5`.

You can select some more stuff on the change set (as an example, you can build a new
custom object or a workflow rule and add them to the change set). When ready, we can
proceed by uploading the change set to the production org.

Uploading a change set

When everything is ready, we can click the **Upload** button to let the change set engine
become an *inbound* change set on the destination org (production) and select the
destination org:

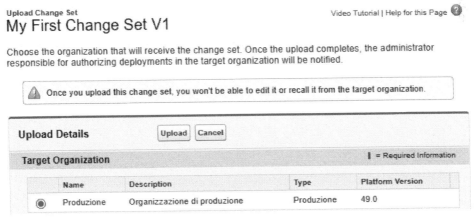

Figure 18.9 – Choosing a destination org

When an org has an outbound connection with more orgs (like the *Integration* sandbox), you'll see more than one org in this list.

By clicking the **Upload** button, the change sets gets a **Closed** status, meaning no more items can be added and the change set becomes available in the destination org within minutes (sometimes it can take up to 30 minutes, just be patient):

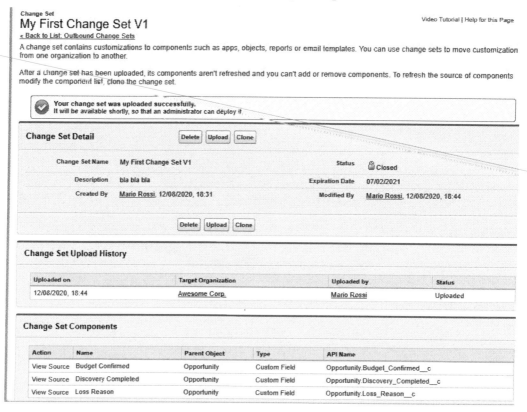

Figure 18.10 – Uploaded change set

If you want to add more components, clone the change set and create a new version.

Let's now move on the destination org to validate and deploy the new metadata items.

Validating, deploying, and monitoring the metadata

Log in to the destination org (our trial production org) and click on **Setup |
Environments | Change Sets | Inbound Change Sets** to get the list of uploaded
change sets:

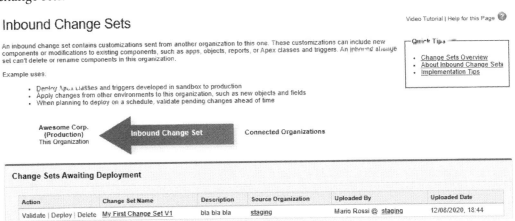

Figure 18.11 – List of incoming change sets

If you don't see any change set or if you get an error message when clicking on the change
set stating that the change set is unavailable, don't panic, this is normal. The change set is
still being set up for you to deploy it. Take a breath and be patient for a little while longer.

Now, we have two options:

- **Validate** the change set.
- **Deploy** the change set.

While the **Validate** action is part of the **Deploy** action, the first is usually preferred when
you want to be sure that the new metadata items are valid on the destination org without
actually deploying them (you'll usually have a given date and time to release your stuff
in production).

Click the **Validate** button to show the following **Test Option** page:

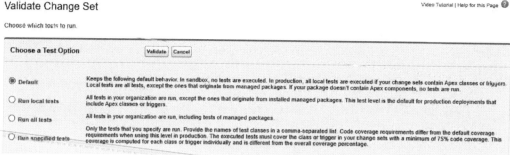

Figure 18.12 – Choosing the test execution policy

When deploying metadata items in orgs with custom Apex code, the metadata deployment engine ensures that all the Apex code is correctly covered by so called *Apex Test Classes*, which are additional Apex coding lines that developers need to write to ensure that the customization they applied with code is safe enough to be brought into production. We don't require a specific Apex testing policy, so we'll use the **Default** value, but you have to remember that Apex tests are one of the most likely failures during deployments.

Now, click the **Validate** button again to start the validation process.

You'll be able to monitor the validation and deployment process from **Setup | Environments | Deploy | Deployment Status**:

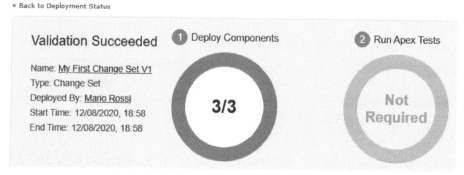

Figure 18.13 – Successful change set deployment

The chances are good that your change set was simple enough that no errors were triggered.

However, this is an example of a failed deploy (caused by a missing custom field on the outbound change set):

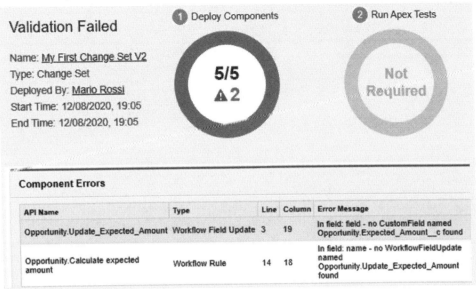

Figure 18.14 – Error caused by a missing custom field

Once all change set misconfiguration is executed on the origin org and validation is successful, proceed with the **Deploy** button to complete the release process.

Before concluding the change sets topic, we'll give some information related to profile configuration release using change sets; that is, how to bring permissions setups along with change sets deploys.

Handling profiles

If we need to include profile-related configurations, such as field level security for a custom field added to the change set, we can configure it in two different ways:

- Add a permission set to the change set (if the permission is granted via a permission set).

- Add the required profiles from the change set's **Profile Settings for Included Components** section.

In both approaches, the change set will bring only the permissions related to the components included in the change set.

> **Further reading**
>
> If you want to know more on change set best practices, refer to
> Salesforce Help at `https://help.salesforce.com/`
> `articleView?id=changesets_best_practices.`
> `htm&type=5`.

In the next section, we'll deploy a feature similar to change sets that can be used with orgs
that are linked – **packages**.

> **Note**
>
> Salesforce is rolling out the DevOps center, which is an improved experience
> for change and release management that will not only deliver a modern and
> robust experience for declarative developers and admins, but also allow for
> collaboration between declarative and programmatic developers throughout
> the DevOps process: this is the evolution of change sets. Have a read of the
> Salesforce administrators blog at `https://admin.salesforce.com/`
> `blog/2020/new-devops-center-is-awesome-for-admins`
> to stay updated.

Releasing with packages

Releasing with packages has some similarities with change sets, mostly in how packages
are created, as we'll see shortly.

Packages can be used to deploy metadata from one org to any other org, whether related
to the same production org or not. They can also be used to distribute metadata libraries
(like open source customizations) or super-secret algorithms that other Salesforce
customers or partners may need in their org and may pay for (in this case, you need to
publish the package on the AppExchange).

> **Further reading**
>
> If you are interested in becoming a Salesforce ISV partner (and want to build
> apps on the AppExchange), complete the **Build Apps as an AppExchange
> Partner** Trailhead trail at `https://trailhead.salesforce.com/`
> `en/content/learn/trails/isv_developer_beginner`.

Also, note that the metadata files you see on this book's GitHub repository at `https://github.com/PacktPublishing/Hands-On-Low-Code-Application-Development-with-Salesforce` have been extracted from a Developer Edition org using `Package` for each single chapter. Then, the package has been extracted with a procedure we'll see in the next subsection. These files are available for deployment using Metadata APIs through the Workbench tool (which we'll see shortly as well).

Now, let's see how to build a new package.

Click on **Setup | Apps | Package Manager**, as shown here:

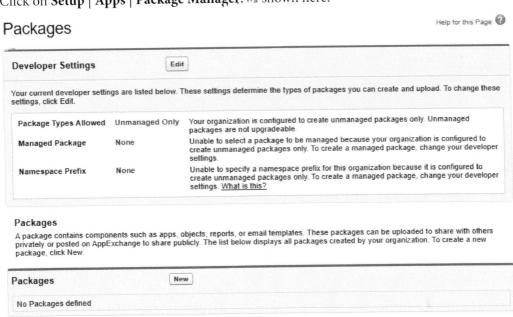

Figure 18.15 – Package Manager landing page

From this page, you can observe that we define a namespace prefix for a **Managed Package**, which is a special kind of protected package used for AppExchange publication. These packages can also be created to publish *hidden* and protected code (meaning no one can read your proprietary Apex algorithms) on customer orgs, although, for security reasons, companies usually don't allow this practice (although no one has certified that your code is safe, the AppExchange apps publication process ensures precisely the safety of any app in its store). Hence, we'll go with *unmanaged* packages.

Create one or more packages. Click the **New** button on the **Packages** section to create a new package:

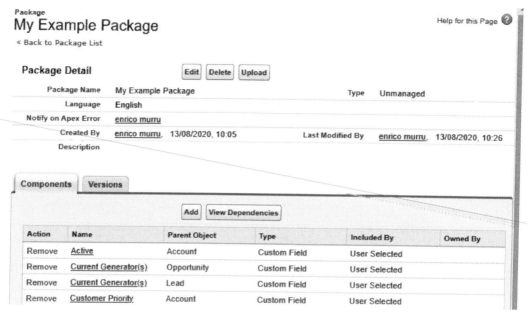

Figure 18.16 – Package creation page

In this package, you can define the following:

- The package's name (use a unique name).

- The package's language.

- The Apex error notification user (this user will be the only recipient in errors generated by this package).

- Select whether you want the package to be managed or unmanaged (we haven't set up the managed options, so you'll only be able to create unmanaged packages).

- Add one or more components: unlike change sets, the engine adds related and required items. For example, if you add a custom field from a custom object but not the custom object itself, the engine will automatically add the custom object, too, to the package. Unlike change sets, no profile can be added to the package (but you are allowed to add permission sets). Moreover, the `Packages` engine seems more powerful than the change set engine in recognizing discrepancies when adding metadata components.

> **Further reading**
>
> To get a full list of all supported metadata types available through packages, have a look at Salesforce Help at `https://help.salesforce.com/articleView?id=packaging_packageable_components.htm&type=5`.

Once you have selected all the necessary metadata items, click the **Upload** button to start the **Upload** wizard that requests the following:

- **Version Name**: This marks a specific version name (you can put whatever value you want (for example YYYYMMDD or simple Month/Year).

- **Version Number**: This defines the version number in the `major_version.minor_version` format (for instance, Version 1.5, where 1 is the major version and 5 the minor version).

- **Release Notes**: This adds a release notes site reference.

- **Post Install Instructions**: This references the name of a Visualforce page or a free URL that displays the info needed for further package configurations.

- **Password**: You can add an optional password to protect the package.

- **Package Requirements**: Here, you can constrain the Salesforce destination org installation by selecting specific features (for example, Communities or Customer Portals or the use of Account record types). These constraints are usually automatically detected by the package manager.

Click the **Upload** button and, just like for change sets, the system will execute all Apex tests to ensure a minimum level of quality of the package. If everything goes well, you'll land on the package version page, shown as follows:

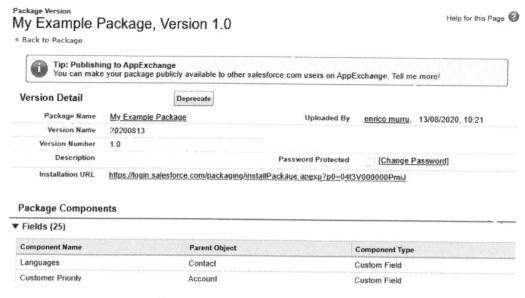

Figure 18.17 – Successful package upload

This page gives you the following options:

- Get the **Installation URL**, so any Salesforce administrator can install the package in their own org (Developer Edition, Trial org, Sandbox or Production org).

- Deprecate a version so no one can install the package anymore.

If you create more versions of the package, you can use the **Versions** tab to get the full list and all installation URLs, shown as follows:

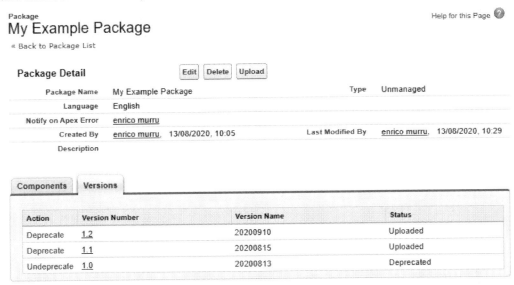

Figure 18.18 – The package's versions list

> **Further reading**
>
> For a complete guide to package development, refer to Salesforce Help at `https://help.salesforce.com/ articleView?id=package_distribute_apps_overview. htm&type=5.`

To keep track of all the implementations and examples I made while writing this book, I created the Developer Edition org, where I developed all customizations, a package for (almost) each chapter:

Packages

A package contains components such as apps, objects, reports, or email templates. These packages can be uploaded to share with others privately or posted on AppExchange to share publicly. The list below displays all packages created by your organization. To create a new package, click New.

Packages		
	New	

Action	Package Name	Description
Edit	Chapter 2	
Edit	Chapter 2 - Advertisement	
Edit	Chapter 3	
Edit	Chapter 4	
Edit	Chapter 5	
Edit	Chapter 6	
Edit	Chapter 7	
Edit	Chapter 8	
Edit	Chapter 9	
Edit	Chapter 10	
Edit	Chapter 11	
Edit	Chapter 12	
Edit	Chapter 13	
Edit	Chapter 14	
Edit	Chapter 16	

Figure 18.19 – Packages with this book's chapters' metadata

Using the Metadata APIs as of the *Summer'20* release, you can get a ZIP file containing all the package metadata. Because we are not learning about APIs or how to code, we'll use a very useful tool that *consumes* Metadata APIs (and more), called **Workbench**.

Retrieving and deploying with Workbench

Although you can use the package URL to deploy a package, let's see how to retrieve and deploy a package using a ZIP file.

> **Note**
>
> The deploy method can be applied to the book's repository at `https://github.com/PacktPublishing/Hands-On-Low-Code-Application-Development-with-Salesforce` to deploy chapter after chapter on your Developer Edition org. Take care to check any `README` file on the repository, as you may be required to manually update some of the XML files in the package so as to get to a successful deploy.

Open up a new browser tab at https://workbench.developerforce.com/, tick the **I agree to the terms of service** checkbox, click the **Login with Salesforce** button, and allow access on the part of the Workbench app to your Developer Edition org:

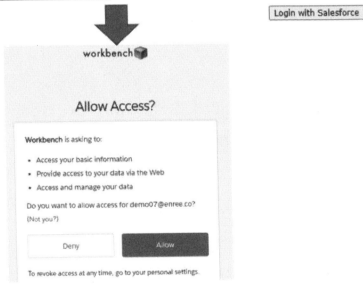

Figure 18.20 – Allowing access to the Workbench app

You may be required to generate a Salesforce login, if you were not already logged in.

Once the org has been enabled, Workbench lets you do things such as the following:

- Get a list of all objects and metadata items available on your org.

- Execute queries.

- Perform all sorts of CRUD operations.

- Retrieve and deploy packages (that's what we want to do now).

We have created a package from the **Package Manager** and now we want to retrieve a package so we can deploy it (with a subsequent deploy) in another org. To do this, click on **Migration | Retrieve**:

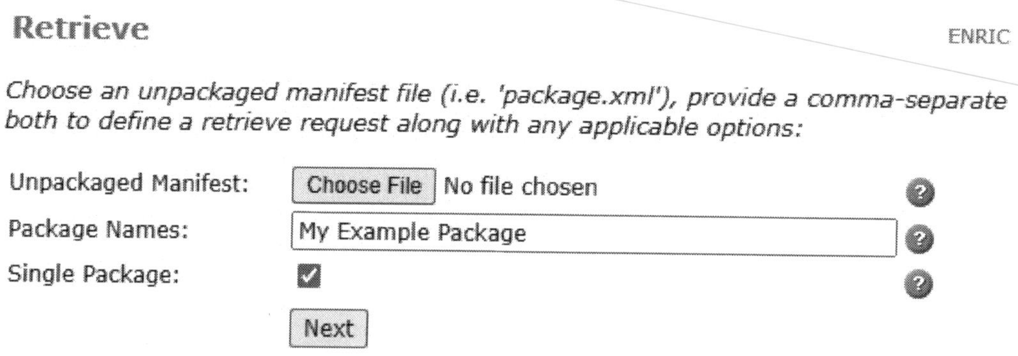

Retrieve   ENRIC

Choose an unpackaged manifest file (i.e. 'package.xml'), provide a comma-separate both to define a retrieve request along with any applicable options:

Unpackaged Manifest:	Choose File No file chosen	?
Package Names:	My Example Package	?
Single Package:	☑	?

Next

Figure 18.21 – Retrieving a package from an org via Workbench

Select the **Single Package** flag, fill in the **Package Names** textbox with the name of the package you created earlier (in our example with My Example Package), and then click **Next** and **Retrieve**. If everything went well (you may have misspelled the package name or there may be more than one package with the same name), this is what you will see:

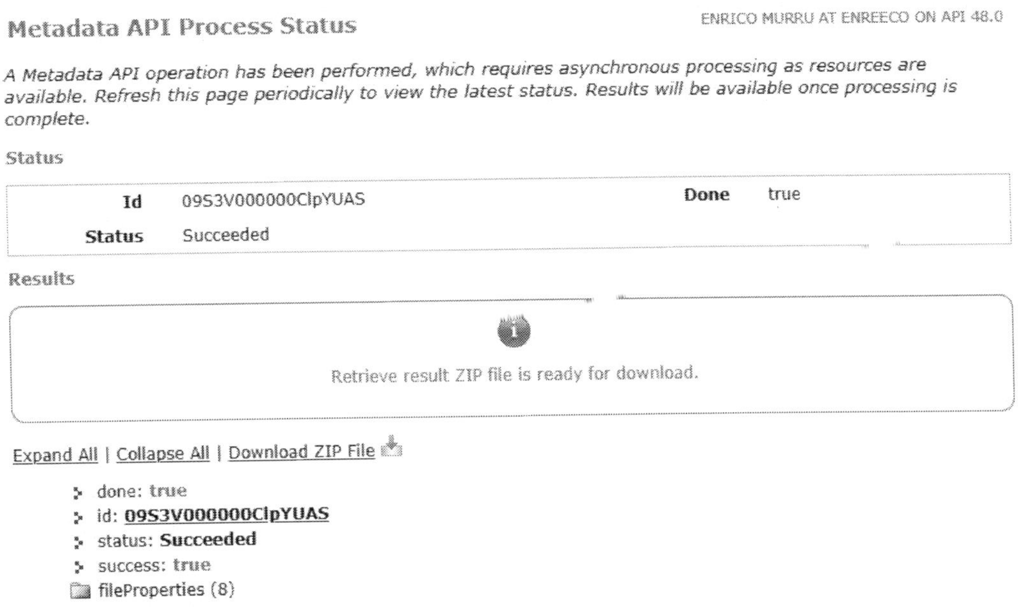

Metadata API Process Status

A Metadata API operation has been performed, which requires asynchronous processing as resources are available. Refresh this page periodically to view the latest status. Results will be available once processing is complete.

Status

Id	09S3V000000ClpYUAS	**Done**	true
Status	Succeeded		

Results

Retrieve result ZIP file is ready for download.

Expand All | Collapse All | Download ZIP File

- done: **true**
- id: **09S3V000000ClpYUAS**
- status: **Succeeded**
- success: **true**
- fileProperties (8)

Figure 18.22 – Package retrieved

Click on the **Download ZIP File** link to get the ZIP file.

If you want to deploy a package instead (for example, to deploy the code from *Chapter 2, Building the Data Model*), click on **Migration | Deploy** and select the ZIP file for *Chapter 2, Building the Data Model* from the GitHub repository (you need to actually ZIP the entire contents by yourself) and flag it again as **Single Package**:

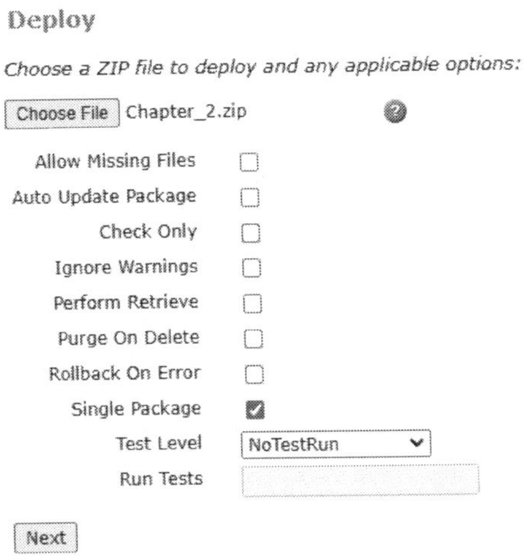

Deploy

Choose a ZIP file to deploy and any applicable options:

Choose File	Chapter_2.zip

Allow Missing Files	☐
Auto Update Package	☐
Check Only	☐
Ignore Warnings	☐
Perform Retrieve	☐
Purge On Delete	☐
Rollback On Error	☐
Single Package	☑
Test Level	NoTestRun
Run Tests	

Next

Figure 18.23 – Deploying a packaged ZIP file

Click **Next** and **Deploy** to start the deploy process. If everything is OK, you'll see a success message on Workbench and on the org under **Setup | Environments | Deploy | Deployment Status**, shown as follows:

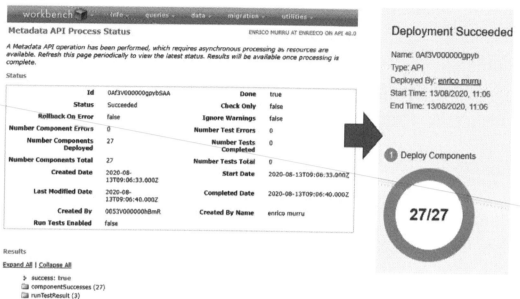

Figure 18.24 – Successful deploy executed from Workbench

> **Further reading**
>
> For a complete guide of the Workbench tool, refer to its GitHub wiki at `https://github.com/forceworkbench/forceworkbench/wiki`.

We have acquired all the basic principles and knowledge on the tools needed to execute deployment from org to org. Before concluding the chapter, we'll devote a few words to AppExchange, the Salesforce app store.

AppExchange – don't reinvent the wheel

AppExchange is Salesforce's marketplace for apps, libraries, services, professional services, and product experts. It also includes Lightning Components, Flows, and apps that are free to use.

Are you trying to build a feature on your CRM that you believe can be generalized? Try to have a look at AppExchange. You may find a free and certified package for that! Are you looking to integrate a **Computer Telephony Integration** (**CTI**) or a digital sign service? Browse AppExchange and you'll probably find a package that meets your needs and lets you integrate with an external service with minimal to no effort (and, again, with certified code).

Navigate to `appexchange.salesforce.com` to browse thousands of pre-built solutions so that you don't need to reinvent the wheel:

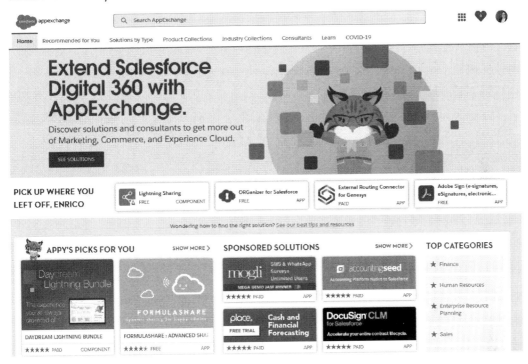

Figure 18.25 – AppExchange landing page

You'll find all kinds of solutions and for all budgets (even for free).

We've already seen how to install a package from AppExchange in the *Adding custom components from the AppExchange* section of *Chapter 13, The Lightning App Builder*, so what are you waiting for? Choose your solution, add it to your org and experiment with it!

As an experienced Salesforce specialist, you need to know exactly when it's time to customize and when it's time to use an AppExchange solution.

Blaze your trail

To increase your knowledge of the topics covered in this chapter, have a look at the following Trailhead content:

- Determine which application life cycle management model is right for you: `https://trailhead.salesforce.com/en/content/learn/trails/determine-which-application-lifecycle-management-model-is-right-for-you`

- Meet your business needs with AppExchange: `https://trailhead.salesforce.com/en/content/learn/trails/meet_your_business_needs-with-appexchange`

Summary

This chapter concludes the *technical* part of this long journey. We have learned a lot about Salesforce platform customization and, with this chapter, we acquired the basics for deploying the changes we make in our daily work in the orgs of our company or those of our customers. With change sets, we learned how to move changes from one sandbox to another, and from a sandbox to production, creating deploy connections between orgs that rely on the same production org. If we want to deploy across orgs that don't reference the same production org (for example, between Developer Edition orgs) or simply if we want to package a configuration that we want to store for future use, packages are what you need. Finally, we used packages with the Workbench tool to let Metadata APIs retrieve a package from an org and deploy it in another org with a few simple clicks.

You now have everything you need to bring your customizations from org to org within your new Salesforce project where a sandbox architecture is in place (through the use of change sets) or delivering components between any kind of Salesforce org (through the use of packages). We'll conclude the book with the next chapter – an overview of the Salesforce culture and a number of tips to get certified.

Section 7:
Before We Say
Goodbye

In this section, we will discover how the Salesforce Community is shaped and which resources you can use to enhance your knowledge.

This section comprises the following chapter:

- *Chapter 19, Salesforce Ohana – The Most Amazing Community Around*

19

Salesforce Ohana – The Most Amazing Community Around

Before closing our journey of Salesforce customization with no code, a word has to be said on the wonderful culture and *ecosystem of people* around Salesforce, which is no doubt one of the key factors that makes the Salesforce community one of the most amazing technologic cultures worldwide and what makes it so successful.

In this chapter, we'll cover the following topics:

- The Ohana culture that is at the basis of the Salesforce world
- The Trailblazer community that is nurtured by the Ohana culture
- The certification process to show the world you know *how to Salesforce*

The Ohana culture

There is a famous animated science fiction comedy-drama film produced by Walt Disney Animation Studios titled *Lilo and Stitch*, which is about a 6-year-old Hawaiian girl named Lilo, raised by her sister Nani after their parents die in an accident, and a blue extraterrestrial creature called Experiment 626, adopted by Lilo as her dog-like pet and renamed Stitch. Stitch, who is a genetically modified alien weapon made by a mad scientist who wanted to cause chaos and destruction throughout the galaxy, initially accepts Lilo's protection to avoid being captured by the intergalactic police.

Quickly, the two main characters develop a close family-like bond, represented by the Hawaiian concept of extended family, Ohana. Thanks to this bond, Stitch reconsiders his destructive nature. The whole movie is centered on the following line: *Ohana means family, and family means nobody gets left behind or forgotten.*

I didn't mean to spoil the movie (after all, it is a 2002 movie), but this small story highlights the concept of Ohana around which Salesforce, thanks to its founder and CEO Marc Benioff, has built an extraordinary and modern corporate culture: a company's purpose should not just be profit, but even more than that.

The Salesforce Ohana is an extended family composed of its employees, its customers, its partners, and a really *big* and supportive community, where everyone tries to help each other through many different ways and touch points. Any stakeholder is included in Ohana in different ways, but Salesforce tries to make the relationship effective for both parties.

If you don't know the story behind how Marc Benioff introduced the concept of Ohana, it has been told in various levels of depth in all Marc's books (just type *Marc Benioff* online and you'll find all his works. I suggest you read *Behind the Cloud*, which is very inspiring), but we can briefly say that in the late 90s, he took a sabbatical year in Hawaii, connected with the local people and customs, discovered the concept of Ohana, and fell in love with the idea of a fully connected network of people and absolutely wanted it to be part of Salesforce's culture.

The Salesforce Ohana culture is based on four core values:

* **Trust**: A trusting relationship is at the base of a sound bond between companies and people. This involves transparency, security, compliance, privacy, and high performance. An example is `https://trust.salesforce.com/en/` with real-time information on Salesforce's systems performance and security, or the security reviews any app on the AppExchange should follow before it is considered safe enough.

- **Customer success**: Salesforce helps its customers to get to the top together, bringing value to the platform by adding more and more products, modules, and features, and also letting people grow their network and skills in the community to support this value. To boast, here are some figures: 30,000+ employees in 25 countries, 150,000+ customers—not bad!

- **Innovation**: As the lead of a small innovation center in my company, I believe innovation (not necessarily only technological but even cultural and social) must be the lifeblood of any company of any size, and Salesforce has innovation in its DNA. New features are added three times a year (thanks to Spring, Summer, and Winter releases), new products are added to the ecosystem, and new ideas are delivered and voted on online (in the **IdeaExchange** you have the power to drive released features. Check it out at `https://trailblazer.salesforce.com/ideaSearch`). Innovation also delivers discomfort, and discomfort lets you go out of your comfort zone, which in turn lets you evolve your social and technical skills (no pain no gain!).

- **Equality**: Everyone should feel included, and everyone should be respected regardless of their background or attitudes. It's no surprise that there is a Chief Equality Officer, in the person of Tony Prophet as of 2020, who is responsible for driving equality policies inside Salesforce. Check out this great video to see how the power of diversity drives the company: `https://youtu.be/BKjq-o9FFXs`.

These values are brought together in Salesforce products (there is more than the CRM out there; check out all the main available products at `www.salesforce.com/products`) and its workplace, but also in events and by giving it all back.

Salesforce events are always huge (no matter the kind), full of Salesforce gadgets and full of people who want to expand their network. The most famous official event is Dreamforce, an annual conference held in San Francisco between the end of August and late November (the date changes every year) that brings together thousands of people interested in technology and new business opportunities. You can find super geeks along with C-level people from all over the world, and you can even have a chit-chat or take a selfie with Marc Benioff if you have the chance to meet him. Unfortunately, because of the COVID-19 pandemic, the 2020 event has been canceled (`https://www.businessinsider.com/salesforce-dreamforce-cancelled-virtual-conference-2020-4?IR=T`).

Here are a few statistics about this great event (have a look at the latest Dreamforce infographic from the Salesforce blog at `www.salesforce.com/blog/2019/12/dreamforce-2019-infographic.html` for 2019, before the COVID-19 emergency):

- 4 days
- 171,000+ registered attendees
- 16,000,000 online viewers
- 120+ countries
- 2,700+ sessions and workshops
- 27 product launches (yes, 27!)

Figure 19.1 – Me at my first Dreamforce in 2011, taking a picture with Sassy, the "No Software" mascot

My happy face is no surprise in this picture taken at my first Dreamforce in 2011. It was huge, funny, full of gadgets, full of learning… absolutely fantastic!

If you cannot afford a trip to San Francisco (during the event, flight and accommodation prices get crazy!), don't despair, as there may be an official event in your country shortly. Have a look at the official events list at `www.salesforce.com/events`.

This great culture led the company to start the **1% Pledge** program (`www.salesforce.org/pledge-1`), a 1-1-1 philanthropic model to leverage technology, people, and resources to improve communities throughout the world, which brought the company to build three (as of 2020) vertical products: **No Profit Cloud**, **Education Cloud**, and **Philanthropy Cloud**. Check out the site if you want your company to be part of the program.

Salesforce Ohana is embraced by a strong and supportive community, the Trailblazer Community, which is the medium through which any *Salesforce person* (whether they are employees, technicians, or customers) is lead into this ecosystem.

The Trailblazer Community

The Trailblazer Community is the lifeblood of Salesforce, because the community has the power to motivate and support Salesforce administrators, developers, architects, users, consultants, and all related stakeholders.

Do you have a doubt about a product? Reach out to the Trailblazer Community.

Did you find a bug on the platform whose fix you believe can benefit others, or that others may have already solved? Reach out to the Trailblazer Community.

Do you want to find nearby geeks to have a Salesforce chat? Reach out to the Trailblazer Community.

Do you want to say hello to community leaders and share with them your opinion? Reach out to the Trailblazer Community.

The first touch point with the community is the Trailblazer Community portal, at `trailblazers.salesforce.com`. This community was formerly known as Success Community, but the Trailblazer re-branding became official in 2019:

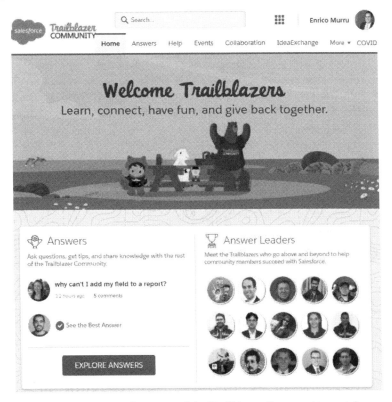

Figure 19.2 – Landing page of the Trailblazer Community portal

Register for free (your Developer Edition org or your Google or LinkedIn account may be enough) and navigate through this endless portal, where you can do the following:

- Collaborate by posting or answering answers.

- Reach the Salesforce Help site for any technical support.

- Check the official Salesforce events list.

- Join thousands of groups created for different purposes (you can even create your own)

- Post and vote on ideas for new or enhanced features.

- Access the **Known Issues** portal to browse between platform issues or bugs and check the plans for a fix.

A trailblazer is anyone capable of leading the way and inspiring like pioneers, they help other people or companies to drive innovation and increase their value and Salesforce's value on the market. Have a read of the official Salesforce blog post titled *What is a Trailblazer?* at `https://www.salesforce.com/blog/2017/07/so-what-is-a-trailblazer.html`.

Among the *most-followed* trailblazers, we can find the **MVPs** (short for **Most Valuable Professionals**) . Once a year, Salesforce experts have the chance to be nominated as MVPs. This nomination comes with a great responsibility; indeed, MVPs must demonstrably contribute to the community yearly in order to have their status renewed, and there are also a few perks, such as community recognition (which can be a great boost for their careers), premier product support (they can open a support case to Salesforce, no matter the customers they work with), dedicated networking events, and a personalized and encouraging training program.

I was an MVP from 2016 to 2019 but unfortunately didn't get renewed in 2020, which I have to admit was demoralizing, but I understood that I had to give more to the community and I started with this book, the idea being to help new trailblazers by providing an accessible place to learn as much and as quickly as possible.

Check out the Salesforce MVP program site at `www.salesforce.com/campaign/mvp`.

Another cool part of the Trailblazer Community is the Salesforce community groups, groups lead by administrators, developers, customers, users, or MVPs that want to share their passion for Salesforce with nearby people of a local community permeated by the Ohana culture. Salesforce groups organize periodic meetings with workshops, hands-on training, and even special guests. As an example of the kinds of event the groups put on, check out the blog post I wrote after a great event we held in November 2017 during a Milan Salesforce Group night, when we had a special Italian Salesforce guest, at `https://blog.enree.co/2017/12/salesforce-celebrities-movember-cloud.html`.

If you want to find a group near you or you want to start a new Salesforce group, go to the official Trailblazer community groups site at `trailblazercommunitygroups.com`.

Salesforce community groups can even be a good source for learning as a lot of them adhere to the **Salesforce Saturdays** model, where people meet in public places on Saturday mornings to study together for Salesforce certification preparation (and more). If you want to be globally acknowledged as a Salesforce professional, official certification is what you need.

Be a certified trailblazer

In the early days of Salesforce CRM, when the platform was a *simple* automation web automated for sales, services, marketing, and even some custom applications, it was easy to know all the features in some depth and also keep pace with all the updates delivered three times a year on the platform.

Today it is quite different because the platform has evolved so much that it makes sense to focus on specific fields (development, administration, field service, marketing, and analytics), as the number of features and frequent new additions to the platform makes staying updated a separate job.

Whether applying to work for a Salesforce customer or a Salesforce consulting partner, it's becoming more and more common for employers to require some kind of evidence of your Salesforce skills, and this can be easily provided with Salesforce certifications. Passing a certification does not guarantee 100% that you are the most skilled professional in that certification field, but it says that you passed it and know what you are talking about.

Given that it is estimated that by 2024 the Salesforce ecosystem will have created about 4.2 million new jobs, it seems more than practical to choose Salesforce as an area to develop.

So, the question might be, what kind of certification do I have to take?

It depends on which career path you want to blaze your trail in:

- **Salesforce administrators**: These people work with stakeholders to define requirements and translate them into Salesforce solutions, customize the platform using declarative automation tools (yep, what you learned in this book), and help Salesforce users to get the most out of Salesforce (`https://trailhead.salesforce.com/credentials/administratoroverview`).

- **Salesforce developers**: These people combine declarative skills (again, what you learned in this book) with programmatic skills to further extend and customize the Salesforce Lightning platform. They are the ones that *crack the code* (`https://trailhead.salesforce.com/credentials/developeroverview`).

- **Salesforce marketers**: These are the experts of marketing strategy implementation (`https://trailhead.salesforce.com/credentials/marketingoverview`).

- **Salesforce consultants**: These people are Salesforce professionals specialized in finding solutions to complex business requirements using the whole gamut of Salesforce products. They are not necessarily highly skilled technical professionals (`https://trailhead.salesforce.com/credentials/consultantoverview`).

- **Salesforce architects**: These people design high-performance solutions that stand against big data volumes and are resilient to critical conditions. They usually have a big-picture view of what's going on and can guide as technical governance leaders of a project. They are often called *technical gurus* (`https://trailhead.salesforce.com/credentials/architectoverview`).

My natural path is the architect path, the objective of which is to be recognized as a Salesforce Technical Architect. To get this certification, the first step is to pass several certifications that are in common with the other careers (as of 2020 there are 10, and they cover diverse Salesforce topics). After passing these certifications, you get automatically qualified with the title of **Application Architect** and **System Architect**. Once you pass all of the prerequisite certifications, you can access the final exam, which consists of a 45-minute live presentation to a panel of judges, after 3 hours of preparation, followed by a 40-minute Q&A session. It's no secret why this is the most difficult certification around (and yes, at the time of writing I missed the last exam to be a Certified Technical Architect, or CTA).

This is the CTA certification path pyramid (as of 2020):

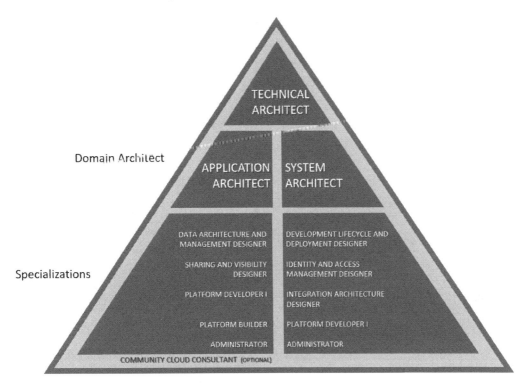

Figure 19.3 – Technical architect certification path

So, which path will you take? I always suggest starting with the *App Builder*, *Administrator*, or *Platform Developer I* certifications, and they are the root of any certification path. Considering that Platform Developer I is meant for Salesforce developers (and after this book, you will be ready to handle programmatic development), you have the other two options. In my opinion, the App Builder certification is a middle-ground certification, as it covers a lot of declarative customization concepts, while the Administrator certification is more focused on all the administrative tasks (such as sharing and security, release, main sales and service features, and monitoring). That's why the Administrator certification is a bit more difficult than the App Builder certification. This of course depends also on your experience of such features.

So, at the end of the day it is up to you to choose, but do not fear failure, because failing is part of success.

It took me 7 years to earn my first certification, but then I reached a count of 20 in 2020, and I still struggle to get more in my portfolio!

Taking your first certification

Before closing this chapter, here's a few words on how the certification process works.

At the time of writing, Salesforce's certification authority is Kryterion (`www.webassessor.com/salesforce`) through the Webassessor app. Create a new Webassessor login and you are ready to book a certification exam.

The process is quite straightforward and there is a cool YouTube video by *Salesforce Hulk* at `https://youtu.be/snHAuRCyt3Q` that shows the entire process, which is summarized in the following steps:

1. Form registration

2. Certification selection

3. Exam schedule

4. Payment

> **Tip**
> Don't procrastinate when booking the exam: schedule an exam date so you know you have a goal and so you are committed and plan things right.

Another requirement is to link your Webassessor account with your Trailhead account. Take a look at the help article at `trailhead.salesforce.com/help?article=Link-Your-Trailhead-and-Webassessor-Accounts`.

When registering for a certification exam, you'll be required to choose between onsite and online. In the first case, you can select a certification center near you, but if you live in a place where no center is available, you can go with the online exam, which you can complete from home or from wherever you want.

For the most official and up-to-date details on how to take an online exam, refer to Salesforce Help at `https://trailhead.salesforce.com/help?article=Online-Proctoring-Completing-Your-Exam-Remotely`, but in any case, pay attention to the following rules:

*   Get a webcam (in COVID-19 times, a laptop webcam is enough, but outside pandemic events, you'll need an external webcam that records the screen, the keyboard, the mouse, and all your upper body).

*   Don't bring books, notes, or any material to copy from.

*   Make your desk clear, with as few devices/cables/things as possible.

- Don't wear watches.

- Put your smartphone in silent or airplane mode and place it away from the webcam's view.

- Don't use multiple screens.

- Don't drink or eat during the exam.

- Don't wear sunglasses. If you need to wear normal glasses (like I do), you may be asked to show that they are normal glasses and not something like *Google glasses* that could record the session (by placing them in front of the webcam for a few seconds).

- Don't read aloud, talk, or point to the screen while taking the exam (I did once when I was concentrating, and I was asked to stop!).

Once you have scheduled the exam and set up your remote location or selected your onsite test center, it's time to finalize your study using all kinds of online available resources:

- Salesforce Help

- Trailblazer community groups

- Salesforce books

- Salesforce blogs (have a look at the good selection at `www.salesforceben.com/salesforce-blogs`)

- Salesforce Stack Exchange community (`salesforce.stackexchange.com`)

- Salesforce certification days, free for all webinars to get in-depth insights about most certifications and even a $70 discount on any $200 exam (`trailhead.salesforce.com/credentials/cert-days`)

What about the exam itself? You'll be facing 60 open and multiple-choice questions with up to five alternatives (I've never seen more) and up to three right answers (the app tells you the kind of question and the required number of correct answers).

You'll generally find one answer that is completely wrong (sometimes more than one) and other ones that may be similar. Choose carefully, reflect, and, if the answers are really similar, choose the best one that fits with your knowledge (I'm not saying to toss a coin). If you are not sure, you can mark the question for a final review, so you'll be able to go back to some answers at the end of the test (you know, sometimes knowledge is hidden by stress and if you get a bit of security, your mind can pick the right answer).

Once you complete the test, you'll immediately receive the result, with a pass percentage for each topic covered by the certification. The list of topics and the final passing score is defined in the exam guide on the Trailhead site (for example, for the Administrator certification, visit `trailhead.salesforce.com/help?article=Salesforce-Certified-Administrator-Exam-Guide`).

If you fail your first exam, don't get down! You can retake it up to twice, paying a 50% fee. Remember, this is perfectly normal, especially for your first certifications.

One last thing: a certification is not forever, and it must be renewed once a year. This is done through the Trailhead portal after completing specific modules (take a look at `trailhead.salesforce.com/en/content/learn/trails/maintain-your-salesforce-certifications`). An automatic email will be sent to your address telling you that new modules are available for certification maintenance and informing you of the due date.

Are you ready to get certified?

I'm sure you are, and that you'll work hard to attain your first certification and finally be recognized as a Salesforce professional.

Good luck!

Blaze your trail

Check out this Trailhead content to find out more about the topics covered in this chapter:

- Salesforce Ohana culture: `https://trailhead.salesforce.com/en/content/learn/modules/manage_the_sfdc_way_ohana`

- Build your career in the Salesforce ecosystem: `https://trailhead.salesforce.com/en/content/learn/trails/build-your-career-with-salesforce-skills`

- Rock your future with Salesforce: `https://trailhead.salesforce.com/en/content/learn/trails/salesforce-for-students`

- Get ready for Dreamforce: `https://trailhead.salesforce.com/en/content/learn/trails/get_ready_for_dreamforce`

- Get started with Trailhead: `https://trailhead.salesforce.com/en/content/learn/trails/learn_salesforce_with_trailhead`

- Study for the Administrator certification exam: `https://trailhead.salesforce.com/en/content/learn/trails/administrator-certification-prep`

- Study for the Platform App Builder exam: `https://trailhead.salesforce.com/en/content/learn/trails/platform-app-builder-certification-prep`

All referenced Trailhead content is available in the **Hands-On Salesforce Application Development without Code** trailmix at `trailhead.salesforce.com/users/enreeco/trailmixes/hands-on-salesforce-application-development-without-code`.

Summary

We've learned about more than technology in this closing chapter.

We've discussed the concept of Salesforce Ohana and the key values Salesforce tries to evangelize across its whole ecosystem, which is composed of customers, employees, technology lovers, partners, consultants, and more.

This big mass of stakeholders creates the base for the diffusion of key values and a fertile land where the Trailblazer community can flourish and grow, where passionate professionals can share their ideas, organize in groups, promote knowledge, and help each other.

After so much learning, a Salesforce certification is what sets you apart as a Salesforce professional and can speed up your career progression. That's why we explained what a certification is and discussed the things to take into account when you're preparing to take a certification exam.

We have reached the end of this path full of learning and, hopefully, fun.

I really hope to have shown you the power of the Salesforce platform and how it can drive customer success through tens of amazing tools, but also to have demonstrated how vital and responsive its community is, and I believe you'll soon become a new member of it, becoming the next Salesforce Trailblazer, evangelizing newcomers in turn or, who knows, becoming the next Salesforce MVP!

Other Books You May Enjoy

If you enjoyed this book, you may be interested in these other books by Packt:

Salesforce for Beginners

Sharif Shaalan

ISBN: 978-1-83898-609-4

- Understand the difference between Salesforce Lightning and Salesforce Classic
- Create and manage leads in Salesforce
- Explore business development with accounts and contacts in Salesforce
- Find out how stages and sales processes help you manage your opportunity pipeline
- Achieve marketing goals using Salesforce campaigns
- Perform business analysis using reports and dashboards
- Gain a high-level overview of the items in the administration section
- Grasp the different aspects needed to build an effective and flexible Salesforce security model

Salesforce Lightning Platform Enterprise Architecture – Third Edition

Andrew Fawcett

ISBN: 978-1-78995-671-9

- Create and deploy AppExchange packages and manage upgrades
- Understand Enterprise Application Architecture patterns
- Customize mobile and desktop user experience with Lightning Web Components
- Manage large data volumes with asynchronous processing and big data strategies
- Implement Source Control and Continuous Integration
- Add AI to your application with Einstein
- Use Lightning External Services to integrate external code and data with your Lightning Application

Leave a review - let other readers know what you think

Please share your thoughts on this book with others by leaving a review on the site that you bought it from. If you purchased the book from Amazon, please leave us an honest review on this book's Amazon page. This is vital so that other potential readers can see and use your unbiased opinion to make purchasing decisions, we can understand what our customers think about our products, and our authors can see your feedback on the title that they have worked with Packt to create. It will only take a few minutes of your time, but is valuable to other potential customers, our authors, and Packt. Thank you!

Index

SUBMIT FOR APPROVAL 279

W

Made in the USA
Columbia, SC
20 May 2021